Revenge of the Forbidden City

Revenge of the Forbidden City

*The Suppression of the Falungong
in China, 1999–2005*

JAMES W. TONG

OXFORD
UNIVERSITY PRESS
2009

OXFORD
UNIVERSITY PRESS

Oxford University Press, Inc., publishes works that further
Oxford University's objective of excellence
in research, scholarship, and education.

Oxford New York
Auckland Cape Town Dar es Salaam Hong Kong Karachi
Kuala Lumpur Madrid Melbourne Mexico City Nairobi
New Delhi Shanghai Taipei Toronto

With offices in
Argentina Austria Brazil Chile Czech Republic France Greece
Guatemala Hungary Italy Japan Poland Portugal Singapore
South Korea Switzerland Thailand Turkey Ukraine Vietnam

Published by Oxford University Press, Inc.
198 Madison Avenue, New York, New York 10016

www.oup.com

Oxford is a registered trademark of Oxford University Press.

Library of Congress Cataloging-in-Publication Data
Tong, James W.
Revenge of the forbidden city : the suppression of the Falungong in China, 1999–2005 / James W. Tong.
    p. cm.
Includes bibliographical references and index.
ISBN 978-0-19-537728-6
1. Falun Gong (Organization) 2. Religion and state—China.
3. Communism and religion—China. 4. Freedom of religion—China. 5. Human rights—China.
6. Political persecution—China. 7. China—Politics and government—21st century.
8. China—Religion—21st century. I. Title.
BP605.F36T66 2009
323.44'20951090511–dc22   2009018042

9 8 7 6 5 4 3 2 1

Printed in the United States of America
on acid-free paper

Contents

Revenge of the Forbidden City

Chapter One

Introduction

April 25, 1999, fell on a Sunday. Jiang Zemin was taking a rest at his residence after breakfast that morning.[1] He had had a busy month.

Two days before, the secretary general of the Chinese Communist Party (CCP) was in Sichuan, wrapping up his six-day tour of the southwest province. After visiting the steel mill in Panzhihua, the hydroelectric power plant in Er Tan, the Wuliangyi Brewery in Yibin, the Changhong Electronic Consumer Company in Mianyang, and the Airplane Industry Corporation in Chengdu, he presided over and addressed the Conference on Reform and Development of State-Owned Enterprises in the provincial capital on April 22.[2] Barely a month before that, his schedule was bound up with the two major national conferences held in Beijing. The National People's Congress (NPC) convened its annual plenary session from March 5 to 15, while the China's People's Political Consultative Conference (CPPCC) held its annual conference from March 3 to 11.[3] As secretary-general, Jiang had to be present at the opening and closing ceremonies of the NPC, listen to reports on revising the Constitution on March 9, and those of the Supreme People's Court and the Supreme People's Procuracy on March 10. He also attended separate breakout sessions with several provincial delegations and that of the People's Liberation Army on March 6, 7, 8, 11, and 12.[4] With the CPPCC, it was not so much attending the formal sessions as meeting the delegates from Hong Kong, Macau, organized religions, and ethnic minorities.[5]

Even after the delegates of the NPC and CPPCC returned to their home provinces, there was no rest for the secretary-general. March 20 took him to Venice, where he kicked off his three-nations state visit to western Europe, luncheoning with 150 corporate elite in Milan, presenting a wreath to the Tomb of the Unknown Soldier in Rome, attending a concert of the Vienna Philharmonic at the Gold Hall at the Musikverein, addressing the Disarmament Conference in Geneva, and touring the European Nuclear Research Center (CERN).[6] The visits were about international politics, as well. While in Italy, Jiang secured a commitment that the European Union would not sponsor a bill critical of China's human rights conditions in the United

Nations Human Rights Convention that year.[7] He conferred with Swiss President Ruth Dreifus on Kosovo when NATO launched its air strike against Yugoslavia on March 24, 1999. The evening before, he made an unscheduled speech at a farewell dinner in Milan deploring the NATO military action.[8] As elaborated in chapter 2, NATO bombing of Belgrade would return as an even more serious problem for Beijing in another two months.

Three other major international political issues were also in the Politburo agenda. On March 17, Li Yafei, the deputy secretary-general of the Association for Relations Across the Taiwan Straits (ARATS), flew to Taipei to prepare for the visit of Wang Daohan, ARATS president, to Taiwan that fall and invited Xu Huiyu, Wang's counterpart in Taiwan, to visit the mainland in June.[9] As also elaborated in chapter 2, both trips would be derailed in May by the "Two State Theory" enunciated by Taiwan President Lee Teng-hui. Off another part of China's coast, national unification was progressing more smoothly. The joint Sino-Portuguese task force to discuss the return of Macau to China completed the last of its 27 meetings on March 24, leaving some technical matters for the experts to resolve and major issues for the Politburo to approve.[10]

A more immediate and knotty political problem was the accession of China to the World Trade Organization (WTO) and Premier Zhu Rongji's visit to the United States. Scheduled to begin on April 6, it would be the first visit of a People's Republic of China premier to the United States in 15 years. The prospective visit, however, was complicated by unexpected developments. The accusations of the congressional report on Chinese espionage, released on January 3, 1999,[11] gathered more steam with the *New York Times* special report on China's alleged theft of U.S. nuclear technology, published as a front-page story on March 6, 1999.[12] The story gained even more momentum with the termination of employment of Wen-ho Lee two days later, and the much-publicized investigation of the Los Alamos lab scientist by the FBI and the U.S. Department of Energy. Further straining Beijing–Washington relations, the U.S.-led NATO began its bombing campaign of Yugoslavia on March 24. Beijing was opposed to the military option and the U.S. position that human rights trumped national sovereignty. With Russian Prime Minister Primarkov canceling his scheduled trip to the United States when NATO launched the air war, the Politburo also deliberated whether Zhu should also postpone his trip. Even after the majority expressed support for the visit, both the process and outcome of the WTO negotiations in Washington was closely followed in Beijing. On April 10, the U.S. trade representative released his version of the "U.S.-China Communiqué" that included the opening of China's telecommunications market to U.S. corporations and the relaxing of inspection requirements on U.S. agriculture produce, conditions that Chinese negotiators had not agreed to. Adding to the U.S. demands that U.S. import textile quotas would continue for another decade and China would accede to the WTO as a nonmarket economy, the news stunned the incumbent and retired CCP leaders in Beijing, with several CCP elders calling Jiang to register displeasure. When the premier returned to China on April 21, none of the other six Politburo Standing Committee (PSC) members greeted him at the Beijing Airport or at the Great Hall of the People.[13] According to a Chinese government insider source, the cold reception was meant to demonstrate Politburo disagreement with the outcome of WTO talks, a position that Jiang Zemin supported, but not without substantial pressure from his current and former Politburo colleagues.[14]

"The Most Serious Political Incident since June 4"

Jiang probably had these issues in his mind when he received a special message from his office staff, who forwarded the phone call from Luo Gan, the Secretary for Legal and Political Affairs on that Sunday morning of April 25. Luo briefed Jiang about a mass rally that was taking place at that very moment at the doorsteps of Zhongnanhai, the CCP headquarters in Beijing.

It turned out that soon after 5 A.M. that morning, a large group of Falungong practitioners began to congregate from different directions toward Zhongnanhai, moving from the main entrance of Beihai Park and toward the Fuyou Street side of the party complex. By 8 A.M., thousands had gathered around the Beimenlu side of Zhongnanhai, stretching from east to west to the northern end of Fuyou Street. In their 20s to their 70s, they were mostly elderly, with women outnumbering men. They formed three to four rows on the sidewalk paralleling the street, with the front row facing the street forming a cordon to keep order and to prevent outsiders from intruding. Those behind either sat or read Falungong publications. They did not display any banners or chant any slogans, taking care not to step into the street to block traffic. Many of them brought their own boxed food and bottled water.[15]

As his initial shock turned to anger, Jiang instructed Luo to handle the crisis, convening a meeting of concerned departments to work out solutions and to engage the demonstrators in dialogue. Luo then called a meeting with the heads of the Ministry of Public Security, the Ministry of State Security, the Armed Police Headquarter, the Central Security Bureau, the Central Committee General Office, and the State Council General Office, as well as related departments in the Beijing municipality, to discuss strategies. In the six-hour marathon dialogue with five representatives of the Falungong that ensued, Luo was joined by the premier to persuade the demonstrators to leave the Zhongnanhai, assuring them that the regime supported physical exercises for health improvements, did not consider the Falungong to be antigovernment, that a recent article criticizing the Falungong represented only the author's personal views, and that the organizers of the rally would not be prosecuted.

Satisfied that those assurances had met their initial purpose to seek under-standing and support from the Beijing leadership, the Falungong represen-tatives then persuaded other practitioners to leave the premise. By 10:30 that evening, the rally that was once 21,000 strong, and that afternoon had stretched 2.5 kilometers, had disappeared. A government insider source reported that the practitioners picked up all trash in plastic bags that they carried away, leaving not a slip of paper, a cigarette butt, or sign of spitting behind. In contrast, on the side of the Zhongnanhai where more than 1,000 public security agents had gathered to monitor the rally, the entire street was littered with food wraps, cigarette cases, and patches of phlegm.[16] During the meeting, Luo and Zhu learned that the five Falungong representatives worked for the Ministry of Railways, the Ministry of Public Security, the People's Lib-eration Army's Chief of Staff Department, the Ministry of Supervision, and Beijing University,[17] all vital institutions of the regime.

In a letter addressed to the PSC and other related leaders that evening, Jiang expressed his personal dismay with the incident on which the Public Security Ministry had not forewarned the Politburo, its potential for further disruption of social order, the mobilizing effect of its religious connotation, and possible foreign connections. He instructed an urgent notice on the event be sent to all provincial party committees and governments, to be communi-cated down to those at the county and bureau levels. He further demanded that the notice reach each employee at the central party and state agencies as well those of the Beijing municipality, requiring each one to respond to the question of whether he or she had practiced Falungong or participated in the sit-in the day before. In a special meeting of the PSC convened the following day, the PSC resolved to launch a program to collect intelligence on the Falungong and to take action against the Falungong after June 4, the tenth anniversary of the Democracy Movement.[18]

The anti-Falungong campaign was born. It would be named "the most serious political incident since June 4" in a Politburo meeting in mid-June.[19]

FALUNGONG: GENERAL INTRODUCTION

"What is the Falungong?" Jiang Zemin asked in ignorance when Luo Gan first reported on the siege of the Zhongnanhai on the morning of April 25, 1999.[20] It is not the focus of the present study to provide a political and religious history of the Falungong, an exposition of its doctrines and practices, the organizational structure, or its financial and communications systems, stud-ies that have been undertaken elsewhere. To provide the background for the subsequent analysis, however, a summary of these aspects of the movement from its origins to April 1999 is in order.

Physical and Spiritual Cultivation

According to Falungong's self-description, it is a system of physical and spiritual cultivation. As physical practice, it is derived from an ancient form of *qigong* that seeks to refine the mind and body through five sets of simple breathing exercises, including seated meditation. Regular pursuit of these exercises, it is claimed, will lead to stress relief, mental clarity, overall health improvement, and peace of mind. Going beyond physical fitness, it also cultivates one's moral character through the principles of truthfulness, benevolence, and forbearance (*zhen, shan, ren*). By practicing the breathing exercises and adhering to the teachings of Master Li Hongzhi, one can not only gain better health but also attain wisdom and enlightenment. At an advanced state, practitioners would ascend to a higher spiritual plane and be assimilated to the cosmos, with the Falun energy rotating inside them (turning of the Falung Wheel).[21]

As presented in David Palmer's book *Qigong Fever* (2007), the core doctrines of Li Hongzhi's teaching are rooted in Buddhism, consisting of four main themes.[22] An apocalyptic theme proclaims that humanity has reached an age of the End of Dharma, marked by moral degeneration, the omnipresence of evil, the adulation of science, and modernity that is created and spread by extraterrestrials, which are descendants of human survivors of prehistoric civilizations. To prevent the apocalypse, the second Messianic theme declares that Li Hongzhi is the savior of his disciples, humanity, and the universe. Initiated into and attaining great supernatural powers as a child, and cultivated by successive Buddhist and Daoist masters, Li embodies all types of special powers of the universe, which he has used to prevent the destruction of the universe, save humanity, and protect and heal his disciples. But in order to be healed, disciples must practice spiritual cultivation, the third theme. To purge bad karma, rid demons from their bodies, and repay karmic debts in previous lives, one should purify the heart, abandon desires, cultivate virtue, and conform to truth, benevolence, and forbearance, the fundamental values of the universe. Finally, disciples must practice Falungong exclusively. They are forbidden to read other religious and medical texts, to mix or even think of other *qigong* methods, to practice *taiji* exercises, or to take medicine when sick.

A Brief History

Breathing exercises and spiritual cultivation were first not mixed in the history of the Falungong, which can be divided into two periods. Both regime and Falungong sources agree that Li Hongzhi founded the Falungong in May 1992.[23] It coincided with the height of the "qigong fever" in China, when *qigong* grand masters Yan Xin and Zhang Hongbao were invited to give packed lectures at large auditoriums at Beijing and Qinghua universities; organize sold-out workshops at the Chinese Academy of Sciences, the Chinese Academy of Social Sciences, and central ministries; and perform at the Chinese New Year special program of China Central Television Corporation (CCTV), the most watched TV program in China. Then the biography of Zhang sold 10 million copies,[24] and *qigong* enjoyed the patronage of several top CCP leaders, including Qian Xuesen and Zhang Zhenhuan.[25] Riding on this nationwide *qigong* wave, Li gave two successful seminars in Changchun and then went to Beijing and held training sessions under the auspices of the China Qigong Scientific Research Society (*Zhongguo qigong keyanhui*, hereafter CQSR),[26] with which the Falungong was accredited as its direct-affiliate branch (*zhishu gongpai*) in 1993, under the title of "Falungong Research Branch Society" (*Falungong yanjiu fenhui*), while Li was accorded the title of Direct-Affiliate Qigong Master (*Zhishu Qigongsi*).[27] From May 1992 to September 1994, Li taught Falungong through 53 training seminars in Changchun, Harbin, and Beijing,[28] from which more than 20,000[29] to 200,000[30] learned Li's unique style of *qigong* exercise. This first period marked the rise of the Falungong, when it established its name among other *qigong* groups in northern Chinese cities, by way of training seminars organized and marketed through the local branches of the CQSR.[31]

A nationwide suppression of *qigong* organizations in 1994 heralded the onset of the second period when the Falungong dissociated from the *qigong* movement and turned to spiritual cultivation. By early 1994, the failure of grand *qigong* masters to reproduce their acts under controlled conditions, the proliferation of self-proclaimed grand masters, the commercialization of *qigong,* and the outbreak of psychological disorders among *qigong* practitioners with vulnerabilities had discredited the *qigong* movement. Its support among top CCP elite waned due to the death of their main patron, Zhang Zhenhuan, and the growing reservations or unwillingness of others to continue their advocacy. A wave of articles critical of *qigong* were published in the national press, accompanied by negative stories in the nightly news. Regulations on registration and income tax of *qigong* organizations were promulgated or more strictly enforced. The International Qigong Service Company of Zhang Hongbao was closed, and the International Qigong Science Federation dissolved in October 1994, its office in Xian sealed, and the home of its secretary-general searched by police. Of the three grand masters, Zhang Hongbao went into hiding and Yan Xin into voluntary exile, while Zhang Xiangyu was arrested for quackery.[32]

Under this hostile environment, the Falungong ended its training seminars, withdrew from the CQSR, made failed attempts to register as a social organization, and shifted to spiritual cultivation. In 1994, Li Hongzhi left for the United States, where he has resided in New York City until the present.[33] In September 1994, Li notified the CQSR that he would terminate the training sessions in China,[34] and then he filed for official withdrawal, which was accepted in March 1996.[35] To provide a legitimate organizational base for the rapidly increasing numbers of Falungong practitioners, Li's lieutenants in Beijing applied for registration as a social organization first to the National Minority Affairs Commission, and then to the China Buddhist Federation and to the United Front Department, all of which denied their application.[36]

At the same time, the Falungong turned to spiritual cultivation. In September 1994, Li Hongzhi declared that he would devote his time to the study of Buddhism. From then on, Li fashioned himself as leader of a religious movement rather than the head of a *qigong* organization. He changed his birthday to that of Sakyamuni, the founder of Buddhism. His writings have become sacred scriptures (*jingwen*). Meditation and reading of the Li's scriptures were added to the daily routine of Falungong practitioners. Falungong congregations were not only practice sessions on breathing exercises but also "Dharma Assemblies" (*fahui*) to study Li's sermons on spiritual cultivation.[37]

Organizational Structure

The organizational structure of the Falungong was also transformed before and after it attempted to register as a social organization.[38] As reported in official media, the movement was led by the Falun Dafa Research Society (*Falun Dafa Yanjiuhui*) in Beijing[39] and presided over by Li Hongzhi. Organized generally along the regime's administrative hierarchy, the "main stations" were found at the provincial, region (*qu*), and municipal levels, overseeing the operations of branch stations (*fenzhan*) at the city and district (*zhou*) levels, with subordinate guidance stations established on the county levels and urban districts within cities. At the lowest level, practice sites, and study groups (*xueshi xiaozu*) beneath them,[40] were established in groups of villages in rural areas and in housing blocks and work units in the cities. The division of main stations, branch stations, guidance stations, and practice sites followed those of the main *qigong* organizations at the time.[41] By the time that the Falungong movement was suppressed in July 22, 1999, the regime claimed that it had 39 main stations, 1,900 guidance stations, 28,000 practice sites (*liangongdian*) nationwide,[42] and 2 million practitioners (*liangongzhe*) inside China.[43] Falungong refers to its adherents as students (*xueyuan*) and practitioners (*xiulianzhe*),[44] while the regime labels them as believers (*xintu*), disciples (*dizhi*),[45] and practitioners (*liangongzhe, lianxizhe, xiulianzhe*).[46] This organizational portrait probably applies to the period before the *qigong* movement was suppressed.

After the Falungong failed in its repeated attempts to register as a social organization, its leaders decided to switch to a loose organizational structure in early 1997. They made a formal declaration that the Falun Dafa Research Society would cease to exist, abolished its administrative and functional offices, and discontinued its services for constituents. To demonstrate that there was no longer a centralized, formal command structure, they abolished the nomenclature of main station (*zhongzhan*) and main station chiefs (*zhongzhan zhang*), calling these guidance stations (*fudaozhan*) as in other stations. To show that the guidance stations were not administrative bodies, they disconnected their telephones and instructed the guidance stations not to maintain financial accounts or hold inventory. Practitioners from thence onward would practice Falungong among themselves, or learn from books and videos.[47] The Falungong could thus claim that it was not a social organization after 1997, a claim disputed by the authorities.

Communications System

Part of the basis of the official claim that the Falungong remained an illegal social organization after 1997 was the fact that the Falungong had an efficient communications system by which its Beijing headquarters could send messages through intermediate levels to the practice sites. Official media report that routine Falungong communications were sent through the postal system, more time-sensitive messages were delivered through telegram,[48] phone, and facsimile, while written notes and word-of-mouth messages, as well as the more high-tech means of cellular phones and pagers were also used.[49] Among these, desk and cellular phones seem to be the predominant mode, especially to call meetings and to mobilize collective action. Internet communication was a recent acquisition, through which confidential messages were sometimes encrypted in secret codes and used extensively especially after the Beijing siege of April 25, 1999, when Li Hongzhi would post his communications on the Web from his New York office.[50] Printed materials were photocopied by each management level and distributed to the next lower level, often overnight.[51] It is not evident whether there were communications at fixed periods from and among different Falungong levels.

Finance

As in its organizational structure, official and Falungong sources differ widely on Falungong finances. Government propaganda portrayed Falungong as having lucrative revenue sources from charging exorbitant admissions to *qigong* seminars and duping practitioners to pay for pricey healing and devotional materials. It claimed that Falungong receipts in its 50-odd training seminars charging 30–60 yuan per head per session amounted to 1.5–2 million yuan.[52] The government also claimed that voluminous sales of Falungong publications, videos, voice tapes, exercise suits and cushions, laminated badges, and Li Hongzhi portraits were filling up Falungong coffers.[53] In defense, Falungong insiders claimed that actual net receipts for Falungong from these sources were much less than those reported by the government. They pointed out that the regime's accounting method for seminar receipts did not allow for half-price discounts for repeat participants, or substantial overhead payments to the CQSR, which organized and marketed the seminars. They also claimed that official sources did not account for material, personnel, travel, and accommodation costs, as well as entertainment expenses for local cadres and special guests.[54] Factoring these cost and expense items, the Falungong claimed that its net income from the training seminars was less than one-tenth of that cited by the government. For book and video sales, Falungong sources claimed that the lion's share of profits went to publishers, distributors, and pirates. Li Hongzhi claimed that total royalty receipts from publishers on all his books inside China was less than 20,000 yuan.[55]

These claims and counterclaims have been assessed in my 2002 *China Quarterly* article "An organizational analysis of the Falungong." Since neither government nor Falungong sources have provided full, itemized accounting of Falungong finances at either the central or provincial levels, available evidence does not permit a more accurate and in-depth assessment of Falungong finance.

Falungong as a Social Movement and Relations with the State

In addition to the above studies on its institutional history, there are also sociological studies on the etiology of the Falungong variously conceptualized as that of a social movement,[56] a quasi-religious movement,[57] a new religious movement,[58] a nonreligious movement,[59] a movement of expression,[60] a global and healing movement,[61] or a spiritual practice that combines Eastern religiosity and quasi-scientific Western modernization,[62] and the attendant socioeconomic ecology of its rise. Three monograph-length studies also approach the subject as social movement history, tracing its historical evolution and explicating its doctrinal system.[63] Closer to the inquiry of the present study, several skillful studies examine or refer to Chinese government actions against the Falungong, focusing on the relationships between state and society,[64] on the source of the conflict,[65] and on the regime's calculus in outlawing the congregation.[66] There are also analyses on the media campaign,[67] regime efforts to regulate Internet use,[68] legal issues involved in the official ban,[69] and a debate on whether the Chinese government used judicial psychiatry as an instrument of oppression.[70]

RESEARCH QUERY

Theoretical Point of Departure

The present study has been informed by the above set of studies on the Falungong. The larger theoretical issues it attempts to address are the theories of Communist decline that suggest that market reforms have eroded the structural basis of party rule and central state capacity, with some prognosticating its final collapse. These theories can be classified as those on the demise of Communist systems in the former Soviet Union and its satellite states, pathological theories on the structural weaknesses of Communism, and institutionalist theories on the decline of the CCP and central state capacity in China.

Theories of Communist Collapse

The sudden collapse of communist systems in central and eastern Europe in the late 1980s has confounded both social scientists and policy makers. In its wake, dozens of research monographs, edited volumes, and special issues of journals have been published on why communist systems fail. Although the empirical referent is generally that of the Soviet Union and the communist states in central and eastern Europe, and some accounts analyze the effects of historical processes occurring in those states,[71] other putative explanations apply more broadly to all communist states, including China.

On a broad level, several studies have examined the institutional flaws of communist economies (Maier, 1997), focusing on its inefficiency to coordinate supply and demand (Arnason, 1993), its failure to manage the exigencies of the world market (Stokes, 1993), the "unfeasibility of socialism" (Przeworski, 1991), the unreformability of communism (Roeder, 1993), its incapacity for accommodation (Remington, 1992), and its inability to learn to adapt to social change (Elster et al., 1998). The disillusion with communism led to an erosion of regime legitimacy (Szelenyi and Szelenyi, 1994; Mason, 1992; Fish, 1995), expressed as widespread cynicism toward the official ideology (Tismaneaunu, 1992; Chirot, 1991), or frustration that the regime failed to honor its social pact to provide material welfare (Przeworski, 1991). Growing cynicism and frustration set the stage for increasing numbers of individuals participating in antiregime demonstrations and crossing the revolutionary threshold (Kuran, 1991) or being mobilized by the information cascade (Lohmann, 1994). Instead of demobilizing collective action, political reforms that introduced accountability and contested elections had the opposite effect, through granting greater freedom of discussion and expression. These political reforms also undermined the authority of the Communist Party, reduced its functions in society (Tompson, 1993; McCauley, 1992), and undercut its administrative and supervisory powers (Gill, 1995). As elaborated in a following section, it is also claimed that market reforms weaken the power of the Communist Party and erode the commitment of its agents to the Party.

Pathological Theories on China's Structural Weakness

In the field of China studies, the economic success of China and the meteoric rise of its status in the international political and economic system have served as the best external validation of its system performance, amplifying accolades of its strength while drowning exposes of its weakness. Nevertheless, the demise of communist systems in central and eastern Europe has also spawned analyses on China's woes. Most of these are in the genre of cataloguing economic and political problems that the authors claim to have reached alarming levels. In two studies that bear almost identical titles, Gordon Chang's *The Coming Collapse of China* (2001) provides a dismal diagnosis of China's economic and political pathologies—bankrupt state-owned enterprises, insolvent banks burdened by mounting nonperforming loans, the absence of laws protecting private property, the lack of credible accounting standards, and the "culture of nonpayment" in commercial transactions. Coupled with top leaders who were unable or unwilling to reform the ailing system, the residual command economy was predicted to crumple under the transparency trading rules of the WTO around 2006.[72] An equally pessimistic account by Jack Goldstone catalogues signs of "The coming Chinese collapse" (1996). Drawing historical parallels from China's dynastic decline, the author lists administrative impotence, regional antagonisms, civil war, and pressures from population growth that are alleged to be unsustainable by economic production. In this account, contemporary China has additional vulnerabilities: conflict between party officials and the nonparty elite (intelligentsia, business leaders, the military), decline in the CCP's direct control of society, rising discontent among peasants and workers, chaotic finance system, and rampant corruption. Already losing its ability to rule effectively, Goldstone predicts that China will face a terminal crisis in the following 10-15 years.[73]

Less deterministic about the collapse of the Chinese state, Charles Wolf and colleagues list the *Fault Lines in China's Economic Terrain* (2003) that might erupt with catastrophic force and disrupt its development. These time bombs include massive unemployment and abject rural poverty, rampant corruption, acute water shortage, a tight energy bottleneck, a fragile financial system, possible major epidemic outbreak, shrinkage of foreign direct investments, and international military conflict.[74] If these fault lines erupt, the aggregated individual adverse effects on China's economy are estimated to be 6.9–10.7% of its gross domestic product per year, and the possible inter-dependent effects are too complex to calculate.[75]

Institutionalist Theories

As has been suggested, these pathologies have not led to system decay for much of CCP's rule, much less to its decline and demise. For the latter, three sets of theories have been proposed to address the question of the viability of the Chinese state and CCP rule under market reforms. All approach China from an institutionalist framework and offer different analyses of its politi-cal economy. All suggest that the capacity of CCP rule or the central state will be undermined by market forces.

Power Dependency Theory.   For Andrew Walder, communist power is based on the distinctive political economy of a Leninist party system and a com-mand economy.[76] The hierarchical structure, strict discipline, and pervasive presence of party organization throughout its political system provide the institutional basis of its formidable power. This is reinforced by the central planning system, where party organizations monopolize property rights over most productive assets and resource allocation decisions in produc-tion, investment, income, and careers. These institutional features lead to a high degree of compliance and discipline among party agents, enforced through arbitrary terror, extensive surveillance, job appointment, and dos-sier systems, as well as reward and punishment schemes. They have the same social control effects on its citizenry, exercised through the pervasive public security system, monopoly of mass media, and suppression of unauthorized political activities and incorrect political discourse.

Within such systems, the strength of communist power varies in relation-ship to three sets of regime capacity. First, it varies with the degree of orga-nized dependence of citizens to the state, agents to party principals, and subordinates to superiors in employment, income, rationing of goods, food, and housing. Second, it depends on the extent to which the regime can mon-itor the political activities and utterances of its constituents, through resi-dence and workplace surveillance, informant networks, party organizations, and affiliate mass organizations. Third, it varies with the state capacity to reward political compliance and punish defiance, through valued economic and social resources.

From this vantage point, economic, social, and political developments in the reform period are seen to converge to erode the institutional basis of CCP power in China. In the economic realm, decollectivization and return to private farming in the rural areas, the legalization of privately owned industries and services in the cities, and the opening of China to foreign direct investments combine to end state monopoly over means of production and resource allocation, as well as to create alternatives in production and consumption independent from party control, state monitoring, and sanctioning institutions. Enterprise reforms that grant greater managerial autonomy to firms likewise erode organized dependence of management and labor to the state through increasing independence from state production quotas, material allocation plans, revenue and expenditure controls, salary scales, and political criteria to tie income, benefits, and promotion to job performance evaluation. Fiscal reforms that allow local governments to retain a larger share of local revenues have similar effects of weakening central control and strengthening local autonomy. An increasing number of constituents existing outside the central planning perimeter of state control, and the weakening of organized dependence of those still inside the perimeter converge to reduce both the fidelity and conformity of party agents to the party line, thereby undermining the monitoring and sanctioning capacity of the state.

Market Transition Theory.   Like power dependence theory, market transition theory arrives at the same conclusion that market reforms weaken the communist state, paving way for its eventual collapse. According to articles by Victor Nee and Lian Peng,[77] the putative process is similar to power dependence theory, where market reforms reduce the proportion of goods and services that are allocated by administrators and create alternative sources of power and privilege outside the control of the state. Unlike power dependence theory, market transition theory contends that market reforms actually increase the power of party agents and bureaucrats. In market transition, transaction costs are higher, as neither rules of the plan nor rules of the market apply in partial reforms. In the absence of private property rights and a legal system to stipulate official procedures and enforce contract compliance, economic actors seek bureaucratic intervention to negotiate transactions, grant operating licenses, or enforce agreements, thus creating new opportunities for party agents to seek rents. At the same time, market expansion also increases entrepreneurship among cadres, who control the allocation of investment credit, market access, and critical resources. Market transition thus increases the payoff for opportunism among party agents.

Commitment to the party declines as market transition progresses. At an early stage of market reform, party control for career advancement and selective incentives, the lack of alternative rewards outside the communist system, and the effectiveness of the monitoring and enforcement mechanism of the party combine to make commitment to the party the dominant strategy for most CCP members. With the expansion of market reforms, the payoff for rent-seeking and entrepreneurship increases relative to rewards provided by the party. While the commitment to the party does not wane among true believers with strong ideological convictions, it does decline among opportunists that succumb to increasing payoff from entrepreneurial and rent-seeking activities, and waiver among middle-of-the-roaders who wager between the party and the market. The balance shifts in favor of market opportunism against party commitment over time, as more opportunists abandon the party, followed by middle-of-the-roaders. When defection reaches a critical mass, even the morale of true believers plunges as they despair about the ability of the party to control political developments and its ultimate survival. With diminishing power, the communist state becomes destabilized and contending social and political forces are unleashed, pushing the weakened regime to its eventual collapse. How stable and durable the party is in the period of market transition would depend on the size of payoff for opportunism, the strength of monitoring capacity of the party, the vigor of its sanctioning capacity, and the degree of successful economic performance.

Market-Preserving Federalism Theory. Another theoretical assault on the capacity of the communist state is launched in institutional economics. In their provocative article "Federalism, Chinese style" (1996), Gabriella Montinola and colleagues argue that the political basis of China's economic success lies in "market-preserving federalism." The fundamental dilemma faced by a government to build and protect markets is, the authors contend, that it has both the capacity to enforce legal rights and rules and the strength to make a creditable commitment to honor those rules. In the absence of such commitments, investors would have no protection against government policies that would diminish their economic welfare, through asset confiscation, exorbitant taxation, or inflationary financing. An institution that provides protection for investors is market-preserving federalism, which is characterized by these traits: (1) a hierarchy of governments each with a delineated scope of authority and jurisdictional autonomy; (2) subnational governments with primary authority over management of economy; (3) a national government with the authority to police the common market and ensure the geographical mobility of goods and factors; (4) limited intergovernmental revenue sharing and constrained borrowing; and (5) durability of the federal structure that cannot be altered by the national government.[78]

The formal and durable decentralization inherent in such an economic system would deny the national government discretionary authority and the power to intervene in the economy. It would also deprive the national government the ability to revoke centralization. Limits on the discretion of local government are placed by competition among jurisdictions. The hard budget constraints to which national and subnational governments are subjected compel both sets of governments to face the consequences of their fiscal decisions. With both the national and subnational governments duly constrained, the institutional arrangement of Chinese federalism offers the credible commitment to preserve the market and to protect investors. To marshal as evidence that the economic system is one of "market-preserving federalism," Montinola et al. cite decentralization policies that transferred enterprise ownership to local governments, the establishment of four special economic zones and 14 coastal cities, fiscal reforms that specify fixed sources of revenue for the central versus local governments, and the spectacular growth of township and village enterprises under local government management. To buttress their argument that market-preserving federalism is durable and irreversible in China, Montinola et al. pointed to the failure of the central government to recentralize investment and financial powers opposed by provincial governors between 1989 and 1991, Deng Xiaoping's southern tour to Guangdong to rally provincial support for market-reform policies, and shift to a formal fiscal federalism system and foreign exchange reform in 1993–94.

Point of Departure of the Present Study

It is not the purpose of this study to validate these theories or to reconcile their differences. Rather, I take their main propositions as a theoretical point of departure to inform my research. I first note that the above three theories are institutionalist arguments, purported to explain the viability of the Chinese state under market reform. For Montinola et al., the remarkable success of the Chinese economy lies in market-preserving federalism, which provides the credible commitment to investors against the arbitrary intervention of a predatory state. For both Walder, Nee, and Peng, the survivability of the Chinese state depends primarily on the institutional features of the Chinese state, not its economic performance, resource base, population pressure, external threats, ideological delegitimation, or other putative challenges to its political economy.[79] The latter act as factors that affect the institutional basis of CCP power: organized dependence, commitment of members to the CCP, and the sanctioning and monitoring capacity of the regime.

Second, it can be deduced from the above institutionalist theories that the capacity of the Chinese state is undermined by the market. For market-preserving federalism, a requisite condition is that the central government be deprived of its power to manage the local finance and local economy (except policing the commons), as well as being constrained by hard budgets in investments. Further, this emasculation of central state power is both formal and durable in market-preserving federalism. For power dependency and market transition theories, the market is antithetical to the communist state. The more expanded the market, the greater the erosion of organized dependence and commitment to the party. The market is the driving force for the decline of communist power.

Third, vital for the survival of the communist state is its monitoring and sanctioning capacity. For market-preserving federalism, the central state needs the policing power to preserve the conditions for a common, national market, by demolishing local trade barriers, to ensure the free movement of goods and services across subnational jurisdictions. For power-dependency theory, the dependency of members to the party and citizens to the single-party state is a function of the extent to which the neoauthoritarian rule is maintained by its ability to monitor the political activities and verbal expressions of its constituents, and its capacity to reward compliance and sanction defiance. For market transition theory, party stability is directly and positively related to its monitoring capacity to identify and prevent opportunism in its members, and to its sanctioning capacity to punish errant and undisciplined party members.

The Present Analysis

The present study begins where the above communist decline theories end. From various theoretical perspectives and with different degrees of deterministic certainty, the repertoire of communist decline theories reviewed above contends that political and economic reforms undermine the basis of power of communist rule and central state capacity and unleash and mobilize the opposition, generating an avalanche of protests until it eventually collapses. Contrary to these dire predictions, China's survival and prosperity have presented an empirical challenge to these theories. Not only has it not crumpled under the endogenous erosion of domestic market reforms, but it has also withstood the exogenous shocks of the Asian financial crisis and the destabilizing force of opening its economy to the WTO regime. Why China did not collapse under what some theorists consider to be the strong gale of a perfect storm remains a theoretical anomaly to be reconciled; its continued illustrious economic performance, newly earned confidence in the international arena, and enhanced international repute, an enigma to be resolved.

The present analysis of China's coercive capacity as displayed in the anti-Falungong campaign is intended to be an empirical negative test to existing theories on decline of Chinese Communism. If CCP rule and state capacity have been eroded by political and economic reforms, it should manifest in the anti-Falungong campaign. Broken into its components, the core of the anti-Falungong campaign involves multiple operations, each of which has high performance thresholds that stretch the administrative capacity of the state, and operational benchmarks with which the coercive operations, the media campaign, and the conversion program can be measured and evaluated. Underlying operational performance, the institutional design and organizational dynamics, the degree of centralization and localization, and the extent of task specialization and coordination can also be discerned. Further, the actual efficiency and effectiveness of its monitoring and sanctioning capacity in intelligence gathering and community surveillance before the crackdown, as well as law enforcement procedures in implementing the ban (arresting Falungong practitioners and dissolving their organizations, confiscating and destroying their inventory, preventing them from staging protests and engaging in sabotage) can be observed and assessed.

In this book, the foregoing campaign operations are analyzed through the prism of theories on communist decline and issues on Chinese political institutions in the reform period. These include the role of the CCP, its monitoring and sanctioning capacity in the era of economic and administrative reforms, and the effects of new institutions (the market and civil society) as well as newfound powers of old institutions (legal institutions, the National People's Congress, the Chinese People's Political Consultative Conference) on the management of the campaign. These research queries are elaborated below.

Role of the Communist Party

A central argument of power dependence and market transition theories hinges on the extent to which the market has weakened the CCP. If the primary task of the CCP is not strengthening the dictatorship of the proletariat through class struggle but promoting economic development through unleashing productive forces, a logical question is whether the present regime and elite cohort have become more friendly toward its domestic challengers. Has the reliance on the invisible hand led to muscular atrophy of its once strong arm? Is the repressive instinct a dominant gene only in its totalitarian past, and has it degenerated into a recessive trait among the gentler and kinder present elite cohort? As Marxist collections languished in public libraries, CCP ideologues and theoreticians departed from the Politburo, and the CCP's theoretical journal stopped waving the *Red Flag* 30 years after its inauguration, can the CCP body operate without its soul, its strong arm still brawny enough to wield the stick, its clarion call to wage ideological battles against antiscience adversaries still confident and credible?

Even if the CCP has remained authoritarian in the era of market reforms, we would still want to question its role in the anti-Falungong campaign. Has it abdicated its coercive powers to the apparatus of the state, content to let the public security establishment to manage the campaign? Or did it reserve the power to set and oversee policy but leaving the government agencies to execute its directives? Or did it insist on the leadership of the CCP in dealing with the Falungong, vesting both policy making and executive powers in central and local CCP agencies? Clearly, there is potential conflict between the CCP and state agencies, and over which institution would formulate policies, manage the campaign, determine priorities, and allocate resources. The institutional and personal rivalry between the general secretary, Hu Yaobang, and the premier, Zhao Ziyang, is well known,[80] as are those between several provincial CCP secretaries and governors (Xu Kangdi and Huang Ju in Shanghai, Zhang Dejiang and Huang Huahua in Guangdong, Wang Maolin and Hu Fuguo in Shanxi, Sun Weiben and Shao Qihui in Heilongjiang, Deng Hongxun and Liu Jianfeng in Hainan).[81] Would the CCP and state at both the central and local levels vie for leadership in the campaign against the Falungong, or would they define turf boundaries, divide the portfolio, and share credit as well as human resource burdens? Or would they, rather, pass the buck to the other agency, justifying their reluctance by the demands of other pressing priorities?

Role of the National People's Congress and China's People's Political Consultative Conference

Going beyond the CCP and the executive branch of the government, I also examine the role of two national political institutions—the legislature (NPC) and the advisory body (CPPCC). During the market reforms era, has the NPC, constitutionally empowered to be the "Supreme Organ of State Power," lived up to its constitutional status? Of the many official stipulations promulgated in the anti-Falungong campaign, how many were issued in the name of the NPC or its Standing Committee? Of the more than 1,000 bills proposed annually in its plenary sessions, how many were aimed at the Falungong or the government campaign? Beyond legislative process, did the NPC Standing Committee also exercise its power of judicial review and question the legality of the legislations on the Falungong or executive acts of the government in the campaign? Did the national legislature also exercise its oversight function, by summoning officials in the executive branch to inquire whether the campaign was implemented within the confines of the law? Did it investigate or ignore reports of torture of Falungong practitioners by public security and labor reform cadres? From its companion national body, the CPPCC has exercised its advisory function in several national political issues. Its delegates have introduced bills or made public speeches against the water pollution in the Three Gorges Reservoir, the urgency of closing small coal mines, the poor quality of public security agents, and corruption among judges. Were they also moved to criticize the official policy on banning the Falungong and its execution?

Market Erosion of Monitoring and Sanctioning Capacity

An analysis of the role of leading political institutions sets the stage for addressing the main question posed by power dependence and market transition theories: in what ways and to what extent have market forces impaired the monitoring and sanctioning capacity of the communist state? First, as the scope of central planning is reduced, does the capacity of the neoauthoritarian state to monitor and sanction its citizens diminish? When the majority of Chinese residents no longer work in rural production teams or urban state-owned enterprises, dine in commune or factory mess halls, or reside in communal housing and government-owned living quarters, can the regime monitor their recreational activities? When individual cellular phones replace the housing block or village common phone, as the Internet supersedes surface mail, can the public security surveillance system still keep track of communications of its usual and unusual suspects? When the state no longer has direct control over local printers, book distribution networks, and clothing stores, can it prohibit the production and sale of Falungong publications, portraits of Li Hongzhi, and practice attire?

Just as important, how credible and effective is state sanction under market reforms? When the central government is no longer the largest or most preferred employer for increasing numbers of its citizens, does its threat to inflict punishment also sound more hollow? Even for those under its direct employ, would not the prospect of alternative placement or the existence of the safe cushions offered by cumulated savings or providing relatives reduce the dire impact of facing dismissal or demotion? More directly, do other demands on community policing created by hardened criminals, triad organizations, and urban transients distract the attention of public security and weaken its coercive hand? For CCP members on the fence, would they be more inclined to choose the Falungong over the CCP now that the latter's monitoring mechanism seems to be less effective and the sanctioning capacity less threatening?

Beyond undermining the effectiveness of state sanction, does the market also erode the coercive capacity of the regime by providing market alternatives? Did it offer safe havens for Falungong practitioners to elude the monitoring and sanctioning system of the neoauthoritarian state? Could Falungong practitioners still find employment after they submerged underground? Did nongovernment landlords rent to fugitive Falungong practitioners, defying household registration requirements? Could Falungong operatives purchase photocopiers, printing paper, and accessories to support their underground press? Did neighbors and colleges not turn them in to the authorities after they had inadvertently blown their covers?

Finally, does market competition affect the effectiveness of the propaganda war? When revolutionary operas no longer provide the main source of public entertainment, how would communist propaganda fare in the competitive media market? In the company of Hollywood classics, World Cup Soccer Finals, Miss China Beauty Pageants, and Hong Kong–styled soirees, did official media repackage anti-Falungong programs to suit popular viewer taste, and editors of the party newspaper *Renmin ribao* loosen its style and liven up the prose of its attack editorials? Would the library of anti-Falungong books still retain the same dogmatic pitch and forbidding tone of revolutionary apologetics? How did television producers balance the marching orders of the CCP secretary with the need for high program ratings, while publishers navigated the narrow channel between the CCP line and the bottom line? In the end, did anti-Falungong books sell or add to the unsold inventory? Did the general public tune in or vote with their remote controls?

Role of Civil Society

Has the market also engendered a civil society with increasing institutional and functional autonomy from the state? After all, the past two decades have seen the blossoming of new emergent trade organizations, Internet groups, and hobby groups in China; the Ministry of Civil Affairs lists more than 137,000 registered social organizations in China for 1999.[82] We can thus ask whether there were human rights groups among these that defended the constitutional right of the Falungong to exist and practice their breathing exercises. If it would be unrealistic to expect overt defiance of official repression, was there at least passive noncompliance? The five organized religions (Buddhist, Daoist, Catholic, Protestant, Islam) often state their public support of the regime's positions in both domestic and international affairs.[83] Have these religious bodies, either individually or collectively, voiced support of the anti-Falungong campaign? Short of organized, collective support, has the less authoritarian market reform fostered the likes of Don Quixote, Wei Jingsheng, or the Tank Man of Tiananmen who would dream the impossible dream and fight the unbeatable foe?

Rule of Law

Aside from their direct effects on reducing organized dependency, creating a less monitored society, providing safe havens for fugitives, and possibility fostering a less compliant civil society, market forces also erode state coercion capacity through indirect effects from the rule of law. A basic argument of the market-preserving federalism theory is the contention that a viable market economy needs to guarantee investor interests, safeguard property rights, and enforce contractual obligations. But in such a market-preserving institution, has the Falungong become the collateral beneficiary of the rule of law? In particular, was the banning of the Falungong premised on extant legal statutes? Was there any evidence that the judiciary was independent from the party and the executive branch? Was the detention, interrogation, arrest, trial, and conviction of Falungong leaders and rank-and-file based on existing laws? Have Chinese courts taken cases initiated by Falungong plaintiffs challenging the legality of official statutes and actions of law enforcement agencies? In cases where Falungong practitioners were defendants, were they given legal representation as provided under Chinese criminal law? Was sentencing fair and fit the alleged crime or extrapunitive?

The rule of law also imposes legal restraints on government behavior. In the administration of justice, this means that the processes of detaining, interrogating, setting bail, surveillance, arresting, trying, convicting, and sending defendants to labor reform are governed by elaborate legal procedures involving filing proper documentation and taking appropriate action by officials with constituted authority within definite time limits. Will the requirement to observe due process and adhere to legal procedures cramp public security agencies in enforcing compliance? Do both physical and legal constraints curb the coercive instincts of the authorities and strengthen the resolve of challengers to defy the regime?

To address these issues, this book examines the monitoring and sanctioning mechanisms suggested by power dependency and market transition theories to be pivotal for the survival of Chinese Communism. In these chapters I analyze the process of how the state prepared for the grand assault, the law enforcement implemented the ban of the Falungong, the propaganda campaign contrived the official spin to the campaign, and the education and conversion programs attempted to rehabilitate errant Falungong practitioners. Going beyond description, I address the question how efficient the anti-Falungong campaign was in implementing the ban, generating propaganda output, and prevailing on Falungong rank-and-file to renounce their affiliation with the congregation. Even more important, I evaluate the effectiveness of monitoring and sanctioning systems, by analyzing performance benchmarks of its communications operations, the extent of media coordination, the reception rates and industry awards for anti-Falungong media programs, and the percentage of recalcitrant Falungong practitioners. Along the way, I examine three sets of regime policy choices: why the regime chose July 22 to be the day to strike, how it triaged Falungong practitioners for prosecution, education, and conversion, and how it attempted to meet the imperatives of the administrative plan and the market in the publications campaign. An accompanying analysis is the institutional design and organizational issues inherent in the anti-Falungong campaign—balancing the conflicting need for central control and local autonomy in campaign operations, calibrating the degree of task specialization among bureaucratic agencies, and managing the campaign through existing institutions or through ad hoc agencies.

Organization of the Book

The explication of these issues is organized into the eight chapters that follow. Chapters 2 and 3 detail the political processes leading to the official
crackdown of July 22, 1999, and those of the implementation of the ban.
Chapter 2 begins with the investigation of whether the timing of the ban was
the result of policy indecision, Politburo agenda, or requisite response time.
This is followed by a description of the three law enforcement tasks: gathering intelligence, preventing protest rallies, and preparing for the propaganda offensive. The chapter closes with a scrutiny of government efforts to
camouflage preparations for the crackdown and a consideration of whether
these were visible in hindsight. Chapter 3 focuses on the five tasks involved
in enforcing the ban: arresting and prosecuting Falungong leaders, dissolving their organizations, destroying their publications stock, establishing a
surveillance network, and preventing Falungong from staging protests and
engaging in sabotage.

The two core programs of propaganda and reeducation in the anti-
Falungong campaign are the subject of chapters 4 and 5. Chapter 4 examines the media campaign, delineating the regular and special programs in
television and radio, as well as the different phases of the campaign in the
national press, tracing how the ban was announced, public support reported,
victory claimed, and the campaign consolidated. Then follows an analysis of
the anti-Falungong publications campaign, in particular, how the regime's
choice of campaign strategy, mode of publisher participation, and product
mix of the propaganda themes was driven by the need to fulfill the political demand for propaganda products on the one hand, and the dynamics of
market forces that shape the publication plans on the other.

Chapter 5 analyzes the education and conversion programs in the campaign. It begins with the need for the regime to sort different classes of
Falungong offenses, assigning each to a different type of reeducation program. It then describes the structure and content of conversion programs
that cater to both individuals and groups, and the responsibility system
that contracts reeducation outcome to the conversion teams. An analysis
of the special soft-sell conversion program in penal institutions in Yunnan
and Heilongjiang follows, ending with a comparison with the brutal methods
reported in Falungong sources.

Chapters 6 and 7 focus on the organizational aspects of the campaign.
Chapter 6 analyzes three institutional choices of how the campaign is managed: existing formal institutions versus ad hoc arrangements, the selection
of which set of CCP and state agencies should handle which set of tasks, and
the mode and extent of top CCP leadership involvement. This analysis at the
system level is complemented with a local-level analysis investigating how

campaign operations were structured at each lower administrative stratum. Chapter 7 focuses on the system of meetings through which announcements of the campaign were communicated through the CCP and government hierarchy. It examines, at each administrative level, how the meetings were organized vertically and horizontally, from central and provincial level agencies down to the enterprise and village levels. It also analyzes how the meetings were managed—who convened, presided over, and attended the meetings, what the agenda items were, and when and where they were held.

Chapters 8 and 9 offer an evaluation of the campaign. Chapter 8 appraises both the media and publications operations, analyzing the quantity of media output, the efficacy of propaganda productions, and the extent of collaboration among different media organizations. An assessment of the effectiveness of the conversion program is also presented that analyzes official statistics on the number of Falungong practitioners that have renounced their ties with the sect. The concluding chapter provides an overall assessment of the nature of Chinese politics as revealed in the anti-Falungong campaign. It addresses the question of whether the CCP played a dominant role in the campaign and whether its operations were overseen by the national legislature and national advisory body. It examines whether campaign management was centralized or characterized by local autonomy, and well coordinated or plagued by bureaucratic politics. It then analyzes the extent to which market forces have undermined the structural basis of CCP and central state capacity in China.

DATA SOURCES

Data for the analyses are largely drawn from official, primary sources that include the national and local press and provincial and municipal yearbooks. The national press sources used are the *Renmin ribao, Guangming ribao, Jiefangjun bao, Jingji ribao, Zhongguo qingnian bao,* and *Gongren ribao,* for their issues of July 23 to August 22, 1999. For a longer analytical period, the *Renmin ribao* from 2000 to 2005 was also consulted, using "Falungong" as a search keyword in its CD-ROM version. For the provincial press, the leading dailies of the 31 provinces were used, covering the same one-month period as the national press, starting July 23. Those of several municipal newspapers that are part of the holdings of the Universities Service Center in Hong Kong were also consulted: *Qiqihaer ribao* in the north; *Lanzhou wanbao* in the northwest; *Dalian ribao, Daqing ribao,* and *Jiemusi ribao* in the northeast; and *Maoming ribao* in the south. While local newspapers cover daily events, annual reviews are drawn from local government yearbooks, including yearbooks of all 31 provinces from 2001 to 2005, and municipal yearbooks from the same period available in the Universities Service Center collection. The sections perused are those on the CCP committee, legal and political affairs, public security, procuracy, judiciary, justice administration, and labor reform. The chapter on the media campaign (chapter 4) drew extensively on the 1999–2004 volumes of the *CCTV Yearbook, China Broadcast and Television Yearbook, China Publications Yearbook, China Journalism Yearbook,* and *China Book Yearbook*. These Chinese periodical sources are listed in the bibliography. Data for the chapters on conversion (chapter 5) and evaluation (chapter 8) are largely based on those in the *China Justice Administration Yearbooks* and the provincial yearbooks. Aside from the above sources, about a dozen anti-Falungong titles published in China from 1999 to 2001 were consulted, largely for chapters 2, 3, and 5.[84]

To introduce balance, extant Falungong sources have also been used. These include the vast media system that the Falungong in the diaspora has built since 1999, consisting of two news agencies,[85] two radio stations,[86] three television networks,[87] a publication series,[88] and a Web site.[89] Much of the content of these media productions can be found in its Web site, *Minghui,* which publishes around 40 news items daily on Falungong in China[90] and is cross-linked with the other Falungong organizations. Its data archive stores information on hundreds of cases of speaking out the truth, allegations of close to 3,000 cases of deaths of practitioners in official custody, more than 20,000 cases of torture against practitioners, and more than 300,000 cases of practitioners recanting their confessions and severance from the Falungong.[91] Among these Falungong sources, this study used mainly the *Minghui* Web site, and referred to other Falungong sources only selectively.

As listed in the notes to various chapters, additional sources include different reference works on Chinese party and government organizations, as well as legal compilations. They also include a special publication on the rehabilitation program in Yunnan's labor reform institutions. Two knowledgeable informants who are current Falungong practitioners have been resource persons clarifying questions on the Falungong. An insider account of Politburo deliberations about the Falungong from May through July 1999,[92] claimed to be written by a high-level government source, was also consulted, as were Hong Kong and U.S. periodicals on Chinese politics.[93]

Source Reliability

Reliability of sources has been a problem in the study of Chinese politics, and for this topic probably more so. Matters relating to security, whether domestic or international, have often be regarded as state secrets, as evidenced by the absence of listings for institutional history, organizational charts, and staff size for the ministries of Public Security, State Security, National Defense, and Foreign Affairs in the official directory for government organizations in China,[94] while those of most other departments are published. Without published government documentation, the analyst has to rely on unofficial sources, the reliability of which is difficult to ascertain. Just as important as the issue of availability, the strategic use of information by both government and Falungong is also a problem, given the adversarial nature of the anti-Falungong campaign, when both antagonists try to score political points through selective use of evidence or even misinformation.

Sources of Bias

In the course of research, I have found different sources of reporting bias from the Chinese government, Falungong, and journalists outside China. In government sources, errors can be made by sloppy reporting. For instance, *Shanxi ribao* reported that the Yongji Thermal Plant organized all cadres and workers to view the TV news banning the Falungong on July 21. Since the news on the Falungong was only broadcast nationwide on the afternoon of July 22, the reporter and editor of the *Shanxi ribao* probably made a mistake on the date of the viewing.[95] Inconsistencies can occur when different bureaucratic agencies use dissimilar counting rules. In the compilation of national and provincial yearbooks, the same agency might be asked by different yearbook editors to submit data by different deadlines. Depending on the cutoff date for submission, the agency may provide estimate figures for one yearbook and final numbers for another. I have found, for instance, that the percentage of Falungong inmates in labor reform institutes who have converted (*Falungong renyuan zhuangfa lu*) for Tianjin in 2003 was listed as more than 82% in the *China Justice Administration Yearbook* (2004),[96] but the same figure was listed as 88% in the *Tianjian Yearbook* (2004).[97] A similar discrepancy can be found in the *China Justice Administration Yearbook* (2004) that reports 45% of Falungong criminals (*Falungong zuifan*) had converted in labor reform institutes in Heilongjiang in 2003, but the *Heilongjiang Yearbook* (2004) lists 50.8% for the same figure.[98]

There were also inconsistencies among different nongovernment sources. For the number of Falungong practitioners apprehended by the government on July 20, the day when the crackdown began, Zong Hairen, in his 2002 book *Zhu Rongji zai Yi Jiujiujiu Nian* [Zhu Rongji in 1999], reported that 5,600 Falungong practitioners were arrested on July 20,[99] whereas *Cheng ming* reported that arrests were made in 22 cities,[100] resulting in the apprehension of 150 Falungong leaders on the same day.[101] Using a different temporal period, the *Hong Kong Standard* reported that 50,000 Falungong followers were arrested in the first week of the crackdown.[102] As elaborated in chapter 3, the large discrepancy in the *Cheng ming* and Zong accounts can be the result of using different counting rules, or using different categories of detainees in criminal processing in China. The *Cheng ming* source is clearly at variance not only with the Zong source but also with sources covered in a Shanghai and Shaanxi newspaper, which reported arrests not in the *Cheng ming* list of cities and much larger numbers of per city arrests.[103]

While Zong's estimate maybe closer to the target in the number of arrests made on July 20, he is clearly mistaken when he reports on what transpired in a Politburo meeting on March 25, 1999. According to Zong, Jiang Zemin convened, presided over, and spoke at a Politburo meeting on March 25 to discuss the U.S. bombing of the Chinese embassy in Belgrade the day before. Zong includes a long quotation of Jiang's speech at the meeting supporting Premier Zhu traveling to the United States despite the bombing.[104] However, Jiang was in Europe from March 20 through 30, meeting President Dreifus on March 25 in Switzerland,[105] and could not have attended and spoken at the Politburo meeting as reported by Zong.

Falungong sources are not immune from erroneous reporting. There was extensive coverage on the atrocities and torture that allegedly took place in labor reform institutions, in particular, a "death concentration camp" located inside the Liaoning Provincial Thrombosis Chinese-Western Medical Hospital at Sujiatun in Shenyang, the provincial capital of Liaoning.[106] Starting on March 9, 2006, a series of more than 200 reports published in the *Epochtimes* and on the *Minghui* Web site claimed that more than 6,000 Falungong practitioners were reportedly tortured to death and had their organs harvested, and their cadavers were incinerated at the hospital.[107] The reports attracted much international attention, including site visits by the international media and diplomatic community.[108]

The story has not been corroborated by other reports. The State Council convened a press conference on the story on April 12, 2006, claiming the hospital had only slightly more than 300 beds and was not equipped for organ transplant.[109] It was visited twice by officers of the U.S. consulate-general in Shenyang, first by consular officer Douglas Kelly on March 22, and again by U.S. Consul-General David Kornbluth with an entourage of five staff members on April 14. Quoting a spokesman of the U.S. embassy in China, an Associated Press release reports that the site was indeed a hospital in function, an indirect affirmation of the Chinese government position. Several media organizations, including the *Dagong bao,* the Phoenix Television Station in Hong Kong, and the Japan Television Network Broadcast company, visited the premises on March 31 and did not confirm the *Epochtimes* story.[110] A discussion of reporting bias in government and Falungong sources relating to the subject matter follows in a later section.

Beyond slopping reporting, adversarial polemics, and alternative use of different counting rules and categories, an additional source of inconsistency in reporting inheres in the convoluted history and political status of Falungong itself. In its seven years of history, the Falungong was an evolving social organization that underwent major metamorphosis from a local to national movement, from one focused exclusively on training in breathing exercises to one grounded on spiritual cultivation, from one where its application for official organizational status was under review to one where its repeated registration filings were summarily rejected. These different states of the movement led to corresponding changes not only in structural forms but also in organizational principles and practices. In addition, the Falungong as an endangered organization was operating outside the law. Like chameleons and other life forms in adversity, it was driven by its self-defense instinct to develop survival structures, dependency relations, and camouflage mechanisms. This means that not only did Falungong structures and functions vary over time, but also their color and anatomy changed according to local conditions, donning camouflage fatigue when it sensed clear and present danger, thus confounding analysts and investigators. Third, unlike most organized religions where official membership often entails an explicit profession of faith, expressed compliance with a set of commandments, and adherence to distinctive and visible religious practices, the Falungong has no institutionalized means to delineate members from nonmembers or authorized from unauthorized agents. It has no rites of induction and expulsion and no formal procedures to deal with overzealous aspirants, black sheep, and false prophets. Falungong sources claimed that some of the profiteering and heterodox practices attributed by official sources to the movement were actually those of charlatans and swindlers masquerading as Li Hongzhi's disciples. In combination, the tortuous history of the Falungong, its structural ambivalence, and the lack of clear identification of its membership provide ample fodder for both the government and Falungong to choose what to report on the basis of "to each according to his need."

Source Bias by Subject Matter

There is thus need for varying degrees of caution in using both the official and Falungong sources, whose reliability varies with respect to subject matter. For much of the analysis of CCP meetings on the Falungong and the organization of anti-Falungong CCP and government agencies, there is probably little strategic utility in fraudulent reporting. Not much can be gained by falsifying the date, timing, location, participants, and agenda of CCP meetings on the Falungong after July 23, 1999, when those meetings were routinely convened and reported. Nor was there much need to misinform the public about the organizational structure and function of anti-Falungong CCP and government agencies. Such reporting was clearly not common and much less mandatory, and either the agency or the media could choose not to release the information rather than report false information. Similarly, it can also be reasoned that official reports on news production, the organization of the media, and publication campaign are probably factual.

The more serious bias in both government and Falungong sources is likely to lie in reports on government coercion in law enforcement as well as the portrayal of Li Hongzhi, the Falungong organization, and its practices. For government sources, the techniques of surveillance, both electronic and human intelligence, as well as security operations (the who, what, when, and where to detain, interrogate, and arrest; the measures adopted to prevent Falungong practitioners from engaging in protest or sabotage activities) are generally covered by a blanket of silence, to keep the public enemies in the dark. In addition to security operations, information on the methods and results of interrogation and conversion programs in prisons and labor reform institutions is likely to be far from complete. The need to report on these methods to the public is outweighed by the cost, especially when these involve coercion. Readers can thus expect official sources to selectively report on the judicial rather than extrajudicial, and on gentle and kind rather than cruel and unusual methods. Conversion success reported in government sources also needs to be qualified. Local public security and labor reform officials were given performance targets to fulfill, and there is likely to be an upward bias in the reported rates. Because conversion success was generally measured by the number of detained practitioners signing the document to renounce ties with the Falungong, it does not capture those who would return to Falungong practice after they were discharged from official detention.

The same polemical bias in government and Falungong sources is also evident in the treatment of Li Hongzhi and the Falungong organizations. To support its propaganda claims, official media accentuated the government claim that the Falungong was an evil cult, Li Hongzhi a fraud, its doctrines irrational and superstitious, and its physical exercises harmful to body and mind. To justify its ban on the Falungong, the regime was intent to show that it was an illegal organization with political agenda and capacity, a well-structured hierarchy, an efficient communications and mobilization network, an abundant financial resource driven by a profiteering motive. Falungong sources are eager to show the contrary, attempting to prove that the Falungong physical exercises have predominantly beneficial health effects, that its spiritual cultivation leads to moral rectitude, that it was only an interest group and not a social organization that required registration, on grounds that it had no command structure, no hierarchy, no leadership, and no formal membership. It claimed that the government allegations about its profiteering practice were disingenuous and that the government used flawed accounting methods, that much of the alleged Falungong income went to third parties, and that it neither required nor encouraged its practitioners to make financial contributions to the congregation. Not content with being apologetic, it went on the offensive to accuse the government of having breached its own laws on freedom of assembly, noncoercive interrogation and detention, and fair and open trial. It accused the authorities of having used extrajudicial methods and draconian torture to force practitioners to renounce their ties with the Falungong.

Dealing with Source Reliability Problems

Disinterested analysts are constrained by the necessity to rely on the government and the Falungong, the only main data sources for much of the subject matter of the present study. Nonetheless, we can be more critical and judicious in their use. Where both differ, their discrepancies are reported, and in some cases (e.g., the organizational and financial structure of the Falungong, and the treatment of its practitioners in detention), analyzed and explained. Where one source has no substantiating evidence and is contradicted by alternative reports (e.g., Falungong allegation that a Shenyang hospital was an organ harvesting center referred to above), the inconsistencies and lack of corroborating evidence are noted. Contrarian logic is applied to establish the opposite of what the source was intent to argue, as when government sources unwittingly suggest that the Falungong had only a loose organization, that torture could have been used on Falungong detainees, and that its campaign was neither effective nor efficient, or when Falungong sources inadvertently disclosed that its practitioners did breach government laws, that official central government policy did not condone torture and detainee abuse, and its projects were unconstrained by hard budgets.

In the analysis that follows, I have attempted to be critical in using both official and Falungong sources where strategic utility outweighs truthful reporting.

Chapter Two

Preparing for the Crackdown

This chapter analyzes the regime's preparations for the crackdown on the Falungong announced on July 22, 1999. First, it investigates whether the timing of the suppression in late July was the result of policy indecision, Politburo agenda, the schedule of the public security apparatus, or the requisite bureaucratic response time. Second, it examines the set of institutions that the regime relied on to formulate and implement the plan of action from April 25 to July 22, and how the Falungong was managed in this critical period, tracing the evolution of the process from makeshift arrangements to the formal establishment of the Central Leading Group on Dealing with the Falungong and its executive arm, the "610 Office." This is followed by an analysis of the regime's efforts to gather intelligence at the central, local, and enterprise levels; to prevent Falungong groups from staging local protests and petition rallies in Beijing; and to prepare for the propaganda warfare that was to begin on July 22. The last section examines the secrecy of presuppression political management, when the official propaganda cannons were silent, officials denied that the regime was planning to ban the Falungong, and the seven members of the Politburo Standing Committee (PSC) kept up their public appearances in the days leading to the suppression. Despite official attempts to mask the imminent suppression, it is precisely these cover-up efforts that reveal its repressive intent on closer examination.

SELECTION OF TIMING OF THE CRACKDOWN

The Falungong siege of the Chinese Communist Party (CCP) and state headquarters was on April 25, but the official dissolution of the Falungong took effect only 90 days later on July 22. An obvious question is whether the choice to ban the Falungong on July 22 was the result of indecision and inaction on the top echelon of the CCP leadership, or the political calendar of the Politburo and that of its public security operative arm, or simply the inherent need for time to investigate and prepare for the case against the Falungong.

There were precedents to Politburo indecision and inaction on how to deal with challenging groups. In 1985–86, the CCP did not crack down on student protests on college campuses, a failure of will for which then Secretary-General Hu Yaobang was purged by CCP elders in January, 1987.[1] Two and a half years later, it was the turn of his successor, Zhao Ziyang, to suffer the same fate for being unwilling and unable to deal resolutely with the two-month-old student movement.[2] As chronicled in Zhang Liang's 2001 *Zhongguo "liusi" zhenxiang* (*The Tiananmen papers*), Zhao's indecision was evident in his failure to convene a Politburo meeting on the student demonstrations after 100,000 students assembled in Tiananmen on April 19, 1989, two armed clashes with security agents on April 19 and 20, and a larger demonstration of 200,000 students and citizens on April 21. Given Zhao's ambivalence, the Politburo was more hesitant than proactive. It was only on the 10th day of the student demonstrations that the first Politburo meeting on the incident was convened on April 24; the first Central Committee notice prescribing action was issued that evening, and the first official document denouncing the student demonstration was published on April 26.[3] Official interactions with the students were to come even later. The first meeting of students with central government officials (Yuan Mu, He Dongchang) was on April 27, and with a Politburo member (Li Peng) only on May 18, after the top party leadership decided to impose martial law.[4] There was no consensus within the PSC on dealing with the students during these two months. Zhao made several attempts to overturn the April 26 *Renmin ribao* editorial characterizing the student demonstrations as turmoil. The vote for imposing martial law at the May 17 PSC meeting was reported to be two affirmative, two negative, and one abstention.[5] Even until his death in January 2005, Zhao refused to recant his opposition to the CCP decision to suppress the student movement.[6]

Resoluteness of the Politburo

In the case of the Falungong, the Politburo was neither indecisive nor inactive after the siege on April 25, 1999. On the day of the siege, Premier Zhu Rongji met with the Falungong representatives, joining Politburo member and security tsar Luo Gan and other top party, state, and Beijing municipal officials.[7] That evening, Jiang Zemin wrote a letter to the CCP's top leaders expressing his bewilderment on the mobilization capacity of Falungong and its discipline, calling it the largest collective action since the 1989 student movement.[8] In stark contrast to Zhao's ambivalence toward the student movement throughout the two months, Jiang denounced the April 25 siege as the boldest public challenge to regime authority since the founding of the Republic, unprecedented even during the Cultural Revolution, and called for resolute action to "nip it in the bud."[9] In a subsequent Politburo meeting on

June 7, Jiang proposed the establishment of a leadership committee to deal with the Falungong and outlined a strategy of gathering intelligence, exposing Li Hongzhi's political motives, and publicizing cases where the practice of Falungong caused deaths, suicides, schizophrenia, and systematic critique of superstition.[10] These latter formed the basic features of the anti-Falungong campaign in July. In yet a later Politburo meeting on July 17, Jiang characterized the April 25 event as "the most serious political incident since June 4."[11] Altogether, Jiang delivered no fewer than three speeches on the Falungong from April 25 to July 20 and issued 13 written policy directives on the Falungong.[12] Li Peng and a majority of PSC members joined Jiang in urging suppression of the Falungong.[13] There was no report of opposition within the PSC to Jiang's hard-line view or the Politburo decision for suppression.[14] The April 26, June 7, and June 17 meetings also approved action items, apparently uncontested, against the Falungong.[15] Clearly, then, Politburo dissent and indecision do not explain its inaction from late April to late July.

Beijing and Politburo Event Calendar, April–July 1999

Even if the top party leadership was resolved to strike at the Falungong, three sets of factors could still affect the timing of the suppression: avoiding negative international media coverage, scheduling around major foreign policy crises, and building a strong case against the Falungong. First, to avoid negative international media coverage, the target dates could not coincide with high-profile international summits or state visits at home and abroad or be temporally close to major anniversaries in Beijing, all of which would attract a large contingent of foreign press alert for stories on continued state repression in China. The regime was quite likely not to repeat its mistake of scheduling the Gorbachev visit and that of the Asian Development Bank in May 1989, when the demonstrating students exploited the presence of the international media.[16] In effect, this would have blocked out a week before and after June 4, the tenth anniversary of the Tiananmen Massacre, and October 1, the 50th anniversary of the founding of the People's Republic of China, as periods when the regime need to abstain from mass arrests. To a lesser extent, the same reasoning would also rule out the two-week period around July 1, when the anniversary of Hong Kong's reversion to Chinese rule would have primed foreign journalists, defiant legislators, resident human rights, and Falungong groups for similar stories.

Intrusion of Foreign Policy Crisis

Second, while the Politburo could avoid major anniversaries and state visits, it could not have prevented major foreign policy crises, two of which have intruded in its timetable. The U.S. bombing of the Chinese embassy in Belgrade on May 8 created an international crisis for the Beijing leaders. At its heels, Taiwan President Lee Teng-hui's enunciation on July 9 of the "Two States Theory," which moved toward independence, also required the Politburo to respond.[17] Beijing regarded this statement as a major departure from the "One China" principle on which it claimed consensus had been reached in 1992, and one that portended movement toward Taiwan independence, which it vigorously opposed. The top leadership reportedly convened more than 10 meetings of the Politburo, the Taiwan Affairs Leading Committee of the Central Committee, and the Military Affairs Commission of the Central Committee to discuss response strategies.[18] The question is whether these events affected the timing of the crackdown. To examine the intensity and durability of the effects of the two crises on the Politburo agenda, an analysis of the relative number of front-page (1) "important news" items (*yaowen*), and (2) authoritative editorials and commentaries of the *Renmin ribao* shows a monotonic decline of front-page coverage of the Belgrade embassy bombing over time, as well as persistence after the crisis erupted on May 8, 1999. In absolute terms, the number of front-page "important news" items on the embassy bombing decreased steadily, from four to five every day in the first eight days (May 9–16) to one to three in the following seven days (May 17–23), and then none or one thereafter through June 8. In terms of persistence, there was daily coverage in the front-page in the first two weeks (May 9–23), and thereafter only intermittently, with days of no coverage increasing in frequency. Front-page editorials and authoritative commentaries on the embassy bombing followed a similar pattern, with the last one published on May 27, three days after the publication of the "important news" on the crisis first became intermittent. The same pattern of front-page coverage, sometimes accompanied by authoritative commentary, also occurred in the response to the two-state theory, where authoritative commentary and front-page coverage began and ceased almost at the same time, from July 13 to 22. In both cases, we can thus infer this pattern of double exit of the last authoritative commentary and last continuous coverage as signaling the weakening of the crisis, freeing the Politburo to turn its attention to other pressing matters.

In combination, the three major anniversaries and the two foreign policy crises effectively ruled out April 30 to May 5 (Labor Day National Holiday), May 8 to June 11 (Embassy bombing and June 4 anniversary), June 24 to July 8 (Return of Hong Kong), and July 9–22 (Lee's Two State Theory) as target dates of the suppression. As shown in table 2.1, this would still leave May 6–7, 24–27, June 12–23, and after July 22 for the regime to take repressive action. Why did it not choose the earlier two windows? The need for due diligence appears to be the reason.

Table 2.1: Political Calendar of Blocked-Out Dates for Crackdown

	M	T	W	Th	F	S	S
April	25	26	27	28	29	30[a]	1
May	2	3	4	5	6	7	8[b]
	9	10	11	12	13	14	15
	16	17	18	19	20	21	22
	23	24	25	26	27	28[c]	29
June	30	31	1	2	3	4	5
	6	7	8	9	10	11	12
	13	14	15	16	17	18	19
	20	21	22	23	24[d]	25	26
	27	28	29	30	1	2	3
July	4	5	6	7	8	9[e]	10
	11	12	13	14	15	16	17
	18	19	20	21	22	23	24
	25	26	27	28	29	30	31

[a]April 30 to May 5 was the National Labor Day holiday.
[b]May 8–23 was the Belgrade embassy bombing and aftermath.
[c]May 28 to June 11 was the sensitive period a week before and after the Tiananmen incident anniversary.
[d]June 24 to July 8 was the week of and week after the return of Hong Kong on July 1.
[e]July 9–22 was Lee Tenghui's Two-State Theory statement and aftermath.

Need for Due Diligence

First, there was need for time to gather the basic intelligence. In the Politburo meeting of April 26, a decision was reached to conduct a full investigation of the Falungong movement at home and abroad,[19] a process detailed further below. The need for such investigation appears to have stemmed from both the need to collect intelligence on the adversary and the Politburo's concern about the overseas connection of the Falungong.[20] Second, it appeared that only after the basic facts of Falungong's membership size, organizational structure, geographical distribution, and evidence of culpability was known did the Politburo move to the next stage of planning the operation. In early June, the 610 Office, named after the inaugural date, was established as the executive arm of a special leading group to described in the next section. Headed by Luo Gan, the office was entrusted with the task to "study, investigate and to come up with a unified approach in terms of specific steps, methods, and measures to resolve the 'Falungong' problem." It was authorized to deal with central and local, party and state agencies, which were called upon to act in close coordination with that office.[21] It can be reasoned, then, that the regime had not worked out its suppression strategy by mid-June.

Third, the regime was apparently intent to declare war on the Falungong only after it had built a strong case against the congregation and when it felt the outcome was certain.

When the regime launched its suppression campaign in late July, due intelligence research had already resulted in a list of the top Falungong leadership in all provinces, information on Li Hongzhi's involvement with the April 25 siege of the Zhongnanhai, previous Falungong protest rallies in the provinces, and cases of deaths, illness, and insanity allegedly caused by practicing Falungong. Information on local Falungong leaders was used to conduct the manhunt. Information on their activities was published on July 23 to show probable cause for their arrests and detention.[22]

PREPARATIONS FOR SUPPRESSION

Preparations for the suppression involved three related tasks: gathering intelligence on the Falungong, preventing its protest rallies and petition activities to be staged locally or in Beijing, and launching propaganda assaults on the sect. Since the Falungong had not been outlawed at this stage, and assembly and demonstrations were legal under the law, these law enforcement actions had to be done with finesse. Much of the intelligence gathering was conducted through covert investigations. Preventive deterrence and interception were used to restrict protest activities, rather than coercive dispersion. Propaganda attacks did not name the Falungong or Li Hongzhi but only generic superstitions.

Intelligence-Gathering Operations

Even before April 25, some local public security establishments conducted investigations on the Falungong. The Guizhou Provincial Bureau of Public Security gathered information on the sect after it received written complaints from local residents sometime in April 1999.[23] That of neighboring Shaanxi Province also conducted investigations before April 25.[24] Both efforts seemed to focus on specific local activities and did not appear to be elaborate. More systematic investigations were launched only after the Falungong rally in Zhongnanhai on April 25, after which the Politburo met and resolved to take punitive action against the sect. The Ministry of Public Security then made a unified plan to collect intelligence both at home and abroad, for efforts on the national as well as local levels.[25] Overseas, security agents stationed in diplomatic missions were instructed to gather information on the political orientation of the movement and on Li Hongzhi. At home, the Political Protection Department of the Ministry of Public Security instructed local public security bureaus to investigate and monitor Falungong activities.[26] In addition, 25 groups of public security and state security agents, reportedly led by Deputy Public Security Ministers Zhao Yongji and Zhu Chunlin, were dispatched to provinces and cities with a strong Falungong presence, to work with their provincial counterparts on intelligence operations.[27]

Local Government Activities

Whether working independently of or in concert with central public security agents, local authorities also carried out their own investigations. In the southernmost region, Hainan provincial authorities initiated an investigation on April 26 on the history of the sect in the province, its leadership profile, organizational structure, pattern of activities, and their characteristics.[28] In North China, the public security establishment of Neimonggu conducted a regionwide investigation of the sect,[29] while that of Gansu Province collected intelligence on different levels of Falungong organizations, which the authorities used to avert Falungong plans to organize protest rallies.[30] At the subprovincial level, Siping municipal law enforcement agents of Liaoning Province placed all 120 core Falungong leaders under surveillance soon after April 25, 1999.[31] Jinzhou Municipality in the same province was reported to have investigated local Falungong structure,[32] while law enforcement agencies of Wulumuqi in Inner Mongolia surveyed the core leadership, its activities, and the geographic distribution of Falungong stations and practice sites.[33] Elsewhere in Henan Province, Zhengzhou Municipal Public Security Bureau acted on the instruction of central, provincial, and municipal authorities to collect prosecutable criminal evidence on the local Falungong core leadership.[34]

More intense efforts were made by three local authorities where the Falungong had been active. In Wuhan, home to a Falungong main station and the nationwide Falungong publication distribution hub, municipal authorities launched a special investigation of Falungong activities in early 1997. The Municipal Public Security Bureau expanded its investigation after the Falungong protest rally in Beijing on April 25.[35] In Jinan Municipality in Shandong Province, close to 1,000 Falungong practitioners had besieged the publication office of the *Qilu Evening News* for two days in June 1998.[36] When news of the Falungong protest rally in Beijing on April 25 reached Jinan, the Municipal Party Committee convened an emergency meeting that evening to conduct an immediate investigation of the organizational structure, core leadership, distribution of practice sites, and pattern of activities, and resolved to send a task force to work with the provincial team to repatriate Falungong petitioners from Beijing. The following day, the Municipal Party Committee convened a meeting of party secretaries of subordinate cities and counties, as well as leading cadres of concerned municipal departments, to set up a "rapid response system" (*quaichu fanying tixi*) and to extend the investigation of Falungong organization and activities in greater depth and wider scope throughout the jurisdiction within the municipality.[37]

The most exhaustive attempts were made by Jilin Province, the home of Falungong movement, where its public security agencies immediately shifted to high gear after April 25. Acting on specific instructions from the Ministry of Public Security in Beijing, the provincial party committee, and the provincial government, the Jilin Bureau of Public Security established a special investigation program on the Falungong. It formed seven special investigation teams, which were dispatched to different localities within the province as well as neighboring Inner Mongolia, to conduct extensive and in-depth investigation on Li Hongzhi and the Falungong. Using both overt interviews and covert techniques, these seven teams worked full time for two months and compiled systematic reports on the alleged (1) organizational structure of the Falungong in Jilin; (2) illegal publication, printing, and distribution of Falungong publications; (3) theft of state secrets; and (4) use of the Internet to mobilize protest rallies, as well as to propagate Falungong doctrine, Li Hongzhi's instructions, and rumors. In all, these investigations resulted in six comprehensive reports on the Falungong, more than 30 special reports, and a documentary film on *Li Hongzhi: The Man, and His Deeds*. These were used not only for due intelligence research as well as prosecutorial evidence in the trial of Falungong leaders by the central and Jilin provincial authorities, they were also later distributed throughout the nation as propaganda feed.[38]

Enterprise-Level Intelligence Gathering

Systematic intelligence gathering was also conducted down to the enterprise level in two subsystems in Jilin Province. First, the public security departments in cultural institutions (*wenbao bumen*) of Jilin issued a notice instructing its agents to step up its surveillance and control (*jiankong*) of Falungong activities. Through investigating 37 publishers, printers, and cultural institutions, security agents identified Falungong core leaders in these enterprises and gathered information on protest rallies being planned. These agencies have collected more than 300 pieces of information on the Falungong, based on which they compiled and submitted more than 50 reports to their superiors.[39] A parallel attempt was initiated by the public security departments in the economic sector (*sheng jingbao bumen*), which also issued a notice to all enterprises under its jurisdiction. The investigation focused on the extent of the Falungong network and assemblies among staff and workers and resulted in the registration of 348 Falungong practitioners. At the same time, action was also taken to prevent possible sabotage by Falungong practitioners to disrupt production. Four different task forces were organized to inspect strategic units and departments and to strengthen their security measures. Intelligence units were established in industrial security departments in different administrative levels to report on Falungong activities and security conditions twice a day. [40]

Elsewhere, enterprise-level investigations were also reported in large industrial corporations in three other cities. The security department of the Hangzhou Steel Consortium, assisted by the local public security bureau, conducted a complete investigation of Falungong practitioners in the company in the end of April and worked out surveillance plans, contingency schemes, and reporting mechanisms to monitor the sect's activities.[41] In South China in June, Liu Xinwen, the Deputy Chief of the Falungong Guangzhou Guidance Station, turned over his large collection of Falungong publications, video tapes, and DVDs to the party committee of the Guangzhou Steel Consortium that employed him.[42] Even earlier, local action took place in Southwest Guizhou Province on the same day as the Zhongnanhai rally, when Chen Jiahua, the deputy head of the Falungong station in Junyi, was requested by her pharmaceutical company employer and the Office of Retired Cadres of the Junyi Military District to cease and desist from practicing Falungong. After 20 visits she complied, and she resigned from the sect at the end of April.[43]

Intelligence-Gathering Methods

In gathering intelligence on the Falungong, public security agencies relied on different sources and methods. Local residents informed public security agents on the activities of the Falungong.[44] More systematic efforts were reported by different public security systems in two localities that were Falungong strongholds. In Shenyang Municipality of Liaoning Province, which had five Falungong main stations, the most numerous among all provinces in China, public security agencies used different methods to collect intelligence on the sect. First, through intercepting the Internet communications of the Falungong, local authorities reaped vital information on the local Falungong network, its program of activities, and protest rallies being planned. Second, through interrogating Falungong practitioners who were detained by public security agents for participating in protest rallies in Beijing, Shenyang authorities also collected information on the command structure, leadership profile, and geographic distribution of Falungong stations and practice sites. Third, through identifying and cultivating informants who were close to core Falungong leaders, authorities infiltrated the top organizational levels of the sect. Based on these techniques, Shenyang authorities compiled a list of more than 1,000 core Falungong leaders and members, who were placed under a special surveillance system overseen by both local Shenyang public security agents as well as the state security operatives.[45]

There was also a report of specific investigations conducted at the residence level. In Shanghai, a party branch secretary in a residential housing committee visited a retired party member and Falungong practitioner in the housing block in June, accompanied with a public security agent. When their request for the meeting was declined, the party branch secretary contacted the practitioner's work unit for assistance.[46] The report suggests that, at least in Shanghai in June, a local party branch secretary and public security agent needed to request a meeting with a Falungong practitioner at the latter's residence, rather than summoning the practitioner to appear at the CCP branch office or the Public Security Office. The report further suggests that the Falungong practitioner was not required by law to meet with the local officials. Elsewhere, however, other reports suggest that local officials were more assertive or persistent and that local high-ranking Falungong officials more compliant. Twice in May and June, authorities in Jilin Province and Changchun Municipality summoned Zhao Lixun, chief of the Falungong main station in Changchun, the birthplace of Li Hongzhi, for interrogation.[47]

In all, over 3,000 public security agents reportedly investigated Falungong activities at home and abroad prior to the official dissolution in July 22, 1999.[48] When the regime launched its suppression campaign in late July, these intelligence-gathering activities had already resulted in an estimate of the basic organizational structure and numerical strength of the Falungong, a list of its top Falungong leadership in all provinces, Li Hongzhi's involvement with the April 25 siege of the Zhongnanhai, previous Falungong protest rallies in the provinces, and cases of deaths, illness, and insanity allegedly caused by practicing Falungong.[49] The intelligence collected thus provided the culpable evidence for arrest and prosecution of Falungong leaders and the material substance for the propaganda campaign against the sect. There was at least one case of arrest, when Dalian Municipal Public Security agents apprehended Yu Xiaode for printing and distributing 6,000 copies of Li Hongzhi's writings on June 4.[50] It appears that the Falungong practitioners were aware of the investigation if not the arrest by the first half of June. They circulated reports that the authorities were likely to take action against the leadership of the Falungong after June 4. To plan for such contingency, the Falungong network in Sichuan's Luoshan County elected second-echelon leaders in case their frontline leaders were arrested.[51]

Demobilization

In tandem with intelligence gathering for the eventual crackdown, public security and other local government agencies also needed to take action to stop the spread of the Falungong, to preempt local demonstrations, and to deter local practitioners traveling to Beijing to stage protest rallies. First, to stop the numerical growth and geographical diffusion of the Falungong, some local party and government agencies adopted measures to deal with party members who joined the sect, the core leaders, and rank-and-file practitioners. Before July 20, party committees in Shandong Province launched an education campaign of "detoxicating" party members who practiced the Falungong, resulting in a conversion rate of 77.8% among sectarian CCP members in the province.[52] In another northern province (Shaanxi), an extensive surveillance system was established by the Public Security Bureau in Xian to keep a close watch over the activities of 21 core Falungong practitioners in the provincial capital.[53] Elsewhere in two coastal cities, athletic bureaus reported efforts to curtail the development of Falungong under their jurisdictions. As early as December 1998, the Athletic Bureau of Wujiang City in Suzhou Municipality included the criterion of controlling the growth of the Falungong when it evaluated the performance of athletic officials for promotion in subordinate townships.[54] Its counterpart in Shanghai issued a notice on May 16, 1999, to dissuade (*chuanzu*) and prohibit (*zhizi*) Falungong practitioners from displaying their banners in practice sites. Sometime before the official ban in July 1999, it also promulgated regulations placing new restrictions on the locations and type of activities where public places could be used for exercise assemblies.[55]

To limit the ripple effect of the April 25 protest rally in Beijing, local authorities were instructed to preempt Falungong practitioners from staging local demonstrations and to prevent the sectarians from petitioning in Beijing. The latter was the more complicated tasks, involving not only setting up road blocks but also dispatching teams of public security agents to Beijing to repatriate Falungong practitioners when interception failed. Most of these cases were reported to have occurred after the ban on July 22, and are discussed in chapter 3 on postban law enforcement operations. There were several reports on preventing local demonstrations that took place before July 22. In Haikou Municipality of Hainan Province, public security agents aborted a sympathetic rally held on April 25 by local Falungong practitioners.[56] Their counterparts in Xian Municipality, together with local governments and party committees, spoke to each practitioner and dissuaded him or her from participating in two large planned Falungong activities on May 1 and May 22.[57] In more preventive action, CCP committee members of its Municipal Public Security Bureau led local police to take up positions in the clock tower and Xincheng city squares at 5 A.M. each morning to preempt Falungong assemblies.[58] Gentler and kinder crowd control strategies were used in Shanghai. To prevent the large Falungong assembly scheduled for Li Hongzhi's birthday on May 29 from taking place along the riverside in Waitan, the Huangpu District Party Committee and government instructed housing block committees and athletic associations to organize a 1,200-citizen exercise troupe to occupy the rally site before the Falungong practitioners assembled. For 15 consecutive days starting June 1, it mobilized 18,000 local residents to participate in the exercise activities, thus depriving the Falungong from staging a mass assembly.[59] As shown chapter 3, the cat-and-mouse game of staging and preventing Falungong rallies continued into the postban period.

The First Propaganda Salvo

As described in the next section, the Falungong was not named in any attack article in the *Renmin ribao* before July 23, 1999. The first propaganda assaults on the Falungong were launched in late June, about two weeks after the establishment of the 610 Office and a month before the announcement of the ban on July 22. They were headed by Ding Guan'gen, deputy head of the Central Leading Committee dealing with the Falungong,[60] and the CCP's propaganda chief who oversaw the content of the nation's vast electronic and printed media network. The assaults were composed of three editorial series denouncing superstition and lauding atheism, while containing veiled attacks on the Falungong, published in the two leading national daily news-papers—*Renmin ribao*, the party newspaper, and *Guangming ribao*, the daily newspaper for intellectuals. The first of the three series was a weekly editorial in the *Renmin ribao* titled "Extol Science, Eradicate Superstition," and reprinted in the *Guangming ribao* on the same day.[61] Both were published on the front page, usually on Mondays, where Falungong was not mentioned by name. A second series with more academic articles extolling atheism was published in irregular intervals from two to five days in the *Renmin ribao*.[62] The third series, also on an irregular schedule, was published in *Guangming ribao* written by scholars denouncing superstition.[63] In this critical month before repression, neither the television stations nor the publications indus-try at the central government level appeared to be involved. The attack was on the general target of superstition, not even religion, and neither the Falungong nor Li Hongzhi was named. There was also no reference to any protest rallies by any religious or *qigong* group, or the malignant medical effects of practicing the Falungong.

As shown in table 2.2, 12 unique articles were published from June 21 to July 21, averaging one between two to three days, and spaced from one to five days apart. The publication dates appear to be coordinated, where no multiple articles in the three series were published on the same date, except July 13. The publication interval did not become shorter as the crackdown approached in late July.

In the meantime, the propaganda machinery was hard at work produc-ing a large number of books, editorials, investigative reports, and special

Table 2.2: Anti-Falungong Coverage in *Renmin ribao* and *Guangming ribao*, June 21 to July 21, 1999

Date	*Renmin ribao* Editorial Series on "Extol Science, Eradicate Superstition"	*Renmin ribao* Atheism Series	*Guangming ribao* "Denounce Superstition" Series
6/21	X		
6/22			
6/23			
6/24			
6/25			X
6/26			
6/27			
6/28	X		
6/29		X	
6/30			
7/1		X	
7/2			
7/3			
7/4			
7/5	X		
7/6		X	
7/7			
7/8		X	
7/9			X
7/10			
7/11			
7/12			
7/13	X	X	X
7/14			
7/15			
7/16			
7/18			
7/19	X		
7/20–21			

Source: *Renmin ribao.*

television programs as propaganda cover to support the ban on the Falungong. As shown in chapter 4, a week after the ban was announced on July 22, 31 anti-Falungong titles were already on the book shelves or available for distribution by the end of July 1999. An additional 50 titles were in the pipeline, ready to be distributed by August. The production of such a library of anti-Falungong books, which involved commissioning writers, editors, publishers and printers, must have been planned and scheduled in the three-month period between the siege of Zhongnanhai in mid-April and the crackdown in late July. Second, as shown chapter 4, Xinhua, the official state news agency, and the party theory journal (*Qiushi*) published authoritative, signed commentaries repudiating the Falungong in July (*Qiushi* on August 1), while the three leading national dailies (the party organ *Renmin ribao*, the military newspaper *Jiefangjun bao*, and the party newspaper for intellectuals *Guangming ribao*) had each published a series of five editorials and authoritative commentaries on the subject from July 23 to 31. Chapter 4 also details the China Central Television Corporation (CCTV) productions of a 68-minute special program on the Falungong, five other documentaries on the sect, and several *Renmin ribao* investigative reports on the alleged irrationality of Li Hongzhi's doctrines, the fraudulent nature of his claims to supernatural powers, the deaths and injuries caused by practicing his breathing exercises, and the organized character and illegal status of the April 25 protest rally. It is reasonable to assume that the production of such programmatic propaganda requires substantial lead time before July 23.

SECRECY OF PRESUPPRESSION POLITICAL MANAGEMENT

Before July 20, when the ban on the Falungong was communicated within party organizations and before the official announcement of the ban on the Falungong at 3 P.M. on July 22, strict secrecy on the impending crackdown was observed, and the regime gave little indication that the prohibition of the sect was in the offing. The extensive investigation that was conducted from April through early June 1999 was a covert operation that did not result in the reported detention, interrogation, and arrest of Falungong rank and file, except for those few cases mentioned above. In the same period, the official media did not report on the enforcement of earlier bans of Falungong publications, promulgated previously on July 24, 1996, August 16, 1996, June 5, 1998, May 10, 1999, and June 1, 1999,[64] or on organized raids on printing presses and book vendors of the banned list that had taken place in the provinces.

From April 25 to July 22, only two official communications related to the Falungong were dispatched by the Xinhua news agency and published in *Renmin ribao*; neither made any threat of an official ban. Two days after the siege of the Zhongnanhai, the Xinhua agency reported an interview with the Bureau of Visitors and Calls (*Xinfangju*) of the Central Committee General Office and the State Council General Office on April 27. In the interview, the bureau chief distinguished two sets of activities. First, physical exercises and practices of martial arts (*liangong jiansheng hedong*) were legal and had not been prohibited by either the central or local governments, but activities that endangered social stability were illegal. Second, the public expression of views was legal, but the gathering around the Zhongnanhai was not, since it disrupted public order and the normal life of the citizenry. The official added that illegal activities would be dealt with according to law. In the interview, the bureau chief did not threaten the prohibition of the sect, detention, and arrest of its leaders, the banning or confiscation of its publications, or dissolution of the practice sites.[65] He did not disclose the decision reached by the PSC meeting the previous day, when Jiang characterized the April 25 siege as a serious political incident that was a meticulously planned, well organized, premeditated, and in open defiance of the regime. Likewise, the PSC decision to undertake a nationwide investigation and not to engage in any mass arrest until after June 4 was kept secret.[66]

Even more explicitly, there was a deceptive denial of any pending crackdown by the same official in a separate Xinhua agency dispatch, released on June 14, 1999, four days after the establishment of the 610 Office.[67] Published as a summary of the meeting between the chief of the Visits and Call Bureau and the Falungong petitioners, the former categorically denied (1) that public security agents were about to suppress Falungong practitioners; (2) that members of the CCP and the Chinese Youth League and party cadres who practiced the Falungong would be dismissed from CCP and league membership and official positions; or (3) that China was prepared to ask for the extradition of an unnamed Falungong leader from the United States at the cost of US$500 million. As events turned out, the first two policies were implemented slightly more than a month later, and were likely to have been the organizational mission and guiding policy of the newfound 610 Office. However, the bureau chief characterized these rumors as completely fabricated and went on to reaffirm the April 27 statements that practicing physical exercise and the public expression of opinions were legal but that large gatherings that disrupted public order and normal life of the citizenry were illegal. Adding a prohibition that was not in the April 27 release, he mentioned that it would be illegal to spread superstition through activities that propagate the Falungong method (*hongfa*).[68]

Likewise, there was no sign of imminent crackdown in the pages of *Renmin ribao* on either the morning or the eve of the official announcement on July 23, even as the "Central Committee Notice on Banning the Falungong" was being transmitted in party organizations throughout the nation, and when public security agents were rounding up Falungong leaders in several localities. The only authoritative commentaries published on July 21 and 22 were editorials and a Xinhua commentary reaffirming the "One China" principle to rebut Lee Teng-hui's "Two States Theory" announced earlier. None of the 10 news items flagged as "important news" in the July 21 issue of *Ren-min ribao* made any explicit or veiled assault on the Falungong.

Public Appearances and Visit Schedules of Top Leaders

There was also little indication from the official media that the top leaders in the PSC were preoccupied with preparations for a major domestic event. As shown in table 2.3, there were multiple reports of activities of each of the seven members of the PSC in the 10-day period from July 12 to July 21, the day before the ban was officially announced nationwide. Reports of activities of Secretary-General Jiang Zemin appeared every day (except July 21) on the front page of *Renmin ribao* categorized as "important news" (*yaowen*) in that period, during which there were reports of two to four activities of Jiang on 7 of the 10 days. Reports of Premier Zhu Rongji's activities also appeared in 8 of the 10 days (except July 12 and 21), and three of these days had reports of multiple activities (July 13, 14, and 16). Aside from textual reports, the *Renmin ribao* published front-page photographs of activities of Jiang Zemin in 7 of the 10 days (except July 11, 12, and 19), and those of Zhu Rongji on July 13, 14, 16, and 19. There was thus front-page photographic coverage of either Jiang Zemin or Zhu Rongji in *Renmin ribao* every day except July 11 and 12. As noted below, some of these textual reports and photographs do not pertain to the leaders' public appearances of the day or the previous day, but concern activities that were not as time sensitive.

Table 2.3: Number of Front-Page Stories in *Renmin Ribao* of Public Appearances of Politburo Standing Committee Members, July 12–22, 1999 versus 1998

Date	Jiang Zemin	Zhu Rongji	Li Peng	Li Ruihuan	Wei Jianxin	Li Lanqing	Hu Jintao
7/12	1		1	1	1	1	1
7/13	2 (3)	2 (1)	1 (1)	1	1 (1)	1 (1)	1
7/14	4 (1)	3 (4)	(1)				
7/15	2 (2)	1 (1)	1 (2)	1	1	1 (1)	2
7/16	4	2			2 (1)		1
7/17	2 (2)	1	1		(1)		(1)
7/18	3	1					(1)
7/19	4	1			1		
7/20	1	1 (1)					
7/21	(2)	(1)		1		1[a]	(1)
7/22	(1)	(1)					

Boldface numbers are those of 1999; numbers parentheses are those for 1998.
[a]On July 21, 1999, Li Lanqing sent his written address to the National Finance Conference without attending the meeting.

In the 10-day period leading to the ban on July 22, not only the secretary-general and the premier but also other members of the PSC kept their schedules of meeting and contacting international figures, as well as taking trips outside Beijing and China. Thus, Li Ruihuan met with the president of the Mexican Supreme Court on July 20, and both Li Ruihuan and Li Peng met with the Romanian parliamentary delegation on July 13. Premier Zhu cabled his greetings to the Pan-African Organization Conference on July 12, met with the New Zealand prime minister on July 18, and received ambassadors of 10 nations on July 20. Jiang Zemin sent a congratulatory letter to President Clinton on the U.S. women's soccer team winning the championship on July 11 and met with the Australian Foreign Minister Downer on July 12, the Rumanian delegation on July 13, the Namibian interior minister on July 16, and the New Zealand prime minister on July 19. In addition to receiving international dignitaries, the premier and the secretary-general also took trips outside Beijing and China in the 10-day period. Zhu Rongji visited the flood-devastated regions in Hubei and Jiangxi provinces on July 12 and 13, while Jiang Zemin toured Outer Mongolia on his state visit from July 15 to 17. On the morning before the crackdown, Jiang met with the Congo ambassador on July 21. The other five members of the PSC did not take trips outside Beijing in the 10-day period prior to the announcement of the ban.

Signs of Imminence of Suppression

For the attentive analysts, clues of an imminent suppression could still be found. First, there were signs that the *Renmin ribao* was reserving front-page space for an important news item in its July 21 and 22 issues. On July 21, an old speech by Jiang Zemin delivered on June 9 at the National Conference on Supporting the Poor was published on the front page. On July 22, the front-page story was on Jiang Zemin signing a set of regulations on the clerical staff of the People's Liberation Army at an unspecified earlier date. The publication of two items that were not important and with a substantial time lag after the events had taken place suggests that these were probably fillers as replacements for stories on the Falungong in case unforeseen developments compelled the crackdown date be advanced. Second, there are indications that the media attempted to create a perception that both Secretary-General Jiang and Premier Zhu were preoccupied with state affairs and not preparing for the crackdown. Both the daily reports on the front page during July 12–20, when the arrests began, with multiple stories on Jiang for 7 of the 10 days and on Zhu for 3 of the 10, and photographic coverage for Jiang for seven days and Zhu for four, appear to be designed to reinforce that impression. The effort seems to be particularly contrived during July 19–22, four consecutive days before the crackdown when Jiang made no daytime public appearances. On July 19, *Renmin ribao* reported that he called President Clinton the night before to talk about Lee Teng-hui's recent speech on the two-state theory. On July 20, the *Renmin ribao* published his photo taken with the New Zealand prime minister on July 19. The publication of an old speech, an old photograph on July 21, and an old story on July 22 was mentioned above. Third, the spin appears to be forced compared with the summer of 1998, when neither Jiang nor Zhu made daily public appearances from July 12 to July 22, as reported in the *Renmin ribao* (table 2.3) without making any attempt to cover up their disappearance.

Absence of Top Public Security Officials

Perhaps the most significant telltale sign of the imminence of the crackdown was the absence of the top two leaders in the 610 Office that was in charge of suppressing the Falungong. Their public appearances were much less frequent and their participation in public events more peripheral, and they made fewer official trips outside the nation's capital in this period. As shown in table 2.4, Li Lanqing, the titular head of that office, had sharply curtailed his public appearances, from more than 14 in an average 10-day period in April through June, to only three from July 12 to 21. Even for these three appearances (July 11, 13, 15), he was merely showing himself and not in any presiding or speaking role. Likewise, as the public security tsar and the operations head of the 610 Office, Luo Gan had reduced his monthly public appearances from eight each in April and May to only two each in June and July, when he attended a conference of procurators on June 25 and a meeting commemorating the anniversary of the founding of the CCP on June 28. In July, Luo received the Romanian parliamentary delegation on July 6, and the minister of the interior of Namibia on July 16. Both Li and Luo used proxies for public appearances during the 10-day period. Luo sent his deputy as proxy to address the July 12 National Conference on Community Safety, while Li sent in his written speech rather than delivering it in person at the National Financial Conference on July 21. Since May 1 if not earlier, both Li and Luo apparently took up on-call positions in Beijing. Luo Gan had reportedly not left the nation's capital since the Falungong siege of Zhongnanhai on April 25, and his last public appearance outside Beijing was to attend a research and study meeting of the public security apparatus in Hebei on February 5–6. Li Lanqing was reportedly away from the national capital on April 21–24 when he toured Jilin province and on April 30 when he addressed the opening ceremony of the World Fair in Kunming. The last event was probably scheduled prior to the Falungong siege of the CCP and state headquarters on April 25, and both travels to Jilin and Kunming in April were scheduled prior to his reported appointment as head of the ad hoc office dealing with the Falungong on June 10.

Table 2.4: Reports of Public Appearances of Li
Lanqing and Luo Gan, January 1 to July 30, 1999

Dates	Li Lanqing	Luo Gan
1/1 – 1/10	5	2
1/11 – 1/20	8	5
1/21 – 1/31	5	1
2/1 – 2/10	9	3
2/11 – 2/20	6	3
2/21 – 2/28	6	1
3/1 – 3/10	9	4
3/11 – 3/20	8	2
3/21 – 3/31	1	1
4/1 – 4/10	4	4
4/11 – 4/20	5	2
4/21 – 4/30	4	5
5/1 – 5/10	7	1
5/11 – 5/20	5	5
5/21 – 5/31	3	2
6/1 – 6/10	5	1
6/11 – 6/20	3	3
6/21 – 6/30	7	4
7/1 – 7/10	4	1
7/11 – 7/20	4	2
7/21 – 7/31	1	0

Source: *Renmin ribao.*

To control for seasonal effect, where top officials may reduce their work schedules in the summer months, table 2.5 compares the public appearances of Li Lanqing and Luo Gan in July 1–21, 1998 versus 1999. It is evident that the reduction of the work schedules of Li Lanqing and Luo Gan in the three-week period preceding the official ban in 1999 was not due to the

Table 2.5: Public Appearances of Li Lanqing and Luo Gan, July 1–21, 1998 versus 1999

Appearance Type	Li Lanqing		Luo Gan	
	1998	1999	1998	1999
Total appearances	12	8	9	2
Presiding/addressing conferences	4	0	1	0
Meeting foreign dignitaries	4	3	1	2
Taking inspection tours outside Beijing	0	0	1	0

Source: *Renmin ribao.*

seasonal effect. Compared with July 1998, Li made fewer public appearances in July 1999 (8 vs. 12). Further, his appearances in July 1999 were low profile, with Li playing no leading role as presiding official or speaker in conferences, which he had done on four occasions in the same period in the previous year.

CONCLUSION

From April 25 to June 22, the regime was busy gathering intelligence both at home and abroad, from the central to the local government levels, to prepare for the eventual showdown with the Falungong. It also attempted to prevent local Falungong groups from staging protest rallies and petitioning in Beijing, while taking defensive measures against possible industrial and economic sabotage by the cornered sectarians. Meantime, its propaganda machinery set the stage by criticizing superstition and placing advance orders for the barrage of anti-Falungong messages that was to come. All these activities remained hidden from the public view, as the regime laid its secret plan to strike at its enemy in the surprise attack on July 22.

To date, no planning document for the anti-Falungong campaign is available for the research community outside China. In law enforcement operations, we do not know whether the intelligence-gathering goals set for the local agencies include the names, addresses, employers, and party memberships of every local Falungong practitioner, or whether they had the more modest scope of specifying the number of local Falungong stations and groups, their practice venues, a roster of their top officials, and an estimate of their numeric strength. It is also unknown whether the operational plan included day-to-day physical or electronic surveillance of the local Falungong leadership, alerting employers of their Falungong affiliation, or home visits by the local residence committees. There is also no available document on reforming and reeducating groups of Falungong practitioners, by which set of party and law enforcement institutions, through what means, and by what time. For the propaganda front, there is a similar lack of published working scripts for the media assault—the respective tasks to be undertaken by the nation's television, radio, newspapers, journals, and printing presses, the type and number of media products, and their publication and broadcast schedules.

Although we do not know the stated goals and specific plans, some of these can be inferred from actual activities. Chapter 3 analyzes law enforcement operations. The propaganda onslaught is examined in chapter 4. How the regime attempted to rehabilitate and detoxify Falungong practitioners is studied in chapter 5.

Chapter Three

Law Enforcement Operations after the Crackdown

In a national televised broadcast at 3 P.M. on July 22, 1999, the Falungong was officially banned. As elaborated in chapter 4, the notice from the Ministry of Civil Affairs promulgating the ban justified the official decision on grounds that it was unregistered, engaging in illegal activities, propagating superstition and fallacies, inciting and creating disturbances, and disrupting social stability. In a supplementary notice, the Ministry of Public Security outlawed Falungong assemblies propagating Falungong beliefs, sit-ins and petitioning activities, the public posting and display of Falungong logos and insignia, and the production and distribution of its publications.[1] To enforce the ban, public security agencies as well as other party and state bureaucracies at all administrative levels were mobilized to engage in the anti-Falungong campaign, which would become the consuming preoccupation for the following months. The campaign involved the following sets of law enforcement tasks: (1) the arrest and prosecution of Falungong leaders, (2) dissolving registered and unregistered Falungong organizations, (3) confiscating and destroying Falungong publications and accessories, (4) establishing a community and residence surveillance network to monitor practitioners, and (5) preventing Falungong from staging protests, petitioning in Beijing, and engaging in sabotage. These tasks are analyzed in order in this chapter. The additional task of reeducating Falungong practitioners is the subject of chapter 5. An analysis of the propaganda assault on the Falungong is presented in chapter 4.

LAW ENFORCEMENT ACTIONS RELATING TO THE BAN

Mass Arrests of July 20

To decapitate the Falungong leadership in a surprise move, mass arrests were made before the official ban was announced. They were to begin at dawn of July 21, one and a half days before the broadcast of the dissolution on July 22.[2] However, the announcement of the ban within party organizations and the public security system nationwide on July 19 caused leaks of the news on the crackdown[3] and led to Falungong protest rallies in several provincial cities (table 3.1). To regain the initiative, the authorities ordered the arrests to begin one day earlier, on July 20.[4]

Arrests were coordinated by the central and local political and legal affairs commissions. The scope of the arrests differs in two sources. Zong Hairen, in his 2001 *Zhu Rongji zai Yi Jiujiujiu Nian* (Zhu Rongji in 1999), reported that 5,600 Falungong practitioners were arrested on July 20, an overwhelming

Table 3.1: Falungong Protest Rallies, July 20–22, 1999

Date	Location	Size
7/20	Yingze Avenue, Taiyuan, Shanxi	Around 100
7/20	People's Square Fountain, Shanghai	N/A
7/20–21	Hebei provincial government office in Shijiazhuang	N/A
7/20–22	Dalian municipal government office	5,000
7/21	Guizhou provincial government office in Guiyang	2,000
7/21	Liaoning provincial government office in Shenyang	More than 1,000
7/21	Hunan provincial government office in Changsha	N/A
7/21	Suzhou	137
7/21	Shenzhen	N/A
7/21	Unspecified localities in Heilongjiang, Guangxi, Henan, Gansu	N/A
7/21	Nanchang, provincial government building	140 in A.M., 400 in P.M.
7/21–22	Jiangsu Provincial Government Office in Nanjing	1,300
7/21–22	Anhui provincial government office in Hefei	700–800
7/21–22	City government offices in Nantong, Yancheng	Several hundred
7/22	Heilongjiang provincial government building in Harbin	6,000–7,000
7/22	Henan provincial government building in Zhengzhou	N/A
7/22	Huayuan Avenue, Hefei, Anhui	N/A
7/22	Nanchang, provincial government building	300
7/22	Nationwide	78 incidents of more than 300 participants each

Source: *Renmin ribao*, August 5, 1999, p. 1, and August 7, 1999, p. 1; Xinhua, Beijing, press release of October 31, 1999; *Jiefang ribao*, July 25, 1999, p. 3; *Heilongjiang ribao*, August 7, 1999, p. 2; *Jiangxi ribao*, August 1, 1999, p. 1.

majority of whom were released after they wrote a repentance statement (*huiguoshu*) and pledged to withdraw from the Falungong.[5] *Cheng ming* (August 1999) reported that arrests were made in 22 cities,[6] resulting in the apprehension of 150 Falungong leaders.[7] The discrepancy of the two accounts on the number of arrests could be due to the latter source reporting only the number of Falungong leaders but not the rank-and-file. It could also result from the *Cheng ming* source including only the actual arrests (*daibu*) and not counting the large majority who were summoned for interrogation (*quanxun*) but later released, those held in custody under administrative or criminal detention (*zhi'an juliu, xingxi juliu*), or those sent to labor education (*laodong jiaoyang*).[8] Three other published reports suggest that the *Cheng ming* figure of 150 arrests is probably understated. The *Cheng ming* source is unlikely to include detention and interrogation of Falungong practitioners within the armed forces, which reportedly took place before July 20 and was not part of the law enforcement procedure in the civilian population.[9] In addition, neither Shanghai nor Qishan was included in the *Cheng ming*'s list of 22 cities. But a Shanghai newspaper reported that 25 Falungong leaders were already in custody in the city on July 22,[10] and a Shaanxi provincial newspaper also disclosed that more than 30 Falungong practitioners were also held in the custody of Qishan County in Shaanxi Province by July 22.[11] The Shanghai and Qishan sources also suggest that the number of Falungong leaders per city in custody by July 22 was much larger than the six to seven per city for 22 cities implied in the *Cheng ming* report. It is possible that the latter reports only arrests made on July 20, whereas the Shanghai and Qishan apprehensions were made before that date. In any case, the authorities arrested or detained a minimum of 150 Falungong practitioners by July 22 before the official ban was announced.

Where names and affiliations of specific individuals were published, the special China Central Television Corporation (CCTV) program announcing the Falungong ban on July 22 included the appearances of the top leaders of the Jilin main station and the head of the Beijing Falun Dafa Research Society, suggesting that they were in official custody before then.[12] Print sources report that Jiang Xiaojun, the head of the Falungong main station in Hainan Province, was detained on July 20,[13] while Xu Xiaohua, the deputy chief of the Falungong main station in Yunnan, had submitted her confession to the Yunnan Party Committee in southwest China before July 21, in which she referred to several days of self-examination.[14] In North China, Wang Yunying, main station chief of Datong in Shanxi Province, announced her withdrawal from the sect on July 21.[15] These reports thus suggest that they were in official custody before the ban was broadcast on July 22. As noted in chapter 2, the Dalian public security agents on June 4, 1999, arrested Yu Xiaode for printing and distributing 6,000 copies of Falungong materials.[16]

Falungong Leaders at Large

But not all top Falungong officials were in custody by July 22. In Anhui, Wang Shengli, chief of the Fouyang main station, was still at large until he turned himself in on July 24.[17] Even after the dissolution of the Chengdu main station in Sichuan Province on July 22, its core leaders were not held in custody and were able to plot a massive protest rally outside the provincial government headquarters.[18] In Hainan, while Jiang Xiaojun, the abovementioned chief of the main station in the province, was arrested on July 21, her deputy and husband, as well as 12 other Falungong leaders, were still at large on July 21, organizing a petition to the provincial government office.[19] Likewise, both the chief of the Guangxi main station (Chen Xueying) and the deputy chief (Guan Haibin) were not in official custody on July 20 and were busy contacting Falungong leaders and organizing protest rallies in Nanning, Guilin, Yulin, Liuzhou, Baixi, Yizhou, Beihai, Fangcheng, Qinzhou, and Liuzhou. At least Guan was still at large on July 21.[20] Xia Ninghua, the chief pro-temp of the Falungong main station in Shanghai, was also able to learn about protest rallies in other provinces and cities on the Internet on July 20 and contacted some members to stage rallies in Shanghai on the same day.[21]

As their top leaders were arrested, second-echelon lieutenants filled their ranks to assume leadership roles. In Wuhan, Tian Wei, a member of the Falungong main station's Visit and Call (*xinfang*) committee and an officer of the Hankou station, was planning a major demonstration on July 21 with more than 10 local Falungong leaders.[22] In another Falungong stronghold, Zhang Belin, chief of the Yanji guidance station in Jilin Province, organized a protest rally to the provincial capital (Changchun) on July 22.[23] In neighboring Liaoning Province, Lin Fuzi, head of the Tieling guidance station, mobilized 1,300 practitioners to protest on rumors of the crackdown on July 20.[24] More details are disclosed in the Nanjing guidance station. On July 20, its core leader, Wang Zhaiyuan, telephoned practitioners Shi Xiuhua, Zhu Haiyu, and Ai Ziqing from his home to plot a protest rally that evening. Shi Xiuhua then convened a meeting for all the heads of the section (*pian*) leaders. At 8 A.M. on July 21, Zhu Haiyu notified practitioners in 7 *pian* in Nantong, Kunshan, Wuxi, and Yancheng to stage the protest. Some 1,300 practitioners assembled in front of the provincial party committee and government headquarters from 10 A.M. on July 21 to 4 A.M. on July 22, including Lu Xiaowei, Shi Xiuhua, Peng Yinhai, and Zhu Haiyu, who led the protest and demanded to meet provincial party and government officials.[25] The presence of these second-echelon Falungong officials who rose to replace their fallen leaders to organize protest rallies thus made it imperative for local authorities to initiate subsequent rounds of arrests in the ensuing months, a topic discussed below in the section on secondary arrests.

Dissolving Falungong Organizations

The official ban of July 22 stipulated that Falungong organizations be disbanded. As part of the process, registered Falungong organizations must be deregistered. At the time of the announcement of the official ban, it was unclear how many Falungong organizations were duly registered. Local newspapers and yearbooks almost never reported on the subject. The Jiangsu Provincial Civil Affairs Department claimed that not even one registered Falungong organization was in the province before the ban.[26] Among the rarely published cases, the Sichuan Provincial Department of Civil Affairs reported that some registered Falungong guidance stations existed in the province as of July 22.[27] In Henan Province, there were no registered Falungong organizations *per se*, but some organizations were under Falungong control, according to the head of the Henan Provincial Department of Civil Affairs.[28] There is no additional information on the abolition (*quti*) of Falungong organizations in Sichuan and Henan, but the process was reported in the case of the Shanghai and Beijing congregations.

Deregistering Falungong Organizations

The Falungong organization in Shanghai was registered not as an independent social organization but as the Falungong Committee of the Shanghai *Qigong* Science Research Society. Sometime before July 22, it was unceremoniously abolished, not by official ministerial action but by the Shanghai Science and Technology Federation with which it was affiliated, after an unspecified investigation.[29] There was no report of involvement of the Shanghai *Qigong* Research Society in the process. The federation completed the legal process of deregistration before the official announcement of the ban.[30] The event was not published in the national newspapers, but did appear in the July 24, 1999, issue of *Jiefang ribao* published in Shanghai, although only inconspicuously on page 2. A related report disclosed that 25 Falungong leaders, presumably officers of the Falungong Committee in Shanghai, were assembled in the City's Science and Technology Hall on 47 Nanchang Road, the official address of the Shanghai Science and Technology Federation. In accordance with legal procedures, the deputy interior bureau chief read the Ministry of Interior notice, while the deputy public security chief of Shanghai read the Ministry of Public Security notice banning the Falungong. The secretary of the Municipal Department for Legal and Political Affairs and chief of Public Security Bureau addressed the 25 defendants, who wrote their statement of repentance and declared their severance from the Falungong.[31]

Unlike the Shanghai organization, the Beijing Falun Dafa Research Society was not registered. It served as the virtual national headquarter of the sect and was abolished by decree of the Ministry of Civil Affairs on July 22.[32] At the time, the detention and interrogation of its officers were not reported in the national press, although the July 22 CCTV special program did show its leader in official custody. More information was reported only on December 26, 1999, when the four leaders of the Beijing Falun Dafa Research Society were tried in Beijing.[33] Then it was reported that the residences of the four were searched with warrant by public security agents on July 20. All four were officially arrested (*daibu*) on October 19, 1999, 90 days after they were first detained. They were thus probably held under administrative detention procedures since July 20,[34] which permitted a maximum of 90 days of being held in custody without prosecution.[35] Their formal arrest on October 19, 1999, thus gave the procuracy an additional three months for investigation provided in the official criminal procedure.[36] The probable reason for the low profile of both cases was the need for official secrecy not to compromise an ongoing criminal investigation, and the weakness of the government case under existing statutes. For Beijing, evidence for the involvement in the April 25 incident was published only on August 9, after a more thorough investigation. Additional time was probably needed to discover their involvements in other charges.

In the case of Shanghai, there was no report of the group engaging in any illegal protest activity. The procurators had to seek new legal ground to charge leaders of the Shanghai Falungong organization in the Decision on Cult Activities, which was promulgated by the Standing Committee of the National People's Congress on October 30, 1999.[37]

Dissolution of Falungong Assemblies

For the unregistered 39 main stations, 1,900 guidance stations, and the nationwide network of 28,000 practice sites, the authorities undertook coercive action to disband these organizations. In many localities, the mere announcement of the ban led to passive compliance, when practitioners simply ceased and desisted from assembling for their morning exercises. In Changchun, the birthplace of Li Hongzhi and the Falungong, no Falungong group assembled in Shengli Park on July 21 and 22.[38] As noted above, the chief of the Jilin main station (Jiao Lixun) was already in official custody by July 22.[39] In south China, the three Falungong practice sites in Fuzhou Dong Street in the Fujian provincial capital were reportedly empty on the morning of July 23.[40] Likewise, the 40 odd Falungong assemblies in Anze County in Shanxi Province in North China did not gather on the same day.[41] Even earlier, practitioners also failed to show in assemblies in Qishan, Pufeng, and Shiquan counties in adjacent Shaanxi Province on July 22.[42] The 600 practitioners in the four Falungong guidance stations in Guang'an City in neighboring Sichuan also ceased to assemble after July 22.[43] In these cases in North, Northeast, South, and Southwest China, there were no reports of coercive action.

Voluntary Compliance

In other localities, the compliance was both active and voluntary, when Falungong assemblies took action to dissolve themselves and practitioners turned themselves in to register with the authorities, declaring their severance from the sect and bringing along Falungong publications, pictorials, and accessories.[44] Sometime before July 28, practitioners in Huajie, Jinsha, Dafang, Qinxi, and Xianning counties in Guizhou Province went to local authorities to renounce their Falungong ties.[45] Elsewhere, from July 23 to 25, the public security bureau of Hexun County in Shanxi received 26 Falungong practitioners, who turned in 120 items of their Falungong possession.[46] The Wuling Region of Hunan Province was besieged by so many Falungong practitioners turning in materials that 88 residence committees of five housing blocks had to set up reception stations to store those items. By July 30, 6,800 items were received from 1,200 practitioners.[47] The Guang'an City public security agencies in Sichuan Province also received more than 2,100 Falungong items from July 22 to 24.[48] In neighboring Shaanxi Province, there were also separate reports from Xian City, Weibin County, the Electric Department of the Railway Bureau of Xingping County, and the Hancheng Mining Bureau's Shuangshuping Coal Mine of practitioners withdrawing from the Falungong on July 22 and 24.[49] At least in Shandong Province, the defection was immediate and *en mass,* where many Falungong practitioners voluntarily withdrew from Falungong within 48 hours of the official announcement of the ban. Some 1,777 Falungong practitioners in Weifang were reported to have withdrawn by 9 P.M. on July 22, six hours after the first broadcast of the ban. Another 1,461 also withdrew in Qingdao by 3 A.M. on July 23, 12 hours after the ban, and 5,689 in nearby Liaocheng by July 24.[50]

Some collective defections were organized by party members in these Falungong organizations. In Dafang County of Guizhou Province, three cadres and 12 party members who practiced Falungong led their congregation of 580 practitioners to terminate their Falungong practice.[51] More often, some local Falungong leaders initiated these collective defections through phone calls, personal visits, and assemblies, activities regarded as accruing merit and grounds for receiving lenient treatment in the July 19 Central Committee document.[52] In Fujian Province, Chen Yue, head of the Jianyang practice site, called all other practice sites of the city on the evening of July 22 to ask them not to assemble the following morning.[53] In Ankang County in Shaanxi Province, the head of a practice site called the secretary of the party branch at his home phone on July 22 and turned over to the local public security bureau his collection of Falungong publications, videos, and exercise attire, valued at 1,100 yuan. He also visited the home of every Falungong practitioner to persuade each of them to cooperate with the government.[54]

In addition, there were also reports that local Falungong leaders organizing group defections, although it is not clear whether they were party members. In Banbishan Farm in Hubei's Yangxin County, the head of the Falungong guidance station convened a meeting of practitioners on the evening of July 22 and disbanded the assembly.[55] Yong Fang, deputy head of the Anshan Station in Liaoning Province, phoned the heads of 40 practice sites in Anshan, beseeching them to cooperate with the authorities, and called the heads of the Liaoyang station twice, enjoining them not to petition in Beijing and the provincial capital and to dissolve all practice sites. He went to different Falungong practice sites at 5 A.M. the following morning to ask practitioners to disassemble.[56] In Hongjiang County in Hunan Province, the Falungong station chief and two deputy heads notified all practitioners on July 22 evening to cease assembling the following day and went door to door to practitioners' homes asking them to turn over Falungong materials to authorities.[57]

Use of Informants and Community Hotlines

Aside from defections, local informants and the establishment of public security hotlines also led officials to search for Falungong assemblies in residential hideouts. In Shanghai, the community hotline "110" and letterbox 110 were established on July 22 for information leading to the detention and arrest of Falungong practitioners in housing blocks and work units.[58] Guiyang, the capital of Guizhou Province, also published informant hotlines at the city's Public Security Bureau, the Bureau of Commercial and Industrial Administration and Management, and the "Eradicate Pornography, Combat Illegal Publications" Office,[59] as did the Shaanxi "Eradicate Pornography Office."[60] In oil-field city Daqing, an informant led city officials to a Falungong assembly in a residential building in the Honggang District, where public security agents detained nine practitioners and confiscated the sect's banner, Li Hongzhi's picture, 44 Falungong books, 29 pictorials, and more than 100 leaflets.[61] Informants' tips also led to the closure of Falungong support services and vendors. In the Beilin District of Xian, a call-in led its Public Security Bureau to a local tailor with an inventory of 700 sets of Falungong practice attire.[62] In Guizhou Province, another local informant in the provincial capital (Guiyang) led local authorities to raid a vendor that stocked 1,081 Falungong books and 11,750 portraits of Li Hongzhi.[63] Acting on an informant's tip, seven public security agents in Hailun City in Heilongjiang

Province raided the "Salon Book Store" of Liu Lizhuan and confiscated her collection of 119 Falungong books, 17 cassette tapes, and 290 paintings, logos, and pictorials.[64]

Use of Coercion

Coercion was used as the last resort in dissolving Falungong assemblies in some localities but the method of first instance in others. To deter Falungong practitioners from assembling in each of the 218 practice sites within the city, Wuhan deployed 800 public security agents in the early hours of July 23.[65] Coastal Jiangsu Province also mobilized 26,000 public security agents to prevent Falungong practitioners from assembling in public places, where none ceased to be operative in the province by the early hours of July 24.[66] Elsewhere in Southwest China, the Provincial Public Security Bureau of Guangxi and its local subordinates organized concerted action on the evening of July 22 to make a sweep to dissolve Falungong guidance stations and practice sites and confiscate their publications. Local law enforcement agents in Guangxi Province disbanded 72 Falungong practice sites in the provincial capital (Nanning), an additional 68 assemblies in Yulin County, and all Falungong sites of Yichun Municipality. In Yibin in the same province, 300 party cadres and public security agents inspected the city at 4 A.M. on July 23 and found no Falungong assemblies in the county seat, townships, and villages.[67] In a more rural setting, the Fu An County Public Security Bureau in Fujian also dispatched its agents to the People's Garden in Wuyi Mountain to prevent Falungong practitioners from gathering for their morning exercises on the same day.[68]

While public security agents were deployed as deterrent, they were actually used for coercion, as reported in some cases. Law enforcement agents in Taiyuan Municipality of Shanxi Province dispersed four groups of 3,500 Falungong practitioners, who assembled in front of the provincial party committee headquarters for three days starting on July 20, 1999.[69] Elsewhere, 6,000 Falungong practitioners assembling on streets around the provincial party committee building in Changchun on the morning of July 22 were escorted by public security agents nearby to the Nanling sports arena and 11 other public places for investigation.[70]

Registering Falungong Practitioners

As part of the dissolution process, Falungong practitioners need to be registered. The task was undertaken by both the party committees (for party members) and the public security agencies (for nonparty members). In Shaanxi Province, party committees at various levels conducted a systematic investigation of Falungong organizations within their jurisdiction and listed each practicing party member in a registry (*dengji zuoce*).[71] In Henan Province, the Party Committee of the Provincial Bureaucratic Agency Work Committee (*shengzhi jiguan gongwei*) convened a meeting of the party secretaries of the provincial departments and bureaus on July 23, requesting the party units to do a systematic investigation of Falungong practitioners within their own party organizations. Within 24 hours, 94 subordinate party organizations had submitted a written report on the number of party members in their units who practiced the Falungong, while an additional 15 have reported the profile by phone.[72]

Falungong practitioners who were not party members were also registered. After disbanding the three Falungong practice sites within its jurisdiction, the Gaoping Public Security Bureau of Jincheng City in Shanxi Province registered the 73 practitioners.[73] Officials in Dafang, Qinxi, and Xianning counties in the Bijei District of Guizhou were also reported to have registered Falungong practitioners when the latter surrendered themselves to local authorities.[74] The task could be time-consuming for some Falungong strongholds, as in Changsha, which reported to have registered 3,649 practitioners,[75] or as in Heilongjiang's Jiamusi City, where municipal authorities registered each of the 8,400 practitioners in its 214 practice sites within 10 days of the imposition of the ban.[76] While there was no additional information on what registration entailed in the above reports, Qian'an City of Hebei Province reported that each of the 1,456 Falungong practitioners of the 79 practice sites in the 18 townships and villages was registered for his or her gender, age, occupation, political/party status, and duration of practicing Falungong. The registry also included data on leaders of the practice sites.[77] In some localities, more information was collected during registration. The Public Security Bureau of Jinzhou Municipality of Liaoning Province set up a data bank for the biographical profile of each of the registered 9,190 Falungong practitioners in the city. For the 988 Falungong leaders, handwriting, fingerprints, and photos were also scanned into the database for easy retrieval and identification.[78] As elaborated in the later section on confiscation of Falungong materials, local governments in Shaanxi Province also registered their number and type of Falungong materials aside from their membership and reported these daily to the provincial "Anti-Pornography, Combat Illegal Publications" Office.[79]

Registration was the first step to identify individual Falungong practitioners and to map out the Falungong organizational presence by each village, township, county, and city. As described in the following section, it enables the regime to monitor the activities of the sect, to introduce residence surveillance, and to build community-based intelligence, as well as to implement other law enforcement programs to prevent and deter Falungong practitioners from engaging in any protest activity.

SECURITY OPERATIONS AFTER THE CRACKDOWN

Even after the initial nationwide banning of the Falungong on July 22, 1999, two law enforcement tasks required more immediate attention of the regime. The first was the confiscation of Falungong materials. The second was to establish a system of local surveillance of Falungong practitioners.

Confiscating Falungong Materials

Along with Falungong practitioners, the existence of millions of copies of their printed publications and videos also presented a problem for authorities. Since the Falungong was banned on July 22, 1999, their publications and materials also became illegal, a fact that was underscored by a joint emergency notice issued on July 26, 1999, by the News and Publications Bureau, Ministry of Public Security, State Bureau of Industry and Commerce, Customs Administration, and the National Office to Eliminate Pornography. The notice authorized the search and seizure of Falungong books, pictorials, and audiovisual and electronic publications and stipulated the investigation and prosecution of those involved in the publication, production, photoduplication, or marketing of those products. The notice further ordered the registration of the seized items by category and quantity and their secure storage until further official notification.[80] A second notice jointly issued a day later by the News and Publications Bureau and the Ministry of Culture specified the list of Falungong publications to be banned, stipulating that these publications were not to be printed and reprinted, existing stock was to be withdrawn from distribution and held in government custody, the master copy was to be surrendered, those already in distribution were to be recovered, and publishers were required to make a serious examination.[81] These notices restated earlier notices listing prohibited Falungong publications promulgated in July and August 1996, June 1998, and May and June 1999, before the ban of July 22, 1999.

Even before the official ban, some cities had launched their operations between July 22 and 28, 1999. The earliest report came from the southwest province of Guangxi, where provincial law enforcement's systematic search and seizure of Falungong publications and accessories began as early as May 6; where around 5,700 volumes were confiscated in Nanning in mid-May, 1,600 volumes in Liuzhou in June, and unknown quantities in Yuli, Guilin and Qinzhou in July.[82] Hainan also seized Falungong publications before the official ban was announced, on July 20,[83] and Beijing began seizing Falungong publications as soon as the ban was announced, confiscating 11,000 volumes of Falungong publications in nearby Sanhe City on July 22.[84] Other cities carried out their raids from July 22 to 28. Yulin Municipal

Public Security Bureau in Guangxi Province deployed 1,630 agent visits to inspect and confiscate Falungong materials from July 22 on.[85] Acting around the same time in neighboring Guangdong Province, Guangzhou public security agents reported having searched a minivan and confiscated its cargo of Falungong publications on July 23.[86] Outside China proper, Wulumuqi in Inner Mongolia seized more than 3,200 volumes of Falungong books and more than 10,000 videos and DVDs before July 24,[87] while law enforcement agents in neighboring Shaanxi province raided 4,098 printers, book stores, vendors, and video rental vendors on July 24 and 25.[88] A late comer in the operation, the Zhejiang provincial bureau of commerce and trade issued the notice to confiscate Falungong publications on July 25 and mobilized 1,685 agent visits to inspect and confiscate such materials by July 28.[89]

In actual search-and-seizure operations, law enforcement officials raided printers, outlets and markets for publishers, vendors, cultural relics dealers, temples and shrines, and tourist spots.[90] Hainan law enforcement agencies carried out the operation at 9 A.M. on July 23, focusing their inspection and confiscation efforts on the nine leading bookstores in Haikou and street vendors in the main thoroughfares.[91] Nanning Municipal authorities in adjacent Guangxi Province conducted a comprehensive inspection of not only all book distribution enterprises in the city but also the publishing and printing establishments,[92] while Liuzhou Railway Bureau in the same province seized 960 Falungong books in a railway container before July 26, 1999.[93] Zhejiang operations appeared rigorous and extensive. Its law enforcement agents not only inspected wholesale markets for books and video products but also paid special attention to the nexus of urban and rural areas that easily fell outside both jurisdictions, including night markets, flea markets, highways, waterways, railroads, and communication thoroughfares.[94]

Once the Falungong books were seized, the confiscated materials needed to be cataloged and reported up the administrative hierarchy.[95] In Shaanxi, localities registered the type and amount of its confiscated Falungong materials daily and reported on the results of its operations to the Provincial Office for Anti-Pornography at noon and to the same office of the national headquarters also daily.[96] While few other provinces had disclosed a similar reporting requirement, the daily tally of total Falungong materials seized in select provinces published in the July 27–29 issues of the *Renmin ribao* and *Guangming ribao* suggests that this was indeed a nationwide policy, as stipulated in a report published in the July 29, 1999, issue of the *Guangming ribao*.[97]

After the confiscated materials were duly registered and reported to higher authorities, a date was set in late July when they would be destroyed in public view. A joint notice was issued by the News and Publications Bureau, Public Security Bureau, State Bureau of Industry and Commerce Management,

Customs, and the National "Eliminate Pornography Office" ordering the destruction of Falungong publications and in a coordinated and orchestrated manner.
Public burning should be organized where government and party officials and
community leaders were invited to participate and make speeches, in a media
event that should be broadcast. To achieve impact, July 29 was selected to be the
day for all provinces and cities.[98] Thereupon, mass rallies in public squares were
held in 17 provincial capitals and major cities to bulldoze Falungong videotapes,
burning Falungong publications or turning them to pulp.[99] In Guangdong, more
than 100 city officials and representatives of mass organizations threw Falungong publications onto conveyor belts of pulp machines.[100]

Enforcement Agencies

The official government agency authorized to lead in the search-and-de-
stroy operation was the "Eliminate Pornography Office," which was originally established to head a nationwide network to eradicate the growing
smut publications proliferating in China. Local authorities were instructed
to report on campaign activities to the local Eliminate Pornography Office,
entrusted to collate and provide a summary report to its national headquarters.[101] The Public Security Bureau was also involved in this operation but appeared to play a supporting role, in collaboration with the
News and Publications Bureau, the State Bureau of Industry and Commerce Management, and the Customs Administration. In actual practice,
the bureaucratic mix of law enforcement teams confiscating the Falungong publications differed from city to city. In Beijing, agents of the Eliminate Pornography Office, together with those of the Ministry of Public
Security, the State Bureau of Industry and Commerce Management, the
Urban Management Bureau (chengguan), the Ministry of Broadcast and
Television, and the News and Publications Bureau, hunted for Falungong
publications. The Public Security Bureau did not take the lead but provided information.[102] Its agents did engage in a joint action with the News
and Publications Bureau to conduct search-and-seizure operations at two
video stores in Dongcheng and Ditan districts in Beijing.[103] In Cangzhou
of Hebei Province, however, it was the public security agents who took the
lead in confiscating Falungong materials,[104] while the Propaganda Department of Pingshan County in the same province organized agents of the
county bureaus of Public Security, Broadcast, and Culture to conduct a
sweep of vendors twice a day.[105] In Wulumuqi, it was the city's Bureau of
Industry and Commerce Management that undertook the raid on bookstores and vendors.[106] In Hainan, a joint committee composed of five provincial agencies (the Propaganda Department, the Literature and Athletic
Bureau, the Public Security Bureau, the News and Publication Bureau,

and the Municipal Literature and Athletic Bureau) was set up to conduct the operations.[107] In Guangxi Province, it was not the Eliminate Pornography Office but several other bureaucratic agencies that participated in the operation. In Nanning, the provincial capital, the News and Publications Bureau was in charge of confiscating Falungong paraphernalia and inspecting all book publishing, printing, and distribution enterprises.[108] In Yulin City in the same province, the Municipal Party Committee organized the Public Security, News and Publications, Industry and Trade, Culture, and Broadcast and Television agencies to undertake the operation.[109] The Provincial Border Patrol of Guangxi also took part in the act and played its role in the inspection and confiscation missions.[110]

Community and Residence Surveillance

The local surveillance network was composed of three interrelated sets of operations. First, community watch groups were formed to monitor Falungong activities, while undercover agents were recruited to serve as informants and infiltrate Falungong groups. Second, public security agents also checked local hotels and vehicles for fugitive Falungong practitioners. Third, a special residence surveillance program provided close scrutiny of Falungong leaders of high to moderate risk. Based on these operations, intelligence information on Falungong organization and activities was reported from local to higher administrative levels.

At the local level, a system of return visits (*huifang*) was introduced to ensure that Falungong members did not lapse back into Falungong practice after registration.[111] In Jinjiang Municipality in Fujian, public security agents visited every registered Falungong practitioner in 2000,[112] as did their counterparts in Wuhan.[113] In Huarong Municipality of Hunan, the Falungong practitioners under surveillance were visited by the hamlet and group monitors every day, the village and township cadres once every five days, and the county "610 Office" once a month. The village and township authorities had to report to the county 610 Office every 20 days.[114]

Local Intelligence Networks

In addition to visiting each registered Falungong practitioner in their residence, a citywide intelligence network was created by Xiangtan Municipality in Hunan that provided up-to-date information on Falungong activities inside the municipality and outside Falungong members visiting Xiangtan. The network was made up of party members and residents who patrolled neighborhoods, monitored the local migrant population, and watched for Falungong practitioners who might put up Falungong posters and banners.[115]

In the same province, the 610 Office of Huarong Municipality seconded veteran party members, heads of villages (*xiang*), hamlets (*cun*), and groups (*zu*) to work with the municipal public security agency to collect local intelligence on Falungong practitioners.[116] Elsewhere in Harbin, a similar 24-hour monitoring system was established in urban districts with dense Falungong presence, where the Communist Youth League organizations in the residential committees and work units kept watchful eyes over Falungong practitioners who were league members.[117] In Southwest China, public security organs in Luoshan Municipality in Sichuan Province also created an "Information Management System for Activities Relating to the Falungong and Other Cults" (*Falungong xiejiao huodong xinxi guanli xitong*) in 2003 to report suspicious activities.[118]

Use of Local Informants

In tandem with community watch groups carrying out overt surveillance activities, intelligence agents were also used by some local authorities to collect information on Falungong activities. The Jinzhou Municipality in Liaoning Province created a network of 2,000 monitor messengers (*jiankong xinxiyuan*) who spied on local Falungong practitioners.[119] Information from a monitor messenger in the Dengshahe District led public security agents to thwart an assembly of 40 Falungong practitioners on May 7, 2001.[120] At the provincial level, Liaoning's Public Security Bureau recruited a group of 65 special agents (*te qing*) to form an elite intelligence network on the Falungong. In 2000, they collected more than 20,000 intelligence items, including more than 2,000 items that were reported to be important.[121] The smaller size of the Liaoning intelligence group compared with that of Jinzhou, the higher administrative level of the recruiting agency, the special designation of the group as special agents, and the quality of intelligence they collected suggest that they were probably local undercover agents recruited in a special program to infiltrate Falungong groups.

Residence Surveillance

Falungong practitioners whose cases did not warrant arrest or might have required extended investigation beyond the legal limit of 10 days were often placed under residence surveillance. In that capacity, they were not free to leave their residence without permission or to meet with other people except their attorneys, were required to present themselves when summoned, and might have to surrender their personal identification document and driver license. Such surveillance appeared tight in some localities, which required daily reporting. In Nenjiang Municipality in Heilongjiang Province, public security agents checked every day on all core Falungong leaders who were placed under residence surveillance.[122] In Hunan's Hengyang Municipality, several public security agents watched over one Falungong leader, whom they met twice a day.[123] In Xinyu Municipality in Jiangxi Province, a daily roll-call system was introduced, where authorities would call on local Falungong leaders twice a day, once in the morning and once in the evening, and met face to face once every day including holidays. Core Falungong leaders were assigned 6, 8, or 12 people to watch over their activities, to ensure that they would never be out of sight of the authorities.[124] Some local enforcement authorities placed under residence surveillance not only those sentenced by the courts but also other core Falungong leaders. In Wanzhou (Sichuan), public security agencies profiled the following six types of Falungong targets for surveillance: (1) those not converted by 2002, (2) those who had been targets of previous law enforcement efforts, (3) missing Falungong practitioners, (4) those who had moved in or out of the community, (5) those who had access to the Internet, and (6) those who knew wireless and cable technology.[125] The last two groups were included in response to the Falungong tactic of communicating via the Internet and media sabotage, elaborated in a later section.

Intelligence Raids and Reporting

In addition to local surveillance, public security agencies also carried out raids to prevent Falungong fugitives from eluding government surveillance. As part of the operation, the Public Security Bureau of Fushun Municipality in Liaoning made a systematic check of rental premises frequented by the city's outlaws. It also checked Internet cafés to deter Falungong practitioners from using public computer stations for e-mail communications.[126] To anticipate Falungong practitioners using the city's photocopiers to duplicate Falungong documents, Shenyang public security officials collected font and ink samples from the city's 3,140 photocopying machines for future identification of Falungong print materials.[127]

Local intelligence on the Falungong was fed to higher administrative levels for systematic processing and law enforcement action. In 2000, Liling public security agents in Hunan Province collected 83 intelligence items on local illegal activities, including 17 on political intelligence and 66 on societal intelligence. Many were on the Falungong, although the precise numbers were not reported.[128] Their counterparts in Jinzhou of Liaoning Province, however, collected 1,800 intelligence items on the organization and activities of the Falungong alone in 1999.[129] The intelligence network established by Huarong Municipality noted above provided 170 intelligence items in 2000, of which 49 were acted on by the municipal party committee, government, and higher public security agencies.[130] Some local law enforcement agencies provided analytical reports on the Falungong as well as raw intelligence. In addition to submitting 172 intelligence items to its provincial superiors, the 610 Office of Xiangtan Municipality also filed 17 analytical reports, edited 14 issues of "important news," produced 14 issues of "brief reports," and distributed 8 "bulletins" on local Falungong activities.[131]

DETERRENCE OPERATIONS

Prevention of Falungong Protests

Despite such extensive community and residence surveillance, some determined Falungong practitioners managed to elude official reconnaissance and continued to put up Falungong posters, display banners, and assemble to practice Falungong exercises in public venues. To prevent such open acts of defiance, law enforcement agencies patrolled public places and took coercive action against Falungong assemblies. Soon after the dissolution of Falungong on July 22, 1999, the extensive public parks network of Guangzhou established a system of daily reporting at 9 A.M. to the municipal parks bureau and local public security agencies. When Falungong assemblies were sighted, park authorities were immediately notified.[132] Two cities in Liaoning Province (Jinzhou and Yingkou) dispatched six and nine police cars to patrol Falungong practice sites, using loudspeakers to add deterrence.[133] Aside from Falungong practice sites, venues where Falungong groups might stage demonstrations were placed on special alert. In Shanghai, 200 public security agents introduced 24-hour patrol of the People's Square and the Bund, as well as the office buildings of the *Jiefang ribao*, the *Wenhui bao*, and the Municipal Civil Affairs Bureau.[134] In Dongying Municipality of Shandong Province, public security officials deployed more than 400 agents to guard the strategic economic departments and the offices and residences of municipal party and government officials and to patrol shopping malls, bus depots, and railway stations soon after the crackdown on July 22, 1999.[135]

Security was upgraded on special occasions and anniversaries of the Falungong. The special sensitive periods were the three major national holidays each lasting at least three days (Chinese New Year Spring Festival, May 1 Labor Day, and October 1 National Day), when Falungong practitioners could more easily commingle with a tidal wave of festive travelers and avoid detection. In addition, public security agencies were also on special alert on the five "special protection" periods (*tewuqi*): the birthday of Li Hongzhi on the eighth day of the fourth month in the lunar calendar,[136] the anniversary of the April 25 Zhongnanhai demonstration and of the July 22 crackdown, and the conventions of the National Party Congress and the National People's Congress, when Falungong practitioners were more likely to protest due to the political significance of these events.[137] Other dates of special local significance are also added to the public security calendar, for example, May 2 for Nanjing, which commemorates the "Hongfa" convention of the Falungong.[138]

When Falungong practitioners assembled, local law enforcement agencies tried different strategies to demobilize their protest activities. In Ma'anshan of Anhui Province, local public security agencies attempted to defuse the assembly before it was staged. Public security agents summoned the core Falungong leaders, the heads of the 22 practice sites, and more than 300 party members and government cadres who practiced the Falungong and ordered them not to participate in such gatherings.[139] Likewise, Long'an County authorities in Jilin province persuaded Falungong practitioners planning to protest in the provincial capital (Changchun) to return home or to their work units.[140] In Jilin Province, public security agents both cordoned off public squares and party and government buildings that were potential targets of Falungong protest. They also closely monitored the activities of Falungong core leaders, thus averting more than 40 large Falungong rallies, as well as 180 smaller incidents.[141]

Interception and Repatriation of Falungong Practitioners

Aside from preventing Falungong practitioners from staging local demonstrations, local governments were also instructed to prevent such gatherings at the national and provincial capitals, since the demonstration in the central party and state headquarters in Beijing on April 25, 1999, was seen as an unacceptable challenge to government authority that was not to be repeated. Interception became the task of local law enforcement and other agencies, which set up checkpoints at major thoroughfares. Repatriation was done through local offices in Beijing.

Local Interception

There were reports of local actions to intercept Falungong travelers on land, sea, and air routes and at both sources and destinations. The most common interception method was setting up checkpoints on major thoroughfares leading to Beijing and the provincial capitals. In Jilin Province, public security agents set up road blocks on highways and checkpoints on provincial railway stations, turning back more than 6,000 Falungong petitioners bound for Beijing.[142] Likewise, Jinzhou Municipality in Liaoning Province sent back 27 groups of 1,885 petitioners.[143] In the provincial capital,

Shenyang Municipality set up nine checkpoints in the city's railway station, long-distance bus depots, and major thoroughfares, which worked around the clock to intercept Falungong petitioners. A supplementary ring of road blocks set up by surrounding counties provided backup support to round up Falungong protestors.[144] Similar reports in Lingyuan City of the same province also disclosed that its Public Security Bureau deployed more than 500 agents to man 17 checkpoints to intercept practitioners heading for Beijing and successfully blocked more than 800 petitioners in the first month after the ban,[145] while Weifang's Public Security Bureau in Shandong Province set up more than 160 checkpoints to intercept Falungong practitioners bound for the national capital.[146] In these operations, vehicle inspection was part of the task. Deploying more than 1,000 policemen at roadblocks, Dongying Municipality of Shandong Province inspected more than 200,000 vehicles and managed to intercept and detain 198 Falungong practitioners bound for Beijing in late July 1999.[147] Likewise, from July 20 to 30, 1999, Changchun public security agents also intercepted 473 vehicles at road blocks where Falungong members made 5,600 attempts to reach the provincial or national capitals to protest the crackdown.[148] Special security requirements were introduced in high-risk periods when Falungong practitioners were more likely to travel to participate in protest activities in the national and provincial capitals. On such days, the public security agents in Nenjiang Municipality of Heilongjiang Province set up checkpoints in major thoroughfares that operated 24 hours, inspected taxicab stations for Falungong suspects and required purchasers of train tickets to show personal identification.[149] Similarly, the Public Security Bureau of Hengyang Municipality in Hunan Province required permits to purchase tickets for trains northbound to the provincial capital of Changsha and to Beijing.[150]

Local law enforcement agencies were not only instructed to intercept locals from traveling to the provincial and national capitals but also required to block Beijing-bound outsiders in transit through the localities. Aside from detaining 12 locals from leaving for Beijing, the public security officials in Huangshi City of Hubei Province also blocked three groups of 120 Falungong practitioners from outside the city bound for the national capital.[151] Likewise, Hubei's Qinhuangdao municipal public security agents also intercepted 470 Falungong practitioners from outside the city *en route* to Beijing, in addition to 1,830 locals headed for the national capital.[152]

Repatriation from Beijing

The interception of Falungong practitioners was not just a local operation; several local governments also set up offices in Beijing to assist Beijing public security agencies in repatriating Falungong petitioners demonstrating in the national capital. These offices appear to have been *ad hoc*. In late July, 1999, the provincial Visit and Call Office of Jilin set up an office in Beijing to receive, resolve, and repatriate petitioners back to Jilin, working even on weekends.[153] It was later joined by the Jilin provincial Public Security Bureau to form the Jilin Provincial Falungong Question Command Post (*zhihuibu*) in Beijing on the eve of the National Day (October 1). Other local governments in Jilin also sent work groups to Beijing to assist in the investigation and repatriation effort.[154] The largest reported Beijing office set up by local public security bureaus was that of Shenyang Municipality, which had more than 100 public security agents stationed in the national capital for repatriating Falungong practitioners.[155] There were more reports of local governments not setting up offices in Beijing but sending work groups. Hengyang Municipality in Hunan Province dispatched a special work group to Beijing to assist in intercepting, investigation, and repatriation of Hengyang Falungong practitioners.[156] Weifang public security agencies sent work teams to the provincial capital of Jinan and to Beijing to assist local law enforcement organs investigate and repatriate Weifang Falungong practitioners back to the city.[157] At the instruction of provincial and municipal authorities, Dongying public security bureau sent more than 20 agents in four large vans to repatriate 189 Falungong practitioners from Beijing on July 23–24, 1999.[158] In all, Dongying sent close to 20 groups of 300 agents to Beijing in 1999 to assist public security officials in the national capital to investigate and repatriate Falungong members back to Dongying.[159] There were similar reports that Liaoning Provincial law enforcement agents blocked, intercepted, and repatriated a total of 7,600 Falungong practitioners bound for and from Beijing in 1999.[160] In Siping, not only did municipal public security agents in Hubei Province intercept 1,030 Falungong practitioners bound for the national and provincial capitals, but also its more than 1,000 agents at 18 road blocks also repatriated 213 Falungong members from Shenyang and Beijing.[161] Sometimes, local law enforcement agents were sent to Beijing at short notice. On learning that Falungong practitioners from the city might be demonstrating in Tiananmen Square the following day on the evening of October 4, 2000, the Jinan Public Security Bureau immediately sent a work group to Beijing to prevent the protest from happening.[162]

Prevention of Sabotage

While much of the law enforcement effort focused on dissolving Falungong assemblies, confiscating their publications, and preventing protest activities, precautions were also taken to prevent industrial, transportation, and media sabotage by Falungong practitioners. In Jilin Province, the public security departments in the economic sector (*sheng jingbao bumen*) issued a notice to all enterprises under its jurisdiction to inspect strategic units and departments and to strengthen their security measures. Intelligence units were established in industrial security departments in different administrative levels from the province to the township to report on Falungong activities and security conditions twice a day.[163] From 1999 through 2003, no specific act of sabotage of industrial production by Falungong practitioners was reported in Jilin Province or elsewhere.

But there was one reported incident of attempted sabotage of railway traffic in Fushun Municipality in adjacent Liaoning Province in January 2001, allegedly perpetrated by Dou Zhengyang and Wang Hongjun, who were both Falungong practitioners. Dou's wife and 80 others were detained by Fushun public security agents for staging a demonstration on December 16, 2001. Placing a call to the Fushun mayor, Dou threatened that he would derail a Fushun–Beijing train the following day. Making two inverted U-shape steel bars in a welding shop at a local auto repair shop, they screwed one of the two bars onto the rail on the Shenyang–Jilin line at 9 P.M. on January 19, 2002.[164] Dou and Wang were apprehended, tried for destroying communications, and sentenced to, respectively, 13 years and life imprisonment. There were no other reports of Falungong practitioners engaging in similar acts of endangering public safety through transportation system sabotage.

There was, however, electronic sabotage. Liaoning provincial public security agents foiled an attempt of Falungong practitioners to post on the Internet the route of the motorcade of the Fifth Asia-Europe Economic Ministers' Meeting (ASEM) in Dalian, ,[165] in an apparent attempt to incite practitioners to protest at the appropriate location. More common were incidents where Falungong practitioners sabotaged television broadcasts. In one of the better reported cases, Zhou Yunjun and 14 coconspirators inserted a Falungong program CD in the main cable television transmission line at around 7 P.M. on March 5, 2002, and disrupted prime-time cable television broadcast for 169,000 cable subscribers in Changchun and Songyuan cities in Jilin Province.[166] Elsewhere, Liling Municipality of Hunan Province adopted measures to prevent the switching of television programs by Falungong programs during airtime around the 16th Party Congress in October 2002.[167] The 610 Office of Huarong Municipality also reported that it had successfully deterred the sabotage of television airwaves by Falungong practitioners in the city.[168] Both Huarong and Liling were municipalities in Hunan Province, which reported that Falungong vendors in international communications used their network services to send Falungong messages to unsuspecting service subscribers.[169] In 2002, Yangzhou Municipality in Jiangsu Province listed the prevention of international telecommunication and television replacement programs as two priority tasks dealing with the Falungong.[170] *Minghui*, the Falungong

Web site, lists 23 cases of successful electronic sabotage from March 2002 to August 2005 where practitioners switched scheduled television programs for Falungong productions.[171]

It is unclear whether there were other cases of media sabotage outside East (Jiangsu), Northeast (Jilin), and Central–South China (Hunan). But the risk of other similar incidents prompted the authorities to convene a national conference on protecting the safe transmission and broadcast of television programs on September 17, 2002, the eve of the opening of the convention of the 16th Party Congress.[172] In Hunan Province, the provincial party committee convened its own conference on September 26, 2002, and signed compliance contracts with 25 broadcast and security units to ensure the smooth transmission of official airwaves.[173] Thereafter, the Television and Broadcast Bureau of Xiangtan Municipality conducted five antisabotage drills in late September, 2002, to ensure that television broadcasts would not be hijacked by Falungong practitioners. Monitors were introduced at every point of the broadcast production when the programs were aired. Two-person teams were installed in studios and machine rooms to watch over each other, and the broadcast rule of "no one leaving the post, no finger leaving the key on the panel" was adopted to ensure that the sabotage of live broadcast programs would be immediately corrected.[174]

Secondary Arrests, Special Cases, and Campaigns

Even as the great majority of Falungong organizations were crushed in July 22, 1999, some hard-core remnants continued to defy the law. There were multiple reports that many local Falungong groups continued to stage local protest rallies, petition to Beijing, print and distribute Falungong publications, and even engage in violent sabotage activities. Four to six years after the ban, twelve provinces in 2003 and six each in 2004 and 2005 still listed the Falungong as a serious law enforcement problem in their annual procuracy reports.[175] To enforce the law, public security agents pursued these defiant Falungong practitioners who were classified according to the severity of their offense. Local suspects became the responsibility of county and city authorities. Provincial suspects were placed on a higher priority, with all local law enforcement authorities within the province admonished to capture them, activities that were supervised by provincial level public security agents. Ministerial suspects (*bu du ban*) were cases filed with the Ministry of Public Security and placed on a nationwide watch-and-capture list. On even a higher level, central suspects (*zhongyang*) were subjects of a multiministry nationwide manhunt.[176] Within the ministerial and central categories, Falungong suspects were further classified as professional fugitives tracked in a nationwide electronic database (*wangshang zuitao duixiang*) of the Ministry of Public Security, and the more serious category of special fugitives, for which the ministry formed special teams to supervise their capture.[177]

The number of Falungong practitioners wanted by different levels of law enforcement agencies varied by locality but could be more than 100. In Anshan Municipality of Liaoning Province, there were six ministerial Falungong fugitives in 2001, who were all captured within the year by local law enforcement agents under the supervision of Ministry of Public Security officials.[178] Ministerial agents also supervised the investigation and arrest of two major Falungong fugitives in Fushun in the same province in 2002.[179] In nearby Jinzhou Municipality, three local practitioners made the Ministerial Special Network list, of whom two were special fugitives who were pursued by ministerial agents in 2001. In the following year, there were 112 missing and fugitive Falungong practitioners, as well as those who escaped surveillance (*sikong*) in the same municipality, in 2002, of whom 81 were captured later than year.[180] In the provincial capital, Shenyang Municipality captured 11 ministerial suspects, 13 provincial suspects, and 15 municipal suspects in 2001, with more than 20 still at large at year's end.[181]

Special-Case Fugitives

For more serious offenders, the "Special Case" (*zhuan'an*) system was introduced to assign specific public security agents who worked full time on the case, with an earmarked budget and special investigatory powers. In Weifang in Shandong Province, public security agents formed special teams to investigate and apprehend Falungong leaders who organized the protest rally in front of municipal party and government headquarter offices on July 14, 1999, the alleged stealing of state secret documents on July 3, 1999, and those who persisted in organizing protest rallies to Beijing after July 20, 1999.[182] These special-case teams were afforded abundant human resources to accomplish their tasks. Even at a lower administrative level in Hunan, the village and township public security agents of Huarong Municipality were able to organize 10 groups of work teams to Guangzhou and Beijing to track three local Falungong fugitives, and managed to capture them within the specified time.[183] At the Shenyang Municipal Public Bureau in Liaoning Province, each suspect was assigned a small teams of agents, who combined both high-tech and human detection techniques and worked with families of fugitives to persuade the fugitives to turn themselves over to law enforcement authorities. Some agents also set up monitoring units near places where fugitives were likely to surface, to wait for the fugitives to appear.[184] These methods appear to have borne fruit, as Shenyang public security agents were commended by the Ministry of Public Security and the Central Legal and Political Affairs Committee in 2002 for solving two major ministerial cases.[185] Elsewhere in Hunan Province, the Xiangtan Municipal Party Committee formed a "Coordination and Command Leading Group to Crack Important Falungong Cases" in April 2002, headed by a member of the Standing Committee of the Municipal Party Committee and Secretary of the Municipal Legal and Political Affairs.[186]

Special Campaigns

Aside from the "Special Case" system that centered on specific Falungong cases, law-enforcement agencies also organized special campaigns targeted at all Falungong operations in a specific spatial-temporal domain with massive deployments. For a major Falungong stronghold such as Changchun, there were several major campaigns in a year. In 2001, four extensive campaigns were launched by public security organs to strike at Falungong remnants in Changchun. Two operations lasting 100 days each were organized, the first one from January 17 to March 27 to prevent Falungong practitioners from traveling to Beijing. Encompassing the more sensitive April 25 and July 22 Falungong anniversaries, the second operation was launched from April 27 to July 27 to consolidate the gains of the first campaign and for mop-up operations. The third and fourth campaigns were initiated by agencies above the municipal public security bureau. Instructed by and working with the municipal party committee and the municipal government, the third campaign on the "Four Preventions" was launched from September 5 to October 15. Between the second and third campaigns, Changchun law enforcement agencies also participated in the four-month nationwide "Strike at the Falungong" campaign to crack down on illegal activities of the Falungong.[187]

There were no details on the operations of the Changchun campaigns, but the Zhuzhou Municipality of Hunan Province reported how its two-month special campaign was organized. Begun in October 8, 2000, the campaign was launched at the instruction of the Ministry of Public Security and the Hunan Provincial Party Committee, targeting at the proliferating Falungong publications that had resurfaced after the July 1999 crackdown. The operation was led by the "Special Campaign Leading Group," headed by the director of the Bureau of Public Security, with the vice chief of the bureau as the deputy head of the campaign. Members of the campaign were agents seconded from the divisions of Political and Legal Affairs, Technological Detection, Foreign Affairs, Patrol Security, and Economic and Cultural Protection and the Computer Management Section of the Public Security Bureau, who were assembled together to work as a team. The campaign confiscated 1,867 Falungong publications, 251 books, 124 video products, 23 pictorials, and 671 other items, eradicating a Falungong printing press and a hideout along the way.[188]

In the following year, while such year-long sustained law enforcement operations were not reported anywhere in China, there were specific operations in some cities targeted against the Falungong on one day in a quarter. In Nankang in Jiangxi Province, concerted and unified activity (*jizhong tongyi xingdong*) was undertaken on February 9, April 22, September 27, and November 11, when public security agents seized nine Falungong letters mailed from outside the province and one Falungong photo album and rearrested a Falungong member who was on parole from labor education.[189] They also investigated those who were taking business trips outside the city and cadres in the municipal bureaucracies.[190] Their counterparts in Xuanwei of Yunnan Province organized four concerted operations to investigate the Falungong practitioners and to tighten surveillance on the 160 registered Falungong practitioners on Falungong special occasions on April 25, May 19, September 29, and November 11 in the same year.[191]

In these single-day campaigns, the number of law enforcement agents mobilized could be substantial. In a special campaign (*zhuangxiang xingdong*) in 2000, the Ma'anshan Municipal Public Security Bureau deployed close to 1,000 agents and checked 282 printing, photocopying, and typesetting stores.[192] On September 27 and November 1, 2002, the Public Security Bureau of Xiangtan Municipality in Hunan Province deployed police 2,580 times to check 4,057 entertainment facilities, printing shops, photocopying shops, Internet cafés, hotels, and rental properties, visiting more than 440 Falungong households, resulting in the capture of two on the special wanted list and an additional bonus of five Falungong fugitives.[193] While Changsha did not report the number of public security agents deployed, it did report that in 2002 it crushed 18 Falungong hideouts (*wodian*) and 6 fellowship groups (*tuanhuo*); captured 89 suspects, including two wanted by the Ministry of Public Security; and cracked 151 Falungong cases.[194] The year before, it investigated 140 leads, cracked 86 cases, and handled 253 people.[195]

CONCLUSION

This chapter analyzes the law enforcement operations of the anti-Falungong campaign. Several of these—the gathering of intelligence and the prevention of Falungong protest rallies, petitioning in Beijing, and sabotage activities—were also law enforcement tasks before the official announcement of the ban on July 22, 1999. Others were operations that were part of the ban: the dissolution of Falungong organizations, the arrest and detention of its leaders, and the confiscation and destruction of Falungong publications. Whether they predated or postdated the official ban, these activities were equally effective in outlawing the Falungong. All registered Falungong organizations were deregistered. Its congregations no longer assembled in its usual venues. The existing stock of publications was confiscated and destroyed; its leaders were captured or went into hiding or voluntary exile. A community-based intelligence network monitored former Falungong practitioners to ensure that they would not misbehave at their residence or work place, using local informants and special agents.

But there were other fronts where the assault on the Falungong needed to be sustained. The propaganda battle to justify the ban had to be continued. The war to recapture the hearts and minds of Falungong practitioners needed to be won. Then there was the important question whether the gains of the law enforcement operations could be consolidated. At the individual level, would those who renounced their Falungong ties regret their act of disloyalty, those who turned in Falungong publications still keep and venerate the portrait of Li Hongzhi, those who signed the severance documents continue to practice breathing exercises and recite Falungong scriptures at night? More ominous for the regime, would the disbanded congregations be able to regroup, the wounded cells metastasize and develop secondary growth, a new cohort of leaders emerge to replace those in labor reform institutions?

These queries are pursued in the following chapters. The effectiveness of how the regime waged the war is examined in chapter 8. Its efforts to recapture the hearts and minds of the misguided Falungong practitioners are analyzed in chapter 5. But our more immediate attention turns to the propaganda operations in the media campaign and the publications campaign examined in chapter 4.

Chapter Four

The Anti-Falungong News Media Campaign

At 3 P.M. on Thursday, July 22, 1999, all television and radio stations in China disrupted their regular programming to announce the official ban of the Falungong, branded as "the most serious political incident since June 4."[1] In the month-long campaign that followed, the elite media agencies in China published news stories and commentaries and dominated the nation's airwaves with television and radio programs denouncing the Falungong and charging its leaders with deluding its followers, exaggerating the benefits and minimizing the risks of its breathing exercises, and disrupting social order. Within four weeks of the official ban, the state Xinhua news agency produced 1,650 releases and 290 articles, the leading party newspaper *Renmin ribao* (*RMRB*) published 780 stories as well as commentaries, and the China Central Television Corporation (CCTV) aired 1,722 news items that totaled more than 100 programming hours on the Falungong.[2] Added to the campaign were the many programs aired by the Central People's Broadcasting Station (CPBS) and a library of 120 titles of anti-Falungong books published by the nation's printing presses in the ensuing nine months, as well as numerous stories with the datelines of provincial and other national media organizations. Thus, the anti-Falungong campaign was arguably the most forceful media assault on a domestic challenger in post-Mao China.[3]

This chapter is focused on the anti-Falungong propaganda campaign. It begins with a description of media programming in the anti-Falungong campaign in the national television and radio broadcasts. This will be followed by an examination of the media campaign in the national press and the publications industry. A last section focuses on coordination among media organizations as well as that between media and other agencies.

ANTI-FALUNGONG CAMPAIGN IN RADIO AND TELEVISION

The anti-Falungong media campaign was kicked off by a special program at the nation's television and radio stations on July 22, 1999. Aired simultaneously at CPBS and CCTV, the special program broadcast separate announcements by the Chinese Communist Party (CCP) Central Committee, the Ministry of

Civil Affairs, and the Ministry of Public Security. Also broadcast was a press conference of the Ministry of Foreign Affairs announcing the ban to foreign agencies, and other investigative reports on the Falungong.[4] Breaking news on public reactions to the Falungong ban were added to the subsequent broadcasts. The prime-time 7 P.M. news program in CCTV on July 23 was a full two hours.[5]

In the month-long media campaign that followed, news on the Falungong was broadcast in the two core daily news programs in the morning and evening at channel I of CPBS, which claimed to have 700 million listeners in 1999.[6] These were rebroadcast and updated in the 5- to 15-minute newsbreaks every hour from 4 A.M. to noon, and at 2, 3, 4, and 6 P.M.[7] In television, the July 22 special program was replayed in segments at the 16 news programs in channel I of CCTV throughout the day. Special reports, interviews, and sometimes more in-depth analysis on the Falungong were broadcast in three news-magazine programs (*News Sweep Length and Breadth, 30 Minutes at Noon,* and *New Century of Rule of Law*) immediately aired after the morning, noon, and evening news programs.[8]

Regular and Special News Programs in Television

As the top medium in China's mass media system in institutional capacity, subscribers, and revenue, television led the charge in the anti-Falungong campaign. Program production on the Falungong campaign was entrusted to its news program center of CCTV, which produced three related sets of regular and special news programs,[9] broadcast mainly on CCTV's channel I (general and news), channel II (economy), and channel IV (international). As shown in table 4.1, news on the Falungong was broadcast in four regular news programs in the morning, noon, and two evening hours.[10] During the four-week anti-Falungong campaign, all four regular news program extended their broadcast schedule to make room for Falungong coverage.[11] As in the national radio network, the anti-Falungong campaign also found airtime in news background programs that were packaged as news magazines, commentaries, talk shows, and investigative reporting, generally broadcast after a regular news program (*Eastern Time and Space, Focused Interview, Plain Speaking,* and *News Investigation*).[12] In all, about half of CCTV's anti-Falungong productions were 66 special programs with a combined airtime of 2,902 minutes produced outside the regular news programs.[13]

Special Television Programs on the Falungong

In addition to the regular and background news programming, five special TV documentaries on the Falungong were produced and aired.[14] *Li Hongzhi:*

Table 4.1: Daily Radio and TV News Programs in CPBS Channel I and CCTV Channel I, 1999

Time	Regular CPBS-I News Programs	Regular CCTV-I News Programs	News Magazine and Special Programs in CCTV-I
6:00–6:15 A.M.		Morning news	
6:30–7:00	News and News-paper Digest		
7:00–7:30	News Sweep Length and Breadth	Rolling news (7–7:20)	
7:20–8:00			Eastern Time and Space, Plainly Speaking
8:00–8:20		Rolling news	
8:22–8:35			Focused Interview
10:00–10:05		Newsbreak	
12:00–12:30 P.M.	Half Hour at Noon (12:05–12:35)	News half-hour	
13:00–13:30	New Century of Rule of Law		
14:00–14:05		Newsbreak	
16:00–16:05		Newsbreak	
18:00–18:05		Rolling news	
18:20–19:00	Evening News Net-work		
19:00–19:30	News Sweep Length and Breadth	National network news	
19:38–19:51			Focused Interview
20:00–20:30	National Network News		
21:00–21:20			Broadcast Live
21:25–21:55			Investigation News
22:00–22:30		Evening news	
00:04–00:09 A.M.		Rolling news	
Total time in news programs	210	170	116

Source: *Zhongguo guangbo dianshi nianjian,* 2000, pp. 85, 246–48; *CCTV Yearbook,* 2000, pp. 382–84.

Abbreviations: CPBS, Central People's Broadcasting Station; CCTV, China Central Television Corporation.

The Man and His Deeds was a 32-minute television movie built on the July 23 *RMRB* article with the same title authored by the Research Office of the Ministry of Public Security,[15] featuring the regime's version of Li's personal history, the disruptive social disorder effects caused by the collective protests of the Falungong, and accusations of the families of those practitioners who died, were injured, or committed suicide after practicing Falungong. "The Truth about the April 25 Illegal Assembly" carried the same title and was based on the same content as another *RMRB* article on July 23.[16] Touting the party line that the April 25 incident was an organized, premeditated, and purposeful political event, it reassured viewers that the regime only targeted a small minority of Falungong ringleaders for prosecution. "Temptation and Control—an Analysis of the Sinister Network of Falungong" plus two five-part episodes of the popular news magazine *Focused Interview* ("Seeing through Li Hongzhi," "Despicable trickery, illogical fallacy") rounded up the five special CCTV programs on the Falungong.[17]

THE PRESS CAMPAIGN

In China's 2,038 newspapers,[18] the full-scale press campaign was launched on July 23, 1999, as the morning's newspapers opened with a full barrage of news stories, authoritative commentaries, and investigative reports announcing and justifying the ban on the Falungong. Some of these had been broadcast mostly in excerpts and some in full text on the nation's television and radio networks the previous afternoon at 3 P.M. The July 23 press salvo was composed of five key authoritative documents described below, and several Xinhua news dispatches publishing notices, press conferences, and interviews of several State Council ministries.

Contents of Five Core Documents of July 23

Cited most often in the press campaign was the Central Committee circular addressing the central and provincial CCP committees, the central organs of the People's Liberation Army, and the CCP cells of mass organizations. It forbade all CCP members to practice Falungong and required them to renounce their membership in Falungong organizations, to refrain from attending their functions, to withhold from providing meeting venues, funds, and other facilities to the Falungong, and to expose and repudiate Li Hongzhi and the Falungong.[19] An accompanying editorial of the *RMRB*, the only such authoritative commentary published by the party organ in the entire anti-Falungong press campaign, provides a policy exegesis of the Central Committee notice. Titled "Elevating understanding" (*tigao renshi*), the editorial underscored the alleged superstitious nature of Falungong teachings, the gravity of its political challenge to the regime, and the need to differentiate the great majority of Falungong followers who practiced breathing exercises for health reasons from the small minority of its leaders who planned and organized political activities, counseling patient education for the former and stern legal sanction for the latter. It emphasized the importance of social stability in managing the Falungong problem and extolled the role of CCP organizations and members in the campaign.

To provide the legal basis for banning the Falungong, the short notice of the Ministry of Civil Affairs stipulated that the Falun Dafa Research Society and its subordinate organizations were held to be illegal and were to be dissolved, on grounds that it had not been registered and that it had engaged in illegal activities, propagated superstition and fallacies, deluded the people, incited and created disturbances, and disrupted social stability.[20] Citing the decision of the Ministry of Civil Affairs, the notice of the Ministry of Public Security then prohibited the public posting and display of Falungong logos and insignia; the distribution of its publications; assemblies propagating Falungong beliefs; sit-ins seeking audiences from authorities pleading for Falungong; fabricating and circulating rumors; and organizing and networking (*chuanlian*) to defy government orders.[21] The fifth document was a systematic critique of Li Hongzhi's doctrines and Falungong practices, by the Research Department of the Public Security Ministry, titled "Li Hongzhi: The Man and His Deeds," described above as a special CCTV program. As presented in table 4.2, these five core documents were published in all national and local daily newspapers in China on July 23, together with an additional set of six policy statements published on July 24.

Table 4.2: Publication Dates and Placement of Central Documents in Major National Dailies, July 23 and 24, 1999

Daily	CC	CA	PS (1)	RMRB Edit.	PS (2)	NPB	OD	PrpD	PD	CYL	UF
RMRB	x	x	x	x	p. 4	p. 2	p. 1	p. 1	p. 4	p. 4	p. 2
GMRB	x	x	x	x	p. 2	p. 3	p. 2	p. 2	p. 2	p. 2	p. 2
JFJB	x	x	x	x	p. 2	p. 5	p. 1	p. 4	p. 4	p. 4	p. 3
JJRB	x	x	x	x	p. 2	p. 3	p. 1	p. 2	p. 1	p. 1	p. 2
ZGQNB	x	x	x	x	p. 2	p. 4	p. 3	P. 2	p. 2	p. 2	p. 2
GRRB	x	x	x	x	p. 2	p. 2	p. 1	p. 2	p. 2	p. 2	–

Abbreviations: *RMRB, Renmin ribao; GMRB, Guangming ribao; JFJG, Jiefang junbao; JJRB, Jingji ribao; ZGQNB, Zhongguo qingnian bao; GRRB, Gongren ribao;* CC, Central Committee notice banning the Falungong (7/19), published 7/23; CA, Ministry of Civil Affairs decision to ban Falungong (7/23); PS (1), Ministry of Public Security notice banning Falungong (7/23); RMRB Edit, *RMRB* 7/23 editorial "Raising Awareness" (7/23); PS (2), Ministry of Public Security special report on Li Hongzhi (7/23); NPB, News and Publication Bureau notice banning Falungong books (7/24); OD, speech of the Organization Minister to the *RMRB* reporter (7/24); PrpD, speech of the Propaganda Minister to the *RMRB* reporter (7/24); PD, Personnel Department notice (7/24); CYL, Chinese Youth League notice (7/24); UF, United Front Minister Wang Zhaoguo meeting leaders of minor political parties (7/24). x indicates publication and placement on 7/23, p. 1.

Supplementary Communications

On day 2 of the press campaign, three sets of six policy documents and authoritative commentaries were also given prominent space in the national and local presses on July 24.[22] First, a notice issued by the News and Publications Bureau (NPB) reaffirmed its previous banning of Falungong publications, listed 11 banned Falungong titles and editions, and restated its prohibitions against the publication, reprinting, and distribution of these Falungong publications and video products that it had previously issued in July 1996 through June 1999.[23] Two *RMRB* interviews of the head of the Department of Organization clarified the purpose and goals of the CCP's Central Committee directive,[24] while that of the Department of Propaganda highlighted the thrust of the anti-Falungong publicity program for the party-controlled media.[25] Three additional documents were companion pieces to the Central Committee circular forbidding CCP members from practicing Falungong, issued by the Communist Youth League, the Ministry of Personnel, and the United Front Department, urging their constituencies not to practice Falungong and to uphold social stability.[26] As shown in table 4.3, the above six documents of July 24, along with the five documents published of July 23, were published not only in the national dailies but also in all the major provincial dailies. There were also other policy statements and attacks on the Falungong, but these were not considered important enough to be published in all national and local daily newspapers.[27]

Thus, within 24 hours after it imposed the ban, the regime had outlawed the public activities and publications of the Falungong, presented criminal charges and built its case against the congregation, and isolated Falungong through the directives to CCP and Communist Youth League members, state cadres, and non-Communist personages that prohibited their continued involvement with the Falungong. This news was broadcast in the electronic media through the national television and radio networks, as well as in all the leading national and provincial newspapers.

Consolidating the Ban, July 24–29

Having announced the ban and formally dissolved the Falungong, the regime moved on to secondary tasks. Media coverage focused on expressions of public support for the official ban, the effectiveness of the ban on dissolving Falungong organizations, and declaring victory of the campaign.

Expressions of Public Support

While media coverage in the first two days of the anti-Falungong campaign was devoted to important policy announcements, numerous reports of public

Table 4.3: Publication Dates and Placement of Central Documents in Leading Provincial Dailies, July 23 and 24, 1999[a]

Provincial Daily[a]	CC	CA	PS (1)	RMRB Edit.	PS (2)	NPB	OD	PrpD	PD	CYL	UF
Beijing	x	x	x	x	p. 2	p. 4	p. 1	p. 1	p. 3	—	p. 3
Tianjin	x	x	x	x	p. 2	p. 3	p. 2	p. 2	p. 2	p. 2	p. 2
Hebei	x	x	x	x	p. 4	p. 4	p. 3	p. 3	p. 3	p. 3	—
Shanxi	x	x	x	x	p. 2	p. 3	p. 2	p. 2	p. 2	p. 2	p. 4
Neimonggu	x	x	x	x	p. 1	p. 2	p. 2	—	p. 4	p. 4	p. 4
Liaoning	x	x	x	x	p. 2	p. 4	p. 1	p. 3	p. 1	p. 3	—
Jilin	x	x	x	x	p. 2	p. 2	p. 3	p. 3	p. 3	p. 3	—
Heilongjiang	x	x	x	x	p. 2	p. 3	p. 1	p. 1	p. 4	p. 4	p. 4
Shanghai	x	x	x	x	p. 3	p. 2	p. 1	p. 1	p. 2	p. 2	p. 2
Jiangsu	p. A1	p. A1	p. A1	p. A3	p. B1	p. 2	p. A2	p. A2	p. A2	p. A2	—
Zhejiang	x	x	x	x	p. 3	p. 1	p. 2	p. 2	p. 2	p. 2	—
Anhui	x	x	x	x	p. 1	p. 1	p. 2	p. 2	p. 2	p. 2	—
Fujian	x	x	x	x	p. 2	p. 2	p. 2	p. 2	p. 3	p. 3	—
Jiangxi	x	x	x	x	p. 3	p. 3	p. 1	p. 1	p. 2	p. 2	—
Shandong	x	x	x	x	p. 2	p. 3	p. 2	p. 2	p. 2	p. 2	p. 2
Henan	x	x	x	x	p. 2	p. 3	p. 2	p. 2	p. 2	p. 2	p. 2
Hubei	x	x	x	x	p. 6	p. 4	p. 3	p. 3	p. 3	p. 3	—
Hunan	x	x	x	x	p. 2	p. 2	p. 4	p. 4	p. 4	p. 4	—
Guangdong	x	x	x	x	p. 2	p. 1	p. 2	p. 2	p. 1	p. 1	—
Guangxi	x	x	x	x	p. 3	p. 2	p. 2	p. 2	p. 2	p. 2	—
Hainan	x	x	x	x	p. 2	p. 2	p. 2	p. 1	p. 2	p. 2	p. 2
Sichuan	X	x	x	x	p. 1	p. 3	p. 2	p. 2	p. 2	p. 2	p. 2
Guizhou	x	x	x	x	p. 2	p. 2	p. 2	p. 1	p. 1	p. 3	p. 3
Yunnan	x	x	x	x	p. 2	p. 2	p. 2	p. 2	p. 2[b]	p. 2	p. 2[b]
Xizhang	x	x	x	x	p. 2	p. 3	p. 2	p. 2	p. 2	p. 2	—
Shaanxi	x	x	x	x	p. 4	p. 3	p. 2	p. 2	p. 2	p. 2	p. 2
Gansu	x	x	x	x	p. 2	p. 2	p. 3	p. 3	p. 3	p. 3	p. 2
Qinghai											
Ningxia	x	x	x	x	p. 2	p. 2	p. 2	p. 2	p. 2	p. 2	—
Xinjiang	x	x	x	x	p. 4	p. 2	p. 2	p. 2	p. 2	p. 2	—
Chongqing	x	x	x	x	p. 4	p. 2	p. 2	p. 2	p. 1	p. 1	p. 2

For abbreviations, see table 4.2.

[a] All provincial dailies are named after their province; hence, *Shanxi ribao* and *Liaoning ribao*. The exceptions are *Dazhong ribao* (Shandong), *Xinhua ribao* (Jiangsu), and *Jiefang ribao* (Shanghai).

[b] Only title of document, no text.

A dash indicates that article was not published.

Source: Provincial newspapers, July 23 and 24, 1999. *Qinghai ribao* was not available to the author at the time of research.

support of the regime decision were also published at the early stage of the media campaign. More prominent coverage was given to public support expressed outside the party and government core, portrayed as unplanned and unmanaged. On July 23, the *RMRB* published two such stories on the front page, one on select pro-Beijing Hong Kong media expressing support of the Falungong ban, and the other on individuals and groups in Beijing, Tianjin, Jiangsu, Shanxi, Guangxi, and Gansu, with quotations from named and titled individuals cheering the government decision.[28] On the following day (July 24), the party newspaper also printed a front-page story reporting support of the Falungong ban from mostly named and titled individuals in Shanghai, Guangzhou, Changchun, and Shandong,[29] while those of ethnic minority leaders, minor noncommunist political parties, and CCP central organizations were published on p. 4. More routine, *pro forma* expression of support for the decision was reported for both the central party and military organizations, with no one mentioned by name or title and no quotations cited.[30]

The above-listed stories report expressions of support largely from the executive branch of the central party and state agencies. Subsequent coverage from July 26 on published more reports on other branches of the central government and provincial agencies, including the standing committees of the National People's Congress and the China Political Consultative Conference, those in provincial meetings, and study sessions convened in several provinces published in p. 1,[31] while those on meetings of central party, state, and military organizations held in Beijing were relegated to p. 4. Table 4.4 presents their dates, placement, and whether the individuals cited were identified by name or with their expressions quoted.

Thus, immediately after the announcement of the Falungong ban, the national press had reported public support for the government action on July 24–26. The earlier reports of July 23 and 24 attempted to convey the message that much of the first reaction was spontaneous and unorganized support both inside and outside the mainland, from a cross section of socioeconomic classes of the nation, from both urban metropolises and more rural areas, covering provinces from all the six regions (North, East, Central–South,

Table 4.4: Coverage of Expression of Support by Source

	Public/Mass	Hong Kong Press	Minorities Parties	Party/State Agencies
First date of report	7/23	7/23	7/24	7/24
Placement in *RMRB*	p. 1	p. 1	p. 4	p. 4
Individual names and titles identified	Yes	No	Yes	No
Individual statements quoted	Yes	No	No	No

Source: *RMRB*.

Northeast, Northwest, Southwest) in China. Those expressed by most party and state organizations, both central and local, mass organizations, and CCP and noncommunist members were published on a later date or on the less conspicuous p. 4.

Pursuing the Enemy

The initial announcement of the ban on the Falungong in the national press on July 23 and the saturation reporting soon thereafter of expressions of support of the ban were followed by a series of media reports on the immediate success of the government campaign and the demise of the Falungong.

The first triumphant reports on the war against the Falungong were that the sect failed to assemble for their daily morning exercises in their usual venues on July 23 and 24 in and outside Beijing.[32] To reinforce the perception that the regime campaign against the Falungong was effective, the official media also published stories on the defection of the Falungong rank-and-file, including more than 2,300 Falungong practitioners in Shandong's Jinan Municipality by July 23,[33] more than 5,000 in Liaocheng in the same province on July 24, and more than 6,000 in the Hebei provincial city of Handan by July 27.[34] There were collateral reports of Falungong leaders defecting, as well, including the deputy chief of the Yunnan Falungong main station, the chiefs of the Changchun and Guangxi main stations, and the top five leaders of the Jinan main station in Shandong.[35] In combination, these reports suggest that the Falungong was decapitated, with its leaders going into hiding or in government custody, and even renouncing their Falungong ties.

In official media, campaign success was evidenced not only by the dissolution of Falungong assemblies and mass defection of Falungong rank and file, but also by the confiscation of Falungong materials. Following the notice issued by the NPB on July 24,[36] and an emergency notice promulgated on July 27 by several agencies calling for the confiscation of such publications,[37] there was extensive reporting of raid and seizure operations of Falungong publications by local authorities, which netted more than 7,000 Falungong volumes in Changsha, more than 20,000 Falungong materials in Guiyang, more than 92,000 volumes in Wuhan, and 10,801 volumes and CD packs in Qingdao.[38] As detailed in the following section, the law enforcement net was cast much wider, and the catch greater.

Declaring Victory

With the dissolution of Falungong assemblies in public places, the arrest and defection of its leaders and rank-and-file, and the seizure and confiscation of its publications and materials, the authorities were ready to declare a successful completion of a campaign that removed a political threat to the regime. To put a face on the outlawed congregation, the Xinhua news agency published the Ministry of Public Security's arrest warrant of Li Hongzhi on July 29, indicting the Falungong founder for propagating superstition, practicing deception, leading to wrongful deaths, and organizing illegal assemblies that disturbed public order. A spokesman of the ministry stated that the law enforcement agency had issued a bulletin informing Interpol that Li was a wanted criminal in China.[39] To add propaganda effect and maximum impact to ending the campaign, public destruction of Falungong publications and materials was staged in major cities. As detailed chapter 3, the extermination of Falungong materiel was done on the same day (July 29) nationwide, in public view, publicized in mass media, cheered on by mass rallies, and attended by local officials and community leaders invited to participate and make speeches. In all, more than two million pieces of Falungong publications, posters, attire, and accessories were set to fire, crushed by bulldozers, or turned into paper pulp in 17 provinces and major cities.[40] Thus, within a week from the first announcement of the ban, official media portray that the Falungong had ceased its public activities, lost its leadership, and deprived its treasured possessions. From its perspective, the government scored a decisive victory over the outlawed sect.

Continuation of the Propaganda War

While August 2 marks the end of the operational phase of the anti-Falungong campaign in television,[41] repudiation of the sect continued. As shown in table 4.5, there was a marked shift in the media campaign against the Falungong after August 2. Prior to that date, there were usually multiple news stories and policy statements on the Falungong every day listed as "important news" (*yaowen*) in the electronic version of the *RMRB*. At the same time, generally no more than one special commentary was published in the same newspaper per day. After August 2, the number of important news and policy announcements has generally dropped, with no stories on August 3, 5, and 6 and from August 9 through 23. In contrast, the number of authoritative commentaries doubled from generally one per day to two starting August 2, with three appearing on August 6 and 14. These authoritative commentaries appeared as a series of editorials, special columns, and signed and unsigned commentaries published by the Xinhua news agency, the CCP's theoretical journal *Qiushi*, and the three major dailies (*RMRB, Guangming ribao,* and *Jiefangjun bao*) that assailed the Falungong along the same propaganda lines as those in the first week of the campaign.

As shown in table 4.6, in the one-month period from July 23 through August 23, the Xinhua news agency published seven "special commentaries" in a single series, the *Qiushi* four (one editorial and three commentaries),

Table 4.5: Important Falungong News in *RMRB*, July 23–August 22, 1999

Date	News, Regime Announcements (A)	Authoritative Commentaries (B)	A + B	Total Important News
7/23	4	1	5	9
7/24	3	0	3	7
7/25	5	1	6	12
7/26	0	2	2	8
7/27	1	1	2	8
7/28	5	0	5	12
7/29	4	1	5	9
7/30	3	1	4	9
7/31	2	1	3	10
8/1	1	1	2	9
8/2	2	1	3	10
8/3	0	2	2	11
8/4	2	2	4	13
8/5	0	2	2	12
8/6	0	3	3	14
8/7	1	2	3	12
8/8	1	2	3	12
8/9	0	1	1	9
8/10	0	2	2	12
8/11	0	2	2	9
8/12	0	2	2	11
8/13	0	0	0	6
8/14	0	3	3	10
8/15	0	2	2	9
8/16	0	1	1	10
8/17	0	2	2	11
8/18	0	1	1	11
8/19	0	1	1	11
8/20	0	1	1	9
8/21	0	0	0	13
8/22	0	2	2	12
8/23	0	1	1	9

Source: *RMRB* (1999), electronic version.

and the *Guangming ribao* a single series of eight editorials. The more productive printed media was the military *Jiefangjun bao,* which contributed a single series of 11 editorials, while the CCP organ *RMRB* generated a total of 27 pieces in four series (1 editorial, 2 special commentaries, 10 commentaries, 15 contributions to the column Talk Today [*jinritan*]). The extent to which these four major official media coordinated the publication schedules

Table 4.6: Reprinting of Authoritative Commentaries among National Press Agencies

Press and Type	Xinhua Dateline	Published same day, full title and text			Published in Qiushi
		RMRB	GMRB	JFJB	
Xinhua special commentary	7/27, 31, 8/2–6	Y	Y/N[a]	Y/N[b]	N
RMRB editorial	7/23	Y	Y	Y	Y
RMRB special commentary	8/18, 20	Y	Y	Y	N
RMRB commentary	7/26, 27, 29, 30 8/4, 6, 9, 12, 13, 16	Y	Y	Y	N
Qiushi editorial	8/1	Y	N	Y	Y
Qiushi commentary	8/16[c]	N	N	Y/N[d]	Y
GMRB editorial	7/25, 27, 28, 29, 30, 8/2, 3, 4	N	Y	N	N
JFJB editorial	7/23, 26, 27, 29, 31, 8/11, 13, 17, 18, 20, 23	N	N	Y	Y/N[e]

[a]*Guangming ribao (GMRB)* published the Xinhua special commentary articles of 7/31 but not those of 8/2–6.
[b]*Jiefang junbao (JFJB)* published the full title and text of Xinhua special commentary articles of 7/31, 8/4, and 8/6 but not 8/5, and only excerpts of those of 8/2 and 8/3.
[c]*Qiushi*'s August 16 issue published three articles signed by *Qiushi* commentators.
[d]*JFJB* published the *Qiushi* commentary articles on 7/26 and 7/29.
[e]Of the 10 *JFJB* editorials, only the 7/23 was published in *Qiushi*.

of these authoritative commentaries on the Falungong and reprint those of others is analyzed in chapter 8.

In addition to the publication of different commentary series in the major national press, periodic assaults against the Falungong continued through the end of 2005. As shown in table 4.7, multiple stories attacking the Falungong in *RMRB* appeared every month from July 1999 to May 2004. While the triple digits in July and August 1999 dissipated to double digits for most months for the remainder of 1999 and from 2000 to 2002, and further to single digits in 2003–4, there were still nine stories on the Falungong in 2005, six years after the official ban. The overall trend is downward, with lower annual averages for 1999–2005, except for 2001.[42]

THE ANTI-FALUNGONG PUBLICATIONS CAMPAIGN

Anti-Falungong books were published in three waves. The first involved uncoordinated efforts in 1998 and up to July 22, 1999, by several presses

Table 4.7: Articles on Falungong in *RMRB,* 1999–2005

Year	Jan	Feb	Mar	Apr	May	June	July	Aug	Sep	Oct	Nov	Dec	Total
1999							170	196	25	41	104	73	609
2000	52	25	63	38	23	34	25	10	14	10	10	21	325
2001	59	66	20	46	25	28	34	6	15	10	12	23	534
2002	20	11	22	24	26	10	25	7	28	17	1	7	198
2003	5	2	9	2	5	2	2	4	4	3	5	3	54
2004	4	1	1	3	1		2	2			1	2	17
2005	2	1	1			2	1				2		9
Grand Total													1,746

Source: RMRB, electronic version.

that published books on science versus superstition, which was the general theme of an earlier policy to counter the abuse of fast-spreading *qigong* in 1996 and 1997.[43] Some of these publications, already in print before July 22, 1999, were later adopted to be part of the official anti-Falungong series described in the following paragraph.[44] The second wave was organized by the NPB in July 1999 to publish more than 30 titles exposing the Falungong and extolling science to fill an immediate government and market need for books on the Falungong when the case broke on July 22. The third wave and main campaign was initiated by the NPB, which convened a conference in Beijing on publishing books criticizing the Falungong on July 30, eight days after the official ban was imposed. It then issued a notice on August 6 to publication houses nationwide to invite them to submit publication proposals on propagating materialism, atheism, and popular science. Soon thereafter, the NPB received proposals on 410 titles from 160 publishers on the above three topics. Among these, the NPB selected 120 titles from 105 publishing houses to be included in its publication plans. These fall into three series: two derived from official communist dogma (20 on Marxian materialism and 40 on atheism), and a third with an equal number (60) on popular scientific knowledge.[45] The following section analyzes the regime's choices of the form of publisher participation, the optimum mix of propaganda themes versus responsiveness to market trends, and the allocation of titles to central versus provincial publishers. The subsequent analyses show that the NPB gave considerable weight to market forces in all these three choices. Why is that so?

Market Competition

Two decades of economic reforms in China had ushered in institutional and market dynamics that severely impaired the monopoly of the propaganda apparatus over the publications industry. Long gone were the golden days of the Maoist era, when propaganda literature was assured of institutional purchases and captive readerships. Propaganda literature now has to compete with popular genres—including literary classics, martial arts, romance novels, sex works sometimes labeled as science, even pornography peddled as art, and a deluge of close to two million copies of Western imports.[46] In particular, there were at least seven times more science and technology titles than those of traditional propaganda (Marxism, materialism, atheism) in the NPB tally of 1999 publications (table 4.8). More daunting competition came from the larger media industry, thanks to a greater than eightfold increase in the number of periodicals and a tenfold increase in the number of newspapers in the reform period,[47] the rapid growth and satellization of its television stations by the 1990s, and extensive use of program ratings and the predominance of advertising income as corporate revenue of China's broadcasting and television stations.[48] In this competitive market, a severe threat for book publishers came from a reinvented periodical and electronic industry. Many of the new-generation dailies and magazines were often glossy productions like their Hong Kong and Taiwan counterparts, reporting Western fashions, human interest stories, overseas vacation spots, and lurid celebrity gossip. In television, the increase from three channels on CCTV in 1991 to eight in 2000, including special economic, sports, music, children, and theater channels, provided specialized programming for different media market segments and demographic consumer groups.[49] Its constant high ratings of more than 360–630 million viewers in its prime-time programs in 1998–2000 testify to the increasing popularity of the reinvented tube.[50]

Table 4.8: Number of Publication Titles by Select Category, 1999

Category	No. Titles
Marxism, Leninism, thoughts of Mao	146
Philosophy	1,346
Social sciences[a]	1,509
Natural sciences	741
Astronomy, earth sciences	674
Biological sciences	455
Chemistry, mathematical sciences	2,010
Medicine, hygiene	5,750

[a]There were separate entries on politics and law (5,567), economics (8,274), and history and geography (4,104).

Source: *Zhongguo chuban nianjian, 2000,* p. 66.

Localization of Book Distribution

A second development that brought gloom to the propaganda book industry was the decentralization of the regulatory and localization of the book distribution system. As a result of the transference of regulatory powers from the NPB to the provinces and local governments,[51] provincial agencies gained control of the publications plan and approval of publications titles. Reinforcing this trend was localization, wherein the Xinhua system also transferred distribution rights to its provincial, municipal, and county stores. Combined with efforts of local distribution networks erecting barriers to block the sale of nonlocal publications, China's book distribution industry was fragmented by these trends. Localization can be seen in the small shares of the top wholesalers, where the combined market share of the leading four wholesalers in 1998 was only 8% of the national wholesale book market.[52] The devastating effect of localization on national distribution can be seen in the approximate parity between the book publishing and distribution markets on the provincial level, where each province distributed about the same share of books that it published. In combination, these media trends have undercut the share of the book market in China. The printed book market has fallen out of the top five media, which in 1998 were, in descending order, television, radio, newspapers, magazines, and the Internet, each of which was rated a more popular medium than printed books by official count.[53] Within the publications industry, per capita book purchases declined from 5.93 copies in 1985 to 5.51 in 1995,[54] and many of these sales were actually of school texts rather than general interest books. At the same time, consumption of other media products had soared, with that of newspaper and periodical circulation increasing 1.45 times and 1.61 times, respectively, that of daily radio broadcasting hours doubling, and that of television programs produced increasing 4.26-fold. Consequently, inventory of unsold books has increased steadily in the late 1990s, amounting to 3.46 billion copies valued at 24.16 billion *yuan* at the end of 1999.[55] All these factors accentuated pressure on publishers to produce books catering to readership trends.

Analysis of NPB Choices

Given these new dynamics in the publications industry, how did the NPB pursue its political goal of repudiating the Falungong? The NPB's decision to adopt the ambidextrous approach, using both the strong arm of the state and the invisible hand of the market, was a compromise for the mixed political economy characteristic of the transitional regime. On the one hand, as noted above, for the great majority of anti-Falungong titles, the NPB invited competitive proposals from central and provincial publishers. On the other hand, it assigned a basic target of 30 anti-Falungong books in the second publication wave to be published by its three in-house presses where it had strong personnel and production controls, thus reinforcing desired propaganda models and also safeguarding against market failure to meet content, quality, and schedule requirements.

Product Mix

The NPB also needed to weigh its apologetics objective against market demand in its selection of topics for the publications campaign. The former would focus on how Falungong beliefs and practices contradicted official dogma, and the latter on physical and social sciences that enjoy brisker book sales. The clear numeric preponderance of publications on natural and social sciences to works on communism and philosophy (table 4.8) suggests that it would be far easier to recruit authors and editors, contract publishers, find shelf space, and sell more titles for the science titles in the series. From this perspective, the NPB's August 6 announcement that the campaign would be more broadly focused on propagating materialism, atheism, and popular science was a clear compromise between propaganda goals and consumer preference. The allocation of 60 titles to popular science, 40 to secular atheism, and 20 to Marxist materialism was in the same order of the overall distribution of published titles in the China book market in 1999, which published 146 titles of Communist dogma, 1,346 on philosophy, and more than 10,000 titles on science (table 4.8).

Selection of Publishers

In selecting which publishers to be awarded publication contracts for the anti-Falungong campaign, the NPB had to select between central and provincial presses. Contracting publishers of central government ministries located in Beijing would reap the advantage of geographical proximity and greater administrative control. In particular, the NPB directly managed a conglomerate of 16 publishing houses,[56] printers, and the Xinhua bookstore with its nationwide points of sale, over which it had close control of production plans, material, and budget. The greater control over the production process, however, would have to be balanced against the more extensive distribution network of the local publications industry. Comparing with those of the central government, the local publications industry in 1999 had 1.6 times more publications presses, produced 1.7 times more titles, printed 5.8 times more volumes, operated 88.6 times more bookstores, sold 16.6 times more books, and earned 45.7 times more profits. To engage the cooperation of the local publications industry, the NPB thus needed to award a substantial number of publication contracts to the local presses.[57]

The interplay between market forces and propaganda needs is evident in the distribution of the types of books among the types of publishers. The central presses in general, and the three NPB presses in particular, shouldered the heaviest burden in publishing the unpopular propaganda titles. The three NPB presses published eight titles on materialism and atheism and no title on popular science. Other central presses published more propaganda titles (18) than science (13), while the provincial presses published more science titles (47) than materialism and atheism combined (22). In all, the NPB and other central presses published 43.3% (26 of 60) of the propaganda titles, while the provincial presses published 78.3% (47 of 60) of the popular science books.

COORDINATION PROBLEMS IN THE ANTI-FALUNGONG PROPAGANDA CAMPAIGN

The sheer scale of the media campaign presented inherent functional and administrative coordination problems for the regime. Functional coordination in the media campaign and the extent to which media organizations participated in news coproduction and coauthorship endeavors, shared news stories and commentaries, and coordinated their publications and broadcast schedules are analyzed in chapter 8. The need for administrative coordination stemmed from the organizational size and increasing competitiveness of the media industry in China, as well as the multiple bureaucracies involved in the campaign. First, when the Falungong was banned in 1999, the media establishment in China included 566 publishers, 2,089 newspapers, 7,583 periodicals, 299 radio broadcasting stations, and 352 television broadcasting stations.[58] The plethora of media institutions were managed by different administrative agencies depending on the type of media (radio, television, newspapers, books, periodicals) and their respective jurisdictions—national and local, party and nonparty. Under the single administration of the party-state, and overseen by the Department of Propaganda, such enormity and complexity called for unified management, functional specialization, and organizational coordination. Second, industry competition has driven media agencies toward a zero-sum game where different media enterprises strive for larger shares of market exposure, corporate profit, and industry prominence.[59] Indeed, in the anti-Falungong campaign, the respective claims of different media organizations that they were able to get exclusive interviews with Falungong leaders as well as investigators and prosecutors illustrate the competitive nature of news production in the campaign.[60] Institutional cooperation among media agencies should thus not be taken for granted.

Third, the media campaign was part of a larger anti-Falungong campaign that required administrative coordination between media organizations and law enforcement, religious policy, public health, and other functional agencies. As noted above, the CCTV television movie titled *Li Hongzhi: The Man and His Deeds,"* aired the afternoon of July 22 and published in *RMRB* the following day, was based on an investigative article written by the Research Office of the Ministry of Public Security. At the same time, just-on-time stories on the expressed contrition and conversion of Falungong leaders and followers suggest that Xinhua and *RMRB* journalists received leads and assistance from public security agencies to interview Falungong practitioners in their custody.[61] To gain access to news sources, media agencies needed to work with a variety of functional bureaucracies, including the courts, procuracy, and public security agents that served as the frontline investigators of the Falungong. Even in the prereform period, coordination was problematic.[62] Their relationships have been complicated by institutional conflicts of interest between media and government bureaucracies. The media's need for timely and newsworthy stories often conflicts with official bureaucratic rules on secrecy to preempt premature, unauthorized disclosure that would leak news of the crackdown and jeopardize investigation and prosecution strategies. The emergence and popularity of investigative journalism in both print media and television news magazines have further strained relations between media organizations and bureaucratic agencies, many of which have become subjects of media exposes.[63]

Some Falungong news stories required close coordination between media organization and state bureaucracies. In announcing the ban on the Falungong on July 22, separate orders of the CCP's Central Committee, the Ministry of Civil Affairs, and the Ministry of Public Security[64] had to be broadcast verbatim in authorized sequential order, and from official releases prepared by these agencies. In the following week, Xinhua and *RMRB* journalists reported on a series of public notices issued by the National People's Congress, the Supreme People's Court, and the Supreme People's Procuracy on outlawing the Falungong, as well as the outpouring of support of the ban by party and government agencies at different administrative levels and by mass organizations and community groups.[65] Many of these were reported in the news programs of CPBS and CCTV on the same day and in the *RMRB* on the following day. Since these were invariably published by all the major national press as important news with prominent placement, editors of these media organizations had to work with the propaganda department and media regulators on conflicting priorities in news publication and planning.

More complex administrative coordination problems rested with cases involving multiple functional agencies with different organizational missions and conflicting priorities. For instance, in the official announcement of the ban on the Falungong on July 22, 1999, not only the regular programming of CCTV and CPBS but also those of the provincial and local radio and television stations had to be interrupted to air the special news program broadcast nationwide at 3 P.M. that day. The much-publicized outdoor destruction of Falungong publications and accessories nationwide on July 29, 1999, in multiple locations on short notice likewise required close and extensive cooperation between the media establishment and the NPB, Public Security Bureau, National Commerce and Trade Management Bureau, Customs, and the National "Eliminate Pornography Office."[66]

As part of the media campaign, then, there is thus need to analyze what campaign activities were coordinated by which set of party and state agencies and whether such coordination was accomplished by the immediate organizational superiors or by the top administrative echelons in the regime. Additionally, there is also need to examine how news organizations coordinated media functions with those of nonmedia party and state agencies.

Administrative Coordination

Within the State Council of the central government, the State Bureau for Broadcast, Film, and Television (SBBFT) oversees the three electronic media outlets (CPBS, CCTV, and the International Broadcasting Station), and the NPB supervises the publications industry. Both the SBBFT and the NPB are directly administered by the State Council, the executive branch of government.[67] On the CCP side, the Department of Propaganda has jurisdiction over propaganda, culture, and publication fields[68] and is subordinated to the Central Committee. At the apex, both the State Council and the Department of Propaganda are led by the Propaganda and Ideology Leading Group of the Politburo in media policy.[69]

Organizational coordination can take the form of "one-level-up" management, where a higher administrative level coordinates activities and resolves disagreements among different subordinate agencies on the next lower administrative level. In this capacity, the NPB and SBBFT serve as the respective coordinating bodies for the print and electronic media for the anti-Falungong campaign. Alternatively, coordination can also take the form of "command and control," where top-echelon administrative organizations initiate and direct campaign operations to be implemented by multiple organizational subordinates in different functional agencies. The bottom-up process of one-level-up coordination is more characteristic of simple tasks requiring coordination within single-line organizations, while the top-down command-and-control process is more congruent with complex operations in multiple-line authority hierarchies.

Limited Coordinating Role of Administrative Agencies

The anti-Falungong campaign appears to be managed by the command-and-control structure that was highly centralized, led by top-echelon central party and state leaders. The two media administrative agencies (NPB and SBBFT) played only a limited management and coordination role. Aside from managing the campaign to publish 120 anti-Falungong titles and participating in the operation to ban and confiscate Falungong publications and video products, there were no reports that the NPB directed or coordinated other campaign activities.[70] At the next higher organizational level, neither the NPB nor SBBFT was reported to have initiated or coordinated news coproduction activities among specific electronic and print media organizations. In reports of Xinhua, *RMRB*, and CCTV in their anti-Falungong campaign, there were references to the leadership of the CCP center and the Propaganda Department but not the NPB and SBBFT.[71]

The limited coordinating role of the media administrative agencies resulted from the compartmentalization of the electronic and print media, the weakened bureaucratic position of the NPB and SBBFT, and the low party rank of its top administrators. First, the NPB and SBBFT operated as relatively independent and vertical bureaucracies with line authority from the central and provincial bureaucracies, to city and county agencies. Strong compartmental barriers appear to exist between the two administrative agencies, as evidenced by the lack of joint notices issued by the NPB and SBBFT addressed to both print and electronic media in 1999. As shown in table 4.9, the NPB issued six notices and orders to the news agencies and the publications industry, while the SBBFT issued 20 notices to the nation's television and broadcast industry in 1999. None of the 26 notices was issued jointly by the two administrative agencies. Indeed, even within the SBBFT, the majority of the 20 notices concerned separate administrative issues in the radio or television media.[72]

Second, the bureaucratic authority of both the NPB and SBBFT was weakened by the State Council reorganization in 1993. In that reorganization, the SBBFT, which had been a ministry since 1982, was demoted to a state bureau. At the same time, the management powers of the two agencies were devolved to local governments and media organizations that gained administrative autonomy. In tandem with their institutional demotion and decentralization, the prescribed staff size of the NPB was reduced from 265 in 1993 to 145 in 1998 while that of the SBBFT was cut from 560 in 1988 to 446 in 1993, and further slashed to only 223 in 1999.[73] The institutional capacity of the NPB and SBBFT to lead and coordinate the nationwide media campaign was thus substantially compromised.

Table 4.9: Public Notices Issued by Media Administrative Organizations

	NPB Orders Only	SBBFT Orders Only	NPB and SBBFT	NPB or SBBFT with Propaganda Department	NPB or SBBFT with Law Enforcement Agencies	NPN or SBBFT with Other Party and State Agencies
Before 4/25/99	**7/24/96,** **8/16/96,** **6/5/98** 3/17/99(2)	3/12/99 3/20/99 3/30/99 4/6/99 4/7/99			4/1/99	2/12/99
4/25/99 to 7/21/99	6/1/99 7/5/99 7/8/99	5/21/99 6/29/99 7/19/99				
7/22/99 to 12/31/99	**11/11/99**	8/2/99 8/10/99 8/12/99 8/18/99 8/23/99 10/99 10/26/99 11/12/99 (4) 12/2/99	**8/23/99** **11/9/99**			7/29/99 9/13/99 9/17/99 9/27/99

Boldface dates are those pertaining to the anti-Falungong campaign.

Source: *Zhongguo xinwen nianjian*, 2000, pp. 30–51; *Zhongguo guangbo dianshi nianjian*, 2000, pp. 198–209.

Third, the administrative authority of the NPB and SBBFT was also cur-tailed by the low party rank of its top administrators. Both agencies were not headed by Central Committee members. They were thus outranked by the heads of Xinhua news agency and the *RMRB*, who were Central Committee members.[74] Outside the media system, the NPB and SBBFT would be even less effective to serve as a coordinating body for the anti-Falungong propa-ganda campaign in their dealings with the public security establishment, State Council ministries, and CCP agencies, some of which were headed by Central Committee members.[75]

Centralization of Anti-Falungong Campaign

Given the institutional weakness of the NPB and SBBFT, several indications suggest the management of the anti-Falungong campaign was centralized at the level of top party and state agencies. First, the preeminent party and state leaders were personally engaged in dealing with the Falungong from the beginning of the crisis. As noted in chapter 2, on April 25 when the Falungong besieged Zhongnanhai, Premier Zhu Rongji met with the representatives of the Falungong, while Secretary-General Jiang Zemin set the guideline to deal with the demands of the protesters, instructed security tsar Luo Gan to convene an emergency meeting, and addressed a letter to top leaders that evening denouncing the Falungong.[76] Second, both the campaign goals and strategies were not proposed by propaganda and public security bureaucratic agencies, but originated from the office of Jiang Zemin. His characterization of the Falungong, the identification of campaign goals, and the specification of its tasks became titles and subtitles of editorials in *RMRB, Guangming ribao,* and *Jiefangjun bao* in the anti-Falungong campaign.[77]

Third, the anti-Falungong campaign was managed by two *ad hoc* agencies within the central party and state apparatus. As elaborated in chapter 6, the "Central Leading Group on Dealing with the Falungong" (CLGDF) was empowered to lead and coordinate various party and state agencies in the campaign, while the "610 Office" was its executive arm. Headed by Politburo Standing Committee member Li Lanqing, the CLGDF was deputized by propaganda chief Ding Guan'gen and security tsar Luo Gan, both Politburo members.[78] The anti-Falungong campaign was thus managed by the top-echelon CCP leaders, several administrative strata above the NPB, SBBFT, the Xinhua news agency, *Qiushi, RMRB, Guangming ribao,* CCTV, CPBS, and the leading publishers.

Fourth, where extant information is available, several operational decisions on how the Xinhua news agency, CCTV and *RMRB* should conduct the anti-Falungong media campaign were reportedly made by CCP central agencies, not by media organizations or regulating bodies (NPB and SBBFT). The official announcement of the banning of Falungong shown at 3 P.M. on July 22 on CCTV was reported to be a central CCP decision. Likewise, both the month-long media blitz in Xinhua from July 22 to August 23 and the phasing of the *RMRB* campaign in three stages were said to be decisions of the CCP central agency. In addition to the timing of the campaign, the *RMRB* also reported that its endeavor to create a Web site to repudiate the Falungong in its Internet edition, and the choice of topics of its three anti-Falungong guest commentaries published on August 13, 18, and 20 were also suggested by the CCP central agency.[79]

The centralized supervision of the anti-Falungong media campaign can also be seen in the top party leaders' and agencies' recognition of the media programs. Two articles on the Falungong, published by *RMRB* on June 24 and December 7, won the praise of Secretary-General Jiang Zemin. The special program banning the Falungong, aired on the morning of July 23, also received the acclaim of unnamed CCP central leaders. An anti-Falungong episode titled "Expelling the God of Plague" in the news magazine program *Speaking Plain Truth* was also singled out for commendation of the Department of Propaganda leaders.[80]

CONCLUSION

Before the Falungong was officially outlawed on July 22, 1999, the *RMRB* published only two stories on the congregation in the entire history of the sect. In the first month since the ban, the party organ published 780 news stories, several investigative reports, an editorial, and three series of commentaries on the Falungong. Together with more than twice this number of releases from the official Xinhua news agency, a similar volume of output from other major national press, enhanced regular programming, and special presentations from the nation's television and radio networks, the anti-Falungong campaign was a media tsunami that dominated the national broadcast and print news in the month-long event.

In deafening decibels and extralarge font, the public was informed that the Falungong was a public enemy, a menace to social order and party rule, a hazard for the physical and mental health for those who practice its craft. Li Hongzhi, esteemed as the venerable master by his followers, was in fact a fraud who falsified his birth date, fabricated healing results, and lived a life of extravagance from ill-gotten gains. Contrary to his public denials, the Falungong was not simply unorganized groups of fitness-conscious citizens who practice breathing exercise for better health, but a disciplined, hierarchically structured organization that mounted illegal collective protest rallies in national and provincial capitals in defiance of China's laws. Consequently, to maintain social order and to protect public health, the Falungong need to be banned and its publications exorcised from public circulation. CCP and Communist Youth League members and government cadres who practiced Falungong should renounce their membership and dissociate from all sect activities. The great majority of practitioners need not fear, since engaging in breathing exercises in public places broke no law. Strict sanctions only befell those who planned and organized protest demonstrations and instigated others to participate in those illegal rallies. For treatment and prevention, both CCP members and the general public should be inoculated against the spiritual virus, through a sustained period of propagandistic education on science, dialectical materialism, and atheism.

The message was publicized in a well-orchestrated propaganda campaign. The official ban was announced on a weekday at 3 P.M., the mid-afternoon slot chosen to allow for in-house public viewing of the announcement at party agencies, government offices, and public enterprises, for commentary by local officials, and for immediate feedback by the masses that would be reported in news dispatches the following morning. Investigative reports painstakingly documented the government's charges and substantiated its claims. Top Falungong officials, former colleagues, neighbors, and an elementary school principal were interviewed as negative character witnesses of Li Hongzhi. Denunciations of the Falungong and support for the regime decision were solicited and published on the day after the announcement of the ban from a careful assortment of academics, professionals, party cadres, government officials, company executives, retirees, and ordinary citizens. At almost the same time, reports on the public disappearance of Falungong assemblies, the confession and repentance of its top leaders, the mass defection of its followers, and the voluntary turnover, forced confiscation, and outdoor destruction of its publications and accessories certified the public death of Falungong inside China. The campaign closely followed the government script, worked out beforehand by the Propaganda Department. There was no surprise ending.

But as a propaganda campaign, was it efficient or effective? Did different media organizations coordinate publication schedules, pool resources, participate in news coproduction, engage in thematic and geographic specialization of content targeted at different market segments, and reprint each other's news stories and commentaries? Were these stories and programs on the Falungong well received by the viewing and reading public? Did any of the investigative reports in the national press or any special television program receive the equivalent of the Pulitzer Prize? Did television ratings rise or fall in the month-long media campaign starting July 22, 1999? Chapter 8 pursues these analyses. But our immediate attention turns now to an analysis of what the regime did with the millions of Falungong practitioners after the ban, presented in chapter 5.

Chapter Five

Curing the Patient—Conversion Programs

After the Falungong organizations were officially dissolved on July 22, 1999, dealing with the large number of Falungong practitioners presented special problems for the regime. Even at the conservative official estimate of 2.3 million, massive detention and incarceration were clearly not options, as the public security, procuracy, court, and labor reform systems lacked the physical space to house the inmates, the procurators and judges to prosecute, indict, convict, and sentence them, and public security agents to enforce coercive detention. To process the much smaller number of 20,000 Falungong core leaders who were detained in the nationwide roundup of July 20-22 immediately before the ban, it would be more than the normal three-month case load based on data from 1998 for criminal cases related to public security and social order issues processed by the procuracy and court systems (table 5.1). Incarcerating all the Falungong practitioners was thus not a realistic solution. The regime needed ways to rehabilitate the multitude of practitioners.

This chapter analyzes the education and conversion programs for Falungong practitioners. It begins with official guidelines on differentiating cate-

Table 5.1: Criminal Case Load and Processing in China's Procuracies and Courts, 1998

Cases	Arrests Authorized		Cases Prosecuted		
	No. Cases	No. Persons	No. Cases	No. Persons	Cases Closed
Total	403,210	598,101	403,145	584,763	480,374
Endangering state security	204	532	186	555	208
Endangering social order	23,575	26,787	27,141	30,015	27,490
Obstructing social order	45,984	76,540	43,520	69,177	46,399

Source: *Zhongguo falu nianjian* [China Law Yearbook, 1999], pp. 1021, 1026.

gories of Falungong practitioners. In a process similar to triage, practitioners were sorted into (1) common practitioners who would be subjected only to public education and study sessions, (2) more hardened practitioners who required personalized indoctrination, and (3) the most committed practitioners destined for labor reform and special rehabilitation programs. Next, it examines the mechanics of conversion programs that focused on both individual and groups, and the responsibility system that assigned Falungong practitioners to conversion teams and tracked the outcome. This is followed by an analysis of conversion programs in penal institutions: the security detention process, the organization of the Heilongjiang system, and the Yunnan special program. The soft, psychological techniques of the Yunnan program is contrasted with the brutal and coercive methods reported in Falungong sources.

GUIDELINES TO DIFFERENTIATE PRACTITIONERS

To differentiate among Falungong practitioners, the regime had already worked out guidelines for separate treatment of different types of offense before suppression. Announced on the same day as the official ban on July 23, a statement of Zheng Qinghong, minister of organization of the Chinese Communist Party (CCP), made four sets of basic distinctions regarding party members who joined the Falungong: (1) common Falungong practitioners should be distinguished from the leaders (*gugan*); (2) common leaders should be distinguished from the planners and organizers with political intentions; (3) the errant but contrite practitioners should be distinguished from those who refused to repent; (4) those who made errors before the CCP announced its official ban should be distinguished from those who made mistakes after the announcement.[1]

Policy guidelines were also specified to deal with five different types of detainees in ascending order of severity in the July 19 Central Committee document. First, general practitioners who voluntarily withdrew organizationally and distanced themselves ideologically from the Falungong would not be treated as problems requiring disciplinary action. Second, the common Falungong leaders who would undergo the same behavioral modification and provide exposés of Falungong problems would not be further investigated (*zhuijiu*). Third, those who had repented or accrued merit after committing serious errors would be dealt with leniently or not be further investigated. Fourth, unrepentant leaders with serious errors would be asked to withdraw from the CCP and would be dismissed if they refused to withdraw voluntarily. Finally, the planners, organizers, and backstage plotters of antigovernment rallies would be resolutely expelled from the CCP.[2]

The above two documents were issued by party organizations and dealt with CCP members who practiced Falungong. Two related documents, issued on July 23 by the Communist Youth League and the State Council, reiterated the same set of guidelines for league members and civil servants.[3] A month after the ban, in an apparent reaction to the uneven and overzealous manner with which the witch hunt was conducted in some localities, the Central Committee and the State Council issued a joint circular on August 24 calling for the "strict observance of policy demarcation lines for promoting the conversion of the great majority of Falungong practitioners."[4] The earlier guidelines for classifying offenses and prescribing disciplinary action were further elaborated.

For the first type of general practitioners, the August 24 joint circular defines this group as those who practice the Falungong to improve their health. In such cases, they would not be asked to make self-examinations and self-criticisms, and their cases should be promptly closed. Core leaders who have participated in protest rallies would also be extricated if they severed their organizational and ideological ties with Falungong, provide a clear account of their activities and an expose of Falungong problems. Lenient punishments will be dealt with core leaders who made serious mistakes but who have clearly separated themselves ideologically from Li Hongzhi and the Falungong, conscientiously confessed their role in illegal activities, recognized and voluntarily examined their mistakes, voluntarily declared that they would withdraw from Falungong organizations, actively exposed the inside story of Falungong, and genuinely desisted from future participation of Falungong activities. They would be exempted from punishment if there were indications that they would accrue merit and redeem themselves. Finally, for the hard-core plotters and organizers, they would be dealt with according to law if they deliberately disrupted social stability and when their actions constituted crimes. The classification scheme is presented in table 5.2.

Within the party system, the specific treatment of different types of offenses was stipulated in an earlier party document distributed to the CCP organizations in the central party and to government agencies, armed forces, mass organizations, and those on the provincial level. Issued on July 19 in the name of the Central Committee, it was first circulated internally within the party and later published in *Renmin ribao* on July 23 as the first salvo of the official ban.[5] The document stipulates the following behavior as evidence of contrition and both mental and organizational separation from the Falungong: (1) cease practicing Falungong, (2) cease participating in its activities, (3) cease holding positions in its organization, (4) cease disseminating its materials, and (5) cease providing venue, funds, and other assistance for its activities. In addition, they should engage in behavior labeled as "accruing

Table 5.2: Classification of Offence Type, Contrition Behavior, and Disciplinary Action for Falungong Detainees

Degree of Involvement	Contritional Behavior	Disciplinary Action
Rank-and-file practitioner	Withdrawal from Falungong Renouncing Falungong	None
Core Leadership who participated in illegal activities	Withdrawal from Falungong Renouncing Falungong Exposing Falungong Accounting for their activities	None
Core leadership with serious errors	Voluntary withdraw from Falungong Renouncing Falungong Exposing Falungong Conscientious confession Voluntary self-examination Abstaining from future Falungong activities Accruing merit	None
	Same as above behavior, but without accruing merit	Lenient
	Unrepentant	Asked to withdrawal from the CCP, involuntary dismissal if refused
Errant core leaders who planned and organized political turmoil	Unrepentant	Expulsion from CCP or Communist Youth Leage or dismissal from government post

merit" (*li gong*), namely, taking the initiative to expose, criticize, and repudiate Li Hongzhi and the Falungong, and to actively coordinate with the CCP and related organizations to propagate the anti-Falungong program to the masses.[6]

Four Modes of Conversion through Education

At the wake of official ban, the regime aimed at not only coercive dissolution of the sect but also reform and rehabilitation of the practitioners. The goal was accomplished through four program initiatives. First, for the great majority of Falungong practitioners and their supporters, a mass campaign through electronic and print media, as well as more traditional forms of propaganda, was launched to exorcise the sectarians of their haunted past.

Second, for those who were more committed to the cause, a more intense effort of individualized reeducation was organized, where one or more agents would work for the repentance of the practitioner. Third, special programs, with emphasis on internal transformation rather than external conformity, were launched to reform the hard-core believers when other efforts failed. Fourth, the group of unreformable practitioners who continued to defy the law or deemed security risks were sent to punitive and rehabilitative labor reform.

Political Education within the CCP

In its notice announcing the official ban, the Central Committee stipulated a nationwide education campaign that would evolve in three stages. Labeled as "Study and Elevate" (*xuexi tigao*), the first stage was designed to inform party members nationwide of the malevolence of the Falungong and the party policy on how to deal with the sect in general and errant party members who had become its practitioners in particular. The second stage, called "education and conversion" (*jiaoyu zhuanhua*), was aimed at redeeming fallen party members and Falungong practitioners who would show contrition and commitment to sever ties with the Falungong. This is followed by the third stage, "organization disposition" (*zhuji chuli*), where the party organization made its judgment on whether the errant party member should be fully rehabilitated, receive censure, or expelled from the party. Except for the last stage, which remained an intraparty process that has not been publicized, both the education and conversion programs in the first two stages involved both party as well as nonparty members.

Chapter 4 analyzes the nationwide campaign waged by the national electronic and print media. This section deals with provinces and municipalities that reported extensive education campaigns that were both prolonged in duration and varied in format. In Xinjiang, all party members and cadres spent at least one full week away from work in the latter half of 1999 in study sessions of the education campaign.[7] In Bangbu Municipality in Jiangxi, the party committee planned to use one month to organize an education campaign that was to be coordinated by a central study and education office, as well as a round-the-clock office system.[8] Showing even greater commitment, the Qinghai Provincial Party Committee ordered a year-long provincewide campaign to commence in late July 1999 and last through the end of June 2000. Defining the scope of the campaign in identical terminology as in the Central Committee notice, all party members and cadres in the province were to be reeducated in Marxian materialism and atheism, in order to strengthen their political sensitivity and sharpen their ability to discriminate the correct from the erroneous doctrine, as well as science from superstition. The goal was to induce the strayed party members to return to the fold and to enable party organizations to preserve their ideological progressiveness and purity.[9]

The mechanics of the first wave of the education campaign followed closely those of a bygone era. For some provincial and municipal party committees, political study programs were launched for the edification of party members. The Jinjiang Municipal Propaganda Bureau in Fujian Province selected publications on atheism and materialism and reprinted these in five issues of its bulletin.[10] The Dandong Municipal Party Committee of Liaoning Province convened study sessions, organized special presentations, and devoted the monthly party meetings to discussing party policy on the Falungong.[11] The Guizhou Provincial Propaganda Department and Organization Department organized 210 classes for its party members and cadres to study materialism and atheism.[12] Meizhou Municipality in Guangdong organized study classes on party policy toward the Falungong, with each party member attending three or more sessions, for a total of 170,000 person-sessions.[13] In a more elaborate effort, the Baoding Municipal Party Committee of Hebei Province put together popular science education forums, organized tests on Marxian materialism, and required top officials in the municipal bureaucracy to make a presentation on dialectic materialism, party-member cadres to write their reflections on the same, and all party members to attend a booster class on the subject.[14]

Political Education for Nonparty Members

Reaching outside the CCP, other local party committees organized public education programs. Hebei Province launched materialism and atheism study seminars to propagate such philosophies to the general public. It also mobilized the legal, science and technology, medicine, and media sectors to expose, criticize, and repudiate Li Hongzhi and Falungong teachings.[15] The "Anti-Cult Federation" of Jinan organized an exhibition on science and superstition, as well as a 10,000-signature drive. Its women and workers federations initiated a program on "families saying 'no' to cults."[16] The Chongqing Municipal Political and Legal Affairs Committee curated exhibitions to repudiate superstition and commissioned academics to publish a popular science monograph series.[17] The Zibo Municipal Propaganda Bureau in Shandong organized a "Science and Technology Publicity Week," arranged media interviews with 20 scientists, and published and distributed 20,000 copies of study materials on strengthening education on materialism.[18] To make the propaganda program more mobile, the Kaifeng Municipal Party Committee and government of Henan Province assembled rehabilitated Falungong practitioners into a speaker program to make presentations at various venues in the city.[19] Similarly, the Hubei Provincial Science Commission and Science Federation established science popularization mobile stations as well as speaker series and assembled Falungong practitioners to receive science education,[20] while the Hebei Provincial Party Committee's Speaker Team collaborated with the provincial broadcast station to produce a radio series of 10 presentations repudiating the Falungong.[21]

The traditional mass mobilization institution of work teams was de-mothballed. As early as July 23, the day after the official ban on the Falungong was promulgated, Xinfeng County of Jiangxi Province deployed 1,200 party members to visit local peasant households to help out with harvesting and persuading Falungong members to withdraw from the sect.[22] In Sichuan Province, 153 work groups were sent to localities by July 26.[23] Elsewhere in Hebei Province, 30,000 party members and cadres were sent from province, municipality, county, township, and enterprises to rural households and urban city block housing committees to educate more than 130,000 Falungong practitioners.[24] In the provincial capital alone, Shijiazhuang Municipality dispatched 3,572 work teams composed of 20,000 cadres from its municipal bureaucracy as well as from county and township enterprises. They deployed a battery of propaganda techniques, known in official parlance as mobile and fixed-point propaganda, seminars, and on-the-spot education, theory guidance, and special topic discussion, through which Falungong practitioners were organized to study the speeches of Jiang Zemin, central documents, and related articles in major newspapers. Special propaganda troupes to repudiate Falungong were formed and sent to 106 residential committees and more than 10 Falungong practice sites. These work teams stayed at the village and the factories and undertook one-to-one reeducation of errant Falungong practitioners. By August 10, 1999, 96% of Falungong practitioners in Shijiazhuang had reportedly withdrawn from the sect.[25]

Going beyond traditional propaganda methods, the Shenyang Propaganda Department organized summer evening soirees in community centers and city parks to propagate science and denounce the Falungong,[26] while the Municipal Theatre Troupe of Jinan dispatched small contingents to stage anti-Falungong performances in different cities and towns.[27] A talk show was organized by the Provincial Television Station in Fuzhou with call-ins from the viewers to express anger at the Falungong siege of Zhongnanhai.[28] Ever creative, Shanghai's Workers Union promoted a package of anti-Falungong activities among its members: (1) visiting nationalistic sites to commemorate the 50th anniversary of the founding of the People's Republic, (2) organizing a discussion session criticizing the sect, (3) engaging in a discussion with a Falungong practitioner of the same work unit, (4) writing an essay repudiating the Falungong in the worker newspaper or the bulletin board, and (5) organizing a forum of workers, cadres, and party members exposing the Falungong, with a keynote address by a converted Falungong practitioner.[29]

CONVERSION PROGRAMS

Targeting Falungong practitioners, a massive program was launched to convert followers of the sect. The first efforts drew on traditional thought-reform methods where the Falungong practitioners underwent group or individual ideological indoctrination sessions. In Fujian's Nanping County, Falungong practitioners were required to view television broadcasts and then participated in discussion, with an unspecified number reportedly repenting.[30] Similarly, Shandong party committees organized Falungong leaders to view television, listen to radio, and read newspapers on official anti-Falungong propaganda.[31] More elaborate efforts took the form of study classes for the reeducation of Falungong practitioners. These were reported in 1999 for Hengyang Municipality and Xinjiang, in 2000 for Changsha, Wuhan, Jinzhou, Luanjiang, Jinan, and Nanyang, in 2001 for Dandong, in 2001 and 2002 for Anshan, in 2002 for Changchun, and in 1999–2001 for Daye. There were no reports on the duration of these sessions except those in Daye, which began in 1998 and lasted through 2001. The nomenclature varied in different localities. Anshan municipalities labeled it "Study Session on Legal System Education" (*Fazi jiaoyu xuexi ban*),[32] while Daye abbreviated it as "Legal Education Session" (*fajiaoban*).[33] Changsha Municipality simply referred to it as study classes for Falungong practitioners.[34] Daye called it "Core Falungong Personnel Legal System Study Session."[35]

Study Sessions

Traditional Marxism and materialism were the core content of these study sessions. Marxist theory was taught at the Luanjiang Municipality in Heilongjiang Province,[36] while lectures on science, culture, and Marxist materialism were given in Nanyang Municipality of Henan Province.[37] Cities and counties of Jinan Municipality assembled Falungong practitioners within their jurisdiction, classified them into separate classes according to education level, and offered instructions on Marxist theory, popular science, scientific exercises, and addresses by converted Falungong practitioners.[38] Both day classes and boarding arrangements were reported. Hengyang Municipality in Hunan Province had non-live-in education sessions,[39] as did Changchun.[40] Xinjiang had live-in arrangements, where party cadre instructors moved in to eat at the same mess hall and lived at the same premises as Falungong practitioners.[41] Wuhan had both.[42]

The number and size of these study sessions varied in different localities. They ranged from two sessions Nanyang Municipality in Henan Province in December 2000,[43] to 100 in Changsha of Hunan Province in 2000.[44] The largest number was reported in Jinzhou Municipality in Liaoning Province,

which organized 178 sessions in 1999 alone.[45] Jinzhou, however, was not
the norm in Liaoning, as other municipalities in the province reported far
fewer study sessions: 8 in Dandong in 2001,[46] 10 in Daye from 1999 through
2001,[47] around 10 Luanjiang in 2000,[48] while Anshan organized 8 to 10 study
sessions in 2001 and 12 in 2002.[49] Jinan organized an unspecified number
of sessions where several hundred Falungong practitioners attended.[50] The
average class size was around 20 for the 100 sessions in Changsha,[51] 19 for
Dandong,[52] 11 for Anshan,[53] and 10 for Nanyang.[54] The largest average class
size was reported to be 26 in Daye,[55] and the smallest in Jinzhou, which had
1.5 participants on average for its 178 study sessions.[56]

Conversion of Individuals

In tandem with the group activity of study sessions, a parallel effort aimed
at individual conversions. In the early weeks after the official ban in July 22,
1999, the program generally took the form of a party cadre in the work unit or
the residence of the practitioner who would meet with the practitioner and
rehash the party line on the irrational nature of the Falungong, the harmful
physical effects on the practitioners, and the adverse impact on the relatives,
colleagues, and society. Thus, in Liaoning Province, Chaoyang Party Secretary Zhang Chuanqing and Mayor Wang Dachao worked on the core leaders
of the two main stations repeatedly until they repented.[57] In the provincial
capital of Jiangsu Province, the party secretary of Nanjing University went
to the Municipal Public Security Bureau to claim its faculty member Professor Wang Zhaiyuan after interrogation and organized his colleagues, relatives, and students to work on his conversion.[58] In the same city, the party
committee of the Jiangsu University of Science and Technology also formed
an informal group to educate and reform its own Associate Professor Wang
Yong.[59] Elsewhere, a Falungong practitioner was assigned to a party cadre in
the practitioner's residence or the work unit. Such conversion dyads of converter and convertee (*yi bang yi*) were reported in Hebei provincial capital
Shijiazhuang on August 10, the municipal departments and enterprises in
Anhui's Bangbu City on August 17, the higher education and research institutions in Nanjing Municipality also on August 17, and party organizations in
Henan's Hui County sometime in the latter half of 1999.[60]

Reforming Hard-Core Practitioners

These early unorganized efforts reported in the first months of the anti-
Falungong campaign gave way to more programmatic initiatives organized for
the conversion of the hard-core Falungong practitioners. Combining the case
approach in social work and the responsibility system in economic reforms,

localities assigned each hard-core Falungong practitioner to an individual party cadre or to a group who would work on the practitioner until the target signed the severance document to break with the sect. The agent was generally a cadre of the local party committee or the Communist Youth League, trained in the art of ideological indoctrination and persuasion. In Harbin, the secretary, deputy secretaries, standing committee members, and department heads of the municipal Communist Youth League were each assigned the task of converting one or two young Falungong practitioners.[61] In Fushun Municipality in neighboring Liaoning Province, each of the 13 standing committee members of the municipal party committee was also paired with one or two Falungong practitioners for the latter's conversion.[62] In Yunnan, the converter–convertee match was based on a mixed criteria of rank and function, with the party secretary pairing with the Falungong leader, the party branch member with the party member practitioner, work unit leader with worker, teacher with student, worker with his or her family, party member with a member of the masses, and the converted practitioner with the one yet to be converted.[63] In Jiangxi's Jingdezhen Municipality, the match was based on official rank and jurisdiction. The conversion of a Falungong practitioner who was a party official of full county-level rank (*zheng xian ji*) would be the responsibility of the leading cadre of the municipal organization department; conversion of the deputy county-level rank (*fu xian ji*) officials became the targets of the departmental superiors or the officials of the county, city, or district, while conversion of the cadres of division (*ke ji*) level or below became the burden of the official of the local unit.[64]

Conversion Teams

When and where the single converter program no longer produced results on some unyielding practitioners, the multiple agent program was implemented. The more elaborate program organized several cadres and significant associates of the Falungong practitioners to form a conversion team. In the Hunan Provincial Capital of Changsha, each unconverted Falungong practitioner in 2000 was assigned "a municipal level cadre, a conversion team, an education assistance committee, a set of education assistance procedures" to work on the target until conversion.[65] In Hengyang Municipality of the same province, the conversion team was made up of the official of the target's work unit, a party member, and a relative of the practitioner.[66] More commonly, the conversion team involved law enforcement officials, administrative superiors, local party officials, and the target's relatives. In Liaoning's Luanjiang Municipality, the conversion team was made up of a member of the party committee of the municipal government, a county-level or department (*chu*)-level cadre, an official of the target's work unit, and a close relative.[67] In the Shangdong provincial capital of Jinan, friends and colleagues of the target were sometimes included in the conversion team.[68] In the Liaoning capital of Shenyang, the conversion team consisted of a local public security agent, an official of the target's work unit, a close relative, and a cadre of the township, village, or residence block.[69] In Yunnan, each unconverted Falungong practitioner was assigned an "Assisting Conversion Committee" made up of the same four constituent categories.[70]

Responsibility Systems in Conversion

More details of the responsibilities of these institutions were reported in Yuxi City in Yunnan, where each "assisting conversion committee" was assigned five tasks. (1) It was entrusted with setting up a management system, conversion program, and case dossier for each practitioner. (2) It needed to organize general education activities aimed at conversion, including sessions to study science and critiques of superstition, laws, and regulations related to Falungong, as well as collective viewing of anti-Falungong films. (3) It had to establish a rigorous surveillance system to monitor the activities of local Falungong activities, submit timely status reports of Falungong practitioners to higher administrative levels, and ensure that each Falungong practitioner is under regime control, undertaking preventive and prohibitive measures to guard Falungong practitioners from distributing Falungong materials in public and abort the Falungong protest rallies and petition trips to Beijing or the provincial capital. (4) It was responsible for enforcing central directives stipulating that local governments should not discriminate against converted practitioners in rank and pay of their current jobs, and (5) it was required to file annual reports of the conversion program and prevention of Falungong protest activities to their organizational superiors.[71]

Superimposed on the responsibility system of individual conversion program were two parallel collective responsibility systems to ensure the individual conversion program would meet its goals. The first is an organizational responsibility system where social and political organizations were assigned the responsibility to convert Falungong practitioners who were functionally related to them. In the oil-field city of Daqing in Heilongjiang, the task to convert Falungong practitioners was assigned to their work units, those of urban residents to the urban district party committees, those of youth league members to the local Communist Youth League, and those of party members assigned to their respective party organizations.[72] In the more elaborate system instituted in the Xinyu County in Hunan Province, student Falungong practitioners were assigned to their teachers, workers to trade unions, youths to the Communist Youth League, villagers to the hamlet and township authorities, urban residents to the housing block committees, urban neighborhoods to local police precincts, local inhabitants to party members, party members to party branches, and core Falungong leaders to top-echelon party elite.[73] This system does not seem to be unique in Xinyu County, as a virtually identical system was also reported in Yunnan Province.[74]

A second collective responsibility system was based on administrative hierarchy where higher level administrators were held responsible for the conversion of Falungong practitioners at the immediate subordinate level. There are reports of this hierarchical administrative responsibility system in party organizations, the Communist Youth League, and labor reform institutions. In Jinan Municipality, the Falungong practitioner conversion program of each urban district and county was assigned to a specific official of deputy municipal or higher rank, those of townships were assigned to select officials of the urban district and county, while those of urban neighborhoods and rural villages were assigned to officials of the township.[75] A related trilevel system can be found in Harbin, where its Communist Youth League organizations and the labor reform establishment adopted a similar system of hierarchical responsibility based on administrative stratification, with the top administrative levels being held responsible for the conversion of Falungong practitioners on the next lower level. In the league organizations, for instance, the top leadership of the municipal Communist Youth League were collectively responsible for the conversion of Falungong practitioners in the municipal party and government agencies; municipal party leaders were responsible for the conversion of those at the cities, counties, and urban districts; and those at the cities, counties, and urban districts were responsible for the conversion program of subordinate village, and hamlets designated for their management. At the lowest administrative level, the league branch in villages and hamlets was assigned the task to convert individual league members who practiced Falungong.[76]

To ensure the designated officials would accomplish their goals of converting Falungong practitioners, a companion "Responsibility Accountability System" (*ziren juejiuji*) was instituted in Anshan and Dandong municipalities of Liaoning Province that stipulated program goals and sanctions of missing performance targets.[77] Although not labeled as such, Xinyu County in Hunan Province appeared to have instituted a similar system when the officials of the municipal commerce bureau, municipal construction bureau, Fenyi County, and Xinyu Textile Company had to make a self-criticism to the municipal party committee for their failure to meet the goals of converting Falungong practitioners under their jurisdiction.[78] To monitor the performance of conversion programs at lower levels, the Jinan municipal party committees established a traveling inspection unit to check on local performance.[79] Three similar teams of traveling supervisors, jointly organized by the provincial organization department, the provincial party committee, and the provincial disciplinary committee, were also established by the Xinjiang Autonomous Region to oversee the conversion programs in localities.[80]

CONVERSION PROGRAMS IN PENAL INSTITUTIONS

From the perspective of the regime, many Falungong practitioners had violated Chinese law and regulations, for which punishment was due. When the Falungong was officially banned on July 22, 1999, several legal statutes were in force that would have criminalized the behavior of many Falungong practitioners. Prosecutable offenses included publishing materials that propagate superstition, failing to declare taxable income from Falungong seminar receipts, the sale of Falungong publications, organizing assemblies without official approval, disturbing social order, and participating in cult activities.[81]

Security Detention

Second-echelon Falungong leaders who were not involved with the Falungong publications program and were not principal ringleaders of major protest rallies could still be charged with lesser offenses of organizing activities of an unregistered social organization, intentionally spreading rumors, and using other means that disturb public order.[82] For such offenses, they are liable to be sanctioned under the Security Management Penalty Regulations of the People's Republic of China (1986), which deal with offenses that are not serious enough to receive criminal punishment. Under such regulations, offenders would be (1) given warning, (2) imposed a fine of 1–200 yuan, and (3) sentenced to security detention (*zhi'an juliu*) of 1–15 days. The regulations stipulate lighter or no sentence for defendants who voluntarily admit their guilt and correct their mistakes in a timely manner, when they were deceived or acted under duress, or when the case was not serious, stipulating more severe punishments for those where these conditions do not obtain and when the defendants were recalcitrant.[83] Reports on Falungong members sent to security detention are generally uninformative about their treatment under this program.

Labor Reform Institutions

The special die-hard Falungong practitioners who were the most committed believers were sentenced to labor reform institutes. Procedures for their treatment were delineated in a series of regulations issued by the Ministry of

Justice Administration, some provincial party committees, and provincial labor reform departments.[84] When held in detention facilities in the public security system or sent to labor reform education (*laogai*) establishments, Falungong practitioners were treated as a special category of inmates (*dandu piandui*), where they were included in a special registry, were enrolled in special education programs, were housed in special wards, followed different daily routines, and were managed by public security or labor reform agents who received special training on how to deal with Falungong practitioners. In the month of July 1999, when the official ban on the Falungong was promulgated, the Labor Reform Bureau of Heilongjiang Province issued a series of 15 regulations on the preparation work, management of Falungong detainees, and the selection, training, and behaviors to be rewarded and punished for public security and reform facility agents dealing with Falungong detainees.[85]

Heilongjiang Labor Reform Programs

Among the 31 provinces in China, Heilongjiang published one of the most detailed reports on the conversion programs in its labor reform system. From November 1999 to late 2000, Heilongjiang labor reform system had registered more than 2,000 Falungong practitioners out of a provincial total of several tens of thousands.[86] The former were classified by the longevity of their Falungong practice, personal interest and personality traits, degree of sincerity of contrition, and characteristics of family members and assigned to security agents who would match their personal profile. They were put under 24-hour surveillance, and institute guards were given special instruction to ensure that Falungong practitioners would be under managed care, control, and surveillance, as well as prevented from escaping, committing suicide or self-mutilation, and staging collective protest. For the education program, the institutes prepared several sets of readers of more than 100,000 words refuting the basic doctrine and practice of Falungong. The average conversion rate of Falungong inmates among all the institutes in the province was more than 80%, with some institutes more than 90%. They were held up as an example to be emulated in a conference on education and conversion of Falungong practitioners convened by the Ministry of Justice Administration in February, 2000. Five units and 14 individuals received special commendation at a meeting where the Heilongjiang provincial government recognized outstanding contributions in Falungong conversion work.[87]

It is not clear which five labor reform institutes in Heilongjiang received the provincial commendation for Falungong conversion work, but it was reported that the Anshan Municipal Labor Reform Institute was certified as a ministerial-rank modern civilized Labor Reform Institute in October 2000.[88] The certification appears to be based on both its inmate conversion program and its outreach program for nonresident Falungong practitioners. For its inmate program, the Municipal Labor Reform Institute was commended for the zero rate of inmates (including Falungong practitioners) dying of unnatural causes or engaged in violent protest in 2000. Its outreach conversion program for Falungong practitioners who were not sentenced to labor reform has received even more public attention from provincial and central authorities. The Anshan labor reform system organized eight study sessions at labor reform institutes, where they invited specialists and converted Falungong practitioners to make presentations to practitioners receiving reeducation. On the eve of Party Day on July 1, 2001, they organized a large singing contest among Falungong inmates. Several Falungong inmates received reduced sentences and were discharged ahead of the sentenced time. The municipal labor reform institute and several agents received the progressive unit and progressive individual award.[89]

More details of the inmate conversion program were reported on the labor reform institutes in the provincial capital, where the labor reform institutes of Harbin Municipality registered 120 Falungong practitioners, of whom 103 were women in 1999. In compliance with the Ministry of Justice Administration regulations noted above, Falungong practitioners were physically segregated from other inmates, where they were grouped into their own brigades with their own programs. To prepare for their confinement and education, institute guards attended a 27-day training session, where they studied policy documents issued by the Ministry of Justice Administration, the National People's Congress, the Supreme People's Court, and the Supreme People's Procuracy. They also practiced drills to prepare them to handle different scenarios of Falungong practitioner behavior. A three-level responsibility system for successful conversion was introduced, where the brigade guards were accountable for Falungong practitioners under their care to midlevel cadres, who in turn were accountable to the institute director.[90]

Elsewhere in Hebei Province, the Qinhuangdao Labor Reform Institute formulated a special program for the confinement and education of Falungong practitioners. They achieved a 100% rate for hard-to-reform inmates in 2000. The labor reform school conducted a follow-up survey on 598 discharged inmates to find out their employment status and social conditions after discharge. They established a gardening and orchard company as a halfway house to ease the transition of inmates back to society.[91]

THE YUNNAN SPECIAL CONVERSION PROGRAM

Beyond programs in penal institutions, a special conversion program was organized in Yunnan Province. The education conversion program was under the jurisdiction of the Provincial Leading Group for Dealing with the Falungong. Inaugurated in late April 2000, the special conversion program was headed by a "Specialist Group" (*zhuangjiazu*) called the "Yunnan Provincial Work Group in Charge of Education Conversion of Falungong Practitioners." They were made up of a multidisciplinary group of close to 10 teaching and research faculty from leading higher education and research institutions in the province,[92] with fields of specialty ranging from biology, astronomy, medicine, psychology, and sociology to philosophy, political science, and religious studies.[93] The group met with the vice provincial party secretary who gave them three tasks: (1) conducting an in-depth study of the Falungong practitioners in the province, (2) assisting and training the public security agents and other cadres who manage the Falungong practitioners, and (3) contacting and interacting with Falungong practitioners undergoing conversion to facilitate their transformation process.

To undertake the above tasks, the specialist group visited in May and June 2000 two labor reform institutes in Yunnan where hard-core Falungong leaders were sentenced to labor reform. In these site visits, the specialist group first reviewed in depth the case history of each Falungong practitioner undergoing labor reform, including their involvement with the Falungong, their alleged illegal activities prior to admission, and their behavior during the conversion program. Second, the group also interviewed all Falungong practitioners individually on their initiation into the Falungong congregation, their motivation to be inducted into the group, their stated reasons for engaging in illegal activities, and their plans for their personal future. Third, a personal dossier for each Falungong practitioner was compiled, with the case history, a report and analysis on the personal interview, and sections on basic personal background, main characteristics, and recommendations for conversion strategies. Fourth, a series of discussions was then conducted among the specialist group with the public security agents and the officials of the Provincial Office for Preventing Cults, over the causes for the rise of the Falungong movement, the classification of different types of Falungong practitioners, and their dominant personality traits. Fifth, suggestions on program features and strategies on how to manage the Falungong practitioners undergoing labor reforms in these two institutes were made by the specialist group.[94]

Features of the Education Conversion Program

The first program was originally scheduled from November 30 to December 15, 2000, but the 16-day program was concluded on December 12 when organizers decided that it had successfully accomplished all program goals three days early. The program was designed for 20 Falungong practitioners from enterprises and residences of the Kunming area, together with close to 40 participants from local anti-Falungong office personnel, the group of professional specialists, and the support group of colleagues, neighbors, and relatives of practitioners, including spouses and next of kin. The ratio of conversion personnel to Falungong practitioners was thus 2:1. The venue was the guest house of the cadre school of the provincial electricity bureau, chosen for its low cost, distance and relative inaccessibility from the city, nonextravagant setting with basic amenities, and close cooperation from leading officials of the provincial electricity bureau, which had six of its personnel among the 20 Falungong practitioners. Meals were buffet style with free seating to facilitate intermingling of staff with participants, who ate, lived, and interacted at the same premises. The nonsegregation arrangement reportedly dissolved the initial fears of practitioners and conveyed a sense of community between practitioners and their handlers.[95]

Three Teams

The education conversion staff was made up of three teams. The first team was the specialist group mentioned above. The second team was composed of the Falungong converts who had switched positions from defender of the faith to regime advocates. Drawing on Falungong scriptures and practice, as well as spiritual journal and personal awakening in the sect, they assumed a role played by none of the participants of the education conversion program. The third team was public security and other personnel that formed the local anti-Falungong network, consisting of staff members of the local party and government Office for Preventing Cults, public security agents, and justice administration agents (*sifa ganjing*) in the courts and the labor reform establishment and basic unit support personnel from the same enterprises and urban residence block or village of the practitioners, who served as the personal contacts for the practitioner in the education conversion program.

Stages of Conversion and Rehabilitation

To sort out Falungong practitioners, the education conversion program employed a classification scheme to categorize four ascending stages of conversion. The first stage is the admission of guilt and of legal violation, expressed as recognition of wrongdoing for having participated in Falungong assemblies, displaying the sect's banners, joining in protest sit-ins, and petitioning to the Office of Visits and Calls after the official ban on July 22, 1999. The second stage is realization of harm incurred from practicing the cult and expression of regret from having joint the sect. This act usually took place during or after viewing the propaganda film on anticult and anti-Falungong documentaries in the program. The third is the act of writing a self-examination report and signing the statement of severance from the Falungong, generally accompanied with other acts of contrition such as turning over Falungong publications, practice attire, and other memorabilia to the conversion staff. The last and consummate stage is demonstrated in voluntarily disclosing self-incriminating behavior unknown to authorities, criticizing the theories and scriptures of Falungong, calling the name of Li Hongzhi without invoking honorific titles, and assisting other practitioners to sever their ties with the Falungong.[96]

The education program was organized around these stages of conversion. It was divided into five sessions corresponding to different stages of conversion, each session building on the psychological effects elicited in the previous session. According to the official report, none of the participating Falungong practitioners showed any sign of contrition when they were first admitted. As they were led through successive stages of the program, their resistance was dissolved and they converted individually or in groups. The first session was built around the opening ceremony of the education conversion class, where the official assured the practitioners that they were good but only misled. The assurance was intended to disarm the practitioners who expected brutal treatment, after having been psychologically and physically traumatized in their preadmission stage by public security officials who arrested and interrogated them. Second, both to understand their sentiments and to give them a chance to relieve their bottled-up anxiety, Falungong practitioners were given time to express their grievances regarding official policy and personnel toward the Falungong. Third, both Falungong practitioners and institute cadres collectively viewed films on national heroes in both war and peace periods, supplemented with presentations by specialists on the altruistic patriotism of these heroes. The session of collective film viewing is designed to build a sense of community between Falungong practitioners and institute cadres, to dissolve part of the mistrust and antagonism of the former toward the latter, and to make the point of what constitutes noble, exemplary behavior. Fourth, the film viewing session was followed by a screening of cults around the world and their malignant effects on the followers and the community, including those of the Davidian and Jonestown cults in the United States and the Aum Shinri Kyu in Japan. To connect the alleged evil of these cults with those in China, the taped accusations of Li Hongzhi by Li Chang and Yao Jie, both leaders in the Falung Dafa organization in Beijing, was shown, followed by moderated discussion of cults in and outside China.

According to the official report, all Falungong practitioners came to the program with apprehension, and most with mistrust. Thinking that enrolling in the conversion program is similar to serving an indefinite sentence or even life imprisonment at labor reform institutes, some had made arrangements with their families over property disposal and care of dependents. They were thus surprised at the apparent supportive and accommodating tone of the opening address of the provincial party secretary, who referred to the practitioners not as antiparty criminals but as good though misguided citizens. Their anxiety was further reduced in the subsequent session where instead of a dreaded browbeating session they were invited to express their grievances with impunity. In the following film-viewing session in which patriotic documentaries were shown, the great majority of women were reportedly moved to tears, and some wanted to purchase the DVD for their relatives. The companion series of video presentation on cults in the United States and Japan made subtle references to the techniques of mass hypnosis, autosuggestion, and personality cults with sectarian leaders, to pave the way for more explicit attack on Falungong practices and techniques that was to come. But even before the frontal assault, some practitioners had already expressed contrition, wrote severance statements, and signed the program discharge papers before returning home by the fifth day of the program. The more stubborn ones persisted, but all eventually succumbed and stayed on to complete the remaining parts of the course, which consisted of a session to repudiate Falungong doctrine and practice, as well as the lack of integrity of Li Hongzhi, to be followed by a pledge to embrace a worldview based on atheistic materialism.[97]

Employment Rehabilitation

The education conversion program did not end when the Falungong practitioners signed their severance papers from the sect. A creative design for the Yunnan conversion program was employment rehabilitation. Administrative detention and education reform uprooted Falungong practitioners from their work units, and they often returned to their community after reeducation to find that they were out of work. To ensure that they would be rehabilitated within their community and restored to their original employment status after the conversion, their employers were invited to meet with the "Assist Conversion Committee" officials on the last day of the conversion program, where they would pledge in the presence of the converted practitioner that their employment status would be restored to their original position, rank, and salary scale. The superior then accompanied the converted practitioner back to his or her domicile after completing the checkout procedures.[98] Sometimes, the nonexclusion and nondiscrimination provision was extended beyond the job security of converted practitioners. In Tonghai County of Yunnan, converted practitioner Guo Dingan regained his contract with county officials to sell cable television subscriptions within the county.[99]

Psychological Features of the Conversion Program

Unlike traditional thought-reform programs that emphasized force-fed ideological indoctrination, the Yunnan program used techniques that fostered self-induced transformation. This was accomplished by creating a supportive atmosphere in the program, developing rapport and trust between Falungong inmates and the conversion staff, and using group conversion techniques and employment rehabilitation.

In the Jianshui County program of March 2, 2001, that catered to hardcore Falungong practitioners, the organizer built in special features to create a supportive environment for program participants. When Falungong practitioners first entered their assigned rooms on the day of registration, they were greeted by a set of stationary supplies on their desks, toiletries in their bathrooms, sentimental greetings on the wall, and a festive floral basket on the table with compliments from the organizer. An extracurricular social program preceded the formal education classes, where participants were treated to a visit to an amusement park, introduced at an evening social dance, and entertained with a variety show. These special features seemed to have their desired effect by the third day of the program, as they attracted a sizable number of unrepentant Falungong practitioners, who volunteered to enroll. Designed for and begun with 16 participants, the program ended with 34 practitioners.[100]

A second novel technique of the Yunnan program was the use of group conversion instead of the traditional method where each inmate underwent education in isolation from other practitioners. The group conversion was reported to have the following advantages. First, the individual program pits the practitioner against the converter in a one-to-one adversarial setting, often resulting in the practitioner closing himself or herself to the converter in self-defense. In a group setting, interaction between converters and convertees becomes less personal, thus ameliorating the anxiety of the convertees and their antagonism with the converter. Second, interactions in an individual conversion setting are dyadic, and interpersonal influence is unilateral, from the converter to the convertee and vice versa. Interactions in a group setting are multilateral and diffuse, where individual practitioners are influenced not only by the converter but also by other practitioners who might be early converters and set an example of conversion for other practitioners. Third, Falungong activities were usually conducted in a group setting, with morning assemblies for breathing exercises, group study of scriptures, and periodic assemblies for special Falungong festivals and holy days. Practitioners have been conditioned to act as a group, to defer to group authority, and be sensitive to the behavior of other members of the group. They are thus more receptive to conversion persuasion in a group setting.

In the Yunnan program, most conversions took place not individually but in groups of three to four or as many as seven to eight 8 practitioners.[101]

CONVERSION ACCORDING TO *MINGHUI*

The practitioner-friendly conversion process emphasizing psychological persuasion in the official version stand, in stark contrast with the disturbing and sinister form described in Falungong sources. In its worldwide Web site *Minghui* ("Clear Wisdom") and its special Web page *zhuichaguoji* ("Uphold Justice"), coercion was the dominant approach and physical and psychological torture were the main instruments of the regime's conversion program. From the Falungong sources, coercive practices are seen as pervasive throughout all regions in China and condoned, if not promoted, by the central authorities in China. These reports appear verifiable, as the great majority of them identify (1) the individual Falungong practitioner, often with age, occupation, and domicile; (2) the time and location that the alleged abuse took place, including not only urban districts and rural townships and villages but also specific penal institutions; and (3) the names and ranks of the alleged perpetrators. Many of these reports include lists of the names of human witnesses and descriptions of physical injuries.

According to *Minghui*, from July 20, 1999, to December 31, 2005, there were no fewer than 14,474 cases of physical torture and psychological abuse by law enforcement agents against Falungong inmates. Most of the latter were named, and the abuse took place at identified public security bureaus, detention centers, and labor reform institutions. The case count is not the same as the number of Falungong victims, which was smaller, because most suffered multiple forms of persecution, with some as many as more than 30 categories in the Falungong classification scheme of abuse and torture. In terms of regional distribution, there were reported cases of such atrocities in every province,[102] with 21 provinces each reporting more than 100 instances of such law enforcement abuse. Among these, the provinces of Hebei, Heilongjiang, Liaoning, Jilin, and Shandong were the top provinces in terms of the number of reported instances of torture and abuse, the number of reported deaths resulting from torture, and the number of law enforcement agents alleged to have committed such atrocities. Each of these five provinces had more than 1,000 cases of reported torture and abuse, more than 200 cases of reported torture-deaths, and more than 1,000 abusive law enforcement agents (table 5.3).

The 14,474 cases are classified by different methods of torture in Falungong sources. Among these, there were 4,724 cases of severe beatings, punching, kicking, striking with baton, or whipping with belts or sharp instruments,

Table 5.3: Reported Cases of Persecution and Tortured Deaths of Falungong Practitioners by Province, July 1999 to December 2005

Province	No. Reported Practitioners Persecuted	No. Reported Tortured Deaths	No. Government Torturers/Persecutors Identified by Name
Hebei	1,651	380	1,649
Heilongjiang	1,697	344	1,855
Liaoning	1,843	335	1,465
Jilin	1,253	327	1,396
Shandong	1,804	282	1,518
Sichuan	969	167	986
Hubei	566	134	595
Henan	306	101	372
Hunan	502	86	440
Beijing	448	77	309
Guangdong	630	64	376
Chongqing	581	62	228
Neimonggu	282	50	288
Gansu	391	48	211
Tianjin	284	40	212
Jiangxi	78	40	54
Anhui	108	38	114
Shanxi	77	38	66
Guizhou	210	30	116
Shaanxi	116	22	79
Xinjiang	97	21	76
Jiangsu	101	21	80
Shanghai	178	15	95
Fujian	21	14	17
Yunnan	116	14	46
Guangxi	75	12	37
Zhejiang	88	9	22
Qinghai	n.d.	5	7
Hainan	3	4	2
Ningxia	18	3	24
Xizhang	n.d.	1	n.d.
Location unknown	136	21	35

Source: library.minghui.org/category/32.226,,1.htm, accessed by author on December 31, 2005.

N.d., no data.

often with the victim bound or handcuffed, as well as hair pulling and arm twisting or bending behind the back to 180 degrees above the head. The 2,466 cases of psychological torment included forcing victims to curse Li Hongzhi, to destroy his portrait and the Falungong publications, and to drink alcohol and to smoke, which are contrary to Falungong injunctions. The 2,154 cases of corporal punishment included being forced to participate in intense, heavy-burden hard labor and being made to squat, crouch, stand, or adopt other painful or exhausting physical postures without moving for hours or days, with threats of beatings or other punishment if they move. There were 1,841 cases of using various restraining devices, including handcuffs and ankle fetters, some designed to inflict severe pain by handcuffing hands behind the back, shackling hands and feet together, chaining to beds, window bars, or tree branches, or using a floor shackle with the victim sitting down cross-legged, the back bent and head stooped to the floor at 180 degrees angle. The 1,063 cases of solitary confinement consist of incarceration in windowless rooms, iron cages, and small cubicles (*xiaohao*) that are dark and damp, with no bed, heating, ventilation, or sanitation, designed to expose prisoners to cold and heat, extreme physical discomfort, deprivation of light, and squalid conditions. Separately, there were cases involving cold treatment that include forcing the victim to stand outdoors barefoot in subzero temperatures with only underwear or sitting on snow piles, pouring cold water continuously on the naked body of the victim, and making the thinly clad, barefoot victim to sit overnight in exposed corridors with cold drafts on wintry nights. Conversely, the 283 cases of heat treatment included exposing the naked bodies of victims to the summer sun for long hours until the skin peeled off, confining victims in small unventilated rooms in mid-summer months with heat turned on at full force; using cigarettes or cigarette lighters to burn the eyebrows and face or red-hot clothing irons to scorch the bodies of victims.

Just as brutal, if not more so, the 1,732 cases of use of electric shocks included those delivered by electric batons, stun guns, and electric chairs to sensitive parts of the body that result in severe pain, damage muscle control, burn skin tissues, and disfigure the face, often leading to victims becoming nauseous, convulsive, or unconscious. The 1,225 cases of devastative forced feeding included punitive forced feeding of excrement, urine, and pepper liquid to victims to punish uncooperative behavior, and forced feeding of food and medicine with tube pushed down the throat for hunger strikers. The 808 cases of suspension in midair included tying prisoners with a rope attached around the wrists, which were lifted above the head, and the Cultural Revolution vintage "hanging aeroplane" position that suspends prisoners by the arms with their hands tied together behind their back so that the arms are contorted when the prisoners are suspended. The 158 cases of using sharp objects include jabbing the hand with screw drivers, slashing the face with glass blades, sticking sharp bamboo strips into fingernails, pulling out fingernails with pliers, and piercing the body with more than 100 pins. In addition, there were 3,153 reported cases of depriving basic physical needs of food, sleep, and use of restrooms; 110 cases of sexual assault, including rape and gang rape by prison guards and female Falungong prisoners being thrown into men's prison cells to be gang-raped; 73 cases of asphyxiation; 1,692 cases of threat and extortion; and 484 cases of terminating employment and student status.

In the most extreme, lethal cases, *Minghui* lists 2,731 instances of named Falungong practitioners who were tortured to death while in official custody, or shortly thereafter as a result of life-threatening injuries sustained during confinement in penal institutions. As shown in table 5.3, the practice appears to be pervasive throughout China, as *Minghui* reports such deaths in each of the 31 provincial units, ranging from 380 in Hebei Province to 1 in Tibet. The obituary does not include 138 cases of missing individuals. These cases of deaths from torture reportedly occurred every year from 1999 to 2005, increasing from 186 in the latter half of 1999 to 245 in 2000, then leaping to 424 in 2001 and remaining greater than 500 cases each year from 2002 to 2004. The lower count of 437 in 2005 can be due to a time lag in reporting (table 5.4).

Minghui also identifies 12,808 public security agents and penal institution staff who were alleged perpetrators of torture by name, a great majority also by rank and title of institution, names of their victims, and time and location of the alleged offense. The alleged perpetrators ranged from prison guards to brigade commanders as well as prison wardens, who were present during, and sometimes participated in, the atrocities. As shown in table 5.3, all 31 provinces (except Tibet) had such named perpetrators, whose numbers correlated highly with the number of reported instances of torture and abuse across provinces. It should be noted that the list of abusive personnel includes only law enforcement agents, and omits some prisoners who were

Table 5.4: Deaths of Falungong Practitioners Caused by Government Persecution, 1999–2005

Year	No. Deaths
1999, July–December	186
2000	245
2001	424
2002	533
2003	516
2004	554
2005	437
Total	2,895[a]

Source: library.minghui.org/category/32.226,,1.htm, accessed by author on December 31, 2005.

[a]The number of deaths in this table is larger than in the third column of table 5.3 due to the later access date of this table.

also accomplices in such atrocities. To avoid culpability and ensure deniability, some jailers used preselected prisoners who were gangsters and hoodlums to apply torture: jailers would bring the victim to the cells of the latter and walk away, and then the gangsters would kick and punch the victim as soon as the guards were gone. In return, the surrogate torturers would be rewarded with food and a reduction of 20 days of prison sentence for each conversion of a Falungong practitioner.[103] As noted above, condoned gang rape of female Falungong prisoners sometimes served as additional reward.

Contrast between Official and Falungong Sources

How can the Falungong version of the prevalent use of brutal coercive methods be reconciled with the kinder and gentler approach of psychological persuasion through self-transformation in official reporting? To be sure, selective presentation and source bias are likely to be present in the adversarial polemics that characterize both regime and Falungong discourse. On close reading of the two accounts, one can still discern some consistency between the official and Falungong sources. One can infer from regime reports that the use of psychological persuasion over physical coercion in conversion is the ideal norm rather than prevalent practice. The use of "no unnatural death" as a performance target in penal institutions suggests that prison abuse is likely to be sufficiently widespread for it to be used as nationwide measure. The rare reports of new inmate-friendly detention facilities that required tens of million yuan to construct only underscore the point that these were exceptional showcases rather than the institutional rule in penitentiary architecture.

On their part, Falungong accounts also refer to the official use of soft-sell and psychological persuasion methods, but with their own spin. A report describes the display of thoughtfulness and considerateness among some of the labor reform institutes and security detention centers, although they regarded these as conversion tactics rather than respect for human rights.[104] There were also reports of more civilized facilities in some labor reform institutions. The dormitories of the Tuanhe Reformatory in Beijing, for instance, had television sets, desks, and aquariums, with outdoor lawns, a basketball court, and a small zoo of deer, rabbits, and peacocks.[105] For cultural enrichment, a detention center of an unspecified location had a well-stocked library, although it was closed most of the time.[106] The Beijing Labor Reform Bureau organized an "IQ contest" in September and October 2001, the Tuanhe Reformatory established a cooking class for its inmates that same year,[107] and the Majiawan Reformatory in Liaoning Province offered volleyball, jump rope, and poker in 2006.[108] These Falungong reports do not fail to note that the civilized facade often hid physical abuse.

From these Falungong reports, it is also clear that there were institutional checks against inmate abuse in these reform institutions. First, several agencies within the labor reform institution system served as institutional watchdogs on inmate abuse. These include the Disciplinary Inspection Division (*jijianke*) that is housed within the labor reform school.[109] There is also an office of the Education Department of the Provincial Labor Reform Bureau that regularly questions inmates on whether they have been abused. Above the labor reform system, the provincial procuracy also has an office inside the Tuanhe Reformatory to monitor and report on the latter's compliance with regulations.[110] In the Tuanhe Reformatory, the standard checkout procedure includes one session the evening before the release with the director of supervision, who routinely asks whether the inmate had been abused during his or her stay.[111]

Outside the labor reform system, Falungong sources also report many visits of media, the judiciary, and international organizations to these labor reformatories. Television crews making site visits were reported in the Wanjia Reformatory in Heilongjiang's Harbin around the Lunar New Year in 2001,[112] the Majiawan Reformatory of Liaoning Province in mid-March 2001,[113] and the Tuanhe Reformatory in the latter half of the same year,[114] often leading reformatory authorities to redecorate the conference room, to unlock the library, and to shuffle more presentable and media-friendly inmates toward where the camera crews would be escorted. Preparation chores were more elaborate when the national CCTV arrived in May 2001 to do a story on the Shibalihe Women's Reformatory in Zhengzhou of Henan Province, or the national "610 Office" announced its inspection of the same facility a month later.[115] Military campaign-style planning was reported for visits by international visitors: foreign journalists at the Women's Ward of the Majiawan Reformatory on March 16, 2001,[116] and the Tuanhe Reformatory in April 2001,[117] and the International Labor Office to the latter on January 9, 2004.[118] Falungong sources invariably reported these visits as staged, where visitors never saw or met with Falungong practitioners who were tortured, but the existence of both in-house and external monitors is likely to have some deterrent effect on the extent and level of inmate abuse. There was at least one case where an inspection by the deputy chief of the Shenyang Municipal Bureau of Justice Administration to the Longshan Labor Reform Institute in late November 1999 resulted in the transfer of the institute's extrapunitive political commissar and all abusive team leaders dealing with Falungong practitioners. The administrative assistant of the director of the Longshan Institute even assembled all Falungong practitioners, apologized for the cadres who brutalized practitioners, and ordered all the electronic batons to be withdrawn from that division.[119]

Some Falungong reports do suggest that the atrocities were unauthorized and unapproved behavior of lower level prison guards sanctioned by the Provincial Bureau of Justice Administration noted above.[120] Reports of use of third-party torture,[121] with hardened criminal inmates carrying out punching and electric shocks with no prison guards present, suggest this deniable behavior was officially prohibited and point to the fact that an official policy to prevent prisoner abuse was in the books, only skirted by lower level prison guards, and probably at the discretion of penal institute administrators. Nevertheless, the publication of such persistent abusive, often brutal behavior by named individuals with their official title, place, and time of torture in the Falungong Web site for more than six years, apparently without official sanction, as well as the substantial year-to-year increase in the number of unnatural deaths of Falungong practitioners in custody and the lack of well-publicized documents reaffirming the official policies, also suggests the regime's lack of will to cease and desist such behavior, and absence of official determination to put an end to such collateral damage.

CONCLUSION

This chapter begins with the given that the institutional capacity of law enforcement in China could not detain, indict, convict, and incarcerate all the 2.3 million Falungong practitioners. In addition to the capacity of penal institutions, it would also be illegal to lock them up for indefinite periods, beyond what is stipulated in the pertinent statutes. The goal of the anti-Falungong campaign was thus not only to rid of the regime of a congregation that staged open defiance of the state, but also to win the hearts and minds of the practitioners. This chapter analyzes regime attempts to redeem those who have fallen from grace.

Much of the conversion program relied on traditional techniques of indoctrination and thought reform, where Falungong practitioners were organized to view anti-Falungong television programs and enroll in Marxism and materialism study sessions, some in live-in arrangements. For the unrepentant, a party member or multiple agents were commissioned to work on the unyielding individual. Borrowing from the economic management system, individual or collective responsibility was assigned to the conversion team, with performance benchmarks. In some localities, supervisors or inspectors were instituted to monitor the progress of these programs. Hardcore practitioners were sentenced to labor reform institutions, where they were segregated from other inmates, put under 24-hour surveillance, and subjected to a daily routine of indoctrination and physical labor. A kinder and gentler program was created by the Yunnan penal institution, which emphasized the use of psychological rather than coercive methods, group dynamics rather than individual indoctrination, and nonsegregated communitarian living of staff and inmates, leading to self-induced transformation. It is not clear the extent to which the soft-sell program was practiced by other provinces. In stark contrast, the more blunt instruments of physical and psychological torture appear to be the dominant approach in many labor reform institutions.

Whether hard or soft sell, what is also unknown is the effect of these conversion programs. Ultimately, the success of the conversion program is measured not by the institutional capacity of the regime to reeducate Falungong practitioners, the level of actual effort, the target hostility, or friendliness of its methods, but by the proportion of Falungong adherents who gave up the practice and never returned to it. To ask a more nuanced set of questions, we would need to know the proportion of its top leaders who have officially renounced their ties with the Falungong versus those of its rank-and-file. Since the party paid special attention to the conversion of party members, we would also need to analyze the rehabilitation rates of the party members. Lastly, we would also need to know whether the conversion was voluntary or coerced, temporary or permanent, by examining evidence on how many of those who have officially severed their ties with the Falungong retracted their renunciations, continued to practice the Falungong, or both. I attempt these analytical tasks in chapter 8.

Chapter Six

Organizational Structure of the Anti-Falungong Campaign

This chapter analyzes how the regime organized its operations against the Falungong, in particular, which set of institutions in the party and state systems the regime relied on to formulate policies and which ones to implement them. It begins with an analysis of three sets of institutional choices at the system level: whether the regime would rely on existing formal institutions or *ad hoc* arrangements to deal with the problem, which set of party and state agencies will be entrusted with which set of tasks, and the mode and extent of top party leadership involvement. This will be followed by an investigation of the organization of structure and function of anti-Falungong operations at each administrative level, from the central through the provincial, municipal, and county down to the township and basic unit levels. The investigations not only are guided by the need to describe institutional arrangements, but also are informed by the degree of variations in organizational structure and institutional nomenclature at each administrative level.

POLICY MAKING AND ENFORCEMENT INSTITUTIONS

Organizational Issues

Dealing with the Falungong presented a set of complex organizational problems in planning and execution for the regime. In considering the institutional design, the organizational issues are operational effectiveness and coordination, policy trade-offs, and institutional choices. The anti-Falungong campaign involved multiple tasks that are national in scope but require local implementation; some of them needed to be executed throughout China at the same time. Task multiplicity and simultaneous execution over different locales in an extensive domain pose problems of both vertical and horizontal integration and coordination. Horizontally, the tasks involved in suppressing the Falungong fall under the jurisdiction of multiple bureaucratic agencies. Foremost were the law enforcement institutions that had the task of disbanding

Falungong organizations, investigating, detaining, arresting, prosecuting, and incarcerating Falungong practitioners. The state media needed to perform the propaganda functions to justify suppression, explain government policies, and mobilize public support. A third set of institutions was given tasks to persuade party members who practiced Falungong to renounce ties with the sect, as well as to educate and convert the rank-and-file Falungong practitioners. Since each of these sets of tasks falls under separate law enforcement, propaganda, and political education bureaucracies, which have different institutional missions and policy priorities, the organization of the campaign becomes problematic. The multijurisdictional nature of these tasks also poses institutional challenges for vertical organization, when the regime needs to ensure that anti-Falungong operations will be executed by the set of party and state agencies that have line authority from the central, top-echelon administration through the intermediary provincial, municipal, county, and township governments, down to the basic unit level of housing block residence committees in cities, villages in the rural areas, enterprises, and factories.

To solve the problem of vertical and horizontal integration and coordination, the regime needs to make three sets of policy trade-offs. The first is the degree of centralization. In meeting an emergent nationwide problem, centralization would specify a uniform set of campaign goals, consistent standards for operations, and a common timetable for fulfillment of tasks. It would also aim to reduce regional and bureaucratic variations as a result of agency shirking, due to differences in willingness or ability of local officials to implement central policy objectives. However, compared to a campaign that would give more operational autonomy to local officials, centralization would also lead to inefficient execution of policies due to information asymmetry between the central and local governments, as central authorities might stipulate inappropriate goals for local achievement, and over- or undercommit resources. The second policy trade-off results from the degree of organizational specialization. The policy to entrust the work of dealing with the Falungong to specialized agencies whose only or primary organizational mission is to manage problems arising from the sect would have the advantage of pinpointing task responsibility, and the campaign would receive the undivided attention of one set of bureaucratic actors. However, given differences in demand for service over time and across space, specialization would also result in underutilization of resources, if the latter is not fungible and if local demand for such specialized services is not consistently high over time. If organizational specialization is chosen along with centralization, then the problem of resource underutilization is compounded by information asymmetry, where the central government lacks local information to optimize policy decisions. The third policy trade-off is the choice of assigning the campaign to an existing formal institution or to an *ad hoc* agency.

An existing organization would have an extant bureaucracy, management team, support staff, office space, and budget line, which can be immediately deployed to work on the campaign and which an *ad hoc* agency does not possess. The institutional disadvantage is the existing bureaucracy might regard the new task as an unfair and additional burden over their existing set of organizational responsibilities. The *ad hoc* agency option, on the other hand, generally relies on seconded personnel on borrowed time, holding offices in loaned space, with the attendant problems of transient corporate existence.

In addition to these organizational issues and policy trade-offs, the regime had to contend with two sets of institutional choices. First, given the multiple bureaucratic actors that had a stake in and jurisdiction over the Falungong, the regime had to decide which set of law enforcement or regulatory agencies should participate in the campaign, what their respective roles would be, and which body would oversee and coordinate these disparate bureaucracies. The second institutional choice was the extent of party leadership and involvement. At the central level, did the Politburo collectively, or its top leaders individually, initiate or merely approve the policy recommendations made by subordinates? How often did it meet to deliberate on the Falungong? At both the central and local levels, which party agency did the Politburo assign to lead and oversee the operation? This section analyses these institutional choices in the light of the foregoing organizational issues and policy trade-offs.

Analysis of Institutional Choice

Answers to these questions can be glimpsed from the initial stage of the campaign when the Politburo had to assign the task to some bureaucratic agency. Since the task involved multiple jurisdictions, a logical candidate would be one of two supraministerial coordinating committees that had jurisdiction over law enforcement and social order—the Central Legal and Political Affairs Committee (CLPAC) and the Central Social Order Unified Management Committee (CSOUMC).[1] Both were umbrella organizations headed by Luo Gan, who specialized on domestic security issues in the Central Secretariat, the executive arm of the Politburo. In this capacity, Luo held leading positions in both the party and state on security and law enforcement and served concurrently as a state councilor, as well as a member of the Politburo and the Central Secretariat. CLPAC had 10 members, composed of Luo as the secretary, with seven members who headed agencies in the regime's law enforcement apparatus.[2] The CSOUMC was a larger organization also headed by Luo Gan as its director, with three deputy directors: Cao Zhi (vice president of the Standing Committee of the National People's Congress), Supreme Court President Xiao Yang, and Chief Procurator Han Xubin. Its 39 members were heads and deputy heads of party organizations (propaganda, organization, disciplinary committee, trade unions, Women's Federation, Communist Youth League), the armed forces (General Political Department, chief of staff), and 29 ministries, commissions, and bureaus in the State Council, including not only the law enforcement agencies (public security, state security, justice, armed police) but most of the noneconomic production ministries.[3] All members of CLPAC not only served on the CSOUMC but were also listed on top of the committee roster.[4] The CLPAC, then, would appear to be on a higher hierarchical stratum than the CSOUMC.

From Makeshift Arrangements to the "610 Office"

Neither the CLPAC nor the CSOUMC appeared to play a leading role in the regime's dealing with the Falungong before the official ban promulgated in July 1999. Instead, the process appeared to have evolved in two stages. In the early stage of the crisis, the regime was in a reactive mode, using different assortments of government agencies assembled in short notice to deal with the Falungong, depending on the task at hand. The point man was invariably Luo Gan, who communicated directly with his immediate superior, the secretary-general of the party (Jiang Zemin), and the premier of the State Council (Zhu Rongji), both of whom were personally involved in the process during this early stage. The process was institutionalized from June 10 on, when the "610 Office" and a separate *ad hoc* committee with regular memberships were created to engage in more proactive planning of the suppression campaign. Luo Gan still headed the first *ad hoc* committee. The appointment of a Politburo Standing Committee (PSC) member later to head a larger committee appeared to have replaced Luo and reduced the need for the intervention of Jiang Zemin and Zhu Rongji.

The makeshift arrangement in the early stage of the crisis was evident during the siege of April 25. The emergency meeting called by Luo Gan at the Zhongnanhai was attended by top officials of the Ministry of Public Security, the Ministry of State Security, the Armed Police Headquarters, the Central Security Forces Bureau, the General Office of the Central Committee, the General Office of the State Council, and related Beijing municipal departments.[5] The meeting was not convened in the name of the CLPAC or CSOUMC, whose roles remained peripheral throughout the process. In the dialogue with the five Falungong representatives later on the day of the siege, it was also not the two committees that represented the regime. Luo Gan was the government's main spokesman, accompanied by Central Committee General Office Deputy Director Wang Gang, Beijing Municipality Executive Deputy Mayor Meng Xueliang, Minister of Public Security Jia Chunwang and State Council Deputy Secretary-General Cui Zhanfu. They were later joined by Premier Zhu Rongji, who persuaded the Falungong practitioners to disperse.[6] Zhu, Wang, and Meng were not members of either committee. In the PSC meeting the following day, it was Luo Gan again who made the main presentation on the Falungong; Jia Qinglin, party secretary for the Beijing Municipality, made a supplementary presentation.[7] Jia served on neither committee. As shown in table 6.1, there was no group with fixed membership dealing with the Falungong from April 25 to June 10.

The process was institutionalized later, when Luo Gan was appointed to head the 610 Office.[8] Thereafter, a designated agency replaced the shifting groups to deal with the Falungong. Instead of merely reacting to events

Table 6.1: Regime Agents Dealing with the Falungong, April 25 through July 20, 1999

Event/Task	Primary Agent	Group	Personal Involvement of Top Party Leaders
Emergency meeting, 4/25	Luo Gan	Top officials of the Ministry of Public Security, Ministry of State Security, Central Security Forces Bureau, Central Committee General Office, State Council General Office, Beijing municipal departments	Jiang instructed Luo to convene meeting
Meeting with Falungong representatives, 4/25	Luo Gan	Central Committee General Office, minister of public security, State Council deputy secretary, Beijing executive mayor	Zhu Rongji participated in the meeting
Politburo meeting, 4/26	Luo Gan	Luo Gan, Beijing party secretary, made presentation	Politburo Standing Committee in attendance
610 Office	Luo Gan	N/A	N/A
Central Leading Group for Dealing with the Falungong, established on 6/17	Li Lanqing	Li Lanqing, Luo Gan, Ding Guangen, minister of public security, minister of state security, Central Committee general office deputy chair, State Council deputy secretary-general	Li Lanqing

Source: Zong Hairen, *Zhu Rongji zai yi jiujiujiu nian* [Zhu Rongji in 1999] (Hong Kong: Mirror Books, 2001); translated in Chinese law and government (January–February 2002), pp. 54–68.

as they arose, the office was given a proactive mission to devise an overall solution for the Falungong problem.[9] The 610 Office became the executive arm of the Central Leading Group on Dealing with the Falungong (CLGDF; *Zhongyang chuli Falungong lingdao xiaozu* in Chinese), established by a Politburo resolution in its June 17 meeting.[10] Headed by PSC member Li Lanqing, the CLGDF was deputized by Luo Gan and Ding Guan'gen, the minister of propaganda and State Council vice premier.[11] In subsequent reports on regime operations dealing with the Falungong, Li Lanqing, rather than Luo Gan, was credited in official reports.

As noted earlier, from April 25 to June 17, responsibility to deal with the Falungong was entrusted to Luo Gan and the Central Political and Legal Affairs Committee. From June 17, 1999, on, the CLGDF and its director, Li Lanqing, took over the reins to take charge of matters relating to the Falungong, with the 610 Office acting as its executive agency. Both Li and Luo were able to call on top government and party officials to work on the case and draw on their institutional resources. In addition, not only PSC member Li, but also Luo appeared to have direct access to Jiang Zemin and Zhu Rongji,[12] both of whom were personally interested and engaged in dealing with the Falungong. During the April 25 siege, Zhu volunteered to meet with the Falungong representatives, while Jiang set the guidelines for Zhu to respond to the demands of the Falungong practitioners.[13] Earlier that day, Jiang instructed Luo Gan to convene the Emergency meeting at Zhongnanhai.[14] As noted in Chapter 2, Jiang's characterization of the Falungong, the *ad hoc* committee he proposed to establish, and the strategy he outlined became the official party policy to deal with the Falungong.

Pattern of Institutional Choice

The creation of the CLGDF as well as the 610 Office as the primary agencies to deal with the Falungong and the composition of their membership suggest a pattern of regime institutional choice that focused on public security issues rather than overall management of the Falungong, used *ad hoc* committees rather than permanent agencies, and invested power in the top party echelon rather than functional state bureaucracies. First, the focus on public security can be seen in the composition of the three *ad hoc* shifting groups that dealt with the Falungong on April 25 and 26, noted above, as well as the CLGDF. As shown below, the core of the seven-member CLGDF was the public security triumvirate (minister of public security, minister of state security, secretary of the Central Legal Political Affairs Commission), constituting the largest functional group in the body, while Li Lanqing represented the PSC, Ding Guan'gen the Department of Propaganda, and Wang Maolin the 610 Office. Conspicuously absent in the CLGDF were two sets of bureaucratic players. There was no representation from the triad of the administration of justice (Ministry of Justice, Supreme People's Court, Supreme People's Procuracy) or the National People's Congress, which enacted laws regulating social order and religious activities, all members of which served on the CLPAC. In addition, absent from the *ad hoc* committee were several regulatory agencies that had jurisdiction over the Falungong—the Ministry of Civil Affairs, which accredited social organizations; and the Bureau of Religious Affairs and the Athletic Commission, which respectively managed religious and *qigong* organizations—and three agencies to which the Falungong applied for registration: the National Minority Affairs Commission, the China Buddhist Federation, and the United Front Department.[15] Recall that these two sets of bureaucratic actors were also absent in the Zhongnanhai emergency meeting of April 25, in the dialogue with Falungong representatives later that day, and in the PSC meeting the following day. It should be thus be evident that the *ad hoc* groups of April 25 and 26, as well as both the 610 Office and the CLGDF, were structured more as a nimble task force to deal with the Falungong and less as an overall organization with a broader mandate to manage other attendant legal and social issues relating to the congregation.

Second, why did the regime also eschew the two supraministerial law enforcement bodies and entrust the task to an *ad hoc* organization? Both the CLPAC and CSOUMC were general-purpose coordinating bodies designed to be inclusive of most central party, state, and military agencies with law enforcement portfolios. They lacked the policy specificity relating to a major case such as the Falungong. Many of the 43 constituent members of the CSOUMC, in particular, those of the State Tourism Bureau, the Ministry of Construction, the Insurance Supervision Management Bureau, and the State Birth Planning Committee, had few policy connections with the Falungong. Both committees were established to manage and formulate policy on major, national law enforcement issues for the regime, the more important of which included armed robberies, drug trafficking, crime syndicates, organized gambling, abduction and sale of women and children, college campus safety, and airline and railroad security.[16] A major case such as the Falungong that required focused attention and sustained executive action would be more appropriate for a task force in the form of an *ad hoc* committee, where members were chosen for their specific functional expertise, personal availability, and institutional resource relating to the mission in question.

Third, the foregoing also suggests that decision-making power was vested in the top party echelon rather than functional state bureaucracies or supraministry coordinating bodies. This can be due, in large measure, to the fragmentary authority structure of the state bureaucracy, which pushes policy issues to higher levels of political organization for consensus building and conflict resolution.[17] In the case of the Falungong, the organizational structure of the 43-member CSOUMC was clearly too diffuse and the coordinating problems too endemic for effective management of a major domestic security issue. While smaller, the 10-member CLPAC was made up of the top executives of the law enforcement agencies too preoccupied with managing their own policy portfolios to devote sustained quality time on the case. The Politburo solution was to exercise strong top-echelon party leadership in dealing with the Falungong. This manifested in the appointment of two Politburo members (Luo Gan and Ding Guangen) and top-ranked PSC member Li Lanqing to handle the case. It can also be seen in the prominent role of the Central Secretariat, in the Politburo agenda, and in the personal involvement of several PSC members noted in chapter 2 on preparing for the crackdown.

CENTRAL ORGANIZATION OF THE ANTI-FALUNGONG CAMPAIGN

In both the central and local levels, the anti-Falungong campaign is organized along similar structural-functional lines. Structurally, at every administrative level, there is an *ad hoc* leadership group in both the party organization and the government bureaucracy that oversees the management of the campaign. In the party system, it is called the "Leading Group for Dealing with the Falungong Question" (*Chuli Falungong Lingdao Xiaozu*), following the nomenclature of the agency established by the Politburo. Within the government bureaucracy, it is generally called the "Leading Group to Prevent and Deal with the Question of Cults" (*Fangfan yu chuli xiejiao wenti lingdao xiaozu*). More often than not, the two groups have overlapping, even identical membership, share the same office, staff, and budget, and convene joint meetings. Known as "One Organization, Two Labels" (*yi ge jigou, liang kuai paizi*),[18] this party–government collaborative arrangement is not exclusive to law enforcement, but is commonly found in other policy arenas.[19] To manage the day-to-day operations of the campaign, a single office was established that serves as the executive arm of the two leading groups, with staff members initially seconded from both party and government agencies. The executive office became institutionalized in 2003, when it had its own permanent staff. Since April 2002, the "Central Leading Group to Deal with the Falungong Question" was renamed the "Leading Group on Work to Maintain Social Stability" (*weihu shehui wending gongzuo lingdao xiaozu*) to include the function to deal with other forms of local protests that have emerged.[20]

Composition of the Party Leading Group

In the party system, leading groups to deal with the Falungong were generally headed by party secretaries for political and legal affairs at that administrative level. As shown below, the secretary or the deputy secretary of the party committee sometimes assumed that position, with other members drawn from top officials of other party and government agencies related to propaganda, organization, and law enforcement. At the central party level, the Politburo meeting resolved to establish the "Central Leading Group to Deal with the Falungong Question" when it met on June 17, 1999. As shown in table 6.2, the group was headed by Li Lanqing, vice premier of the State Council, with five deputy directors—Luo Gan, secretary of the Political and Legal Affairs Committee, Ding Guan'gen, minister of propaganda, Jia Chunwang, minister of public security, Xu Yongyue, minister of state security, and Wang Maolin, director of the 610 Office.[21] All six held top party ranks at the time of their appointment. Li was a PSC member, Ding and Luo were both Politburo members, Jia and Wang Central Committee members, and Xu was an alternate member of the Central Committee.[22] This practice of appointing cadres with top party ranks to head the agency to deal with the Falungong was to invest it with proper formal powers, where its leaders outranked other departmental officials at the administrative level. To provide administra-

Table 6.2: Composition of Central Leading Groups to Handle the Falungong

Group Position	Name	Party Rank	Bureaucratic Position
Head	Li Lanqing	Member of Standing Committee, Politburo	Vice Premier, State Council
Deputy Head	Luo Gan	Member of Politburo	Secretary of Political and Legal Affairs Committee
Deputy Head	Ding Guan'gen	Member of Politburo	Minister of propaganda
Deputy Head	Jia Chunwang	Member of Central Committee	Minister of public security
Deputy Head	Xu Yongyue	Alternate member of Central Committee	Minister of state security
Deputy Head	Wang Maolin	Member of Central Committee	Deputy head, Central Leading Group on Propaganda and Ideological Work

Source: http://www.epochtimes.com/gb/4/10/26/n700451.htm, accessed by author on July 31, 2005.

tive support, the "Office of the Central Leading Group for Dealing with the Falungong Question" became the executive arm of the CLGDF. Nicknamed the 610 Office after the date of its creation, it was reportedly headed by Wang Maolin, with four deputy directors—Liu Jing, deputy minister of public security, Yuan Yin, a secretary of the State Council office, Li Dongsheng, party secretary of CCTV, and Wang Xiaoxiang, deputy director of the State Council office on dealing with the Falungong.[23] Three additional members of the office were reported to be Dong Zhuifa, the visiting inspector (*qinshiyuan*) of the office, Gao Xiaodong, its deputy bureau chief, and Liu Yuanshan, deputy minister of propaganda.[24]

Organization of the State Council Office

On the state government side, the "State Council Office for Preventing and Dealing with the Question of Cults" (*Guowuyuan Fangfan he chuli xiejiao wenti bangongsi*) was reportedly established on September 30, 2000.[25] Unlike its counterpart in the party system, the State Council agency was thus established more than a year after the official ban on the Falungong, and a month before the Standing Committee of the National People's Congress promulgated its decision to dissolve cult organizations to prevent and punish cult activities.[26] The first announcement of the presence of the agency was made on February 26, 2001, when that office held a joint conference with different party and state agencies reporting their accomplishments in dealing with the Falungong.[27] The following day, Office Director Liu Jing held a press conference to introduce the State Council office, the functions of which were stated as (1) to provide integrated coordination of dealing with the Falungong in different agencies, (2) to launch investigative research on preventing and dealing with the Falungong, (3) to strengthen the collaboration and cooperation with organizations of different nations, (4) to protect the basic human rights of citizens, and (5) to shelter citizens from being harmed by cults.[28] In its official notice on establishing bureaucratic agencies of March 21, 2003, the State Council stipulated that the "State Council Office for Preventing and Dealing with the Question of Cults" would be listed as an agency directly administered by the central party (*Zhonggong zhongyang zhishu jigou*). It would hold office together with the "Office of the Central Leading Group on Dealing with the Falungong Question," in a "One Organization, Two Labels" arrangement.[29]

Functions and Activities of the 610 Office

The foregoing reports suggest that the central 610 Office served the special agencies dealing with the Falungong in both the Politburo and the State

Council. The State Council office, however, cannot be found in the printed *Directory of State Council Organizations* or in the Web sites of the State Council or of the *Renmin ribao*. Reports on its functions and activities in the official media are rare. They include those on its participation in the State Council Press briefing noted above, in two conferences on anti-Falungong activities in the national capital and in the provinces, and organizing anti-Falungong exhibitions in the Beijing as well as in elementary and secondary schools.[30] Reports on its budget and personnel are also uncommon. The 610 Office budget generally included personnel salaries, the 610 subsidy, and special subsidy. The central 610 Office has stipulated that such subsidies should be provided. But as noted below, the 610 Offices of some local governments such as the Laiyang Municipality were not budgeted for any operating funds.[31] In the rare few cases where the source of funding are identified, the budget of the office appears to come from both the party and government fiscal accounts (under Political and Legal Affairs). As noted below, the staff of some local 610 Offices were generally seconded from different party and state agencies, with some local offices also recruiting their own staff from college graduates or even those with advanced degrees.[32]

PROVINCIAL AND MUNICIPAL ORGANIZATION
OF THE ANTI-FALUNGONG CAMPAIGN

Provincial and municipal organization paralleled the structure at the central party and government level. Party committees on the provincial, municipal, county, and township levels had generally established "Leading Groups to Deal with the Falungong," while its corresponding government agency instituted the "Leading Group to Prevent and Deal with the Question of Cults." A single executive office is generally established to serve both the party and government leading groups under the "One Organization, Two Labels" arrangement. Like its central counterparts, the local 610 Offices were generally part of the party organization and headed by the party secretary or deputy party secretary. Established first as *ad hoc* organs without their own permanent staff and office space to deal with the immediate crisis in the aftermath of dissolving the Falungong, they were often attached to the Political and Legal Affairs Committee of the local party committee, but were changed to permanent agencies soon thereafter. Following the example of the central state agency, some local governments' "Leading Groups to Deal with the Problems of Cults" were also renamed "Leading Group on Work to Maintain Social Stability" after April 2002.

As in its central counterpart, most of the local agencies handling the Falungong were called 610 Offices. But there were a few exceptions. The

Heilongjiang Provincial Office was called the "615 Office."[33] The Dandong Municipal Office was called the "621 Office."[34] The one in Xinjin County was named the "July 16 Office" after its inaugural dates.[35] In bureaucratic classification, the central 610 Office was ranked as a ministerial (*bu*) agency, the provincial office as department (*si*) agency, the municipal-level office as a bureau (*chu*) agency, the county-level office as a division (*ke*) agency, and those below the county-level as a branch (*gu*) agency.[36]

Provincial-Level Organization

On the province level, specialized agencies dealing with the Falungong have been reported in Heilongjiang, Jilin, Hunan, Shandong, Zhejiang, Shanxi, Henan, Sichuan, and Yunnan.[37] The organization in Zhejiang parallels those at the central administrative level, where the provincial party committee had an Office of the Leading Group to Handle the Falungong Question (*chuli Falungong wenti lingdao xiaozu bangongsi*), while the provincial government had an Office on Preventing and Handling the Problems of Cults. Both offices were headed by the same office director and probably had the same staff and office.[38] The provincial party committee of Henan had an "Office of the Leading Group on Preventing and Handling the Problems of Cults" that also appeared to hold office with the Provincial Government Office on Preventing and Handling Cult Questions. Both were headed by a deputy party secretary in charge of the Provincial Legal and Political Affairs Committee.[39]

There were few reports with additional descriptions about their internal organization or operations. Yunnan did report that its "Leading Group to Handle the Falungong" was headed by the deputy provincial party secretary, assisted by two deputy directors—a deputy provincial governor, and the provincial secretary for legal and political affairs who was also a member of the standing committee of the provincial party committee, with 19 additional members who were heads of provincial departments. The leading group had an office and clerical staff.[40] Elsewhere, there was also a report on the organization and operations of the anti-Falungong agency in Sichuan, where the provincial party committee established an office of the Leading Committee to Handle the Falungong by early August 1999. Meeting daily in the afternoon in the immediate aftermath of the ban, the leading committee established a leadership responsibility system, a reporting system, and monitoring system on dealing with the Falungong. It also required subordinate party committees to make a progress report on alternate business days and to implement a departmental accountability system, a locality accountability system, and a responsibility tracking system.[41]

Some provincial bureaucracies also had specialized agencies dealing with the Falungong. In the State Asset Supervision and Management Committee of Shanxi Province, the party committee established a Leading Group for Preventing and Handling the Problems of Cults, whose work was assisted by an office. Its day-to-day operations, however, were handled by the general department (*zonghe chu*) of the Provincial State Asset Supervision and Management Committee.[42] The Organization Department of Sichuan Province that manages job assignments for party members also established a special office dealing with the Falungong,[43] as did organization bureaus of all local municipal, district, and county party committees. In all, 5,000 staff members were assigned to their offices to handle the problems of Falungong relating to party membership and organization in Sichuan.[44]

Municipal 610 Offices

At the municipal level, there was also a high level of nomenclature, structural, and functional similarities in the organization and activities of anti-Falungong agencies. Table 6.3 lists these features in four cities in different parts of China (Sanya in Hainan, Hengyang in Hunan, Yangquan in Shanxi, and Wuhai in Inner Mongolia). In all four cities, the anti-Falungong office was invariably subordinated to the municipal party committee and served both the municipal party and government agencies dealing with the Falungong. Within the government bureaucracy, it was generally called the "Office in Preventing and Handling the Problems of Cults." There are more variations in the nomenclature among the party agencies, as a result of time. Before 2002, they are generally called the "Leading Group of the Municipal Party Committee Dealing with the Falungong." From 2003 to 2005, the referent "and Harmful *Qigong* Organizations" was added to the title in some municipalities.[45] As noted above, sometime since the latter half of 2002, the agency was often renamed as the "Office of the Party Committee to Maintain Social Stability," to broaden its functions to include the prevention of proliferating protest rallies against local land confiscation. In some municipal 610 Offices (Hengyang and Wuhai), two specialized departments are instituted, one dealing with general office business and administrative matters (communications, personnel, finance) and the other dealing with special functions (education, policy research). The Sanya office did not have specialized departments.[46] There were also some variations in the prescribed staff size, with up to eight in Hengyang on the high end. Ranks vary from branch (*gu*) cadre in smaller agencies to division (*ke*) cadres in larger ones.

The Hengyang Municipal 610 Office

Among the four municipalities, Hengyang of Hunan Province is rather typical. Its Leading Group to Deal with the Falungong at the municipal party

Table 6.3: Organization of "610 Offices" in Municipalities

	Municipality			
Characteristic	Sanya	Hengyang	Yangquan	Wuhai
Province Name	Hainan Office of Leading Group of Sanya Municipal Party Committee in Dealing with the Falungong	Hunan Office of Leading Group of Hengyang Municipal Party Committee in Dealing with the Falungong	Shanxi 610 Office of the Yangquan Municipal Party Committee	Inner Mongolia Office of the Leading Group of Wuhai Municipal Party Committee on Dealing with Falungong and Harmful *Qigong* Organizations
Other names	Office of Municipal Party Committee Leading Group to Maintain Stability	Office of Municipal Government in Preventing and Handling Cult Questions	Office of Municipal Government in Preventing and Handling Cult Questions	Office of Municipal Government in Preventing and Handling Cult Questions
External label	Office of Municipal Government to Prevent and Deal with Cult Questions	Office of Municipal Government in Preventing and Handling Cult Questions		Office of Municipal Government in Preventing and Handling Cult Questions
Organizational superior	Sanya Municipal Party Committee	Hengyang Municipal Party Committee	Yangquan Municipal Party Committee	Wuhai Municipal Party Committee
Prescribed FTE staff Size and Rank	One full-time deputy director of deputy section-rank	Eight (including one director, two deputy directors), of which two at branch cadre rank	Four (including one director and one deputy director)	N/A
Departments	None	General branch, education branch	N/A	Two (Secretariat, General Policy Research Branch)
Functions	See text			

committee and the Leading Group to Prevent and Handle the Problems of Cults at the municipal government were served by the same office that was established in 2001 and abbreviated as the 610 Office. Managed by the Political and Legal Affairs Committee of the municipal party committee, it has a prescribed staff of eight, including a director, two deputy directors, with two cadres of division-level (*keji*) rank. The office has two departments—the general branch (*zonghe ke*) that manages intelligence collection, analysis, convening meetings, logistics, and maintaining secrecy, and the education branch (*jiaoyu ke*) is in charge of propaganda, education conversion of Falungong practitioners, and inspecting, coordinating, and supervising the operations of different municipal agencies and urban districts.[47]

The Laiyang and Xinyu Municipal 610 Offices

More information is available on the organizational structure and institutional history of the 610 Office in Laiyang and Xinyu municipalities, both also in Hunan Province. In the Laiyang Municipal Party Committee, the "Laiyang Committee on Handling the Falungong" was established on July 23, 1999, one day after the formal announcement of the dissolution of the Falungong. The top three officials of the committee were those of the municipal party committee—the deputy party secretary and two members of the its standing committee, who were also its Propaganda Department head, and its Department of Legal and Political Affairs head. Listed as the fourth and fifth officials of the committee were two deputy mayors. Members of the committee were the top officials of the general office of the municipal party committee, the general office of the municipal government office, the Organizational Department, the Propaganda Department, the Political and Legal Affairs Committee, the Public Security Bureau, the Education Bureau, and those of mass organizations (Chief Worker's Union, the Women's Federation, the Communist Youth League, and the Federation of Scientists).[48]

The executive arm of the committee was the 610 Office, which managed the day-to-day operations of the committee. The nominal head of the office was the director of the general office of the municipal party committee, and the two deputies were the deputy heads of the Municipal Propaganda Department and the Deputy Director of the General Office of the Municipal Party Committee. The last mentioned was the executive head of the 610 Office. Initially, the 12 staff members were seconded and drew their salaries from the above municipal party and government agencies. Effective January 18, 2001, the 610 Office was formally instituted as a permanent (*changxie*) unit at the first-ranked divisional level (*zheng keji*). Headed by the deputy director of the general office of the municipal party committee, it has its own prescribed staff of eight people who would be detached from their original employers. The 610

Office is located in the Secretariat Building of the Municipal Party Committee and managed by the latter. The 610 Office is authorized to command, coordinate, and handle all Falungong matters within the municipal jurisdictional territory, including provincial and regional managed mines and enterprises. It is not provided with its own operating budget or office equipment.[49]

In Xinyu Municipality in Hunan, the 610 Office was created by a resolution of the standing committee of the municipal party committee, which met on January 12, 2001. Its creation history illustrates the local bureaucratic red tape involved in setting up a new local agency even for a national priority. It was formally approved by the municipal organization staffing committee (*jigou bianji huiyuanhui*) on April 20 of the same year as a first-ranked bureau-level unit (*zheng chuji*), affiliated with the municipal political and legal affairs committee. The office was headed by the deputy secretary of legal and political affairs; the two deputies were the deputy chief of the municipal public security bureau, and an assistant county judge. The office has two departments—a general department and an education propaganda department. Its seven prescribed staff members were seconded mostly from the law-enforcement agencies—the municipal public security bureau, the municipal courts, municipal justice administration bureau, municipal organizational department and municipal procuracy. To second the seven agents without creating new staff positions, the municipal organization staffing committee (MOSC), which managed municipal personnel, had to juggle the numbers. It had to cut two staff positions from the municipal organization department and the municipal propaganda department and assign these to the 610 Office. For the remaining five positions, the MOSC separated the accounting from actual use of the five positions. Two agents remained on the payroll of the municipal justice administration bureau, and one each on that of the municipal public security bureau, the municipal courts, and the municipal procuracy. The seven staff positions were classified as three bureau-level, second-class (*fu keji*) and two bureau-level, first-class (*zheng keji*) ranks.[50]

Functions of the Sanya 610 Office

A detailed description of the functions of the 610 Office was provided by the Sanya Municipality in Hainan Province. They were listed as (1) proposing measures and suggestions to the Municipal Party Committee Leading Group on Dealing with the Falungong, according to the strategic plan (*bushu*) of the Central Committee, provincial party committee, and municipal party committee; (2) making operational plans to deal with the Falungong within a fixed time period and to supervise its implementation, based on the arrangements of the municipal party committee Leading Group on Dealing with the Falungong; (3) unifying, urging, and inspecting the work of various districts and departments in implementing the policies and plans of the central, provincial, and municipal party committees, and reporting the local implementations to the provincial 610 Office and the municipal party committee Leading Group to deal with the Falungong; (4) organizing and pushing forward the work of investigating and analyzing the Falungong question; (5) proposing policies and suggestions for the reference of the municipal leadership; (6) integrating, analyzing, and handling intelligence on the Falungong; (7) reporting on a fixed schedule the movements and situations of the Falungong to different districts and departments; (8) directing and coordinating the work on the Falungong of different districts and departments; (9) planning and managing citywide meetings on the Falungong convened by the municipal party committee as instructed by the head of the municipal party committee Leading Group on dealing with the Falungong; (10) organizing, directing, and coordinating the work of different districts and departments on preventing and handling other cults and harmful *qigong* organizations; and (11) undertaking tasks given by the provincial 610 Office and the provincial party committee Leading Group on Dealing with the Falungong.[51]

Not all municipal organizations dealing with the Falungong were specialized agencies with their own prescribed staff and office space. In Ordos of Neimonggu province, the 610 Office was not a separate agency in the municipal table of organization an agency within the office of the municipal party committee, although it had an almost identical job description of the Sanya 610 Office.[52] In Huizhou Municipality of Guangdong Province, there was also no separate 610 Office. The task of dealing with the Falungong was entrusted to two of the seven agencies within the committee on political and legal affairs of the municipal party committee, where the 610 Office Intelligence Branch (*610 Ban xinxike*) was given the charge to collect, analyze, and report on intelligence and propose policies on dealing with the Falungong; and the 610 Office General Coordinating Branch (*610 Ban zonghe xietiaoke*) was responsible for organizing, coordinating, and directing operations to deal with emergencies and unforeseen events relating to the Falungong.[53]

Urban District-Level Organization

At the urban district (*qu*) administrative level immediately below the municipalities, specialized agencies established to deal with the Falungong have a similar structure and function as those on the municipal level, and worked closely with municipal authorities. The 610 Office of the Dongli urban district in Harbin had a prescribed staff of five, including four administrative staff (*xingzheng bianzhi*) and one undertaking staff (*shiye bianzhi*), with one of section-level cadre (*chuji lingdao*) and one branch-level cadre (*keji lingdao*). In July 2005, it had the following job description: (1) to conduct investigations, analyze present situations, summarize experiences, study work regularities, and offer policies and recommendations to the district party committee and government on how to maintain political stability, in order to fulfill its mission to be the assistant and chief of staff; (2) to understand and grasp the direction of development of cults, to collect intelligence within the district, and to transmit important information to the district party committee and district government in a timely manner, to coordinate and manage the work on preventing and handling cults in the district; (3) to coordinate and direct the work of the district party committee and district government on dealing and solving the Falungong, other cults, and harmful *qigong* organizations; (4) to handle the daily work of the district party committee's Leading Group on Dealing with and Solving the Falungong Question; and (5) to supervise and urge (*duchu*) the implementation of assigned tasks, and to fulfill other tasks given by the district party committee's Leading Group on Dealing with and Solving the Falungong Question.[54]

There is further description on the division of labor and respective functions of its two departments. The functions of the general investigation and research branch (*zonghe diaoyan ke*) include (1) conducting investigations, analyzing present situations, summarizing experiences, and studying work regularities of work on the Falungong, other cults, and harmful *qigong* organizations; (2) drafting summary reports, work plans, speeches for the officials, and other documents of the district party committee Leading Group on Dealing with the Falungong Question; (3) convening meetings of the 610 Office; (4) identifying and propagating model experiences; (5) preparing statistical tables on the education and conversion program of the district party committee Leading Group on Dealing with the Falungong; (6) attending to matters relating to convening meetings of that office; (7) handling the distribution, reception, filing, and archiving of official documents on the Falungong; (8) taking care of maintaining secrecy and the office seal; (9) compiling and editing the office newsletter and chronology bulletin; (10) managing the administrative and financial matters of the office; and (11) participating in the district party committee's work on inspecting and directing the operations of the basic levels.[55]

The second agency was the "Coordination and Command Branch" (*xietiao zhidao ke*), which has the responsibility of (1) collecting, understanding, and grasping the movements of the Falungong, other cults, and harmful *qigong* organizations; (2) coordinating and directing the work of preventing and handling the Falungong, other cults, and harmful *qigong* organizations by related agencies of subordinate township, streets, and urban wards; (3) coordinating and directing the implementation of the leadership responsibility system as well as accountability system in the work on preventing, controlling, and striking at the Falungong, other cults, and harmful *qigong* organizations by the public security, procuracy, and courts; (4) preparing statistical tables on the organization and illegal activities of the Falungong and other cults, as

Table 6.4: Organization of 610 Offices in Urban Districts

Characteristic	Urban District			
	Dongli	Zhengxiang	Donghu	Xicheng
Municipality	Harbin	Hengyang	Nanchang	Beijing
Province	Heilongjiang	Hunan	Jiangxi	Beijing
Name	Office of Leading Group of District Party Committee on Dealing with the Falungong	Office of Leading Group of District Party Committee on Dealing with the Falungong	Office of Leading Group of District Party Committee on Dealing with the Falungong	Office of Xicheng Urban District on Integrated Treatment of Social Order
Other name	Office of Leading Group of Municipal Government on Preventing and Dealing with Falungong and Other Cults	Office of Leading Group of Municipal Government on Preventing and Dealing with Cults	Urban District 610 Office	
Organizational superior	Urban district party committee	Urban district party committee	Urban district	Urban district party committee
Prescribed staff size and rank	Five (including four in administrative staffing, one in undertaking staffing), of whom one was section ranked cadre, two were branch-level cadres	One in administrative staffing, one director, one deputy director	Four (including a music department), of whom one each was director and deputy director	One deputy director of 610 Office, one deputy director of Office on Integrated Social Order
Departments	Two (General Investigation and Analysis Branch, Coordination and Command Branch)	N/A	N/A	N/A

well as harmful *qigong* organizations; and (5) participating in the drafting of important documents of the 610 Office.[56]

Table 6.4 compares the organizational structure of the 610 Offices of four urban districts in Dongli (Heilongjiang), Zhengxiang (Hunan), Donghu (Jiangxi), and Xicheng (Beijing).

COUNTY, TOWNSHIP, AND BASIC-LEVEL ORGANIZATION

County-Level Organization

Among the 2,861 counties in China,[57] there were more reported variations in the organizational structure of agencies dealing with the Falungong. By and large, many counties have a similar structural arrangement as those of the central, provincial, and municipal levels. In Xianghe County of Hebei Province, Longhui County of Hunan Province, and Antu County of Jilin Province, a Leading Group on Preventing and Handling the Falungong was established in the county party committee, and a separate Leading Group on Preventing and Handling the Problems of Cults was established in the county government. Each leading group was assisted by an executive agency (the 610 Office), which held office together, headed by the same office director, or deputy directors.[58] This is the "Two Organizations, One Label" arrangement of higher administrative levels.

Variations in County-Level Organizations

Beyond this common organizational structure, there were variations in institutional arrangements, where three sets of the latter could be found. First, the 610 Office was a specialized agency in the county bureaucracy. It might hold office with the Committee for Legal and Political Affairs of the County Party Committee but was not listed as subordinate to it. This appears to be the institutional arrangement of Xinjin County of Hunan Province, where the 610 Office was a distinct administrative unit in the county table of organization, with a first-ranked bureau unit classification and a prescribed staff. A similar arrangement existed in Tonghai County of Yunnan Province, where its 610 Office was a distinct county bureau and held office with the County Legal and Political Affairs Committee.[59] In the second arrangement, the 610 Office was subordinate to the County Committee for Legal and Political Affairs as one of its administrative agencies and held office with the County Government Office on Preventing and Handling the Problems of Cults. This was the institutional arrangement in Heilongjiang's Tahe County and Guangdong's Guangning County.[60] Third, in Raohe County of Heilongjiang

Province and Daozhang County in Guizhou Province, where there was no 610 Office. The work of dealing with the Falungong was handled by the county party committee's Political and Legal Affairs Committee, with similar functions as other 610 Offices.[61]

Structure and Function of County Agencies

More detailed information is available for the organizational mission and functions of the Antu County of Jilin Province. The Leading Group for Preventing and Handling the Problems of Cults in Antu County of Jilin Province was assisted by an executive agency, which was also the county government office serving the same function. The mission of the office consisted of (1) implementing the laws, regulations, and policies of party and government agencies of higher administrative levels, as well as the operational tasks of the county party committee and government; (2) conducting investigations and analyses on the organization of Falungong and other cults and their effects on the community; (3) collecting intelligence on the activities and organizations of cults within the county and reporting these to the county party committee and government in a timely manner; and (4) coordinating and directing different county agencies and subordinate townships and villages in law enforcement operations against the illegal activities of cults and harmful *qigong* organizations, as well as education activities aimed at converting the same. These tasks were managed respectively by three separate departments of the office. The general research department (*zhonghe yanjiu ke*) collected intelligence, proposed policy measures, and served as the general business office on dealing with cults, with attendant communications, filing, and financial management functions. A second prevention and disposition department (*fangfan chuzi ke*) acted as the operational arm that dissolved cult organizations, cracked down on cult activities, organized preventive operations that deterred cult activities, and handled sudden and unforeseen cult activities that affected community political stability. A third coordination and command department (*xietiao zhidao ke*) provided coordination among the leading group and different county agencies, directed the operations of township and villages on cults, organized the education activities aimed at converting cult members, and implemented the propaganda programs on cults and harmful *qigong* activities.[62]

A similar description of agency tasks can be found in Tonghai County.[63] The relative importance of these tasks can be seen in an enumeration of organizational goals and an evaluation scheme that assigns merit points on the degree of effectiveness with which county agencies and subordinate townships and villages of Lingtai County of Gansu Province accomplish their anti-Falungong and anticult activities (table 6.5).

Table 6.5: Assignment of Merit Points for Different Tasks in the Anticult Campaign in Lingtai County, Gansu Province, 2005

Task Performance	Merit Points
Four or more special meetings documented with minutes, with task assignment on the cult problem	10
Establishment of a leading group to deal with cults, with specific leaders and working staff	3
Signing responsibility contracts by different levels, with clear task objectives	4
Having a "4 in 1" system of conversion and reeducation teams	3
Having an annual plan with specific task arrangements	3
Organizing systematic investigation of the cult problems in the locality/unit	6
Having a prevention and crisis management plan with budget allocation	3
Integrating the task of preventing and handling cults in the work agenda, with quarterly inspection, annual evaluation, and work summary	3
No resurgence of Falungong activities	10
No resurgence of the "Mentu" cult	10
Regular propaganda and criticism activities against cults, with clear social impact	20
Serious and complete fulfillment of anticult campaign in the rural areas and timely summary of work and reporting	10
Having varieties of anticult education activities, reaching 80% of the masses and 90% of the primary and secondary students	10
No practicing Falungong members and no "Mentu" member activities within year	10
No Falungong or Mentu members producing or distributing propaganda materials; no Falungong practitioners committing suicide or mutilation; no Falungong members petitioning to the city, province, or Beijing; no local employees participating in "Mentu" assemblies	5
Forceful investigation and prohibition of emergent cult activities and timely reporting	10
Total:	120

Source: www.lingtai.gansu.gov.cn/new/ReadNews.asp?NewsId=1081 accessed August 2006.

Township-Level Organization

At administrative levels below the county, reports on township agencies dealing with the Falungong are rare, but these do not seem to deviate from those on the organizational structure and activities of higher administrative levels. The report on the Sitang Township of Sinan County in Guizhou Province was particularly informative about the operations of the 610 Office at the township level. At the Sitang Party Committee, a Leading Group for Preventing and Handling the Problems of Cults was formed with the party secretary as the head, after township authorities received a secret cable from its counterpart at the county level and the instructions of the county 610 Office. Subsequently, the township party and government committees convened three joint meetings on the matter and allocated 1,500 *yuan* to fund an education program on preventing and dealing with the Falungong, which was implemented in three stages. First, from January 1 to 25, 2005, the program mobilized and trained core leaders, which include 92 village and community cadres, all officials of agencies directly administered by the Township, and the principals and prefects of studies in 19 primary and secondary schools. In the second stage, from March 1 to 25, 2005, village and community cadres went door to door to propagate the program. The third, concluding stage lasted from March 25 to April 5, when the branch party secretaries and village cadres undertook investigations and reported on operations preventing and dealing with cults to the leading group of the township. At the same time, a propaganda campaign was launched throughout the township, where 350 pictorials, 324 manuals, 2 DVDs, and 1,490 sets of anti-Falungong materials compiled by the leading group were used to educate the masses in the township. A major target of the campaign were the primary and secondary schools, which the township authorities encouraged to organize classroom activities to denounce the Falungong, including writing slogans, displaying banners, and posting news on the chalk boards and school periodicals. Four-year or higher students were assembled to hear a lesson on opposing the Falungong. Every student had to write a journal on the education program, which would be corrected by the teachers and brought home by the student to show to parents and relatives. The journals would be returned by the parents to the party and government agency, to be stored in the school archive. To state in the form of a written agreement, 48 responsibility contracts were signed by school administrators where they committed to implementing provisions in the township anti-Falungong program.[64]

Basic-Level Organizations

At the lowest level of the administrative system in China, there were also reports on agencies dealing with the Falungong in party committees in one street block in Ningbo Municipality, a machinery factory in Xian, and several universities.

Street-Block 610 Office in Ningbo

In Dongliu Street of Jiangdong Urban District in Ningbo Municipality, the street block serves as the first line of defense against the Falungong, where the tasks to deal with local Falungong activities were organized into four subsystems: (1) classified investigation, (2) situation analysis, (3) desk filing data, and (4) early warning. Falungong practitioners were categorized as those who were (1) not yet converted, (2) beginning to convert, (3) basically converted, and (4) completely converted. They were managed separately, according to their classificatory categories, where a case file and a treatment plan were created for each practitioner in the first two categories. These high-risk residents were visited at a fixed schedule, and written reports on their mental states were to be filed. Category 2 practitioners (those beginning to be converted) were introduced to different organized activities, with the aim to integrate them into mainstream community life. New residents were registered after a thorough investigation of their political background. A network of resident monitors was created, where each community designated one resident as the contact person for Falungong matters. Two such monitors were appointed in the Huaguang Cheng and Dongliu ward communities, where there was a stronger Falungong presence. A separate network of education and assistance for Falungong converts was also established, composed of resident professionals, volunteers, and cadres who were retired, old, or on leave. In combination, these organizational components formed a system of "total participation" (*chuanmin chanyu*) by street-block residents, based on the principle of prevention by the public, management by the public, and control by the public (*chunfang, chunzhi, chun kong*).[65]

Dongfang Machine Factory Organization

While there were many reports on enterprises engaging in activities repudiating the Falungong, those reporting on the organizational structure were rare. In one such report, the party committee of the Dongfang Machinery Factory in Xian convened a leading cadre conference for mid- and top-level cadres, and a separate one for retired cadres and those on leave, both on the morning of July 22, 1999. Also on the same morning, a leading group to deal with the Falungong was established by the party committee of the Dongfang Machinery Factory in Xian. The leading group was headed by the Factory's party secretary, with the general manager and assistant general managers serving as deputy directors. There was no reference to a 610 Office. It is not clear what were the constituents of the leading group, but it was reported that the factory's organization department, the community relations department (*chungongchu*), and the propaganda department spoke with the 50 Falungong practitioners.[66]

610 Offices at Universities

More reports of 610 Offices were found in several universities. The earliest report of a special agency dealing with the Falungong was that of the China Agricultural University in Beijing, where a Leading Group to Resolve the Falungong Question (*jiejue Falungong wenti lingdao xiaozu*) was formed in April 1999, three months before the official ban, and probably immediately after the Falungong protest rally in Zhongnanhai. The top officials of the leading group were the school's party secretary, assisted by the deputy party secretary, with the heads of the party committee office, the security department, organization department, worker's union, Department of Retired and On-leave Cadres, and Student Affairs Office as members. The group conducted an in-depth investigation of Falungong organization and activities on campus and convened several meetings of the main party branches and departments. From July through August 1999, the work of the leading group was focused on three sets of tasks—establishing study sessions for all party members of the school, forming small groups to assist party members undergoing the conversion process, and organizing operations to confiscate Falungong publications and videos.[67] A similar organizational structure was found at the Agricultural College of Neimonggu and the Xibei University in Xian.[68]

Elsewhere, Lanzhou University in Gansu Province had an Office of the Leading Group on Preventing and Handling the Problems of Cults that was attached to the party committee office.[69] But the director of the 610 Office was neither the party secretary of the university nor one of its four deputy party secretaries.[70] Not all universities had 610 Offices. In its campus emergency plan, the Central China Science and Technology University's Wuchang campus (*Huazhong Keji Daxue Wuchang fenxiao*) stipulated that events relating to the Falungong would be handled not by a campus agency but by the city's Office on Preventing and Handling Cult Questions.[71]

Below the university level, there were no reports of specialized agencies dealing with the Falungong. The only exception was the School of Medicine of Beijing University, which had a Leading Group on Preventing and Handling the Problems of Cults. Its day-to-day operations were undertaken by the Political Protection Office of the security department of the medical school.[72] The School of Medicine of Beijing University, however, was an autonomous college before its merger with Beijing University several years ago.

The power and functions of the 610 Office in a university can be seen in a report on the Dongbei University, where the agency was headed by the deputy party secretary. The latter withheld salary payments of five campus employees who were Falungong practitioners and who refused to sign the statement of conversion to sever ties with the Falungong, and transferred them from their jobs. The director also forbade university academic departments from recruiting faculty and students who were known Falungong practitioners.[73]

CONCLUSION

This chapter analyzes how the regime organizes its operations against the Falungong. The foregoing sections suggest that the organization structure is highly centralized, with a similar set of institutional arrangements from the central government through the provincial, municipal, and county levels down through the township level to the basic units of villages, housing blocks, enterprises, and universities. At each administrative level, a leading group was established in both the party and government committees that are generally affiliated with the political and legal affairs committees and share the same executive agency and office staff. The similarities in structure and function across geographical regions and administrative strata, and the almost uniform nomenclature of these agencies despite changes over time, attest to the centralized organizational structure of the regime's anti-Falungong initiatives.

On the institutional choice of which set of party and government agencies would strike at the Falungong, it appears that the regime focused on public security issues rather than the overall management of the Falungong, and invested power in the top party echelon rather than functional state agencies. The core constituents of the CLGDF and its informal antecedent were public security *apparatchiks,* not top officials of the Ministry of Justice, Supreme People's Court, or the Supreme People's Procuracy, or regulatory agencies that had jurisdiction over registering Falungong organizations and approving their publications. At both the central and local levels, leadership of the anti-Falungong campaign rest with party agencies rather than government bureaucracies, as the secretary-general and several other PSC members took personal interest and became engaged in the campaign. This pattern of institutional choice suggests the predominance of public security concerns, the primacy of party leadership, especially that of the Central Secretariat and the secretary-general, and the need and the preference for extrabureaucratic organizational solution for crisis management.

An evolutionary process can also be seen in the regime's response. At the beginning of the policy cycle, the state relied on *ad hoc* arrangements rather than existing formal institutions. The first three regime responses to the Falungong challenge at the central level—meeting Falungong representatives on April 25, the emergency meeting of the Politburo on the same day, and the second Politburo meeting on the following day—were not made by the same set of bureaucratic actors. Makeshift arrangements characterized the regime's initial responses to the Falungong, until the 610 Office was established on June 10, 1999, that provided a more permanent organization to manage the domestic threat. At the local government level, a similar *ad hoc* arrangement was evident in the staffing of the local 610 Offices, which were generally seconded from other party and government agencies on that administrative level, before they acquired their own prescribed office staff after April 2002. A second evolutionary organizational feature can be seen in the dilution of the anti-Falungong functions of the local 610 Offices. As indicated in its nomenclature, the operations of these agencies were initially almost exclusively focused on the Falungong. Their functions were later broadened to include other cults and "harmful *qigong* organizations," reflected in the change of the names of these agencies. After April 2002, there were renamed "Leading Group for Handling Social Stability," to handle the increasing incidents of local protests triggered by forced land acquisition and tenant eviction by local governments.

Chapter Seven

Party Meetings Announcing the Ban

The first announcements of the ban on the Falungong were made internally, when the Central Committee issued the notice to ban the Falungong on July 19 to central and provincial levels of party organizations, three days before the order was televised nationally at 3 p.m. on July 22, along with notices of the ministries of Public Security, Personnel, and Civil Affairs.[1] The notice was addressed to the following list of institutional recipients: (1) central party departments, (2) ministries and commissions in the State Council, (3) provincial units, (4) military regions, (5) national headquarters of the Military Affairs Commission, (6) armed services (*bing zong*), and (7) mass organizations.[2] As per party convention, an important policy needs to be disseminated to all party members prior to its official announcement in the national media, through a series of intraparty meetings.

This chapter analyzes the institutional aspects of party meetings on announcing the ban on the Falungong. The inquiry is prompted by the enormity of the task. In 1997, there were more than 60 million party members in the 158,596 party committees, 179,884 main party branches, and 3,175,393 party branches in China.[3] Disseminating the policy document to so many in so short a time constitutes a colossal undertaking with formidable logistical problems. This analysis first focuses on the organizational framework of these meetings, to scrutinize how these meetings are structured vertically and horizontally in the party system. It then proceeds in descending order of the party hierarchy, analyzing how these meetings were organized at each administrative level, from the central and provincial agencies, through those at the municipalities and counties, down to the lowest level in townships, enterprises, and villages. At each administrative level, attention is paid to who convened, presided, and attended the meeting, whether the agenda included both informational items as well as operational tasks, and when and where the meetings took place. I also note where variations obtained between administrative levels or among bureaucratic agencies. I begin with a consideration of general regulations on party meetings.

GENERAL REGULATIONS ON PARTY MEETINGS

Party manuals prescribe general guidelines on how party meetings are to be convened.[4] Three types of such meetings are differentiated: (1) a party committee meeting (*dangweihui*); (2) a party committee standing committee meeting (*changweihui*), and (3) a party secretary business meeting (*dangwei bangonghuiyi*).[5] All three types of meetings are convened and presided by the party secretary, who also chooses the venue and time, sets the agenda, and prepares the documents to be discussed. The party secretary may delegate the task to convene and preside the meeting to the deputy party secretary.[6] Participants of the all-member party conferences are fixed, but those of other party committees are not. The latter are generally set or suggested by the party secretary office staff, and determined by the party secretary.[7] Meetings of party committees and their standing committees require a quorum of half of the members of the appropriate committee before they can be convened and for their resolutions to be legitimate.[8] To reduce the time that administrators have to spend on organizing party meetings and traveling to and attending conventions, the 2000 party manual urges party leaders to cut the number of meetings and to simplify the format. Restated in a document jointly issued by the Central Committee and State Council on December 4, 2001, party organizations are instructed to require party committee approval for convention of meetings and to restrict the number of business meetings per agency to once per year and twice including special circumstances. They are encouraged to combine meetings that are functionally related within the same agency, or those on the same policy issue convened by different agencies into a single, larger meeting for multiple agencies. National conferences organized by central party and state agencies should not exceed three days and 300 participants. Convenors are required to inform the Central Committee Business Office or the State Council Business Office about the conference title, theme, time, location, and participants for approval. To enforce these regulations, party secretaries are instructed not to approve the conventional expenditures even after these are incurred.[9] The party secretary decides whether minutes will be kept for the meeting, and whether and to whom these will be distributed as a committee meeting report (*baogao*), summary (*jiyao*), decision (*jueding*), or notice (*tongji*).

CENTRAL PARTY AND STATE AGENCY MEETINGS

Meetings on the Falungong were structured along the organizational framework of the political system, both vertically and horizontally. Vertically, there were meetings on all administrative levels of political authority: (1) central, (2) provincial, (3) municipal, (4) county, (5) township, and (6) basic levels (housing block residence committees in urban areas, villages in the countryside, and enterprises and factories). Horizontally, separate meetings were also convened at each administrative level for (1) the core party and government leadership, (2) party and government agencies, (3) mass organizations, (4) heads of subordinate administrative levels, and (5) enterprises administered by those agencies. Regardless whether the agencies were party or government organizations, the meetings were generally convened by the party committees at that level.

Almost immediately after receipt of the Central Committee notice, party committees at all administrative levels lost no time to announce the ban to party members before the televised broadcast. At the top level of the political system, discussion meetings and study sessions were convened by party organizations in (1) the Chinese Communist Party system, (2) the State Council, (3) the armed forces, and (4) the party-controlled mass organizations.[10] Added to these four basic subdivisions of the traditional Chinese communist state, generally abbreviated as the *dang, zheng, jun, qun* subsystems, are the (5) judiciary and procuracy and (6) minority political parties, which gain newfound respect in the postcommunist emphasis on the rule of law and democratic reform. The meetings were convened both to communicate the ban to the core group of party faithful and regime supporters, and to engage their support in the regime's assault on the outlawed congregation.

Meetings in Central Party Agencies

In the central party system, meetings were held at (1) leadership organs (*lingdao jikou*), (2) working departments (*gongzuo jikou*), and (3) mass organizations.[11] As shown in table 7.1, of the three leadership organs within the party system, the Central Committee issued the notice to ban the Falungong and the Central Disciplinary Committee held a discussion meeting by July 23. While there was no report that the Central Military Commission had convened any meeting on the Falungong ban by that day, the four main departments of the People's Liberation Army (general chief of staff, political affairs, logistics, equipment) have reported convening meetings on July 23.[12] Among the 30 working departments in the party system, meetings were reported in all except two agencies (the Central Party Archive and the Security Committee Office).[13] Likewise, seven of the eight party-controlled mass organizations and professional associations (National Federation of Workers' Union, Communist Youth League, National Federation of Women, China Federation of Literati and Artists, China Federation of Scientists, China Federation of Writers, and China Federation of Journalists) reported convening discussion meetings by July 23, with the exception of the Federation of Overseas Chinese.[14] There is little additional information on the size of attendance or the category of participants in these meetings.

Table 7.1: Reported Meetings of Central Party Agencies

Central Party Agency	Meeting by 7/23
Leadership organs	
Central Committee	Sender of official notice
Central Disciplinary Committee	Yes
Central Military Commission	No
Working departments	
Organization, Propaganda, United Front, International Liaison, Political and Legal Affairs, Policy Research, Taiwan Affairs, External Propaganda, Central Directly Affiliated Organs Work Committee, Central State Organs Work Committee, Central Party School, Party History Research Office, Mao Tse-tung Writings Editorial Committee, Central Compilation and Translation Bureau, People's Daily, Qiushi Magazine, Guangming Daily (*n* = 28)	Yes
Central Party Archive, Security Committee Office	No
Mass organizations	
National Federation of Workers' Unions, Communist Youth League, National Federation of Women, China Federation of Scientists, China Federation of Literati and Artists, China Federation of Writers, China Federation of Journalists (*n* = 7)	Yes
National Federation of Overseas Chinese	No

Source: *Renmin ribao*, July 24, 1999, p. 1; *Zhongguo gongchandang zhujishi zhiliao (1921-1997)*, vol. 7, pp. 47–222.

Meetings in Central State Agencies

In the government organization, the official directory of the central state apparatus lists six categories of agencies: (1) leadership organs, (2) depart-ments, (3) directly affiliated organizations, (4) agencies, (5) direct undertak-ings, and (6) administrations under the ministries and commissions.[15] With the exception of the leadership organs, the other five sets of agencies are constituents of the State Council, the executive arm of the Chinese state. As shown in table 7.2, the three leadership organs (the National People's Congress, the Supreme People's Court, the Supreme People's Procuracy) reportedly met on banning the Falungong by July 23,[16] as did 21 of the 29 departments at the next lower echelon in the State Council organization.[17]

There are no published reports of meetings convened at the Ministries of National Defense, Supervision, Finance, Water Resources, the State Ethnic Affairs Commission, State Planning Commission, the People's Bank of China, and the National Audit Office.[18] A even smaller percentage of the other four types of agencies in the State Council have reported meetings. Only 7 of the 17 "organizations directly affiliated to the State Council" (*jishu jigou*), 2 of the 7 agencies (*banshi jigou*), 4 of the 11 direct undertakings (*jishu shiye danwei*), and only 1 of the 13 "state administrations under the jurisdiction of the ministries and commissions of the State Council (*buwei guanli guojia ju*) have reportedly convened meetings on the Falungong by July 23.[19]

Table 7.2: Reported Meetings of Central State Agencies

Central State Agency	Meeting by 7/23
Leadership organs	
National People's Congress (Standing Committee), Supreme People's Court, Supreme People's Procuracy	Yes
State Chairman, State Council, Central Military Affairs Commission	No
Departments (ministry, commission, office)	
Foreign Affairs, State Development Planning Commission, State Economic and Trade Commission, Education, Science and Technology, Science Technology and Industry for National Defense, Public Security, State Security, Civil Affairs, Justice, Personnel, Labor and Social Security, Land Resources, Construction, Railways, Communications, Agriculture, Foreign Trade and Economic Cooperation, Culture, Health, Family Planning (*n* = 21)	Yes
National Defense, Supervision, Finance, Water Resources State Ethnic Affairs Commission, State Planning Commission, People's Bank of China, National Audit Office (*n* = 8)	No
Directly affiliated organizations	
Taxation; Civil Aviation; Radio, Film, and TV; Press and Publication; Forestry; Drug Administration; Religious Affairs (*n* = 7)	Yes
Customs; Industry and Commerce; Quality Supervision, Inspection, and Quarantine; Environmental Protection; Sport; Statistics; Intellectual Property; Tourism; Counsel's Office; Government Offices Administration (*n* = 10)	No

(Continued)

Table 7.2: Continued

Central State Agency	Meeting by 7/23
Agencies	
Economic Restructuring, Taiwan Affairs Office ($n = 2$)	Yes
Overseas Chinese Affairs, Hong Kong and Macao Affairs, Legislative Affairs, Research, Information ($n = 5$)	No
Direct Undertakings	
Xinhua News Agency, Academy of Sciences, Academy of Social Sciences, Social Security Fund ($n = 4$)	Yes
Chinese Academy of Engineering, Development Research Center, National School of Administration, Seismological Bureau, Meteorological Bureau; Securities Regulatory Commission, Natural Science Foundation ($n = 7$)	No
Administrations under the ministries and commissions	
Traditional Chinese Medicine ($n = 1$)	Yes
Bureau of Letters and Calls, Grain, Work Safety, Tobacco Monopoly, Foreign Expert Affairs, Oceanic Administration, Surveying and Mapping, Post, Cultural Heritage, Foreign Exchange, State Archives, Protection of State Secrets ($n = 12$)	No

Source: Xinhua, Beijing, July 23, 1999; *Zhonghua renmin gongheguo zhengfu jigou wushinian*, pp. 506–8.

Format of Meetings

Where meetings were held, they appeared to follow a fixed format. First, three levels of meetings were held in several ministries in top-down widening scope of participation: top leaders, administrative cadres, and all party members. At the apex of the organization, the party group of the ministry first convened its own meeting. For most central ministries and commissions, the party group is composed of six to eight members, headed by a party secretary and a deputy party secretary. The party group of large ministries like the Ministry of Education has 10 members.[20] This was followed by a second, larger meeting of the department- and bureau-level cadres, whose numbers vary across ministries. As shown in table 7.3, among the 34 departments of the State Council in 1998, they range from 10–20 in smaller departments (Cultural Relics, Chinese Medicine, Foreign Experts, State Surveying) to more than 60 in larger ones (Finance, Education, Foreign Trade and Economic Cooperation, National Audit Office). The third was a still larger meeting where all the cadres of the ministry as well as party members participated, with the party secretary presiding or delivering a speech. The number of ministry cadres range from 60–70 in smaller ministries to more than

500 in large ones (table 7.3). In central party agencies, virtually all cadres are party members. In central state agencies, the latter make up 97.8% of cadres in 1998.[21] All three levels of meetings were convened and led by the party committee in the respective ministry. Outside the ruling Chinese Communist Party, the Democratic Nation-Building Party also had this format and structure of meetings, with a first meeting of the top party leadership (chairman and vice chairmen, secretary-general), followed by a second meeting of cadres in the bureau level or higher, and a third meeting for all cadres of that party.[22]

Table 7.3: Bureaucratic Size of Departments and Bureaus in the State Council, 1998

Ministry	No. Departments	No. Bureaus	Total Prescribed Staff
Education	18	65	470
Science and Technology	9	34	230
National Minority Affairs	8	27	150
Civil Affairs	10	35	215
Justice Administration	9	34	220
Finance	20	74	610
Personnel	11	39	258
Foreign Experts	5	18	64
Labor and Social Security	12	38	245
Land Resources	14	48	300
Oceanic Administration	6	20	100
State Surveying	5	16	70
Construction	12	45	275
Railway	12	47	400
Communications	10	37	300
Information Industry	13	45	320
Postal Service	8	27	180
Water Resources	10	37	220
Agriculture	16	59	483
Foreign Trade and Economic Cooperation	19	67	457
Culture	10	37	275
Cultural Relics	3	10	60
Health	10	34	225
Chinese Medicine	5	18	71
State Planning Commission	7	22	120
People's Bank	13	49	500
Foreign Exchange	6	12	140
National Audit Office	12	60	450

Source: *Zhongguo zhengfu zhuji jigou* [Government Organization of China] (Beijing: Gaige chubanshe, 1998), pp. 174–351. The organizational charts and staff size of the ministries of Foreign Affairs, National Defense, Committee of National Defense Science and Technology, Public Security, and State Security are not published.

Meeting Status and Bureaucratic Size

For both central party and state agencies, the lack of reported meetings cannot be accounted for by the absence of party organizations in these units. In the party organization, party committees (*dangwei*) are instituted in central party agencies, and party groups (*dangzu*) in central state agencies. Even the smaller agencies in the central and state establishments have party committees and party groups.[23] However, it remains uncertain whether the absence of reported meetings in these agencies is because no meetings were actually held or because meetings were held but not reported. There is no clear set of organizational characteristics that differentiate those with reported meetings by July 23 from those that have not. In terms of institutional status, it is not clear why large and important ministries such as the Ministry of Finance and the National Audit Office did not report having convened any meetings on the Falungong, when small and less consequential agency such as Traditional Chinese Medicine and the Social Security Fund did. Some working departments without reported meetings (the Central Party Archive, Security Committee Office) actually enjoyed greater organizational prestige than those that had convened meetings (Party History Research Office, Mao Tse-tung Writings Editorial Committee). Some mass organizations that met (China Federation of Literati and Artists) are not necessarily more prominent than the one that did not—the State Council Overseas Chinese Office was headed by a Central Committee member.[24] As shown in table 7.3, it appears that a large number of central state agencies that did not report meetings were either the largest or smallest ministries. These include three of the six central ministries with staff sizes of more than 450 (Finance, People's Bank, National Audit Office), and all the five ministries with total staff sizes of fewer than 100 (Foreign Experts, Oceanic Administration, State Surveying, Cultural Relics, Chinese Medicine).

PROVINCIAL-LEVEL MEETINGS

At the next lower administrative stratum, three levels of multiple meetings were also convened in a majority of the 31 provincial units to announce the ban: the top provincial leadership, several provincial bureaucratic agencies, and provincial-level mass organizations, corresponding to the triple stratification at the central level. These meetings were held by the afternoon of July 22.

Provincial Party Committee Meetings

At the top stratum of the provincial political system, the provincial party committee generally convened a meeting for the core leadership of the province,

Table 7.4: Leadership of Provincial Organs

	Province					
Characteristic	Shanxi	Liaoning	Gansu	Jiangsu	Guangdong	Yunnan
Region in China	North	Northeast	Northwest	East	Central-South	Southwest
Party Committee						
No. secretaries	1	1	1	1	1	1
No. deputy secretaries	3	4	5	4	4	3
Provincial Government						
No. governors	1	1	1	1	1	1
No. deputy governors	8	7	6	8	7	7
People's Congress Standing Committee						
No. directors	1	1	1	1	1	1
No. deputy directors	11	8	8	8	7	9
Political Consultative Conference						
No. chairmen	1	1	1	1	1	1
No. vice chairmen	11	11	11	9	10	10
Party Disciplinary Committee						
No. secretaries	1	1	1	1	1	1
No. deputy secretaries	3	3	3	3	3	2

Source: Data for the provincial party committee, provincial government, provincial people's congress, and provincial party disciplinary committees are drawn from ZGZZ, vol. 7, which lists appointments that ended on September 1997. Data for the provincial political consultative conferences are drawn from the latter's Web sites, which list data for 2006.

which is generally made up of the four branches of provincial authorities: (1) the provincial party committee, (2) the provincial government, (3) the provincial people's congress, and (4) the provincial political consultative conference. These are generally referred to as the "Four Leadership Teams" (*sitao banzi*). Sometimes the provincial party disciplinary inspection committee is included as the fifth branch of the provincial core leadership. As shown in table 7.4, the leadership in a selection of provinces across the six administrative regions in China is generally made up of a party secretary (*shuji*), three to five deputy party secretaries, and a standing committee that includes all the secretaries in addition to four to nine party member cadres. The top leadership of the other four branches consists of one director and 7-11 deputy directors (*zhuren*) in the standing committee of the provincial people's congress, one governor (*shengzhang*) and 6-8 deputy governors in the provincial government, one chairman (*zhuxi*) and 9-11 deputy chairmen in the provincial political consultative conference, a secretary, two or three deputy secretaries, and five to seven additional cadres in the standing committee of the provincial party disciplinary committee.[25] As shown in table 7.4, there is not much variation in the top provincial leadership stratum across the six administrative regions in China. The heads of these four or five branches generally constitute the standing committee of the provincial party committee, which have 10-13 members. Those of the provincial party committee are larger and are proportional to the number of party members in the province.

Meetings of Provincial Party and Government Agencies

A second group of provincial-level meetings were those convened in separate venues by the provincial party and government agencies for party cadres and members in their own units. These include both the four to five leadership organs described in the above paragraph and provincial departments. In the former, separate meetings for all party members to view the July 22 CCTV special program announcing the ban were held by the Fujian Provincial People's Congress and the Fujian Provincial Political Consultative Conference, presided respectively by the chairman of the standing committee of the two bodies.[26] Hainan Province convened three meetings for the same two provincial agencies, plus the provincial government general office.[27] On top of these three agencies, Hubei Province also held separate meetings for the provincial disciplinary inspection commission and the standing committee of the party committee of the military district.[28]

Among provincial departments that organized their own study and discussion meetings, the most prominent were those that are functionally related to the banning of the Falungong and have extensive subordinate organizational constituencies. These include several provincial organization departments that convened multiple meetings not only for cadres and party members within their own agencies, but also for subordinate and affiliate organization departments, as well as those in other provincial agencies.[29] Similarly, several provincial propaganda departments also convened meetings for their own bureaucrats and subordinate propaganda departments, as well as media organizations, cultural bureaus, and newspaper editors.[30] Multiple, separate meetings were necessitated by the sheer size of the provincial bureaucracy. Heilongjiang, for instance, which had a population of 36.2 million in 2000,[31] with close to 30,000 cadres and party members in 100 provincial-level party agencies.[32]

Other clusters of provincial agencies that reported convening party meetings include the coercive apparatus of the armed services and public security agencies,[33] party-controlled mass organizations and minor political parties,[34] and higher education agencies.[35]

A glimpse of the extensiveness of provincial agencies that convened meetings on the Falungong can be seen in the news stories in Shanxi Province, which reported separate meetings on banning the Falungong held by its Geology Department, Prison Management Bureau, Agricultural Science Academy, Social Science Academy, Telecommunications Bureau, and the Agricultural Machinery Bureau.[36]

Size and Participants of Provincial Party Committee Meetings

Unlike those at the central level, where the first meeting was a small group of the six to eight top leaders who constitute the party committee in a central party agency or the party group in a central state agency, the first provincial-level meeting was attended by more participants. As shown in table 7.5, this first meeting generally encompassed not only the provincial party secretaries, but also the heads of three other institutions: (1) the provincial bureaucracy—*bu* or *ting* (departments), *wei* (commissions), *ban* (offices), *ju* (bureaus); (2) local governments—*qu* (districts), *zhou* (prefectures), *shi* (cities), *xian* (counties); and (3) field offices of central party and state agencies stationed in the provincial capital (e.g., the People's Liberation Army and Armed Police, State Tax Bureau, Customs Administration, Xinhua news agency). As also shown table 7.5, some provinces also included law enforcement agencies (the Provincial People's Court, Procuracy, Public Security, the Armed Police, Border Patrol, and the Fire Fighting Brigade), and/or heads of party-controlled mass organizations (the Federation of Women, Workers' Union) or those of leading institutes of higher education and research,[37] and those of major enterprises. Although the top leaders of both groups may have been included in the Provincial Party Committee, the enlarged party committee meetings permit larger representation from these agencies. These second-tier political elite generally do not hold membership in the Provincial Party Committee and its more exclusive Standing Committee. As also shown in table 7.5, a majority of

Table 7.5: Reported Meetings of Provincial Party Committees

Province (Source)[a]	Date	Type of Meeting	Role of Party Secretary or Deputy	Participants[b]
Hainan (*HNRB*, 7/23:1)	7/20 P.M.	Party member cadres	Party secretary spoke, deputy party secretary presided the meeting	1A members, 1B,C,D; 2A; 3A (cities, counties, and concerned departments); 4A; 6A; 7A
Xinjiang (*XJRB*, 7/24:1)	7/21 A.M.	Party committee emergency telephone conference	Party secretary presided	2B,2D; 3A; 4A; leaders of divisions of garrison forces
Ningxia (*NXRB*, 7/23:1)	7/21 A.M.	Leading cadres meeting	Party secretary and two deputy secretaries attended	1A,B,C,D; 2A,C; 3A; 4A
Neimonggu (*NMGRB*, 7/24:1)	7/21 A.M.	Enlarged PC SC meeting	Party secretary presided, spoke	
Sichuan (*SCRB*, 7/23:1)	7/21	Chengdu work conference	Chairman of the provincial people's congress standing committee spoke	Responsible persons of 1A,B,C,D; concerned 2A; 3A; 4A
Hubei (*HBRB*, 7/23:1)	7/21	Enlarged meeting of party committee	Provincial party committee standing committee deputy provincial governor presided	
Jilin (*JLRB*, 7/23:1)	7/21	Enlarged meeting of party committee		
Tianjin (*TJRB*, 7/23:1)	7/22, 3 P.M.	Enlarged meeting of party committee	Party secretary presided	Responsible persons of 1A,B,C,D
Beijing (*BJRB*, 7/23:1)	7/22, P.M.	Enlarged meeting of party committee	Party secretary, Mayor presided	
Chongqing (*CQRB*, 7/23:1)	7/22 P.M.	Viewing TV announcement	Party secretary spoke	Municipal leaders
Gansu (*GSRB*, 7/23:1)	7/22 P.M.	Viewing TV announcement	Party secretary spoke	Leaders of 1A,B,C,D
Liaoning (*LNRB*, 7/23:1)	7/22 P.M.	Viewing TV announcement		Leading cadres of 1C, 1A standing committee

(*Continued*)

Table 7.5: Continued

Province (Source)[a]	Date	Type of Meeting	Role of Party Secretary or Deputy	Participants[b]
Yunnan (*YNRB*, 7/23:1)	7/22	Leading cadres of county level or higher	Party secretary spoke	
Guizhou (*GZRB*, 7/23:1)	Before 7/23	1) Meeting of party committee standing committee; 2) provincial leading cadres	Deputy party secretary and provincial governor presided meeting and spoke	Leading responsible persons of 1A,B,C,D; concerned 2A; 3A; 4A; selected 5A, B
Guangdong (*Nanfang RB*, 7/24:1)	7/23 A.M.	Enlarged meeting of party committee standing committee	Party secretary presided	Leaders of 1A,B,C,D; concerned 2A
Guangdong (*MR*, 7/25:1)	7/21	Meeting of leading cadres of cities and counties		
Zhejiang (*ZJRB*, 7/24:1)	Before 7/24	Enlarged meeting of party committee standing committee	Party secretary presided	
Fujian (*FJRB* 7/24:1)	Before 7/24	Enlarged meeting of party committee standing committee	Party secretary presided, spoke	
Guangxi (*GXRB*, 7/25:1)	7/24 A.M.	Enlarged meeting of party committee standing committee		
Jiangsu (*YHRB*, 7/26:1)	7/25 A.M.	Discussion meeting of party committee standing committee and Provincial People's Political Consultative Conference	[a]	

[a]*Hainan ribao, Xinjiang ribao, Ningxia ribao, Neimonggu ribao, Sichuan ribao, Hubei ribao, Jilin ribao, Tianjin ribao, Beijing ribao, Chongqing ribao.*

[b]1A, provincial party committee; 1B, provincial people's congress; 1C, provincial government; 1D, provincial people's political consultative conference; 1E, provincial disciplinary committee. 2A, provincial departments; 2B, provincial departments, committees, offices, bureaus; 2C, provincial units; 2D, provincial directly managed enterprises. 3A, districts, *zhou*, cities, counties. 4A, central party and state agencies stationed in province. 5A, colleges and research institutes; 5B, mass organizations (Women's Federation, Communist Youth League, Workers' Unions); 5C, minority political parties; 5D, business and trade organizations, 6A, provincial armed police, border troops, firefighters. 7A, high court, procuracy.

this first provincial party organization meeting on the Falungong is generally called an Enlarged Meeting of the Provincial Party Committee or its Standing Committee to accommodate these second echelon leaders, a practice stipulated in party manuals.[38] As a result, the size of attendance varies. The April 3, 2002, Guangdong Provincial Party Committee was attended by 880 participants. But at year's end, the same provincial party committee meeting convened on December 23–24 had only around 500 attendees.[39]

Procedure and Venue of Provincial-Level Meetings

Almost all provincial party committees were convened at the provincial capital, at the provincial party and government buildings,[40] as the first of a series of specific conventions on how to deal with the Falungong, and presided by the party secretary. But there are exceptions. The four Gansu Province core leadership group meetings were held not at the provincial or government buildings but at the provincial guest house.[41] Probably due to its vast territory with few air flights among cities in the autonomous region, the Xinjiang Party Committee was convened as a telephone conference (*dianhua huiyi*).[42] In Guangdong Province, the Enlarged Meeting of the Standing Committee of the Provincial Party Committee convened on the morning of July 23 was not the first provincial meeting held on the Falungong. It was convened two days after the provincial meeting for heads of cities and counties on the same subject.[43] There were also exceptions to the rule of the party secretary presiding over party committee meetings at the given administrative level. In lieu of the party secretary, meetings had been presided by the provincial governor in Guizhou, the mayor in Beijing, and the deputy provincial governor in Hubei.[44] It should be noted that while they were not the top party cadres in their province, these officials also held concurrent top positions in their respective provincial party committees.

There were also cases where the Central Committee notice to ban the Falungong was not announced at a special party committee meeting, but was communicated through another provincewide meeting convened on another subject matter at the same time. Henan did not convene any specific party committee meeting on the Falungong on July 22 to July 27 and was likely to have raised the issue in its 6th provincial party congress convened on July 21 and 22.[45] Chongqing Municipality also discussed the Falungong issue in its "Three Represents" Conference when the five core municipal leadership organs met on July 23,[46] as did Gansu Province on the same day.[47] The Yunnan Provincial Party Committee meeting with minor political parties, the Federation of Trade and Industries, and nonparty personnel was probably held during the provincial economy conference around July 23 in the provincial capital.[48]

Timing of Provincial-Level Meetings

By July 22, when the official ban was announced in the media network at 3 P.M., almost all provincial party committees had convened a provincial-level meeting on the Falungong. There were no reports of any such provincial-level meetings held on or before July 19, the date on which the notice was issued. The earliest provincial meetings were reported on July 20, when the Hainan Provincial Party Committee convened a meeting for party cadres that evening.[49] As shown in table 7.5, six other provinces (Xinjiang, Ningxia, Neimonggu, Sichuan, Hubei, and Jilin) had convened meetings by July 21, and six additional provinces (Tianjin, Beijing, Chongqing, Gansu, Liaoning, Yunnan, Guizhou) by July 22. While not reporting any specific dates for its provincial party committee meetings, publication of such meetings in the provincial newspapers from July 22 to 24 suggests that those in Guangdong, Zhejiang, Fujian, and Guangxi were held before July 24. Jiangsu Province convened a discussion meeting of the party committee's standing committee and the provincial political consultative conference on July 25. No provincial-level meetings on the Falungong were reported in Heilongjiang, Jilin, Shanxi, Shaanxi, Anhui, Jiangxi, Shandong, Henan, Tibet, and Qinghai in the July 22–27 issues of the provincial newspapers.[50]

In addition to separate meetings convened by different party and government agencies at different local administrative levels, much larger mobilization efforts were organized to inform party members on the party line on the Falungong. In Shanxi, the provincial government bureaucracy organized a two-day conference for its 60,000 party members on July 21 and 22 to announce the ban, in addition to the other meetings convened by specific provincial bureaucratic agencies.[51] In Guangxi, the provincial party committee organized a even larger event, where the 1.5 million party members spent a special thematic party day (*zhuanti dangri hedong*) on July 24 studying party policy. The event involved 80,000 grassroot party branches from the township level or higher, in the provincial party committee, provincial bureaucracy, armed forces, institutes of higher education, local party and government agencies, enterprises, and urban and rural residential units.[52]

MUNICIPAL AND COUNTY AGENCIES

Below the province level, municipal and county party committees also convened meetings in their own jurisdictions. These meetings have similar stratified structure, participant lists, choice of venues, and timetables as those on the central and provincial levels. At this administrative level, more information on the procedure, agenda, and operational tasks deliberated in these meetings is available in local newspaper reports.

Stratified Structure and Timing

As in higher administrative levels, there was not a single meeting but a series of meetings at the municipal level. Dalian reports the same meeting structure of triple stratification in the afternoon of July 22. Mirroring the provincial level, party members and cadres of the core leadership organs—the municipal party committee, municipal government, municipal people's congress standing committee, and municipal political consultative committee convened a meeting to view the special CCTV program announcing the official ban, after which the municipal party secretary spoke.[53] Simultaneously, a second set of meetings were convened by the justice administration triumvirate (municipal public security bureau, the municipal procuracy, the municipal intermediate court) and mass organizations (the Municipal Main Worker Union, the Communist Youth League, the Women's Federation, and the Municipal Science Federation). As shown in table 7.6, a third set of meetings was convened for cadres and party members of the municipal bureaucracy—from the Bureau of Industry, Finance, and Trade to the Municipal Cultural Bureau—as well as science and research institutes.[54] For comparison, a list of meetings of municipal party, government, and mass organizations of the Qiqihaer Municipality in Heilongjiang Province is presented in table 7.6. In both cities, additional meetings were convened by the party committees in large city-managed enterprises, including both heavy industrial companies as well as commercial and financial consortia. In addition, Dalian reported meetings for urban districts within the municipality and subordinate cities under its jurisdiction.

Reports from several provinces suggest that these meetings were held by July 24. Where specific dates for these local meetings are available, the subprovincial party committees of Anhui, Heilongjiang, Henan, Hubei, and Liaoning had convened meetings on July 22 and 23 (table 7.7). Elsewhere, the party committees of 14 districts and municipalities of Fujian Province each convened separate meetings for its cadres on July 22.[55] Those of 14 districts and municipalities of Guangxi Province had done so by July 23, while those of 19 municipalities and counties of Hainan Province had also convened their meetings by July 24.[56]

Participants, Venues, and Size of Municipal-Level Meetings

Participants of municipal-level meetings also resembled those of central and provincial levels in institutional divisions. As shown in table 7.8, participant lists of meetings in the 16 subordinate cities in Hubei Province are rather typical. The core municipal party and government leadership is generally

Table 7.6: Convention of Meetings in Dalian and Qiqihaer Municipalities

Agency	Dalian (Liaoning), 7/22 P.M.	Qiqihaer (Heilongjiang)
Core municipal leadership organs	Party Committee, Government, People's Congress Standing Committee, Political Consultative Conference	Party Committee, People's Congress, Political Consultative Conference, Disciplinary Committee
Municipal bureaucracy	Public Security, Procuracy, Intermediate Courts, Industry, Finance, Trade, Supplies and Marketing Association, Urban Construction, Planning, Real Estate, Environment Protection, Culture Bureau	Disciplinary, Procuracy, and Surveillance cadres convened by the Party Disciplinary Committee; Urban and Village Enterprises Management Bureau; Culture Market Management Office
Mass organizations	Main Workers' Union, Communist Youth League, Women's Federation, Science Federation	Main Workers' Union, Communist Youth League, Minor political parties; Federation of Industries and Commerce; Democratic Federation; Science Federation; Qigong Society; Literature Federation
Enterprises	New Boat Construction Plant, Elevator Enterprises, Heavy Machinery Co., Commercial Group, Friendship Group, Tianbai Group	Heilong Group, Hongying Group, Faluerji Power Plant, Beibo Plant
Subordinate cities	Luxun, Jingzhou, Wafangdian, Pulandian, Zhuanghe, Changhai	
Urban districts	Zhongshan, Sigang, Shahekou, Ganjingji	

Source: *Dalian ribao*, July 23 and 24, 1999, p. 1; *Qiqihaer ribao*, July 24, 1999, p. 1.

represented by the standing committee of the municipal party committee, which includes the heads of the municipal government, the chairman of the standing committee of the municipal people's congress, the chairman of the standing committee of the municipal political consultative conference, and often the chairman of the municipal party disciplinary committee as well. The top officials of the municipal party and government agencies include

Table 7.7: Dates of Convention of City and County Party Committee Meetings in Five Provinces

Date	Henan	Hubei	Anhui	Liaoning	Heilongjiang
			Province		
July 21			Liu An, Chuzhou		
July 22	Anyang, Luoyang, Kaifeng, Luhe, Sanmenxia, Zhumadian, Zhaozuo, Zhiyuan, Xinyang, Hebi, Zhoukou	Huangshi, Suizhou, Xiantao, Shennongjia Forestry Region	An Qing, Tongling	Shenyang, Dalian, Fuxun, Benxi, Jinzhou, Chaoyang	Heihe, Yichun, Harbin, Jiamusi, Binxian, Qiqihaer, Suihua, Daqing, (Mingshui, Anda City, Wangqui, Zhaodong, Hailun), Shuangyashan, Hegang, Qitaihe
July 23		Jingzhou, Huanggang, Jingmen, Xiangfan, Xinaming, Shiyan, Qianjiang	Chizhou		
July 22 and 23		Yichang, Xiaogan, Yuezhou, Ensi, Tianmen	Huaibei, Maanshan, Wuhu, Hefei, Fuyang		
July 24			Chaohu		
Unspecified	Xuchang				
Unreported					

Source: *Hubei ribao*, July 24, 1999, pp. 1, 4; *Henan ribao*, July 26, 1999, pp. 1, 5; *Anhui ribao*, July 2, 1999, July 27, 1999, p. 1; *Heilongjiang ribao*, July 24, 1999, pp. 1, 2.

those of municipal departments (*bu*), offices (*ban*), committees (*wei*), and bureaus (*ju*). Those of subordinate cities and counties include county-level cadres above deputy rank (*fuxianji*), as specified in Yichang, Jingman, and Huangshi cities. There was explicit mention of attendance by "some retired and on-leave cadres" in Huangshi and Shiyan cities. Participation of representatives from mass organizations was not the norm and was reported only in Tianmen City, Ensi District, and Shennongjia Forest District.[57]

Table 7.8: City and County Meetings in Hubei Province

City/County	Date	Meetings
Yichang City	7/22, 23	Meetings of (1) standing committee of municipal Party committee; (2) heads of municipal party and government departments (*bu*), offices (*ban*), committees (*hui*), and bureaus (*ju*); (3) county-level cadres above deputy rank (*fuxianji*)
Jingzhou City	7/23	Thematic meetings (*zhuanti huiyi*) of (1) municipal party committee and (2) district party committees of city and counties
Xiaogan City	7/22. 23	Emergency meetings of (1) municipal party committee and (2) municipal government
Huanggang City	7/23	Discussion meeting and viewing of special TV program convened by the municipal party committee and municipal government
Jingmen City	7/23	Meeting of county-level cadres above deputy rank
Huangshi City	7/22	Meeting and viewing of special TV program of county-level cadres above deputy rank and some retired and on-leave cadres
Xiangfan City	7/23	Party and government cadres meeting for subordinate districts of cities and counties and municipal party and government agencies
Xianning City	7/23	Discussion meeting for party cadres of municipal party committee and government
Shiyan City	7/22, 23	Meeting for county-level cadres and some retired and on-leave cadres
Yuezhou City	7/23	Meeting for heads of agencies of Municipal Party Committee and government
Ensi District (zhou)	7/23	Study meeting for cadres and masses convened by the district party committee and government
Qianjiang City	7/22, 23	Meeting for party cadres in municipal party and government agencies to view TV program
Chuizhou	7/22	Emergency meeting for party cadres convened by municipal party committee
Tianmen City	7/22, 23	Meeting for cadres and masses to view TV program
Xiantao City	7/23	Study and discussion meeting of party cadres convened by municipal party committee and government
Shennongjia Forest District	7/22	Meeting for cadres and masses to view TV program

Source: *Hubei ribao*, July 24, 1999, pp. 1, 4.

Most news stories did not report on the venues and size of municipal meetings. Where available, many were held in the premises of their respective organizations, as were the 11 districts and cities of Jiangxi Province.[58] The Dalian meeting for its core leadership organs was convened in the electronic room of the municipal party committee office, where viewing of the special television program was done in high-tech style.[59] Sometimes, the municipal meeting was not convened in a single venue but multiple sites, as was the Harbin meeting for its municipal bureaucracy, where its 20,000 party members and cadres assembled in 150 sites to view the special television program and listen to speeches by municipal leaders followed by discussion within each separate site, where slightly more than 100 individuals engaged in face-to-face interaction.[60] Elsewhere, Qiqihaer Municipality also reported separate breakout sessions after the collective viewing of the television program and the party secretary speech.[61]

Procedures and Agenda of Municipal Meetings

As in the central and provincial levels, municipal party committee meetings are generally presided by the party secretary.[62] If the meeting was held at 3 P.M. on July 22, the basic agenda was to view the two-hour special television program announcing the ban on the Falungong. For party meetings convened before the nationally televised program, the common agenda item was studying the July 19 Central Committee notice banning the Falungong. The task was generally introduced by the party secretary, who summarized the document and expounded on the "spirit" of the document.[63] Municipal meetings convened after July 22 might also include documents promulgated by the ministries of Civil Affairs, Personnel, and Public Security issued that day,[64] while those that were convened after the provincial party committee meeting might also include a discussion of the provincial party secretary speech and the provincial party committee notice as well as the Central Committee notice.[65] Where the study of multiple documents were tasked, the party secretary first made introductory remarks, followed by one or two deputy party secretaries speaking respectively on the Central Committee notice and provincial party committee document or provincial party secretary speech.[66] Expression of support of the Central Committee decision and endorsement of the documents and speeches were part of the standard routine of these meetings. To illustrate with the report on the Harbin municipal bureaucracy meeting, the named and titled individuals voicing support of the Central Committee decision included six leaders of the minor, democratic political parties, two students from the Harbin Medical College and from the Mechanical Engineering Department of the Harbin Industrial University, the deputy party secretary of the Northeast Agricultural University, a director of the residence committee of the city's Taiping District, the party secretary of the Harbin Airplane Manufacturing Co., and a staff person of the Hexin Company.[67]

Report and Assignment of Operational Tasks

Municipal meetings on the Falungong often include business items where operational tasks on the banning of the Falungong were discussed and assigned. A Lanzhou municipal meeting included a report of the registration of Falungong practitioners in its Chengguan District.[68] The meeting of cadres of the Women's Federation in Daqing received a briefing on how various municipal units carried out activities to ban the Falungong,[69] as did the leading cadres of Maoming Municipality.[70] In its meeting of municipal agency cadres, the Jiamusi municipal party committee established a leading work group to deal with the Falungong, made plans for Falungong work, and issued a notice on initiating study and education activities.[71] More detailed information was reported in various meetings of municipal agencies in Dalian. Its marine court meeting deliberated on plans to investigate and educate security agents and their families who practiced Falungong. The meeting of the Federation of Handicapped People organized visits to homes of the disabled to identify the extent of Falungong penetration. The judiciary bureau meeting discussed strategies to contact attorneys who undertook cases of Falungong practitioners. The procuracy meetings arranged procuracy leaders to meet with Falungong practitioners within the procuracy system. The Jingzhou District compiled a detailed registry for each practitioner and assigned individual projects to educate Falungong leaders.[72]

Study Sessions

To comply with the stipulation in the Central Committee notice that a study program needs to be launched to educate every party member on the Falungong, study meetings often follow municipal party committee meetings.[73] In a rare report of such meetings, the Department of Propaganda in Maoming City in Guangdong Province disclosed its education program for party members, stipulating that party branches in party and government agencies, enterprises, mass organizations, schools, and urban communities should work mornings but spend afternoons studying the official policy on the Falungong from July 26 through the end of the month. A lighter study schedule was prescribed from August 1 on for an indefinite period where party members were required to spend two to three and a half days per week in such studies. The least burdensome study load was imposed on party committees in industrial plants and mines, where they were expected to spend at least half a day per week in the study.[74]

The Maoming Propaganda Department also published a list of party and state documents that formed the content in these study meetings: (1) the

Central Committee notice banning the Falungong; (2) the Xinhua news agency list of deaths, injuries, and sickness allegedly caused by Falungong; (3) the Xinhua special report on Li Hongzhi; (4) the notices of the ministries of Civil Affairs, Personnel, and Public Security; (5) *Renmin ribao* editorials on Falungong; (6) the Constitution of the Chinese Communist Party, Preamble and chapters 1 and 7; and (7) reference materials published by the Guangdong Province Propaganda Department.[75] The study list was by no means uniform in the number or documents across localities in China. As shown in table 7.9, the study lists of another two municipalities had only four documents, and a Xinjiang County list consisted of only three. Only the Central Committee notice was common among the four study lists. The Xinhua list of deaths and injuries

Table 7.9: Documents in Study Meetings

Documents	Tianjin	Maoming City, Guangdong	Qiqihar City, Heilongjiang	Bachu County, Xinjiang
Central Committee notice on banning the Falungong	X	X	X	X
Xinhua list of deaths, injuries, and sickness allegedly caused by the Falungong	X	X		X
Xinhua special report on Li Hongzhi	X	X		
Notices of the ministries of Civil Affairs, Personnel, and Public Security	X	X		
Renmin ribao editorials on the Falungong		X		X
Jiang Zemin's speeches and comments to the Politburo on the Falungong			X	
Constitution, Preamble and chapters 1 and 7		X		
Regulations of the Chinese Communist Party			X	
Reference materials published by Guangdong Province Propaganda Department		X		
Speeches by the Heilongjiang and Qiqihaer party secretaries			X	

Sources: *Tianjin ribao*, July 26, 1999, p. 1; *Maoming ribao*, July 27, 1999, p. 1; *Qiqihar ribao*, July 27, 1999, p. 1; *Xinjiang ribao*, August 9, 1999, p. 2.

Table 7.10: Urban District Meetings

Date/Time	City/Urban District	Meeting	Agenda
7/22	Lanzhou/Qilihe	Party committee and district government, party member cadres and masses	Viewing CCTV news
7/22 A.M.	Lanzhou/ Chengguang	Standing Committee	Analyzed situation of Falungong practitioners registered on July 21 and organized them to view CCTV news
7/22 P.M.	Jiamusi/Sijiao	Party committee	Viewing CCTV news, studying municipal meeting speeches
7/22	Daqing/Honggang	Party committee cadres	Studying Central Committee notice
After 7/22 but before 7/26	Daqing/Honggang	Two meetings of party members subdivision (*ke*)-level cadres, retired and on-leave cadres, enterprise management cadres	
Before 7/26	Daqing/Xianhulu	Party member cadres	Viewing notices of Central Committee, ministries of Civil Affairs and Public Security
Before 7/26	Daqing/Datong	Party member cadres	Studying Central Committee notice, provincial and municipal party committee speeches

Source: *Lanzhou wanbao*, July 24, 1999, p. 1; *Jiamusi ribao*, July 23, 1999, p. 1; *Daqing ribao*, July 26, 1999, p. 1.

allegedly caused by Falungong practice was included in three, the Xinhua special report on Li Hongzi and *Renmin ribao* editorials were each included in two study lists. Conspicuously absent in most study lists were the Chinese Communist Party Constitution and Jiang Zemin's speeches, which were stipulated twice in the Central Committee notice as part of the required reading material in the study session. Each of these was included in only one of the four study lists.[76]

SUBMUNICIPAL-LEVEL MEETINGS

Below the municipal level, urban districts in cities, and counties under the municipal jurisdiction also held meetings on the Falungong. There is little difference in the timing, structure, scope of participation, and agenda setting in these meetings compared with those on the municipal and higher administrative levels. As shown in table 7.10, most of the reported meetings were convened on July 22, when the ban was televised nationally on CCTV. Most urban district meetings were attended by party member cadres, although mass organizations were also included in the Qilihe District in Lanzhou Municipality.[77] At least the Honggang District of Daqing Municipality convened multiple meetings, where the first meeting was attended by party member cadres, and two subsequent meetings by party member cadres who were at the subdivision level, those managing enterprises, retired cadres, and cadres on leave.[78] The meeting agenda was similar to those on higher administrative levels, with viewing and studying the Central Committee notice as the dominant task. The content of the study also included provincial- and municipal-level party committee speeches. There was at least one report with a business agenda item in the Chengguan District meeting in Lanzhou Municipality, when its standing committee analyzed the situation of Falungong practitioners who have registered the evening before.[79]

County-Level Meetings

At the county level, most reported meetings were held by July 23, when both the Benlan and Yuzhong counties of Lanzhou Municipality convened their meetings. The Benlan County meeting was attended by all county-level cadres of counties, townships, and villages, as well as cadres of provincial and city units stationed in the county. The types of participants at the Yuzhong County meeting were not reported, but 1,000 people attended the meeting.[80] That size of county-level meetings was apparently not uncommon. Fujian's Xiapu County also convened three separate meetings each with more than 1,000 for party members, cadres, and nonparty cadres on July 22.[81]

More detailed information is available for Dianbai County in Maoming Municipality in Guangdong Province. As shown in table 7.11, no fewer than five meetings were convened, the first on the morning of July 21, when party member cadres of county-bureau level and higher met to study central party and state documents. A second meeting was held on the following morning with a business item, attended by cadres of the five core county organizations (party committee, people's congress, government, party disciplinary committee, political consultative committee), who studied the spirit of the July 21 meeting and discussed its implementation in the county. The

Table 7.11: Meetings in Dianbai County, Maoming Municipality, Guangdong

Date/Time	Meeting Participants	Agenda
7/21 a.m.	Party member cadres of county-bureau level of higher	Studying the central party and state documents
7/22 a.m.	Leaders of the five core county organizations (party committee, people's congress, government, party disciplinary committee, political consultative committee)	Studying the spirit of the 7/21 meeting of leading cadres of cities and counties of the province and discussing its implementation in the county
7/22 p.m.	2,000 party member cadres of division (*ke*) or higher, directors of party committee offices, public security precincts of subordinate townships, party member cadres of branch (*gu*) level or higher in county-administered enterprises, party member cadres who are retired or on leave, principals of high schools, main responsible people of state-owned enterprises, province and city agencies stationed in the county	Studying the Central Committee and the spirit of provincial party committee conference
7/22 P.M.	Party member cadres of the five core county organizations, those of townships and enterprises	Viewing the special news program of CCTV
7/23 P.M.	Discussion meeting of various social groups	Repudiating the Falungong

Source: *Maoming ribao*, July 25, 1999, p. 1.

largest meeting was convened in the afternoon of July 22, when 2,000 party member cadres gathered to view the CCTV announcement and study the Central Committee and provincial party documents. The categories of participants in this large county meeting are shown in table 7.11.[82] A meeting held later that evening was attended by party member cadres of five core county organizations and those of township enterprises. A fifth meeting was reported on the morning of July 23, when representatives of social groups gathered to express support for the ban on Falungong.[83]

Meetings in Townships, Enterprises, and Villages

On an even lower administrative echelon, there were also reports of meetings on the Falungong at the township, enterprise, and village levels. It is not clear when they were convened. The publication dates on July 29 and 31 in the municipal newspapers could mean that they were convened several days later than municipal and urban district-level meetings, or that these were held around the same time but considered less newsworthy and published later. At this administrative level, multiple meetings were also convened at the Changqi Township of Huazhou in Guangdong's Maoming City, respectively, for (1) the core township authorities (party committee, government, people's congress); (2) party member cadres of township government and villages; (3) party members of the township bureaucracy; and (4) party members of party branches at the village level.[84] Elsewhere, Yangzao Township of the same city also convened separate emergency meetings for the township's party committee, government, people's congress, and political consultative conference and secretaries of subordinate party branches, followed by separate meetings for all party members convened by each of the 46 party branches. The agenda was similar to its organizational superiors, consisting of studying the Central Committee notice and the decisions of the Ministry of Civil Affairs and the Ministry of Public Security.[85] Provincial, municipal, and urban district-level directives were included in the study session of neighboring Shengzheng Township, which studied documents issued by the Central Committee, Guangdong Province, Maoming City, and Southern Maoming District.[86]

There were also sporadic reports of meetings at the enterprise level, which were convened from July 22 though 24, and almost all in urban areas. It should be noted that the Yongji Thermal Plant in Shanxi was reported to have organized a meeting for all cadres and workers to view the television news on July 21.[87] As noted in chapter 1, the meeting was most probably convened on July 22 rather than a day earlier. The enterprises included large industrial manufactories (First Auto Group in Changchun, Auto Tire Co. of Hangzhou, the Shaanxi Eastern Machinery Factory, Qilu Petrochemical in

Jinan, Shandong), a public utility (Yongji Thermal Plant in Shanxi), a commercial retail company (First Department Store of Qiqihaer), and hospitality service (Gold Coast Luodun Hotel in Haikou, Hainan Province). At the Qilu Petrochemical Co., the meeting was convened by the company party committee for subordinate party branches and party cells also on July 23.[88] The agenda was generally to view the CCTV news program, and to study the Central Committee notice.[89] But now and then some special effort was reported. In the Auto Tire Group of Hangzhou, the senior engineer Huang Zhuyuan wrote an article on the evening of July 22 repudiating the Falungong and sent to the company broadcast station, which broadcast it during the lunch break the following day.[90] These meetings appeared to have been held on company time, at least for the television viewing, which was broadcast on a Thursday at 3 P.M. In addition to scheduling several viewings of the CCTV news program, the First Department Store in Qiqihaer also convened discussion meetings at least from July 23 to 25 before the store opened for business.[91] Several enterprises organized multiple meetings. The Shaanxi Eastern Machinery Factory convened six, while the First Auto Group reported a first emergency meeting for heads of party organization and enterprise management on the afternoon of July 24, followed by separate study classes for party secretaries of basic unit party committees in its No. 1 Casting Plant.[92]

There is a virtual absence of reports on meetings at the village level. The absence could be due to the lack of party committees at the lowest organizational level. The only reported such meetings were convened by the Gao An City Party Committee of Jiangxi Province, which convened seven meetings for leaders of Huabinshan Village and 14 for its *apparatchiks* to deal with the Falungong.[93]

CONCLUSION

From top-level party and state agencies in the national capital to the basic-level enterprises, residential committees, and villages, a series of meetings on the Falungong were convened by party committees on the central, provincial, municipal, county, township, and village levels, following the official ban of the Falungong announced on July 22, 1999. At each administrative level, multiple meetings were convened for different substrata. The first meeting was generally attended by the core leadership organs of political authority, consisting of the party committee, the government, the people's congress, the political consultative committee, and sometimes the party disciplinary committee. A second meeting was held for officials who head the party and government agencies, followed by a third meeting of the cadres and all party members. Often, other meetings are convened for party members in the outer ring of mass organizations, colleges, and research institutes and those in government-owned enterprises. While the timing of the meetings within each administrative stratum is generally sequential, they were not in descending chronological order as one moves from a higher to lower administrative levels. Provincial-level meetings did not begin only after those on the central level ended, and those on the municipal and county levels did not follow those on the central and provincial levels. They were convened mostly in the 72-hour period from July 20 to the afternoon of July 22, when the news to ban the Falungong was broadcast nationwide. By then, a great majority of the more than 60 million party members in the 158,596 party committees, 179,884 main party branches, and 3,175,393 party branches would have attended a party committee meeting announcing the ban on the Falungong.[94]

The foregoing suggests a system of convening intraparty meetings that are highly orchestrated across administrative levels and among different party and state agencies, where the Politburo took the initiative and prepared the document that set the meeting agenda, and subordinate levels disseminated the political message through a series of meetings that cloned the structure, procedure, agenda, format, and participants of central-level conventions. The goal was to forge a consensus among all members of the party, who are expected to voice support for the policy. Bred to conform and nurtured to comply, the entire party then acts as the proverbial chess game, where different pieces move with one mind at the marching order of the Politburo. As far as party meetings are concerned, in 1999 as in 1949, democratic centralism still reigns.

Chapter Eight

Evaluation of the Anti-Falungong Campaign

This chapter presents an assessment of the capacity and effectiveness of China's anti-Falungong efforts. It begins with an evaluation of the media campaign waged by the official television, radio, and national press, followed by that of the publication campaign. Both assessments examine not only the quantity of the official media output but also the efficacy of propaganda productions, as well as the degree of collaboration among different media institutions. The last section presents an analysis of the effectiveness of the conversion program, official statistics on the number of Falungong practitioners who have severed their ties with the sect, and those of Falungong sources that show the number of practitioners who have publicly retracted such statements.

EVALUATION OF THE MEDIA CAMPAIGN

In the media campaign against the Falungong, the regime had at its disposal the vast resources of a colossal establishment, which consisted of 2,038 newspapers, 566 publishers, 352 television stations, and 299 radio stations.[1] Given the market reforms where leading national media organizations now derive the lion's share of their corporate revenue from advertising income rather than state subsidies, the question is whether China's newspapers, television, and radio would be responsive to the state's propaganda needs. Chapter 4 showed that in the first month of the government assault on the Falungong, the national media generated 1,650 Xinhua news releases, 780 *Renmin ribao* (*RMRB*) stories, and 1,722 news clips from the apex of its establishment alone. There is thus no doubt that the regime-controlled media network in China could generate the propaganda output on regime demand. I now address the issue of efficacy and efficiency of these propaganda productions. Specifically, were these anti-Falungong news stories and programs quality products that have won industry awards, and received high reception ratings? After all, the ultimate test of the propaganda pudding is in the consumption rather than production.

Given the competitive nature of the media market in China, there is also need to examine the extent to which different media acted in a coordinated or competitive fashion in content production and dissemination. In particular, this section analyzes the degree to which different media agencies participated in news coproduction and coauthorship endeavors and engaged in thematic and geographic specialization of news and commentary production. For content dissemination, I investigate the extent to which media organizations shared news stories and commentaries and coordinated their publication and broadcast schedules, and whether the phasing of the campaign was coterminous among different media agencies. I identified collaboration in using the official Xinhua news releases, in commentary distribution, and in residual publication, but this was rare in news coproduction and thematic specialization, program and publication scheduling, and the phasing of the campaign.

Vertical Coordination

Coordination of the complex anti-Falungong campaign could be achieved vertically or horizontally. Vertical coordination can result from hierarchical management, where administrative superordinates instruct organizational subordinates to march in locked step to the rhythm of the same martial tune. In contrast to this top-down imposed uniformity, coordination can also result from horizontal collaboration among different media organizations, where they can engage in joint production and distribution for mutual benefit. In the Falungong media campaign, there was strong vertical but weak horizontal coordination among the media organizations. Vertical coordination is clearly evidenced by (1) the uniform publication and placement of important policy statements and news items, (2) the role of Xinhua news agency in producing and disseminating important releases, and (3) the reprinting of special commentaries composed by authoritative organizations. Horizontal coordination among media organizations was infrequent and can be seen in the areas of broadcast scheduling, cosponsorship, and residual publication. It was rare in news coproduction and thematic specialization and in program and publication scheduling.

Uniform Publication and Placement of News Items

Vertical coordination can be seen in the pattern of uniform publication of important news items and policy announcements. As shown in table 4.2 (see chapter 4), the 10 major central party and state policy statements promulgated on July 23 and July 24 were all published in their full texts by the six leading national dailies in China (*RMRB, Guangming ribao* [*GMRB*], *Jiefangjun bao* [*JFJB*], *Jingji ribao* [*JJRB*], *Zhongguo qingnian bao* [*ZGQNB*], and *Gongren ribao* [*GRRB*]). For the five policy documents on July 23, four (the notices of the Central Committee, Ministry of Civil Affairs, and Ministry of Public Security and the *RMRB* editorial) were identically placed on the front page of the national dailies. The fifth, a special report of the Ministry of Public Security on Li Hongzhi, was placed not on p. 1 but on p. 4 in *RMRB*, and p. 2 in the other five dailies. Aside from these five important documents, an additional 18 news stories on the July 23 issue of *RMRB* were classified as "important news," but these were not published by all the other five major national dailies on July 24. The same pattern of uniform publication of a separate set of the same five central policy documents (out of 32 important news items in *RMRB*) on the six major dailies on July 24 confirms the pattern. In this case, all five major government policy documents (notices of the News and Publications Bureau [NPB], the Personnel Department, the Communist Youth League; speeches to reporters by the organization department and the propaganda department) were all published in their full texts on the same day. As presented in table 4.3 (see chapter 4), the 31 provincial newspapers also show the same publication and placement pattern, printing the same set of four policy documents on the front page, the Public Security Ministry's special report on Li Hongzhi on a separate page on July 23, and the same separate set of five policy documents on July 24 outside the front page. This pattern of (1) publishing the full text and title of five important documents on July 23 in all six major national dailies and 31 provincial dailies, (2) uniform placement of the same set of four on p. 1, (3) placement of the five items mostly outside the front page, (4) publishing the same set of five policy documents in full text on July 24 in all six major national and 31 provincial dailies, and (5) placement of these outside the front page, is clear evidence of vertical coordination probably dictated by the Propaganda Department, the organizational superiors of all the national and provincial dailies.

Special Role of Xinhua in Authoritative News Production and Dissemination

The special role of the Xinhua as China's official news agency in news production and dissemination is also part of the vertical coordination scheme in the anti-Falungong media campaign. First, Xinhua acts as the official news hub and distributor, dispatching editorials, commentaries, and special articles from one national daily to another.[2] News stories and commentaries reprinted in newspapers carry not only bylines of the original publisher but also Xinhua datelines. Suggestive of Xinhua's authoritativeness, state and party notices published in printed media carry Xinhua datelines, while radio and television announcers give specific attribution to each Xinhua story.

Second, both during and outside the media campaign, China's media organizations published authoritative news releases and commentaries prepared

Table 8.1: Anti-Falungong Authoritative Commentaries of Xinhua in *RMRB, GMRB,* and *JFJB*

Date	RMRB	GMRB	JFJB
7/23	*RMRB* Ed. 1 (1); Ministry of Public Security article on life of Li Hongzhi (2)	Reprints 1, 2	*JFJB* Ed. 1; reprints 1, 2;
7/24	NPB article repudiating Li Hongzhi's theory (3)	Reprints 3	Reprints 3
7/26	*RMRB* C-1 (4)	*GMRB* Ed. 1; reprints 4	*JFJB* Ed. 2; reprints 4; *Qiushi* commentary
7/27	Xinhua GC (5); *RMRB* C-2 (6)	Reprints 5, 6; *GMRB* Ed. 2	*JFJB* Ed. 3; excerpts 5, reprints 6
7/28		*GMRB* Ed. 3	
7/29	*RMRB* C-3 (7)	Reprints 7, *GMRB* Ed. 4	*JFJB* Ed. 4; reprints 7, *Qiushi* commentary
7/30	*RMRB* C-4 (8); Xinhua story (9)	Reprints 8; 9; *GMRB* Ed. 5	Reprints 8, 9
7/31	Xinhua GC (10)	Reprints 10	*JFJB* Ed. 5; reprints 10, and *Qiushi* commentary
8/1	*Qiushi* Ed. (11)		Reprints 11
8/2	Xinhua GC (12)	*GMRB* Ed. 6	Reprints 12, excerpts
8/3	Xinhua GC (13)	*GMRB* Ed. 7	Reprints 13, excerpts
8/4	*RMRB* C-5 (14); Xinhua GC (15)	Xinhua reporters (16); Reprints 14, *GMRB* Ed. 8	Reprints 15, 16
8/5	Xinhua GC (17)	Xinhua reporters (18)	Exp. 17, reprints 18
8/6	*RMRB* C-6 (19), Xinhua GC (20), excerpts	Reprints 19	Reprints 19, 20, *JJRB* commentary
8/9	*RMRB* C-7 (21)	Reprints 21	Reprints 21
8/11			*JFJB* Ed. 6
8/12	*RMRB* C-8 (22)	Reprints 22	Reprints 22
8/13	Xinhua, *RMRB* reporters on 4/25 (23); *RMRB* commentary (24)	Reprints 23, 24	*JFJB* Ed. 7; reprints 23, 24
8/16	*RMRB* C-9 (25)	Reprints 25	Reprints 25
8/17			*JFJB* Ed. II-1
8/18	*RMRB* SC (26)	Reprints 26	*JFJB* Ed. II-2; reprints 26
8/20	*RMRB* SC (27)	Reprints 27	*JFJB* Ed. II-3; reprints 27
8/22		*GMRB* SC	
8/23	*RMRB* SC (27)	Reprints 27	Reprints 27; *JFJB* Ed. II-4

Abbreviations: C, Ed., editorial; GC, guest commentator; SC, special commentary; Numbers with no parentheses in the *GMRB* and *JFJB* columns refer to the parenthesized number in the *RMRB* and *GMRB* columns.

by Xinhua. In that capacity, Xinhua acted as the primary producer of three types of authoritative news releases on the Falungong. First, the set of official notices to ban the Falungong announced on July 22 and 23, 1999, all carried Xinhua datelines: the three core announcements by the Central Committee, the Ministry of Civil Affairs, and the Ministry of Public Security, issued on July 22 and referred to in the preceding section, as well as supplementary communications and press conferences by leading party and state agencies published on the following day.[3] Second, Xinhua also prepared special investigative reports on the Falungong that were based on extensive intelligence gathering and in-depth research supported by expert legal opinion that less resourceful media channels lacked the capacity to produce. Its reports on the April 25 siege of the Zhongnanhai, the 18 major protest rallies organized by the Falungong, and the 180 cases of deaths, injuries, and insanity allegedly caused by Falungong practice[4] all required sustained painstaking research on classified information in multiple locations. Third, Xinhua also organized the writing of a set of special commentaries on the Falungong by top party and state agencies, including the Central Organization Department, the Ministry of Civil Affairs, the Ministry of Justice, the Ministry of Health, and the Communist Youth League, signed under the name of "Xinhua Guest Commentator" (*Xinhua Teyao Pinglunyuan*). These investigative reports and authoritative commentaries were generally published with their original titles and full text on the front page on the same or following day in China's major national dailies,[5] as shown in table 8.1.

Collaboration in News Commentary Production and Reprinting

Aside from Xinhua, leading national printed media also compose their own news commentaries on the Falungong, and reprint those of other major media organizations. The Party's theoretical journal *Qiushi*, and the three major national dailies—the party organ *RMRB*, the military daily *JFJB*, and the newspaper for intellectuals *GMRB* each published its own commentary series that included (1) the editorial, (2) official in-house commentary, (3) guest commentary written by outside authors, and (4) special investigative reports prepared by Xinhua and/or *RMRB* reporters, authored by party and state agencies. As shown in table 8.2, *GMRB* and *JFJB* published only one set of authoritative commentary (the editorial), *Qiushi* had two (*Qiushi* editorial and commentary), *RMRB* had four (editorial, commentary, guest commentary, *Jinritan* column), and Xinhua had one guest commentary series and special investigative reports.

These special commentaries and reports were reprinted with different timing and level of completeness by the elite national printed media, generally reflecting the authoritativeness of the source. As shown in table 8.2, all

Table 8.2: Reprinting of Authoritative Commentaries among National Press

Commentary Type	Xinhua Dateline	Published Same Day, Full title and Text			
		In *RMRB,*	In *GMRB,*	In *JFJB,*	In *Qiushi*
Xinhua special commentary	7/27, 31; 8/2–6	Y	Y/N[a]	Y/N[b]	N
RMRB editorial	7/23	Y	Y	Y	Y
RMRB special commentary	8/18, 20	Y	Y	Y	N
RMRB commentary	7/26, 27, 29, 30; 8/4, 6, 9, 12, 13, 16	Y	Y	Y	N
RMRB column *Jinritan*	7/25; 8/3, 4, 5, 6, 7, 8, 10, 11, 12, 14, 15, 17, 19, 22[c]	Y	N	N	N
Qiushi editorial	8/1	Y	N	Y	Y
Qiushi commentary	8/16[d]	N	N	Y/N[d]	Y
GMRB editorial	7/25, 27, 28, 29, 30; 8/2, 3, 4	N	Y	N	N
JFJB editorial	7/23, 26, 27, 29, 31; 8/11, 13, 17, 18, 20, 23	N	N	Y	Y/N[e]

Of the 10 *JFJB* editorials, only the 7/23 editorial was published in *Qiushi.*
[a]*GMRB* published the Xinhua special commentary articles of 7/31, but not those of 8/2–6.
[b]*JFJB* published the full title and text of Xinhua special Commentary articles of 7/31, 8/4, and 8/6 but not 8/5 and only in excerpts of 8/2 and 8/3.
[c]There were two *Jinritan* columns published on August 12.
[d]*Qiushi,* August 16 issue published three articles signed "*Qiushi* commentator."
[e]*JFJB* published the *Qiushi* commentaries on 7/26 and 7/29.

13 items in the three sets of *RMRB* commentaries (1 editorial, 2 commentaries, and 10 guest commentaries) were published by *GMRB* and *JFJB,* on the same day, with their original titles and full text. But all 14 contributions of *RMRB*'s fourth minor series (*Jinritan*) were not published in any other dailies. The seven Xinhua guest commentaries were published in *RMRB* on the same day with their original title and text; four of these were also published by *JFJB* in the same mode, and the other three were excerpted.[6] The *GMRB* published only the July 31, 1999, Xinhua guest commentary, but not the other six. As a general rule, *GMRB* and *JFJB* editorials were not published or excerpted by *RMRB* or by each other. As a monthly periodical, *Qiushi* generally does not reprint special commentaries and investigative reports of other news organizations that would have appeared in print in multiple publications by *Qiushi*'s monthly publication dates.[7]

Table 8.3: Publication Dates of Anti-Falungong Book Series, 1999–2000

Publication Date	On Materialism	On Atheism	On Popular Science	Cumulative Total
Before July 1999	3	2	15	20
July 1999	5	10	0	35
August 1999	4	14	3	56
September 1999	2	2	10	70
October 1999	3	2	6	81
November 1999	1	0	3	85
December 1999	1	8	9	103
2000	1	2	12	117
Unscheduled	0	1	2	120
Total	20	40	60	120

Source: *Zhongguo chuban nianjian*, 2000, pp. 470–472.

Cosponsorship and Residual Publication

Media organizations also engaged in two forms of collaborative ventures that required less editorial control and hence lower coordination costs. First, the party newspaper *RMRB* jointly organized a seminar with the theory journal *Qiushi* to repudiate the Falungong on July 27, 1999, and separately, with *GMRB* on July 29, 1999.[8] The three media agencies also coorganized a forum on November 4, 1999, after the National People's Congress, the Supreme People's Court, and the Supreme People's Procuracy determined that the Falungong was an evil cult that breached Chinese law.[9] Second, both the Xinhua and *Qiushi* compiled collections of articles on the Falungong originally published in other presses. The editor's note in the Xinhua anthology acknowledges the contribution of the *RMRB*, *GMRB*, and *JJRB*, as well as the *Qiushi* magazine, for making their news items available for the publication.[10] The special issue of *Qiushi* included major notices of party and state agen-

Table 8.4: Comparison of Subscription Rate of Anti-Falungong and People's Republic of China 50th Anniversary

Measure	Anti-Falungong	PRC Anniversary
Target	120	100
Publishers submitting proposals	160	234
No. publication proposals submitted	410	765
Oversubscription rate	3.4	7.6

Source: *Zhongguo chuban nianjian*, 2000, p. 78.

cies banning the Falungong; investigative reports of the Xinhua news agency, the NPB, and Ministry of Public Security; editorials of *RMRB* and *JFJB;* and *RMRB* press interviews of the organization and propaganda departments.[11]

Horizontal Cooperation

Horizontal coordination among media organizations was more marked by its absence than presence. Compared to what media organizations could jointly produce and disseminate in the anti-Falungong campaign, their cooperative ventures in news production, thematic specialization, and publication scheduling were feeble.

Absence of News Coproduction

Coproduction of news stories on the Falungong was rare among media organizations. The important investigative report on the April 25 siege of the Zhongnanhai was jointly written by an *RMRB* journalist and three Xinhua reporters as a Xinhua release, published in the *RMRB*, and broadcast as a China Central Television Corporation (CCTV) movie on the same day.[12] A separate CCTV biographic movie titled *Li Hongzhi: The Man and His Deeds* was built on the investigation by the Research Office of the Ministry of Public Security published in *RMRB* on July 27. A less important story on a seminar on repudiating the Falungong was jointly filed by a Xinhua reporter and two *RMRB* journalists.[13] Other than these, no news stories on the Falungong were jointly written by more than one major printed media organization among the thousands of stories in the three elite national dailies. There was a similar lack of news coproduction between the national television and radio networks, with an absence of joint coverage or production of anti-Falungong programs in Central People's Broadcasting Station (CPBS) and CCTV.[14] Within CCTV, there was also no report of the five news magazine programs (*Eastern Time and Space, Living Space, Focused Interview, Plain Speaking,* and *News Probe*) engaging in coproduction on Falungong programs,[15] except for a joint effort coproduced by *Eastern Time and Space* and *News Probe* aired on August 5, 1999.[16] The absence of such news coauthorship and coproduction is probably the result of the small marginal utility of collaboration, the organizational structure of CCTV news production that favors unit autonomy and accountability, the high coordination cost imposed by the requirement for multiple hierarchical layers of editorial control and approval for news stories, and the competitiveness of the industry.

Lack of Thematic Coordination

There was also no explicit thematic coordination, where one medium would specialize on a given theme. The official campaign had different lines of attack, faulting the Falungong for being unscientific and irrational in its doctrinal beliefs, for exaggerating the healing powers and health benefits of its breathing exercises, for making fraudulent claims of the supernatural powers of its leader Li Hongzhi, and for disrupting social order and breaching China's laws. There was thus ample room for thematic specialization of commentaries, with one medium focusing on a specific issue. Indeed, one would expect this to be the case, given the different organizational missions of the national dailies, where *RMRB* focuses on party and ideology, *GMRB*, the paper for the intelligentsia, on the intellectual content of Falungong beliefs and practices, and the military's *JFJB*, on the negative social impact on domestic security. Instead, the thematic content of commentaries and editorials of various media overlap one another, with no explicit specialization and division of labor. The absence of specialization in thematic commentaries suggests a lack of vertical coordination at higher levels to provide an overall plan for media commentaries, as well as a similar lack of horizontal collaboration among editorial boards of major national dailies. It may also be the result of deliberate policy where different media focus on the same thematic issues to show unity of purpose and strategy in the campaign. While plausible, the latter explanation is not likely, since each media organization can still collaborate while engaging in the same line of attack.

Publication and Program Scheduling and Campaign Phasing

Coordinated scheduling is not evident in the publication dates of the *RMRB*, *GMRB*, and *JFJB* commentaries. As shown in table 8.2, the *RMRB* commentary series on the Falungong was published on July 26, 27, 29, and 30 and August 4, 6, 9, 12, 13, and 16; those of *GMRB* on July 25, 27, 28, 29, and 30 and August 2, 3, and 4; while the *JFJB* published its editorials on July 23, 26, 27, 29, and 31 and August 11, 13, 17, 18, 20, and 23. There were thus multiple authoritative commentaries published on the same day (three on July 27, two on July 29, and August 4), and days where one or more national dailies did not publish or reprint a single authoritative commentary (none on July 25 and 28 for both *RMRB* and *JFJB*, and none on August 7 and 8 for all three major national dailies). This suggests that there was no publication spacing or rotational scheduling, where each national daily would coordinate the publication dates of their editorials and commentaries to avoid reader fatigue over commentary saturation and to ensure that the electronic media would have a daily staple of authoritative commentaries for sustained release and public consumption.

Within the broadcast industry, it is also not evident that the CPBS and CCTV coordinated their specific broadcast schedules on Falungong programming. The two national stations do appear to coordinate their regular daily news programming schedules of channel I in CPBS and CCTV. This is especially the case in prime-time news programming, both during the morning breakfast hour and during the evening golden slot between 7–7:30 P.M., where both the reception and advertising rates are the highest. CPBS, the weaker medium, schedules its morning and evening news programs to begin half an hour before those of the more popular CCTV. The second half-hour of CPBS news programs, both morning and evening, does overlap with the news programs of CCTV. As shown earlier in table 4.1 (see chapter 4), the daily news programs of CPBS channel I and CCTV channel I overlap at 7:00–7:20, 12:05–12:30, and 19:00–19:30. Of the 210 minutes of daily news programs in CPBS channel I and 170 minutes of news programs in CCTV channel I, the overlap was slightly under 20%.[17] If the news magazines and special news programs of CCTV channel I are included in the calculation, then the overlap in the news programs of the two electronic media is 15% in the same period.[18]

At a higher organizational level, there was also no coordination in campaign scheduling among different types of media. The publications industry, printed and electronic media structured their anti-Falungong campaign in different stages with different begin and end dates. There is also no clear evidence where the content of an earlier phase of one medium fed into those of other media that began later. The marching orders for the Xinhua new agency was to launch a month-long campaign against the Falungong that was to last from July 22 to August 23.[19] In television, there was distinct phasing of the campaign, which was demarcated in three stages: (1) July 22–23, (2) July 24–29, and (3) July 30 to August 2, 1999.[20] The press campaign was also reported to be composed of three phases that do not appear to be coterminous with the television campaign.[21] Probably due to the much longer production cycle for publishing books, there was even less overlap between the phasing of publication campaign and those of the television and press campaigns. There was no clearly enunciated timeline in the publication campaign that produced 120 titles of anti-Falungong books.[22]

RESULTS OF THE PUBLICATION CAMPAIGN

The results of the publication campaign seemed to have achieved the intended propaganda goals by several basic measures. As elaborated in chapter 4, the propaganda machinery and the regime-controlled publications industry still possessed formidable institutional capacity to mount a forceful assault on the regime's adversaries. As shown in table 8.5, the publication target of 120 titles was less than 0.1% of the production output of the industry's 566 presses in 1999. The smallest of the three in-house presses of the NPB alone published more titles and printed more volumes and pages than that of the entire anti-Falungong campaign. To implement its publication goals, the NPB was quick to act on the directive to launch the anti-Falungong drive. Within the same month that the Falungong was banned, it had already commissioned its in-house presses that published 30 anti-Falungong titles. Beyond publishers it had direct control, it was also able to convene a national conference to solicit publication projects from the publishers, only eight days after the Falungong was banned. It drew a volume of proposals more than three times the publication target, a result that suggests that the NPB wielded strong influence on the nation's publications industry, which was responsive to the demands of its propaganda superiors. Further, the speed with which the publications industry produced anti-Falungong books was impressive. As shown in table 8.3, 31 titles were already on the book shelves or available for distribution by the end of July 1999, a week after the official ban was first promulgated. There were multiple publications on each of the three series stipulated by the Propaganda Department—materialism (7), atheism (9), and popular science (15)—to meet the demand of different market segments. The list grew to 50 by the following month, and 95 by year's end, enough to fill many shelves in a Xinhua book store in major cities. Finally, by April 2002, the entire series had appeared in print, meeting the original publication target date.[23] The Propaganda Department also claimed that it was able to recruit some leading scientists to participate in the project, including Zhou Guangshao, Lu Yongxiang, and Zhu Guangya, all of whom were prominent scholars with international reputation in their professions.[24] The publication industry, then, appeared to be both efficient and responsive to support the regime's call to suppress the Falungong.

Table 8.5: Institutional Capacity of Publications Industry in China, 1999

Publishers	No. Publishers	Total Titles	Total Printed Volumes/ Sheets (in Millions)	Total Printed Pages (in Millions)	Total List Sale Price (in Million Yuan)
Total national	566	141,831	7,316.3	39,090	43,600
Central party/ state direct subordinates	66	3,394	65.1	705	931.9
People's Press	1	335	3.19	37	58.6
People's Fine Arts Press	1	207	4.6	16.8	58.3
China Books Publishing Co.	1	146	1.57	15.99	19.16
Total three NPB Presses	3	688	8.36	69.79	136.06

Source: *Zhongguo chuban nianjian*, 2000, pp. 67–71, 699.

Mobilization Achievements

These mobilization results were achieved in trying circumstances. First, since the Falungong was officially banned only in late July 1999, the publication series was not part of the annual publication plan of 1999 approved at the beginning of the year,[25] or part of the larger publication plan of the Ninth Five Year Plan from 1996 to 2000.[26] The publications industry would thus need to commission writers and editors, contract publishers, and finance the project in mid-course. In addition, 1999 was a vintage year of special anniversaries, all of which competed for resources and imposed deadlines on the publication industry. Like its counterparts outside China, the publishers need to fill high-volume orders for special calendars, retrospective albums, and other commemorative titles on the new century and the millennium. Within China, the year was the 50th anniversary of the founding of the People's Republic of China, an event to be marked by the publication of 100 extravaganza monographs, 500 CDs, and an additional 100 video and electronic products.[27] The 1999 publication plan also included producing a special series to mark the 80th anniversary of the May Fourth Movement that heralded the advent of communism and modern culture in China, and the historic return to China's sovereignty of Macau, the first European settlement in Asia, after more than 400 years of Portuguese rule.[28] The propaganda department and the publications industry in China thus deserve special credit for meeting publication goals and on schedule under these challenging circumstances.

Measuring Policy Effect

However, the above measures are indicators of production effort, not policy effect. Were these anti-Falungong titles widely purchased and read, or shunned by the general public, and were they considered quality productions by the publishing industry? To determine how effective the anti-Falungong publication campaign was, the following section compares the publication volume of the campaign with that of the industry and that published by the Falungong, and three measures of overall quality of the 120 anti-Falungong titles. The section begins with a comparison of the subscription rates of two publication series.

Comparison of Subscription Rates

As noted in chapter 4, when the NPB solicited publication proposals from the publishers, they received 410 subscriptions from 160 publishers for the 120 anti-Falungong titles. The 3.4 times oversubscription rate is indeed enviable but should be compared with other responses of the publications industry to other publication projects. Earlier in 1999, the NPB also solicited publication proposals from the nation's publishers for 100 titles to commemorate the 50th anniversary of the Founding of the People's Republic of China on October 1, 1999. As shown in table 8.4, the NPB received 765 proposals from 234 publishers. In terms of both the number of publication proposals received and the number of publishers submitting proposals, the 50th anniversary publication project was much better received by the industry than the anti-Falungong publication project. The oversubscription rate of the former (7.6) is more than double that of the anti-Falungong publication project (3.4).

Comparison of Circulation Numbers with Other Publications

To determine the extent to which the anti-Falungong titles were purchased and read by the public, the most direct measure would be total sales figures of these publications. However, aggregate data on sales were not published, nor were the numbers of copies produced and the numbers of printings made of the 120 anti-Falungong titles. Only a few of the anti-Falungong publications list the number of editions and printings on their back covers, and even fewer list the number of copies made for those printings and editions. My preliminary search found no title with subsequent editions and only one with a second printing.[29] Of those that list the number of copies, they range from 5,000 to 30,000 copies, with most less than 10,000 copies. The circulation was thus much smaller than the most popular publication titles in China, which range from 100,000 to the millions.[30]

Compared to the average printed volume of other publications in China, the circulation of anti-Falungong titles was also small. As shown in table 8.5, the 566 publishing houses overall produced 141,831 titles with a total 7.3 billion copies in 1999, or 51,582 copies per title on average, many more times that of an average anti-Falungong title.[31] Since many of the publication titles are large-volume school texts by the provincial education presses, I have also examined data with two sets of publishers that are more comparable. As also shown in table 8.5, the 66 central party state publishers and their direct subordinates produced a total of 3,394 titles with an aggregate volume of 65.1 million, or 19,180 copies per title. Table 8.5 also shows that three NPB presses produced a total of 688 titles with 8.36 million volumes, amounting to 12,151 copies per title. These numbers suggest that the anti-Falungong titles have a much smaller distribution than the average publication title in China in 1999, smaller than those of the average publication of the central and party presses, and even smaller than those of the three NPB in-house presses.

Comparison with Falungong Publications

The small circulation of the anti-Falungong publications can also be shown by comparing book sales by the Falungong. In the court trial of the Beijing Falungong leaders on December 26, 1999, the government prosecutor charged that the Falun Dafa Research Society directly produced, edited, and distributed 11.08 million copies of Falungong titles.[32] Since there were 11 banned Falungong titles,[33] each Falungong title sold an average of more than one million copies. The actual circulation of Falungong publications in China could actually be higher, since the above figures exclude those distributed outside China, those produced but not distributed by the Falun Dafa Research Society, or those produced and distributed by its subordinates in the provinces and by private vendors. Assuming that 120 anti-Falungong titles had an average printing of 10,000 copies, and that all of these were sold, then the total circulation of the 120 titles was 1.2 million copies, or less than 12% of the total books directly produced and distributed by the Falun Dafa Research Society. Whether measured in terms of total distribution or per title sales, the Falungong titles had a much wider readership than those of the government publication campaign.

Evaluation of Publication Quality

As alternative measures of propaganda impact, I have also searched for indicators of publication quality among China's Best Publications Awards, Best Sellers, and Book Review lists, to find how many of the 120 titles made these coveted ranks. For printed monographs and series, there were three prestigious overall best book awards in China, each one presented in a media event by the director of the NPB, as well as minister or deputy minister of propaganda.[34]

Analysis of Best Publication Awards

The National Best Book Prize (*Guojia tushu jiang*) was established in October 1992 by the Bureau of Book Management of the NPB,[35] the same agency that was in charge of managing the publication of the 120 anti-Falungong titles. For the 1999 competition, 148 titles received awards, from 1,800 entries submitted by 430 publishers.[36] The 148 titles include 52 Best Book Prizes and 96 Honorable Mentions. For the year 2000, the National Best Book Prize was presented to 214 titles.[37] Another national publication contest is the China Book Prize (*Zhongguo tushujiang*), chosen after at least four rounds of screening and selected on the basis of secret ballots by panels of distinguished judges. One hundred fifty books from 156 publishers were chosen from 1,291 titles published in 1998 and 1999 that were submitted by 403 publishers.[38] The "Five Best Project" (*Wu Ge Yi Gongcheng*) Prize was established in 1992 by the Department of Propaganda to commemorate the 50th anniversary of Mao's speech in Yenan on literature and art and to recognize outstanding publications, music, film, television, and theatrical productions. For the 1999 competition, 63 books were selected from 214 entries.[39]

Table 8.6 lists the number of awards given by these five national book competitions in China.[40] Only one of the 120 anti-Falungong monographs was among the 575 winning titles in the five national best book competitions in 1999 and 2000. Even the title of this sole anti-Falungong book, however, was ambiguous: a book in a children's nature book series whose title did not mention the Falungong.[41] The short summary of the publication in the introduction of the award series also made no reference to the Falungong. Further, the title appeared in print in May 1999, and the series was published before 1997. In other words, both the publication of the title and that of the larger series preceded the anti-Falungong campaign. It is thus questionable that it was its anti-Falungong content that merited the award selection. It should also be noted that there was no apparent anti-party publication bias in these competitions. Other publications on party history,[42] communist theory,[43] party leaders,[44] and nationalistic history[45] received the Best Book Prizes in 1999 and 2000. It can be deduced, then, that a probable reason why the 120 anti-Falungong titles did not receive best book awards was the lesser quality of the content of the anti-Falungong publications, which did not make the grade for award-winning titles. The fact that at most one anti-Falungong title won a prize in five separate competitions with at least three distinct panels of judges in official NPB and Department of Propaganda contests suggests that the overall quality of the 120 anti-Falungong titles was low.

Table 8.6: National Best Book Awards and Anti-Falungong Books, 1999 and 2000

Category	No. Awards	No. Anti-Falungong Books
National Best Book Prize Award, 1999	52	0
National Best Book Prize Honorable Mention, 1999	96	0
National Best Book Prize, 2000	214	0
China Book Prize, 2000	150	0
"Five Best Project," 1999	63	1
Total	575	1

Source: *Zhongguo chuban nianjian*, 2000, pp. 208–14; www.people.com.cn, August 17, 2001.

Table 8.7: Number of titles of Best Sellers of CFBPP and Anti-Falungong Books, 2000

	National Best-Sellers	Anti-Falungong Books
Social sciences	127	0
Economics	73	0
Science and technology	185	0
Literature	97	0
Culture and education	136	0
Children	63	1
Total	681	1

Source: *Zhongguo chuban nianjian*, 2000, pp. 658–62.

Analysis of Best Sellers

To provide an alternative measure on the social impact of the anti-Falungong publication series, I also examined how the anti-Falungong series did in the marketplace. Since data on sales and printing of these titles have not been published, I relied on the next best data source. A trade group, the China Federation of Books and Periodicals Publishers (CFBPP), instituted the Best-selling Good Books List (*yiuxiu changxiao shu*), to differentiate what it considers to be quality publications from dictionaries, school texts, and exam preparatory manuals that are market leaders in book sales.[46] For 1998–99, the CFBPP National Best Sellers list only included books on social sciences, economics, and science and technology, showing 296 titles as best sellers, out of more than 141,000 publications.[47] For 2000, the listing categories were literature, culture and education, and children's books, showing 385 best-selling titles.[48] For these two years, then, 681 titles made the list (table 8.7). Among these, only one of the 120 anti-Falungong titles could be found, and it was the same above-mentioned children's book, from whose title or summary Falungong content cannot be inferred, which appeared in print before the Falungong was banned. It is thus questionable that any anti-Falungong book made the best-seller list of the publishing industry in China in 1999 and 2000. The convergence of the best book awards and best seller lists leaves little doubt that the quality of the 120 anti-Falungong titles is wanting.

RATINGS OF TV PROGRAMS

To examine whether television programs on the Falungong also had the same low public reception as those in the printed media, this section analyzes three sets of ratings on Falungong programs: evening news programs, award-winning television, and award-winning news programs.

Ratings of Evening News and Prime-Time Special Programs

The first set of ratings are those of the evening news programs in CCTV. Scheduled prime-time daily from 7:00 to 7:30 P.M., aired throughout China via satellite, and broadcast through provincial stations, these were by far the most popular television programs in 1999, topping all 12 monthly charts and commanding a reception rate between 37.11% to 52.10%, with an estimated viewership of 406 million to 570 million per day.[49] The ratings were based on surveys of television viewing of 10,500 households in 49–55 survey stations, projected on a nationwide representative sampling frame completed in 1997. Since 2000, the ratings were contracted to a joint venture between CCTV and Taylor Nelson Sofres, a leading international marketing research group, and used electronic viewing recorders.[50] While longitudinal comparisons of program ratings overtime would thus be confounded by the change in the methodology in 2000, within-year comparisons should not be affected.

Ratings for the evening network news for 1999 were aggregated by four- to five-week intervals and published by CCTV. As shown in table 8.8, the evening news programs in the four-week period from July 18 to August 14 during which the anti-Falungong campaign took place had an average 432.9 million viewers and 39.57% reception rate, the second lowest of 12 periods. Only the last period from November 15 to December 31 had a lower rating in 1999. The low ratings could be due to the special viewing habits of summer months, where outdoor activities could have lured some viewers to leave the

Table 8.8: Reception Rates of Evening Network News in Millions, 1997–99

Dates (based on 1999)	No. Viewers			Reception Rates		
	1999	1998	1997	1999	1998	1997
12/20/98 – /1/16/99	506.6	404.8	361.3	46.31	47.51	42.4
1/17 – 2/13	497.7	419.6	386.0	45.44	49.25	45.3
2/14 – 3/13	498.9	414.8	409.0	45.60	48.69	48.0
3/14 – 4/24	492.5	403.6	400.0	45.02	47.37	46.95
4/25 – 5/15	570.0	385.5	404.3	52.10	45.25	47.45
5/16 – 6/12	520.1	389.7	419.6	47.54	45.74	49.25
6/13 – 7/17	458.3	361.4	492.5	41.89	42.42	57.80
7/18 – 8/14	432.9	363.5	387.1	39.57	42.66	45.43
8/15 – 9/18	444.3	409.4	397.2	40.61	48.05	46.62
9/19 – 10/16	470.9	500.6	405.1	43.04	45.76	47.55
10/17 – 11/14	471.3	497.3	404.1	43.08	45.46	47.43
11/15 – 12/31	406.0	498.1	403.5	37.11	45.53	47.36

These dates vary by the year, since ratings were aggregated by the week. The dates in the table were those of 1999. Those in 1997 and 1998 were closest dates to the periods in 1999.

Table 8.9: Reception Rates (in Millions) of Special Feature Program on Falungong
(Air time: 7:30 – 8:10 P.M.)

Airing Period	Program	No. Viewers (in Millions)	Reception Rate (%)
12/20–1/16	Focused Interview	311.79	28.50
	Science and Technology Survey	269.34	24.62
	Epidemic prevention	232.80	21.28
1/17–2/13	Focused Interview	298.33	27.27
	Science and Technology survey	249.43	22.80
	Special news topic	245.82	22.47
2/14–3/13	Science and Technology survey (year of rabbit)	413.64	37.81
	Focused Interview	412.66	37.72
	Special report on two conferences	222.96	20.38
3/14–4/24	Focused Interview	291.33	26.63
	Science and Technology survey	245.93	22.48
	Special report on two conferences	233.35	21.33
4/25–5/15	Focused Interview	346.03	31.63
	Science and Technology survey	252.71	23.10
	News Survey	134.45	12.29
5/16–6/21	Focused Interview	325.90	29.79
	Science and Technology Survey	235.76	21.55
	Topical News	103.38	9.45
6/13–7/17	Focused Interview	277.00	25.32
	Science and Technology Survey	199.33	18.22
	Towards a New Era (special feature)	107.32	9.81
7/18–8/14	Focused Interview	251.90	23.03
	Science and Technology survey	180.29	16.84
	Towards a New Era (special feature)	123.40	11.28
8/15–9/18	The Evil Falungong	157.21	14.37
	Focused Interview	270.66	24.74
	Science and Technology survey	200.09	18.29
9/19–10/16	Focused Interview	329.73	30.14
	Science and Technology survey	292.32	26.72
	Fortune Forum '99	239.91	21.93
10/17–11/14	New Focus	285.75	26.12
	Science and Technology survey	208.08	19.02
	State council press conference	105.13	9.46
11/15–12/31	Focused Interview	299.79	27.40
	Olympic Games opening ceremony	242.78	22.19
	Macau sovereignty return ceremony	240.15	21.19

Source: *CCTV Yearbook*, 2000, pp. 324–29.

tube for the lake or the park. To control for seasonal effects, we also examined corresponding data for adjacent years. Since CCTV had not published equivalent figures for 2000–2, we compared the data for 1997 and 1998. We did find a seasonal effect, where the months of July and August had the second or third lowest ratings for the years 1997, 1998, and 1999. Our results are thus indeterminate as to whether anti-Falungong programs depressed ratings.

CCTV also published reception data on ratings for the top three prime-time special programs (*zhuangti jiemu*) for each of the 12 periods, aired at 7:30–8:10 P.M. immediately after the evening network news. There are thus ratings on 36 special prime-time programs. Of the anti-Falungong special programs, only *The Evil Falungong* (*xiewu di Falungong*) made the list of the top three special programs in the period from August 15 through September 18, with 157.2 million viewers and 14.37% reception rate.[51] It placed 33 among the 36 top special programs for 1999, or in the bottom 10% (table 8.9).

Analysis of TV and News Programs Winning Awards

To assess the quality of anti-Falungong news programs in CCTV and other news media organizations, we also scrutinize the winners of three major, national television, and news program awards in China. Established by the China News Journalists Association, the China News Awards are open to competition from more than 5,000 media organizations in China. Its 2000 awards were presented to outstanding news programs in television, radio, news agencies, and newspapers produced in 1999. The award categories were news, commentary, special features, series, on-site production, photography, broadcast organization, page layout, and cartoons.[52] The May Fourth News Awards were instituted by the Communist Youth League and the China Society for News Workers, covering a similar list of award categories and open to competition from the same group of media organizations.[53] The China Television Broadcast News Awards were established by the State Bureau for Television and Broadcast and receives nominations from its provincial subordinate bureaus, CCTV, and the China International Television Station. The finalists are adjudicated by a panel of judges selected by three trade associations: the China Television and Broadcast Society, the China Television Arts Commission, and the China Television and Broadcast Journalists Association.[54] Its 1999 awards were presented to television news programs produced in the 1999 calendar year. The award categories were short news, long news, commentary, special features, news program editing, and on-site production.[55]

As presented in table 8.10, no anti-Falungong news program won any of the 106 prizes in the Sixth May Fourth News Awards. CCTV's production titled: *Fact: Li Hongzhi Did Fall Ill and Did Take Medicine* won a third prize in the 1999 TV and Broadcast News Award, but no anti-Falungong production by other media organizations won any prize in that competition. In the grand 2000 China News Awards, CCTV did not win any of the 24 first prizes, none of the 57 second prizes, and none of the 102 third prizes. Anti-Falungong programs produced by other media organizations did win at least one first prize, three second prizes, and one third prize. They may have won an additional first prize and one additional third prize. These two news productions had titles suggesting that they might be aimed at the Falungong,[56] but whether that is actually the case needs to be verified.

EVALUATION OF CONVERSION AND COERCION

This section examines what coercive methods did and did not achieve in rehabilitating Falungong practitioners. As a law enforcement operation, the anti-Falungong campaign was successful. When the ban was officially

Table 8.10: Anti-Falungong News Programs Winning National Media Awards, 1999–2000

Awards	Total Prizes	CCTV Anti-Falungong Programs	Non-CCTV Anti-Falungong Productions[a]
2000 China News Awards			
Special Prize	1	0	0
First prize	24	0	1 (2)
Second prize	57	0	3
Third prize	102	0	1 (2)
6th May Fourth News Awards			
First prize	23	0	0
Second prize	33	0	0
Third prize	50	0	0
1999 Calendar Year TV and Broadcast News Awards			
Special prize	2	0	0
First prize	5	0	0
Second prize	5	0	0
Third prize	2	1	0
Total	210	1	5 (7)

[a]Figures within parenthesis denote award entries that may or may not be anti-Falungong productions.

Source: *CCTV Yearbook*, 2001, pp. 154–55; *Zhongguo xinwen nianjian, 2001*, pp. 252–61.

promulgated at 3 P.M. on July 22, the regime had already gathered the basic intelligence on the Falungong organization and leadership and its local networks, communications patterns, and prosecutorial evidence. Many leaders of Falungong stations and main stations were in government custody by the time the ban was announced, and there was no evidence of reported leaks before July 19, when the ban was first communicated through party organizations. The enforcement of the ban appeared to be effective, with the great majority of local Falungong congregations dissolved and more than two million pieces of Falungong publications and accessories confiscated and destroyed within a week of the ban. At least by July 30 if not earlier, there were no more large groups of Falungong practitioners protesting in front of government buildings and broadcasting stations in the national and provincial capitals, and assemblies gathering for daily breathing exercises in public venues had virtually disappeared after the ban. The prairie fire has been contained by July 23, and only local smothering remained afterward. After the ban, the once rapidly metastasizing movement ceased to be a threat to the regime.

But the regime also waged another war. For the Falungong, winning over hearts and minds is just as important if not more so than locking up their bodies. Even if the regime succeeded in putting all Falungong practitioners behind the walls of labor reform institutions, if they did not reform, the regime still lost. The degree of success of the anti-Falungong campaign thus needs to be measured not by the numbers of Falungong organizations crushed, activities eliminated, and practitioners detained or incarcerated, but by the share of practitioners who gave up their practice and never returned to it.

Measures of Conversion Success

To analyze the effectiveness of the conversion program, the most direct and measures are statistics of detoxification success. The regime, however, has not published any summary statistics on the number of Falungong rank-and-file who quit the practice or at least submitted to regime authority and withdrew from the sect. Nevertheless, the degree of success of the conversion program can be gleaned from three sets of relatively systematic data on the defection of both Falungong leaders and followers. The first is on the top Falungong leaders, the heads and deputy heads of the 38 main Stations who renounced their Falungong ties, and the approximate dates of renunciation. The second is the percentage of practicing Falungong party members who signed severance papers to withdraw from the sect by early August 1999. The third is the conversion rates of the Falungong practitioners declared to be successfully rehabilitated at provincial labor reform institutions. As discussed in the sections that follow, the validity of these claims of mission accomplishment needs to be qualified by contradictory evidence.

Defection of Top Falungong Officials

Both to declare victory as well as to encourage imitation, the official media published the names and ranks of Falungong provincial leadership who defected, including the chiefs (*zongzhang zhangzhang*) and deputy chiefs (*zongzhang fu zhangzhang*) of its 38 main stations. As presented in table 8.11, defections of these leaders have been reported in 32 of the 38 main stations. in terms of time to defection, there were few main station chiefs of little faith, and only six were reported to have severed their ties with the Falung-ong within the first week, 9 by the second, 13 by the third, an additional 2 by the fourth week, while 8 appear to have held on beyond the end of August, more than five weeks after the crackdown. For those of deputy ranks, seven have capitulated by the first week, nine by the second, and six by the third week. As discussed in the following paragraph, it is unclear how many dep-uty chiefs have not defected.

The ratio of defection of main station chiefs is relatively easy to calcu-late. Since there was only one head for each main station, the percentage of those who had defected versus those who remained recalcitrant by a given date can be determined. Table 8.12 shows that 28 of the 38 main station chiefs had defected by the end of August 1999, leaving 10 who were still unrepentant. Those of deputy chiefs are less clear for two reasons. First, the total number of such positions is unknown, so the denomina-

Table 8.11: Defection of Top Falungong Leaders, July–August 1999

Main Stations	Name and Date of Main Station Chief Defection	Names and Date of Main Station Deputy Chief Defection
Beijing	Tang Xuehua (8/7)	Liu Shuwen (8/7)
Tianjin	Xu Jinfang (8/4)	
Hebei-Shijiazhuang	Duan Rongxin (8/7)	
Hebei-Handan		Wang Zhenzhong (8/3)
Shanxi-Datong	Wang Yuanying (7/21)	
Shanxi-Taiyuan	Wang Zuowu (7/29)	
Liaoning-Shenyang	Chen Suo (7/31)	
Liaoning-Lingyuan	Tong Cuilian (7/31)	Zhang Yali (8/1)
Liaoning-Jinzhou	Li Bingheng (8/9)	Wu Baogui (8/3)
Liaoning-Chaoyang	Wang Zhicheng (7/31)	
Liaoning-Dalian	Gao Qiuju (8/7)	
Jilin-Changchun	Jiao Lixun (7/25)	Xu Yinquan (7/28)

Heilongjiang-Harbin	Zhang Shengjie (8/7)	
Heilongjiang-Jiamusi	Ma Jun (8/7)	
Heilongjiang-Qitaishi	Guan Maohui (8/7)	
Heilongjiang-Qiqihaer	Lu Mengjian (7/29)	
Shanghai	Xia Ninghua (protemp, 8/1)	Zhang Ziyun, Song Xuewen (8/1)
Jiangsu-Nanjing	Ma Zhenyu (8/5)	Shi Xiuhua (7/28)
Anhui		Gao Qingyin (7/31)
Anhui-Fouyang	Wang Shengli (7/24)	
Fujian	Chen Gong (after 7/22)	Chen Ridong, Huang Jinfan (8/6)
Jiangxi	Zhou Hongwen (8/7)	
Shandong	Zhang Shouqiang (7/27)	Zhang Zigang, Liu Qingyu, Jing Guixia, Cheng Huiping (7/27)
Henan	Yu Ruichen (7/30)	Li Honglin (7/30)
Hubei	Xu Xianglan (8/5)	Wang Xiaoming (8/5)
Hunan-Changsha	Cao Xuwu (8/6)	
Hunan-Changde	Chen Li (8/2)	
Guangdong	Gao Dawei (not defected as of 8/6)	
Guangxi	Chen Xueying (7/25)	Pen Chaoyue (7/24) Guan Haibin (7/26)
Hainan	Jiang Xiaojun (8/28)	
Sichuan-Chengdu	Kuang Minggai (7/26)	
Yunnan	Wang Lan (8/17)	Xu Xiaohua (7/21) Wang Taiyuan (not defected as of 8/6)
Shaanxi	Song Xiujuan (8/6)	Shou Shunfu (8/6)
Gansu	Yuan Jiang (not defected as of 8/5)	
Ningxia-Yinchuan		Luan Ning (8/5)

Source: *Renmin ribao,* July 26, 27 and 28 and August 2, 5, 6, 7, and 8, 1999; *Anhui ribao,* July 28, 1999; *Hunan ribao,* August 2 and 9, 1999; *Xinhua,* Kunming, press release of Aug. 17; *Xinhua ribao,* July 29, 1999, p. A2; Aug. 5, 1999, p. A1.

tor cannot be determined. From table 8.11, it can be inferred that the number of deputy chief defections varies from one to four, with two being the mode. These numbers, however, pertain to only those defected, not the total number of deputy chiefs in those main stations. If we assume that the average number of deputy chiefs is two per main station, then the total number of such positions for the 38 main stations is 76. Increasing the average number to 2.5 per main station, then the total number of deputy chiefs is 95. Using 76 as the total, there would be 22 main

Table 8.12: Dates of Conversion of Provincial Falungong Main Stations Leaders

	7/20-26	7/28–8/3	8/4-11	After 8/11	Not Reported	Total
Chiefs of main stations	6	9	13	2	8	38
Cumulative conversion rate of main station chiefs	15.8%	39.5%	73.7%	79.0%		
Deputy chiefs of main stations	7	9	6		(54)	76 (assuming two per main station)
					(73)	95 (assuming two and a half per main station)

station deputy chiefs who have defected, while 54 have remained stead-
fast. The latter number increases to 73 if we used 95 as the total number of
deputy chiefs. Second, these large numbers of loyal main station deputy
chiefs may not be valid, as the official media might regard the defection
of deputy ranks less newsworthy than those of the full-ranked heads of
main stations and thus not reporting all such instances. Available data do
not allow us to ascertain the extent of selective underreporting of deputy
ranks. The latter is clearly not the explanation in Jiangsu, Anhui, Ningxia,
and Hebei-Handan, which reported only defections of its deputy chiefs
and not the main station chiefs. But we do not know whether such is the
case for other main station deputy chiefs.

Renunciation of Falungong Ties by Party Members

Official media also published the percentage of party members who were
practitioners and renounced their Falungong affiliation for 11 provinces by
the end of August 1999. As explained in chapter 5, these were the results
of an intensive campaign within basic-level party organizations to persuade
party members to withdraw from the Falungong, often assigning two or
more party members and leaders to work with one strayed member, sometimes involving the leading cadres of the employing unit, as well. Shown in
the second column of table 8.13, the percentage of party members who had
renounced their Falungong ties were all in the upper 90%. Thus, at least
for these 11 provinces, an overwhelming majority of Falungong practitioners

who were party members had declared their severance from the sect, a percentage that can be considered impressive. The reported times of these withdrawals were July 31 and August 2, or within 10 days of the Falungong ban first being imposed. Both the high conversion rate and the short time period where conversion was accomplished suggest an effective rehabilitation program. There are, however, grounds for skepticism of these numbers. First, the eleven constitutes around a third of the 31 provinces in China. In particular, two of the provinces with the largest Falungong presence (Heilongjiang and Liaoning) did not report figures. Second, the high conversion numbers reported in the eleven provinces also do not inform us of the number who later recanted their forced conversions, or party members who subsequently heeded the call of Li Hongzhi to withdraw from the party. Both official and Falungong sources reported on these recantations and withdrawal of party membership, a subject analyzed in the next section.

Conversion Rates of Labor Reform Inmates

The *Zhongguo Sifa Xingzheng Nianjian* (China Yearbook on Justice Administration) has published conversion rates of Falungong practitioners who served time in labor reform institutes for most provinces. These refer to the less severe category of Falungong practitioners who were sanctioned by public security agencies to serve up to 15 days' time in labor reform institutes, as stipulated in the "Security Management Penalty Regulations of the People's Republic of China" (1986).[57] They were distinct from Falungong practitioners who received prison sentences imposed by courts for having violated state laws, a category labeled as "criminals" in official data, which are available for only a minority of provinces. As shown in table 8.13, in 2000–2003, 22 of the 31 provinces published conversion rates of total practitioners who were inmates in the labor reform institutions in the province at least for one year (2003 is the last year for which such data are available). Among these, conversion rates range from a low of 29.3% for Qinghai in 2001 to a high of 98.7% in Neimonggu in 2003.

Limits of Conversion Success

Two trends in the conversion rates are noteworthy. First, they show that four years after the ban, law enforcement had not relaxed its vigilance and was able to apprehend and incarcerate errant Falungong practitioners, who were not immune from official sanction. The published conversion rates are high, and a majority of Falungong practitioners who spent time in labor reform institutions were rehabilitated after their short tenure in labor reform. As more Falungong practitioners passed through the conversion process over

Table 8.13: Conversion Rates of Falungong Practitioners by Province, 1999–2003 (%)

| Province | Conversion of Party Members in 1999 | | Conversion of Falungong Inmates in Labor Reform Institution | | | |
	(A) (%)	Date of Report	2000	2001	2002	2003
Beijing	98.9	7/31				
Tianjin	99.5				>84	>82
Hebei	97.7[a]					
Shanxi	97.0[b]					
Neimonggu				>65		98.7
Liaoning	95.5[c]	8/2			87.2	
Jilin	95.5	8/2	87.4	85.7	91.5 (cumulative)	
Heilongjiang			70.6	73	82 (51 for Falungon criminals)	>90
Shanghai					85	90
Jiangsu						
Zhejiang	99.4	7/31			89	91.6
Anhui	98	8/1	>90	68	72.4	
Fujian			82.6	85.6		
Jiangxi	97.78	7/28				
Shandong			>80		96	
Henan				>80		
Hubei			87			88
Hunan			>80			
Guangdong			83.4			
Guangxi			91.97	78.9	79.43	
Hainan	62.8			90	93	96
Sichuan	90	7/30	77.9	70.1	78	63
Guizhou			89.7			
Yunnan						
Xizhang						
Shaanxi				46	>90	>95
Gansu				70	84	68
Qinghai			96	29.3	70	72
Ningxia				54.8		
Xinjiang			68.7	83.3	46	87
Chongqing					92.7	

[a]The figures are for Hebei's Handan Main Station only.

[b]The figures are for Shansi's Datong Main Station only; in Taiyuan, 16,000 practitioners were also reported to have converted.

[c]It is unclear whether the figures are for Liaoning's Shenyang Main Station or for the entire province.

[d]Only the seven provinces in this column specified the dates of conversion.

Source: *Zhongguo sifa Xingzheng nianjian*, 2003, pp. 53–172; *Zhongguo sifa Xingzheng nianjian*, 2004, pp. 47–178.

the years, the cumulative result would be fewer and fewer recalcitrant practitioners. As the latter remain in captivity, the institutional capacity of the
Falungong to reorganize and reinvent itself would decrease over time. This
optimistic inference from the published conversion rates, however, must
be balanced with the following observed trends. It will be noted that more
than four years after the regime had banned the Falungong, a significant
number of Falungong practitioners still defied the official ban and chose
prison sentences over a declaration of severance from the congregation. The
conversion rates do not increase over time, suggesting that the labor reform
institutions had not perfected their craft to be more effective in converting Falungong inmates. It should be further noted that the conversion rates
among the more hardened Falungong practitioners, convicted by the courts
to serve prison sentences in labor reform institutions, were invariably lower
than those of Falungong practitioner inmates. In addition, it may well be the
case that a sizable number of those declared to have been converted by labor
reform officials later rescinded their severance declarations and returned
to the Falungong fold. Falungong sources published a total of 331,470 such
recantation statements alleged to be sent by Falungong practitioners who
signed severance papers with the authorities from January 2001 through
July 2006.[58] However, the veracity of these statements cannot be certified.

CONCLUSION

This chapter evaluates the capacity and effectiveness of the anti-Falungong
campaign. There is little question that the regime was able to mobilize its
institutional resources, launching a full-scale assault on the Falungong in
the three fronts of the campaign. The regime-controlled television, radio,
and Xinhua news agency were able to dominate the nation's media during
the entire duration of the campaign, saturating the airwaves and printed
pages with news releases, press conferences, background analyses, special programs, and editorial series repudiating the Falungong. Its publication houses were also able to produce the 120 anti-Falungong titles by the
regime's deadline, even filling the shelves of the nation's Xinhua book stores
with 31 anti-Falungong titles a week after the ban, and 50 by the end of the
following month. The enforcement of the ban on the Falungong was clearly
visible, with many of the latter's top leaders in official custody, a great majority of its congregations dissolved, the bulk of the Falungong publication stock
destroyed within weeks if not days. Many provinces reported that more than
90% of party members who were Falungong practitioners had renounced
their affiliations with the sect. For the following four years, provinces also
reported that a great majority of its rank-and-file had formally severed its
ties with the Falungong when they underwent labor education.

That the regime would prevail with overwhelming force and asymmetrical power was a foregone conclusion even before the anti-Falungong campaign began. In the foregoing pages, the analytical focus was on the effectiveness rather than capacity. Here my examination of the evidence yields a different answer. In all three fronts, the campaign was executed with the effectiveness of blunt instruments. In the media campaign, there was vertical integration but little horizontal coordination among the media organizations, which rarely collaborated in news production, thematic specialization, campaign phasing, and program publication. The great majority of its propaganda outputs did not pass the quality test and popularity contest. At most one of the 120 anti-Falungong monographs won a Best Book Prize. Per title, the series had smaller distribution than an average book in the central and party presses, those directly controlled by the NPB, and much smaller circulation than an average book published by the Falungong. Similarly, the NPB's television, radio, and news agencies produced few award-winning titles, and reception rates that have been published suggest that during the campaign, both the prime-time evening news in CCTV and its special programs on the Falungong had relatively low ratings. For its conversion program, the double-digit percentage of Falungong inmates in labor education who chose not to renounce their ties with the Falungong in the fourth year after the ban cast doubt on the effectiveness of the program.

But is the more important question not how effective the campaign was waged but whether the regime had won? The concluding chapter 9 takes up this question from the perspective, analyzing what the campaign has achieved, as well as what it failed to do.

Chapter Nine

Concluding Remarks

As we reach the end of the study, what answers can it offer for the larger questions on the fate of the party state under market reforms? In particular, in managing the most serious political challenge to the regime since the Tiananmen incident of June 1989, is it evident that the role of the Chinese Communist Party has diminished in the reform period, the power of the central state giving way to local governments, the legislature, and the Chinese People's Political Consultative Conference (CPPCC)? Has its monitoring and sanctioning capacity been eroded by market forces, handicapped by physical and legal constraints, the emergent civil society taking advantage of the new political opportunity structure opened by the rule of law?

FEATURES OF THE AUTHORITARIAN COMMUNIST STATE

In dealing with domestic challengers, the foregoing chapters suggest that the communist state has remained highly authoritarian. The Chinese Communist Party played a dominant role in leading the campaign, the management of which was highly centralized. The National People's Congress (NPC) did not exercise its constitutional authority of judicial review, legislative, and oversight functions, while the CPPCC played a subordinate and supportive role to the Central Committee. There was no report of interagency conflict or intergovernmental bargaining over cost-sharing burdens in managing the Anti-Falungong campaign.

Dominant Role of the Chinese Communist Party

Rumors on the demise of the institutional power of the Chinese Communist Party are premature. As evident in the anti-Falungong campaign, the party still exercises its leadership in the political realm in China. In crisis management, it was the party, not the State Council, that took the lead. All major policies were deliberated and made at the Politburo, not in the State Council.

The main policy-making body was the Central Leading Group for Dealing with the Falungong, established by and subordinated to the Politburo. All top officials in the group and the its executive arm, the 610 Office, were top party officials, most of whom were members of the Politburo, its Standing Committee, and the Central Committee. In political communications, the main policy document was issued by the party's Central Committee. The main editorials were written by and published in the main party newspapers. The decision to ban the Falungong was communicated not through the state government structure, but through party committees of various administrative levels and bureaucratic agencies. All party members were expected to know about the ban before it was officially announced in the national media on July 22. In specific campaign operations, the anti-Falungong program in the media was directed by the Department of Propaganda of the Chinese Communist Party, not the related agencies in the State Council—the Ministry of Television and Broadcast, the State Bureau of News and Information, or the Ministry of Culture. The decision of whether to continue to employ Falungong practitioners in government or party positions was made by the Organizational Department of the party, not the Ministry of Personnel. In rehabilitating Falungong practitioners, the basic policy document was issued by the party's Central Committee, stipulating what to do in the conversion of party members who practiced the Falungong. The first conversion program was political education within party organizations. In study sessions for both party and nonparty members, traditional Marxism and materialism formed the core content of instruction. It should thus be clear that the party took a dominant role in the anti-Falungong campaign at the central government level.

Below the central level, party organizations also took the lead in the local anti-Falungong campaign. Party organizations were the first to convene meetings to announce the ban, deliberate policies, and set tasks to launch the local campaign. The party committees, not the government, directed the work of the local public security and law enforcement agencies and oversaw the operation. From the province and municipality, down to the township, enterprises, and schools, the local policy-making Leading Group for Dealing with the Falungong and its executive 610 Office were headed by party secretaries, not the governor or mayor, enterprise managers, or school principals. In sum, party leadership is still dominant in both the central and local levels, in bureaucratic agencies, media, public security, and law enforcement in the anti-Falungong campaign, and in almost all major campaign operations. While the role of the party may have become ambivalent in some policy areas and some party leaders may have suffered identity problems in the era of market reforms, its role in dealing with the enemy of the state and communist rule has not been in doubt.

Centralization of the Chinese State

Contrary to the analysis of market-preserving federalism theory, the state has not lost its capacity to extract and enforce local compliance. In managing the campaign, the Chinese regime is a highly centralized state. This is evident in the relative lack of local autonomy in the organizational structure and campaign operations. From the province down to the enterprise level, the campaign was headed by the Leading Group for Dealing with the Falungong, managed by the executive 610 Office, affiliated with the local political and legal affairs committee and supervised by the party committee. At different administrative strata, these organizations have very similar mission statements and task descriptions. The similarity of structure and function and the uniformity of the nomenclature are clearly attributes of the highly centralized organization of the campaign.

The centralization of the campaign can also be seen in the uniformity of meetings convened at different administrative levels, across different bureaucratic agencies, and in both urban areas and the countryside. At each administrative level, and sometimes within each bureaucratic agency, multiple meetings were convened, the first for the core leadership organs, the second for the heads of party and government agencies, and a third for cadres and all party members. These were scheduled in a narrow three-day time frame from July 21 to 23 at the provincial, municipal, and county levels, attended by a similar list of participants in bureaucratic rank and position. Convened and presided by the party secretary, the meetings had agendas generally included the study of the party and government documents announcing the ban on the Falungong, viewing of CCTV special programs, discussion of campaign tasks, and expressing support of the party position. The relative lack of local variations in the structure, format, procedure, agenda, conveners, and participants in these meetings is another manifestation of the centralization of the campaign.

The pattern of campaign operations analyzed in the preceding chapters also suggests that the central state capacity in managing the campaign was virtually intact. There was synchronization of the timing of several important events nationwide—mass arrests of top Falungong leaders on July 20–22, announcement of the ban throughout different television and radio stations at 3 P.M. on July 22, and public destruction of Falungong publications and accessories in different cities on July 29. The same five policy documents were published in the front page of all major national and provincial dailies on July 23, as was another set of five documents on July 24. An invisible hand also appears to be orchestrating the reporting of local implementation and results of the campaign. Different provincial newspapers reported on the arrest and detention of the heads and deputy heads of the Falungong main stations and the percentages of Falungong party members who renounced their ties with sect in the first two weeks after the ban. Provincial and municipal yearbooks also published the percentage of Falungong inmates in local labor reform institutions in the same reporting format and comparable statistics. Despite the substantial variations in the local strength of Falungong presence and its history in staging protest rallies, there were few local variations in the reporting format and categories.

Absence of Bureaucratic Politics

Centralism is also evidenced by the lack of bureaucratic politics among different institutional players in the Chinese political system. Within law enforcement, there were no published references to shirking among different bureaucratic agencies. There were no reports of local public security agencies objecting or resisting the task to intercept Falungong groups passing through their jurisdiction to petition in the provincial capital or in Beijing, or complaining about using local funds to go to the national capital to repatriate local Falungong practitioners. The Anti-Pornography Office did not voice its chagrin over its new responsibility to confiscate, register, and destroy all Falungong publications, a task that could have been assigned to other law enforcement agencies. There were no reports of media organizations complaining of denial of interview or obstruction of media coverage by party and state agencies on Falungong stories, and no law enforcement officials charging the media with biased reporting, or unauthorized and premature publication jeopardizing their cases under investigation. In the annual financial reports of the CCTV, there was no suggestion that the extended hours of covering the anti-Falungong campaign had reduced program ratings, viewership, or advertising revenue. Similarly, there were no published reports of the publications industry complaining that the rush production of anti-Falungong monograph series disrupted their production schedules and hurt their overall sales and financial bottom line, although both seem to be the case, as analyses in chapter 8 demonstrated. No bureaucratic agency at the central or local level was reported to have demanded supplementary funds to augment the local budget for the added administrative burden to deal with the Falungong, and there was no report of interagency or intergovernmental bargaining over the sharing of financial or human resource burdens in managing the Falungong campaign.

Impotence of the National People's Congress

The highly centralized feature of the anti-Falungong campaign manifested not only in the relative lack of local autonomy in campaign operations but also in the executive dominance, and absence of institutional checks and balances from other branches of government. The NPC, the legislature at the central government, played only a limited legislative role and exercised no oversight function in the campaign. None of the five major policy documents promulgating and enforcing the ban on the Falungong on July 22, 1999, was issued by the NPC. After July 23, its standing committee, and not the entire NPC, issued two legislative decisions relating to the Falungong: "Decision on Dissolving, Preventing, and Punishing Activities of Cults" (October 30, 1999), and "Decision to Protect the Security of the Internet" (December 28, 2000), part of which criminalizes the use of the Internet for Falungong activities.[1] Neither of these legislations has the full legal authority of national law deliberated and promulgated by a plenary session of the NPC. Neither was deliberated by the entire body of the national legislature, and both documents took the same positions as the Politburo and the State Council. Promulgated three to five months after the ban, they only ratified the decision to outlaw the Falungong made by the party and State Council.

Aside from exercising only a peripheral role in promulgating legislations on the Falungong, the NPC was also derelict in discharging two of its formal duties. First, none of its special committees or deputies was reported to have exercised its oversight function as provided by the constitution, by summoning officials of the executive branch to inquire how the campaign was implemented in the public security and law enforcement realm. Reports on torture of Falungong practitioners by local public security and labor reform officials, at least some of which appear to be credible, were ignored.[2] Second, the legislators did propose more than a thousand bills annually in recent years to be drafted into law.[3] As shown in table 9.1, among more than 5,000

Table 9.1: Numbers of Sponsored Bills at the National People's Congress, 2000–2004

Year	Total	On the Falungong	On Public Security Management and Punishment	On Enacting the Labor Reform Law
2000	195	0	3	5
2001	268	0	3	6
2002	285	0	5	6
2003	338	0	0	2
2004	641	0	0	12
Total	1,727	0	11	31

Source: *Bulletin of the Standing Committee of the National People's Congress of the People's Republic of China*, 2000, pp. 176–86; 2001, pp. 267–75; 2002, pp. 167–70; 2003, pp. 253–63; 2004: 218–36.

proposed bills from 2000 through 2004, 1,727 bills were referred to special committees for further processing in the same legislative period. Among the latter, there was not a single bill on how to manage the Falungong, or relating to the conduct of the law enforcement agents in their dealings with the congregation. Bills either on enacting laws for public security management and punishment or on labor reform education were generally in the single digits in a given year with hundreds of sponsored bills. Taken together, the absence of published congressional queries and the lack of sponsored bills on the regime's management of the Falungong suggest that the national legislature has abdicated its constitutional powers of judicial review, legislative, and oversight powers over the regime's handling of the Falungong.

Passivity of the Chinese People's Political Consultative Conference

A similar curtain of silence on the Falungong fell on the meetings of the CPPCC, an advisory body established at different administrative levels and regarded as one of the four main political institutions of the regime.[4] Like the NPC, the intellectual, social, and cultural elite that form the core members of the CPPCC also propose bills, some of which have been critical of government policies and the performance of bureaucratic agencies, ranging from the low standards in vocational training institutes and the disadvantaged position of

Table 9.2: Numbers of Speeches at the CPPCC on Falungong and Civil Rights of Labor Education Inmates, 1999–2002

CPPCC Session	Archived Speeches	Repudiating the Falungong	Questioning State Agents' Treatment of Falungong Practitioners	Advocating Better Protection of Labor Reform Inmates
1999	460	0	0	0
2000	491	0	0	1[a]
2001[b]	228	N/D	N/D	N/D
2002	49	2[c]	0	0

[a]The 2000 speech advocating better protection of labor reform inmates was made by Zhang Tongmen of the Democratic National Development party (No. 185)
[b]There is no information on the content and title of the 2001 speeches.
[c]The two 2002 speeches repudiating the Falungong was made by Kong Lingren (no. 691) and Zhang Jiyu (no. 716).

Source: http://www.cppcc.gov.cn/htm/ziliao/mulu91.htm, http://www.cppcc.gov.cn/htm/ziliao/mulu92.htm, http://www.cppcc.gov.cn/htm/ziliao/mulu93.htm, and http://www.cppcc.gov.cn/htm/ziliao/mulu94.htm.

privately owned enterprises versus state-owned enterprises in marketing to the danger of opening the domestic financial market to international corporations and the proliferation of soiree extravaganzas in television programs. As shown in table 9.2, among the speeches made by delegates of the CPPCC from 1999 to 2002, only two concerned the Falungong, and both were titled with official slogans on carrying out the repudiation of the Falungong in depth and to the bitter end. Using a broader conception, only one speech advocated better protection of civil rights of labor reform inmates.[5] At least in its public position, the CPPCC thus served as a supportive institution, not an advisory body to the regime on managing the Falungong. Neither the NPC nor the CPPCC, then, provided the institutional checks and balances vis-à-vis the communist state in dealing with domestic challengers. The later section on the rule of law also shows the lack of judiciary independence.

COERCIVE CAPACITY AND ITS DETRACTORS

While the communist state has remained disciplined under dominant party leadership, highly centralized under Beijing control, and unencumbered by the national legislature, the advisory body, and bureaucratic politics, have its monitoring and sanctioning capacity been eroded by market reforms as power dependency and market transition theories suggest? Has the strong arm of the state been tied by legal constraints imposed by the rule of law? Has the emergent civil society been emboldened to lend support to the beleaguered Falungong?

Monitoring and Sanctioning Capacity

By and large, the monitoring and sanctioning capacity of the communist state remained effective in banning the Falungong. Prior to the ban on July 22, 1999, public security agents had already collected systematic information on the organizational structure, venues, membership, and activities of local Falungong congregations in preparation for the grand assault. They also seemed to have compiled intelligence on the identity, location, and daily schedules of the sect's central and provincial level leaders, as well as their alleged legal violations of laws on publications, social organizations, and assembly. For Falungong strongholds such as Jilin and Wuhan, special investigative reports were prepared on the publications and distribution network, their communications web with subordinate Falungong organizations, and their financial structure and revenue sources. Both human and electronic surveillance was deployed, by both residence- and workplace-based security agents as well as paid informants. At least the Jinzhou Municipality in Liaoning Province created a network of "monitor messengers" to spy on local Falungong practitioners. By the time the ban was implemented, the regime had already at its disposal actionable intelligence to dissolve Falungong gatherings, as well as sufficient evidence for detaining and prosecuting its leaders as well as the rank-and-file. The monitoring reports also provided ammunition for the propaganda war on the alleged doctrinal fallacies and financial profiteering of Li Hongzhi, as well as damage of the Falungong exercise to the body and mind of practitioners. The scrutiny of party members who practiced the Falungong was especially extensive, where each was subjected to an ideological inquisition and required to sever relations with the Falungong. Continued prosecution of Falungong practitioners to the present day, the classification of different types of Falungong fugitives wanted by the regime, and new Falungong registrants at labor reform institutions suggest that the monitoring system has not been terminated.

The state was just as effective in its sanctioning capacity. Falungong daily exercise gatherings in public parks, larger convocations held in sports arenas on special anniversaries, and 3- to 4-day training sessions have virtually disappeared after July 23, 1999. All known Falungong organizations were duly deregistered and their assemblies effectively dissolved. The nationwide distribution of Falungong publications has been outlawed, their editors and publishers censured, and their existing stock of books, practice attire, founder's portraits confiscated and set to flames. Falungong leaders were arrested and put on trial, or went into hiding or to self-exile. Recalcitrant followers were sent to labor reform institutions, where reported conversion rates were high. Within the party, there was a thorough housecleaning, where members practicing Falungong were purged or required to make a formal declaration of their severance from the Falungong. To date, there has been no reversal of fortune for the outlawed congregation. None of the above organizations and banned activities has outlived the repression inside China.

Nevertheless, economic and political reforms did have some effect on eroding the monitoring and sanctioning capacity of the state. Despite an official ban, Falungong books were published by government printing presses, some under the direct management of central agencies. Top Falungong provincial leaders in Anhui, Chengdu, Hainan, Guangxi, and Shanghai were able to elude capture by the time of the ban was promulgated, thanks to Internet communications. At least 10 of the 38 main station chiefs and a much larger number of deputy station chiefs remained at large or unrepentant by the end of August 1999. Four years into the ban, a double-digit percentage of Falungong inmates in labor education still chose not to renounce their ties with the Falungong by the end of 2003. Official media continue to report Falungong practitioners staging protests in provincial and national capitals, sabotaging media broadcasts, and printing and distributing Falungong materials. The

Falungong was still cited as a major law enforcement problem in 21 provincial procuracy reports in 2002, where eight highlighted the congregation in the front page of its report and four mentioned the Falungong as security risk in their 2003 procuracy reports.[6]

The Rule of Law and Its Compromises

Was there rule of law in the anti-Falungong campaign? Did campaign operations breach existing Chinese laws? To justify the ban on the Falungong, the Ministry of Civic Affairs based its decision on the fact that the Falungong was not a registered social organization, and hence its activities were illegal, citing the provisions of the "Regulations on the Registration and Management of Social Organizations," which prohibits any activity of unregistered organizations. Based on the above registration notice, the Ministry of Public Security also issued its own notice outlawing the public posting and display of Falungong logos and insignia, the distribution of its publications, assembling for Falungong activities, sit-ins seeking audiences from authorities pleading for Falungong, fabricating and circulating rumors, and organizing and networking (*chuanlian*) to defy government orders.[7] It would thus appear that the official dissolution of the Falungong was in accordance with existing law, as was the prohibition and prosecution of Falungong assemblies, protest activities, and the distribution of Falungong publications after the ban.

As for the legality of the detention, arrest, trial, and conviction of Falungong practitioners for their activities before July 22, much would depend on the facts of the individual cases. Since neither official nor Falungong sources publish the full case histories of judicial proceedings, it is difficult to ascertain whether public security, procuracy, and the courts were acting in accordance with the law. But it appears that many alleged activities of individual Falungong practitioners or groups before July 22 had breached laws of the People's Republic of China. At least its leaders could have been charged with violating the State Council "Regulations on Registering and Managing Social Organizations," which prohibits all activities of any social organizations that have not been officially registered.[8] Under this statute, some Falungong leaders, including those of the Falun Dafa Research Society in Beijing, could also be charged with breaching tax laws for failing to declare income derived from seminar fees and sales from publications and Falungong materials.[9] Those who played a leading role in the more than 300 Falungong protest rallies from April 25 to July 22, 1999, could have also violated official sanctions against organizing assemblies without official approval, and ones that besieged state organs and disturb social order, in violation of the "Law on Assembly, Parade, and Protest of the People's Republic of China."[10]

On court proceedings, the published trials of Falungong practitioners also appeared to have followed extant laws. A majority of the cases involve downloading, reproducing, and distributing Falungong materials, and there were also cases of displaying Falungong slogans in public, broadcasting Falungong tapes outside labor reform institute, sending mass Falungong text messages through cellular phones, and replacing public broadcast with Falungong programs.[11] That the defendants had committed most of these alleged acts does not seem to be disputed, since the Falungong Web site, newspaper, and radio had published numerous cases of Falungong practitioners committing these acts, which many defendants also acknowledged in court. Aside from the legality of criminal charges, the trial process also seems to be in compliance with the law. There was also the appearance of rule of law in some cases, which presented material evidence (receipts for property rental, phone installations, forensic test reports) and witness testimonies.[12] At least in one case, the judge dismissed charges against one Falungong practitioner on grounds that the evidence presented by the procurator was insufficient.[13] The publication of sentencing guidelines jointly by the Supreme People's Court and the Supreme People's Procuracy to determine the seriousness of the offense and appropriate punishment may also have the effect of reducing arbitrary and capricious sentencing.[14]

But several law enforcement practices compromise the integrity of the rule of law in the anti-Falungong campaign. First, there is no report that any court in China has agreed to take cases initiated by Falungong plaintiffs challenging the legality of official statutes and action of the law enforcement agencies. Except for the case of the judge dismissing charges against the Falungong practitioner noted in the above paragraph, there are no reports of any court in any administrative level in China dismissing or reducing charges in Falungong cases prosecuted by the local procuracy. There is likewise no report of any procurator who has refused to issue any warrant for the arrest, search, or wiretap of any Falungong practitioner or group. On the other hand, the Dalian Municipal Judiciary Bureau reportedly discussed strategies to persuade the local lawyer community not to take Falungong cases.[15] Similarly, there is an additional report that three separate intermediate courts in Shijiazhuang, the provincial capital of Hebei, refusing to consider the case of alleged wrongful sentencing of a Falungong practitioner brought by defense attorneys,[16] a practice that Falungong sources suggest was quite prevalent.[17] The allegation may be true since most reports of court proceedings did not mention the presence of defense counsel. The extent of denial of legal representation or judicial tampering of defense attorneys is not clear. There was at least one Falungong source that reports a practicing lawyer mounting an eloquent defense of a practitioner distributing Falungong materials in a court case in Guangxi Province on December 8, 2005,[18] and one other well-publicized case involving Falungong defendants reportedly retaining their own lawyers.[19]

Along with the denial of legal representation was extrapunitive sentencing. Despite the publication of sentencing guidelines, the Supreme People's Procuracy could not have anticipated the broad range of offenses committed by Falungong practitioners. Consequently, local judges still had wide latitudes in sentencing, resulting in some unusually heavy convictions. For instance, a practitioner in Beijing who downloaded and distributed around 800 copies of Falungong materials to other practitioners received a three-year prison sentence in April 2003 for her first-time offense.[20] Two other practitioners were sentenced to 12 and 13 years respectively for posting news on a Web site about ill treatment of a student Falungong member in prison.[21] For their role in replacing regular television programs with those of Falungong, a group of Falungong conspirators in Changchun received heavy prison sentences, with 8 of the 15 defendants condemned to 17–20 years' imprisonment.[22]

A more prevalent and less disputed infraction is the practice of physical abuse and torture of Falungong inmates in labor reform institutions, which is clearly prohibited by law and regulations of the Re-education through Labor Reform Administration.[23] As elaborated in chapter 5, such practices appear to be widespread in many locations in China, as suggested by the use of "no unnatural death" as a nationwide performance target in labor reform institutions. Less draconian, but probably more common and less documented, were instances of law enforcement agencies taking procedural shortcuts. In the reform period, both the NPC and the Ministry of Justice promulgated extensive laws and regulations on administering criminal justice, including elaborate legal procedures involving filing proper documentation and taking appropriate action by officials within definite time limits. In criminal detention (*xingxi juliu*), for instance, public security agents are authorized to detain a suspect only under seven given conditions when a crime is suspected. Four sets of legal documents need to be filed: "Report to Request Detention," "Detention Certificate," "Detention Notice," and "Notice to Release," to be completed or approved by, or shown to, different parties (suspect, suspect's family or employer, administrative or law enforcement official). Family members or employer needs to be informed in writing within 24 hours of detention; interrogation to determine arrest or release is required to be completed within 24 hours. If arrest is warranted, the arrest warrant needs to be issued within three days of detention, up to seven days in special circumstances, and up to 30 days when the case involves multiple offenses or multiple locations. Elaborate procedures also govern the processes of setting bail, surveillance, court trial, and labor reform. There is a paucity of published information on whether law enforcement agencies complied with these elaborate procedures. One can reason when a city or county was inundated with up to several thousand practitioners who need to be handled in the law enforcement system within a few weeks or even days, the temptation was to skirt these procedures. Falungong sources often mention that families were not notified about the detention of Falungong practitioners, contrary to stipulations requiring that they be informed within 24 hours.[24] They also frequently refer to the practice as "kidnapping,"[25] suggesting that proper legal documentation and procedure had not been filed. Available documentation, however, is insufficient to verify these allegations.

Stunted Growth of Civil Society

It is true that revolutionary regimes always claim paramount power and terrorize society into submission. Chapter 1 noted that the new political opportunity structure in the market reform period in China has spawned nongovernmental organizations and emboldened discontented groups to stage protests. Has the activism of these groups inspired other social organizations to support the Falungong out of solidarity? In particular, have the five organized religions taken an official position on the Falungong? These religious organizations often state their public support of the regime's positions in both domestic and international affairs. On domestic events, the five religious bodies voiced support for the resolutions of the 15th Party Congress in September 1997; called for renewed patriotism in a seminar commemorating the 50th anniversary of the anti-Japanese War in September 25, 1999, and participated in the National Day Parade on the Founding of the People's Republic on October 1999.[26] In international affairs, the five religions also protested the alleged biased portrayal of Chinese religion in the U.S. State Department's "Report on World Religions" in August 1997, denounced the NATO bombing of the Chinese Embassy in Belgrade in May 1999, and condemned Taiwan President Lee Teng-hui's Two-State Theory in July 1999.[27]

Neither official nor Falungong sources suggest that any human rights group inside China has defended the Falungong. While five official religions have expressed public support for the regime's policies, they have not taken a collective position or issue a joint statement on the Falungong. In a statement published in the *Renmin ribao* on August 4, 1999, Ding Guangxun, the honorary president of the Chinese Federation of Protestants, declared his church's support of the ban on the Falungong.[28] In separate statements published in the *Renmin ribao* on August 2 and 4, the Chinese Federation of Buddhists' president (Zhao Puchu) and vice president (Ming Shan) also echoed their support.[29] In contrast, the Chinese Federation of Daoists, the Chinese Catholic Patriotic Church, and the Chinese Federation of Islam did not issue any statement on the anti-Falungong campaign from July 22 through the end of 1999. Their silence on the issue is mystifying given their previous support of the regime's position in major domestic and international issues. An inference can thus be drawn that these three religious organizations did not want to lend their public support to the anti-Falungong campaign.

But if it would be unrealistic to expect human rights groups or official religions to defend the Falungong, has the more liberal political climate in the reform period fostered individuals to provide moral or material support of the banned sect? Thus far, the closest report of a "white knight" appears as a defense attorney in the case referred to above. There are, however, more reports of anonymous sympathizers who chose the congregation over the state. Falungong sources have published several reports of people not turning their practitioners in to the authorities. They include employers who continued to hire unrepentant Falungong practitioners despite official prohibition,[30] colleagues and superiors tolerating practitioners reading Falungong publications openly during office hours[31] and even tipping them off about impending police arrests,[32] departmental security chiefs closing an eye to the presence of Falungong publications, and landlords who knowingly ignored the premises being used as an underground Falungong press.[33] There was also a report that public security agents did not detain a Falungong practitioner after the latter sermonized them on the morality of the Falungong,[34] and a separate report that the local public security agents had warned a Falungong operator of a materials center that agents of the 610 Office were coming.[35] But these were all covert assistance, and the sources do not explain their motivation. Providing protective cover in secret is not the same as publically declaring support for the Falungong.

The State and Its Enemies

As the first major political campaign in the post-Mao era, the anti-Falungong campaign was a powerful show of force that testifies to the centrality of state monopoly of coercive and propaganda institutions and the efficacy of the sanctioning and monitoring capacity of the communist state. The effective campaign with which the Falungong was crushed is witness to the enduring power of China's authoritarian regime. Contrary to postulations that the power of the Chinese Communist Party has declined, that its monitoring and sanctioning capacity is eroded by market reform, and that its collapse is probable, even imminent and certain,[36] this study demonstrates that the regime does not lack the capacity to respond to political challenges, the will to utilize that capacity, and the ability to achieve intended results. Even in this reform era, as the communist state's ideological machinery lapses in its control of the minds of its citizenry, its household registration system fails in keeping peasants on their farms and youths in their domiciles, and as its neoauthoritarian system in the work place offers fewer carrots to coax and sticks to coerce than before, the regime has not lost its will and capacity to crush its domestic adversaries. Compared to the hesitant regime reaction in the 1986 and 1989 student movements, the Politburo under Jiang Zemin was much more resolute and effective in dealing with the Falungong than its predecessors were with the students.

Though resolute and ready, it should be noted that the post-Mao regime is not an indiscriminate oppressor. The study illuminates how the regime chose which battle to fight, when to engage the enemy, and where it drew the scrimmage line. Ten years after the democracy movement in 1989, unregistered organizations were tolerated, even one whose publications were repeatedly banned and that had mounted numerous protest rallies against local government agencies, provided it did not challenge the authority of the regime. The trip wire is laid around Zhongnanhai, the cloistered national headquarters of the party and state, where it is still the Forbidden City that offers no quarter for trespassers, the sanctuary into which the unordained and unanointed cannot enter, much less demonstrate. Indeed, the prohibition applies not only to territorial space but also organizational membership. A main reason why the Falungong was suppressed so resolutely was its successful penetration into the inner core and top echelon of the party, a fact that Jiang Zemin found both disturbing and intolerable.[37]

But will the same scenario play out at some future time? Will the coming of the party decline and system collapse be hastened by market expansion that further erodes organized dependency and the political commitment of party members, until the entire system collapses rapidly and smoothly as those in Russia and Eastern Europe? In the wake of the 17th Party Congress, it is uncertain what the future portends. To paraphrase Heraclitus, the regime may not use the same methods and achieve the same results twice. For one, the regime, with four new members in the nine-person new Politburo Standing Committee, is likely to differ from the present regime. Yet whether it will be a gentler and kinder horticulturist who allows the blooming of some unplanted flowers or an overvigilant gardener who nips any uncultivated sprout in the bud remains to be seen. The post-Mao Chinese garden has seen both varieties of leaders. On their part, the next-generation dissident groups may have learned from the mistakes of the Falungong and will adapt their strategies accordingly. They would probably exist as a subterranean life form for a relatively long period, developing survival structures, dependency relations, and camouflage mechanisms. Depending on how benign or threatening the external environment is, they may mimic their surroundings, change their colors, and contort their anatomy to avoid predation. Or like the Catholic Church in China, they may develop a schizophrenic persona, with an above-ground institution that swears loyalty to the communist state and an underground body that pledges allegiance to the Pope. There may also be unity in duality, with some members living a double life of above- and below-ground existence.

Between the state and its domestic challengers, society itself may also change. Civil society may also come of age, with more lawyer associations, journalist federations, and chambers of commerce organizing to advance their corporate interests. Given new autonomy from the state,[38] religious groups may even press for greater independence from the local Religious Affairs Bureau. As the private sphere becomes larger relative to the public realm, dissident groups will also have more foraging space before they reach the limits of regime tolerance. The state may also grow more accustomed to the proliferation of civil groups, even becoming more assured that their ascendancy does not mean the demise of its own power. As civil society becomes more mature and the state more mellow, both may become more sophisticated in relating to each other, as they learn how to play the non-zero-sum game of coexistence.

From this perspective, Heraclitus, rather than George Orwell or Crane Brinton, may provide a more appropriate framework to understand authoritarian rule in the market reform period. Brinton did little to forecast how the post-Thermidorian state after the brutal Reign of Terror would deal with its challengers, except that it would be less resolute and its methods less draconian.[39] For Orwell, power corrupts the revolutionary elite and corrodes the revolutionary cause, as they compromise their lofty principles and betray their ideological commitment. In the end, the new rulers of *Animal Farm* are indistinguishable from the old masters that they drove out. But for Heraclitus, not only do the rulers change, so do its enemies and society, and also how these three interact. Contrary to Orwell's script and Brinton's dissection, the postrevolutionary state will not return to the political culture of the ancient regime. Future clashes between the Chinese state and challengers are thus less likely to be competition déjà vu than the less predictable confrontation de jour.

Notes

CHAPTER 1

1. Zong Hairen, *Zhu Rongji zai yi jiujiujiu nian* [Zhu Rongji in 1999] (Hong Kong: Mirror Books, 2001) [hereafter Zong, 2001], p. 48; translated in *Chinese law and government* (January-February 2002) [hereafter Zong (2002a)], p. 54.

2. *Renmin ribao*, April 23, 24, 1999, p. 1.

3. *Renmin ribao*, March 1, 3, 5, 11, 15, 1999, p. 1.

4. *Renmin ribao*, March 6, 7, 8, 9, 10, 11, 12, 13, 16, 1999, p. 1.

5. *Renmin ribao*, March 5, 6, 1999, p. 1.

6. *Renmin ribao*, March 21, 24, 25, 26, 28, 29, 1999, p. 1.

7. *Renmin ribao*, March 21, 23, 24, 25, 26, 28, 29, 1999, p. 1.

8. *Renmin ribao*, March 25, 1999, p. 4; March 26, 1999, p. 1.

9. *Renmin ribao*, March 18, 19, 1999, p. 4.

10. *Renmin ribao*, March 24, 25, 1999, p. 4.

11. Known as the Cox Report, after Californian Republican Congressman Christopher Cox, who chaired the committee that produced it, "The Report of the Select Committee on U.S. National Security and Military/Commercial Concerns with the People's Republic of China" charges that China stole U.S. nuclear technology. The summary of the opening paragraph reads,

> The People's Republic of China (PRC) has stolen design information on the United States' most advanced thermonuclear weapons. The Select Committee judges that the PRC's next generation of thermonuclear weapons, currently under development, will exploit elements of stolen U.S. design information. PRC penetration of our national nuclear weapons laboratories spans at least the past several decades and almost certainly continues today.

12. The full title was "Breach at Los Alamos: a special report; China stole nuclear secrets for bomb, U.S. aide says," *New York Times*, March 6, 1999, p. 1.

13. *Renmin ribao*, April 22, 1999, p. 1.

14. Zong (2002a, p. 51) suggests that it was a deliberate signal of Jiang Zemin, who tried to dissociate himself with Zhu's handling of the WTO accession issue.

15. Zong (2002a), p. 53.

16. Zong (2002a), p. 60.

17. Zong (2002a), p. 55.

18. Zong (2002a, p. 65) mentioned that action would be taken after "May 4." The original Chinese states that it was "June 4"; see Zong (2001), p. 14.

19. Zong (2002a), p. 66.

20. Zong (2002a), p. 54.

21. This portrait of the Falungong is largely drawn from the Falungong Web page (www.falundafa.org/eng/index.htm).

22. David Palmer, *Qigong fever: body, science and utopia in China* (New York: Columbia University Press, 2007) [hereafter Palmer (2007)], pp. 236–57.

23. *Renmin ribao*, July 23, 1999; "Qian suo Falungong" [A brief discussion on Falungong] (August 14, 1999), *Minghui* Web site (www.minghui.org). Elsewhere, Falungong publications claim that the Great Falun Method (Falun Dafa) is an ancient practice.

24. Palmer (2007), pp. 236–57.

25. Palmer (2007), pp. 69–72. Qian played a leading role in the development of China's nuclear program. Zhang was a brigadier-general in the People's Liberation Army.

26. Ye Hao, "Youguan Falungong shifou you zuzhi di zhenxiang" [An explanation on whether the Falungong was organized] (July 31, 1999), *Minghui* Web site (www. minghui.org) [hereafter Ye Hao (1999)].

27. Ye Hao (1999).

28. The total number of training seminars varies according to different reports. "Falungong zhenshi gushi" [The real story of Falungong], http://minghui.org/mh/article/2000/6/25/12501p.html, stated 53 seminars. Jennifer Zeng mentioned 54 seminars in *Witnessing history: one Chinese woman's fight for freedom* (New York: Soho Press, 2006), p. 329; while a *Beijing wanbao* (August 7, 1999) report gave the total number of training seminars as 56.

29. "Falungong zhenshi gushi" [The real story of Falungong], *Minghui* Web site (www.minghui.org).

30. Zhao Jiemin, "Qiefa jianju jianghu pianzi Li Hongzhi cailiao" [Materials exposing the swindler Li Hongzhi], Web site (www.xy.org/_ppfl/).

31. Ye Hao (1999).

32. Palmer (2007), pp. 170–72.

33. *Renmin ribao*, July 30, 1999, p. 4; see also Yan Shi, ed., *Shiji jupian: Li Hongzhi* [Swindler of the century: Li Hongzhi] (Beijing: Dazhong wenyi chubanshe, 1999), p. 75.

34. "Yu fa bu rong, yu li bu tong" [Incompatible with law, illogical in reason], *Minghui* Web site (www.minghui.org). It signatory was "A group of China law workers," dated August 11, 1999 [hereafter A group of China law workers (1999)].

35. "Falungong di zhenshi gushi," Minghui Web site (www.minghui.org).

36. There were no special organizational links between the Falungong and the National Minority Commission. A Falungong source suggested that the choice to affiliate with the commission could be due to personal connections in the top leadership of both organizations.

37. James Tong, "An organizational analysis of the Falungong: structure, communications, financing," *China Quarterly*, no. 171 (September 2002), pp. 641–65 [hereafter Tong (2002a)].

38. For an organizational analysis of the Falungong, see Tong (2002a).

39. In Falungong publications, "Falun Dafa" is synonymous with Falungong.

40. *Beijing wanbao*, August 7, 1999.

41. This is suggested by a Falungong source.

42. *Guangming ribao*, August 3, 1999, p. 1.

43. *Renmin ribao,* August 15, 1999, p. 1. See also Tong (2002a) for another official estimate.

44. A group of China law workers (1999).

45. *Guangming ribao,* August 3, 1999; *Henan ribao,* August 1, 1999, p. 2.

46. *Guangming ribao,* August 3 (reported in Shandong) and August 6 (reported in Nanjing), 1999; *Gansu ribao,* August 6, p. 4, both *lianxizhe* and *liangongzhe; Gansu ribao,* August 22; *xiulianzhe* in *Tianjin ribao,* November 1, 1999, p. 1.

47. *Renmin ribao,* August 4, 1999, p. 1.

48. *Guangming ribao,* August 3, 1999; August 5, 1999, p. 1.

49. *Renmin ribao,* July 30, 1999, p. 4; July 31, 1999, p. 1; August 2, 1999, p. 4.

50. *Renmin ribao,* August 2, 1999, p. 4; *Guangming ribao,* August 3, 1999; *Fujian ribao,* August 6, 1999; see Stephen O'Leary, "Falungong and the Internet," *Online Journalism Review* (2000), www.ojr/ethics/1017964337.php.

51. *Guangming ribao,* August 3, 1999; Xinhua, Beijing, press release of August 2, 1999.

52. The 1.5 million *yuan* figure was cited by Tang Xuehua, former Beijing main station chief, in his confession; see *Beijing wanbao,* August 7, 1999. The 2 million *yuan* figure was mentioned by a Falungong source referring to a government allegation ("Falungong xueyuan tan jingji wuxian," *Minghui* Web site, www.minghui.org).

53. *Renmin ribao,* August 1, 2, 15, 1999, p. 1.

54. "Falungong zhenshi di gushi," *Minghui* Web site (www.minghui.org); Hao (1999).

55. From Li Hongzhi's response to a reporter's inquiry in his press conference in Sydney, May 2, 1999, published in Shi, *Shiji jupian,* p. 56.

56. Patricia Thornton, "Framing dissent in contemporary China: irony, ambiguity and metonymy," *China Quarterly,* no. 171 (September 2002), pp. 661-81.

57. Beatrice Leung, "China and the Falun Gong: party and society relations in the modern era," *Journal of Contemporary China,* 11/33 (November 2002), pp. 761-85.

58. David Ownby, "The Falun Gong in the new world," *European Journal of East Asian Studies,* 2/2 (December 2003), pp. 303-21.

59. Cheris S.C. Chan, "The Falun Gong in China: a sociological perspective," *China Quarterly,* no. 179 (September 2004), pp. 665-84.

60. Kevin McDonald, "Oneself as another: from social movement to experience movement," *Current Sociology,* 52/4 (July 2004), pp. 575-90, 665-81.

61. Kevin McDonald, *Global movements: action and culture* (Oxford: Blackwell Publishing, 2006), pp. 14-17, 140-68.

62. Vaughan McTernan, "The Falun Gong: a virtual meeting of East and West," *Bucknell Review,* 47/2 (June 2003), pp. 104-28.

63. Maria Hsia Chang, *Falun Gong: the end of days* (New Haven: Yale University Press, 2004); Ian Adams, Riley Adams, and Rocco Galati, *Power of the wheel: the Falun Gong revolution* (Toronto: Stoddart Publishing Co., 2000); see also Palmer (2007).

64. John Wong and William T. Liu, *The mystery of the China's Falun Gong: its rise and its sociological implications.* East Asian Institute Contemporary China Series, no. 22 (Singapore: Singapore University Press, 1999).

65. Hongyan Xiao, "Falun Gong and the ideological crisis of the Chinese Communist Party: Marxist atheism vs. vulgar theism," *East Asia: An International Quarterly,* 19/1-2 (Spring-Summer 2001), pp. 123-44; Patsy Rahn, "The chemistry of a conflict:

the Chinese government and the Falun Gong," *Terrorism and Political Violence*, 14/4 (Winter 2002), pp. 41-66.

66. Jason Kindopp, "China's war on 'cults,'" *Current History*, 101/656 (September 2002), pp. 259-67.

67. Chiung Hwang Chen, "Framing Falun Gong: Xinhua news agency's coverage of the new religious movement in China," *Asian Journal of Communication*, 15/1 (March 2005), pp. 16-37.

68. Alex Wyatt, "The global economy and the on-line world: consequences of WTO accession on the regulation of the Internet in China," *Melbourne Journal of International Law*, 3/2 (October 2002), pp. 436-53; Bill Hancock, "China's internal war with the Falun Gong sect spills onto the Internet," *Computers and Security*, 18/6 (October 1999), pp. 464-66.

69. Bryan Edelman and James T. Richardson, "Imposed limitations on freedom of religion in China and the margin of appreciation doctrine: a legal analysis of the crackdown on the Falun Gong on other 'evil cults,'" *Journal of Church and State*, 47/2 (Spring 2005), pp. 243-68; Janice Casil, "Falun Gong and China's human rights violations," *Peace Review*, 16/2 (June 2004), pp. 225-31.

70. Alan A. Stone, "The plight of the Falun Gong," *Psychiatric Times* (November 2004), pp. 1-13; Alan A. Stone, "The China psychiatric crisis: following up on the plight of the Falun Gong," *Psychiatric Times* (May 2005), pp. 1-13; Robin Munro, *Dangerous minds: political psychiatry in China today and its origins in the Mao era* (New York: Human Rights Watch, 2002).

71. See, e.g., Jerry F. Hough, *Democratization and revolution in the USSR, 1985-1991* (Washington, DC: Brookings Institution, 1997); Ivan Szelenyi and Balazs Szelenyi, "Why socialism failed: towards a theory of system breakdown," *Theory and Society*, 23/2 (1994), pp. 211-31; Marek M. Kaminski, "How communism could have been saved: formal analysis of electoral bargaining in Poland in 1989," *Public Choice*, 98/1-2 (1999), pp. 83-109; Johann P. Arnason, *The future that failed: origins and destinies of the Soviet model* (London: Routledge, 1993); Timur Kuran, "Now out of never: the element of surprise in the East European revolution of 1989," *World Politics*, 44/1 (1991), pp. 7-48; Laszlo Bruszt and David Stark, "Remaking of the political field in Hungary: from the politics of confrontation to the politics of competition," *Journal of International Affairs*, 45/1 (1991), pp. 201-45; Arpad Szakolczai and Agnes Horváth, "Political instructors and the decline of communism in Hungary: apparatus, nomenclatura and the issue of legacy," *British Journal of Political Science*, 21/4 (1991), pp. 469-88; Rasma Karklins and Roger Petersen, "Decision calculus of protesters and regimes: Eastern Europe 1989," *Journal of Politics*, 55/3 (1993), pp. 588-614; Grzegorz Ekiert, "Democratization processes in East Central Europe: a theoretical reconsideration," *British Journal of Political Science*, 21/3 (1991), pp. 285-313.

72. Gordon G. Chang, *The coming collapse of China* (New York: Random House, 2001).

73. Jack A. Goldstone, "The coming Chinese collapse," *Foreign Policy*, no. 99 (Summer 1996), pp. 35-52.

74. Charles Wolf, Jr., K.C. Yeh, Benjamin Zycher, Nicholas Eberstadt, and Sung-ho Lee, *Fault lines in China's economic terrain* (Santa Monica, Calif.: Rand Corporation, 2003).

75. Wolf et al., *Fault lines*, tables 10-1 and 10-2, pp. 176-77.

76. Andrew Walder, "The decline of communist power: elements of a theory of institutional change," *Theory and Society,* 23 (1994), pp. 297-323.

77. Victor Nee, "A theory of market transition: from redistribution to markets in state socialism," *American Sociological Review,* 54 (1989), pp. 663-81; Victor Nee and Lian Peng, "Sleeping with the enemy: a dynamic model of declining commitment in state socialism" *Theory and Society,* 23 (1994), pp. 253-96.

78. Gabriella Montinola, Yingyi Qian, and Barry R. Weingast, "Federalism, Chinese style: the political basis for economic success," *World Politics,* 48/1 (1996), pp. 50-81.

79. Walder, "The decline of communist power," p. 303.

80. See, e.g., Susan Shirk, *The political logic of economic reform in China* (Berkeley: University of California Press, 1993), pp. 222-24; Richard Baum, *Burying Mao: Chinese politics in the age of Deng Xiaoping* (Princeton, NJ: Princeton University Press, 1994), pp. 151-53.

81. *Cheng ming,* no. 296 (June 2002), pp. 16-18, and no. 335 (September 2005), pp. 14-15; Ho Pin, *Zhongguo xin zhuhou* [The new lords of the People's Republic of China] (Mississauga, Ont.: Mirror Books, 1996), p. 30.

82. *Zhongguo minzheng nianjian, 2004* [China civil affairs yearbook, 2004] (Beijing: Zhonguo shehui chubanshe, 2005), p. 494.

83. *Renmin ribao,* August 7, 1997, p. 4; May 9, 1999, p. 4; July 17, 1999, p. 2.

84. Ju Mengjun, ed., *Chanchu xiejia qiankun lang* [The universe will be bright after the cult is eradicated] (Beijing: Xinhua chubanshe, 2001); Dou Wentao, *Falungong daqidi* [Great expose of the Falungong] (Beijing: Xiandai chubanshe, 2000); Wang Zhigang and Song Jianfeng, *"Falungong" xiejiaobenji mianmianguan* [Different perspectives of the essence of the Falungong cult] (Beijing: Lantian chubanshe, 2001); Yan Shi ed., *Shiji jupian: Li Hongzhi* [Swindler of the century: Li Hongzhi] (Beijing: Dazhong wenyi chubanshe, 1999); Zhao Jianxun ed., *Zui-e—Falungong shouhaizhe xuelei kongsu* [Crimes—the blood and tears accusations of Falungong victims] (Beijing: Zhongguo minzhu fazi chubanshe, 2000); *Toushi xiejiao jiepou Falungong* [Cult penetrated—anatomy of Falungong] (Beijing: Zhongguo qingnian chubanshe, 2001); *Zhuan Falun pipan* [A critique of Zhuan Falun] (Beijing: Beijing chubanshe, 2001); *Xiandai Huangyan: Li Hongzhi wailixieshuo pingxi* [Contemporary lies: a critical analysis of the crooked theories and evil teachings of Li Hongzhi] (Beijing: Zhongguo shuji chubanshe, 1999); *Falungong xianxiang pingxi* [A critical analysis of the Falungong phenomenon] (Beijing: Shehui kexue wenxian chubanshe, 2001); *Bushi "zhen shan ren" er shi "zhen chan ren"* [It is not "truth, kindness, forbearance" but real cruelty] (Beijing: Xuexi chubanshe, 2001); Tang Zhongren, ed., *Tiaochu jingshen xianjing* [Jumping out from the spiritual trap] (Shanghai: Shanghai renmin chubanshe, 2001); Zhuang Fenggan, *"Falungong" xianxiang di xinli fenxi* [A psychological analysis of the Falungong phenomenon] (Beijing: Kexue chubanshe, 2002).

85. These are the "News and information about Falungong around the world" (chinese.faluninfo.net/fdi/gb/index.htm), which publishes daily news releases in 10 languages, and the *Epochtimes* (www.epochtimes.com, www.ntdtv.org), which has news releases in 13 languages and publishes a daily newspaper, *Dajiyuan* (Epochtimes), distributed free in overseas Chinese communities.

86. "Friends of the Falung Dafa Radio" (fofld.radio.org) and the "Sound of Hope International Radio" (www.soundofhope.org).

87. Fangguangming (International), Fangguangming (Taiwan), and New Tang Dynasty TV, which broadcasts in three languages (www.fgmtv.org).

88. The publications series include the basic Falungong doctrinal scripture, *Zhuangfalun*, which has been translated into 25 languages, in addition to five commentaries on the mantra, four titles of Li Hongzhi's poetry, and around 20 sets of lecture notes. The series also comprises 60 e-books on counterofficial propaganda; six titles in its publications series, *Minghui congshu*, which includes children's books, a biography of a Falungong practitioner, a compilation of 81 cases where practicing Falungong leads to dramatic health improvements, two anthologies of poetry by practitioners, and an indictment of Jiang Zemin; and more than 6,000 titles of local Falungong newsletters; see www.minghui.org.

89. See www.minghui.org.

90. These daily news items are published under six headings: (1) atrocities against Falungong practitioners inside detention and labor reform education institutions; (2) local reports of persecution against practitioners; (3) hall of infamy of public security and "610 Office" cadres and their contact information; (4) discussion forum on doctrinal and physical exercise issues; (5) stories on practitioners; and (6) short news items. See search.minghui.org/mh/articles/2005/12/21/115659.html, www.falundafa.ca, and www.minghui.org.

91. See *Minghui* (www.minghui.org), various sections, accessed on July 31, 2006.

92. Zong (2001, 2002a, 2002b).

93. The Hong Kong periodicals *Cheng ming* and *Dongxiang* were consulted, as was the U.S. publication *Beijing zhichun*.

94. *Zhongguo zhengfu zhuji jigou* [Government organization of China] (Beijing: Gaige chubanshe, 1998), pp. 174–351. The organizational charts and staff size of all other ministries are published.

95. *Shanxi ribao*, August 8, 1999, p. 1.

96. *Zhongguo sifa xingzheng nianjian* (2004), p. 54.

97. *Tianjian nianjian* (2004), p. 168.

98. *Zhongguo sifa xingzheng nianjian* (2004); *Heilongjiang nianjian* (2004), p. 126. In labor reform institutes, "Falungong criminals" refer to those who were indicted and sentenced for criminal offenses, whereas "inmates" refer to those being held under the administrative detention procedure and not charged with criminal violations; see chapter 5.

99. Zong (2002a, p. 70) reports that an overwhelming majority of these 5,600 were released after they wrote a repentance statement [*huiguoshu*] and pledged to withdraw from the Falungong.

100. These cities were Beijing, Tianjin, Shijiazhuang, Dalian, Shenyang, Weifang, Yiantai, Wuhan, Guangzhou, Shenzhen, Linyungang, Taiyuan, Datong, Changzhi, Zhangjiakou, Benxi, Yanchuan, Jinzhou, and four other unnamed cities; *Cheng ming* (August 1999), p. 8.

101. *Cheng ming* (August 1999), p. 8.

102. *Hong Kong Standard,* July 27, 1999.

103. *Cheng ming* (August, 1999), p. 8; *Jiefang ribao*, July 24, 1999, *Shaanxi ribao*, July 27, 1999, p. 1.

104. Zong (2002a), pp. 40–41.

105. *Renmin ribao*, March 26, 1999, p. 1.

106. See minghui.org/mh/articles/2006/3/19/123176.html.

107. See www.minghui.ca/mh/articles/2006/3/8/122394p.html and library.minghui.org/search.asp?sss=%CB%D5%BC%D2%CD%CD&category_id=&dynamic=0.

108. See www.lskj.gov.cn/Association/AssociationShow.aspx?ID=8980&subclass=2.

109. See www.lskj.gov.cn/Association/AssociationShow.aspx?ID=8980&subclass=2.

110. See www.lskj.gov.cn/Association/AssociationShow.aspx?ID=8980&subclass=2.

CHAPTER 2

1. Richard Baum, *Burying Mao: Chinese politics in the age of Deng Xiaoping* (Princeton: Princeton University Press, 1994) [hereafter Baum (1994)], pp. 200–208.

2. Baum (1994), pp. 247–70.

3. Contrary to the advice of his personal secretary Tian Ziyun, Zhao did not postpone his trip to Pyongyang on April 23–29. It was only in his absence that the Politburo deliberated on what to do with the Falungong. See Zhang Liang, *Zhongguo "liusi" zhenxiang* [*The Tiananmen Papers*] (New York: Mingjing chubanshe, 2001) [hereafter Zhang (2001)], pp. 47, 57–96.

4. Li Peng was also a member of the Politburo Standing Committee. The decision to impose martial law was made by a meeting of the Politburo Standing Committee on the morning of May 17. See Zhang (2001), pp. 184–90.

5. Zhang (2001), p. 193.

6. Zhang (2001), pp. 441–46.

7. Zong Hairen, *Zhu Rongji zai yi jiujiujiu nian* [Zhu Rongji in 1999] (Hong Kong: Mirror Books, 2001); translated in *Chinese law and government* (January–February 2002) [hereafter Zong (2002a)], pp. 55–56.

8. The letter was addressed to the members of the Politburo Standing Committee and other concerned leaders, dated April 25, 1999, and was transmitted by the General Office of the Central Committee for broader circulation on April 27, 1999. The text of the letter was published in *Beijing zhichun* (Beijing Spring), no. 97 (June 2001), pp. 9–10.

9. Zong (2002a), p. 63.

10. *Beijing zhichun*, no. 97 (June 2001), pp. 10–12.

11. Zong (2002a), p. 66.

12. Zong (2002a), pp. 67–68.

13. Zong (2002a), p. 64.

14. Zhu Rongji did not speak for suppression of the Falungong in the April 26 meeting, but he also did not voice opposition to the policy. See Zong (2002a), p. 64.

15. Zong (2002a), p. 66.

16. Baum (1994), pp. 254–62.

17. In his interview with the German Radio program *Deutsche Welles* on July 9, President Lee Teng-hui stated that relations across the Taiwan Straits should be one of "state to state," or at least a "special state-to-state relations," and not one "between the central and local governments within China"; Central News Agency, Taipei, July 9, 1999. For the text of his speech, see www.taipei.org and www.future-China.org.tw.

18. Zong Hairan, *Zhu Rongji zai Yi Jiujiujiu Nian* [Zhu Rongji in 1999]. Hong Kong: Mirror Books, 2001, translated in *Chinese Law and Government* (March-April), pp. 3–91. hereafter Zong (2002b), p. 16.

19. Zong (2002a), p. 65.

20. For the Politburo's concern for the overseas connection of the Falungong, see James Tong, "Anatomy of regime repression in China: timing, enforcement institutions, and target selection in banning the Falungong, July, 1999," *Asian Survey* (November–December 2002), pp. 795–820.

21. Shiyu Zhou, "The '610 Office'–the primary organ mechanism of Jiang Zemin's terrorism policy against Falun Gong," presented at the Panel Discussion on China's State Terrorism at National Press Club, Washington D.C., October 10, 2001.

22. Research Department, Ministry of Public Security, "Li Hongzhi: the man and his deeds," *Renmin ribao*, July 23, 1999. Reports of arrests of top local Falungong leaderships were published in *Renmin ribao* in late July and early August 1999.

23. *Guizhou nianjian*, 2000, p. 143.

24. *Shaanxi nianjian*, 2000, p. 103.

25. *Zhongguo gongan nianjian, 2000* [China public security yearbook, 2000] (Beijing: Chunzhong chubanshe, 2001), p. 405; *Zhengzhou nianjian*, 2000, p. 90.

26. *Hebei ribao*, August 1, 1999, p. 1.

27. *Cheng ming*, no. 262 (August 1999), p. 6.

28. *Hainan ribao*, August 18, 1999, p. 1.

29. *Zhongguo gongan nianjian, 2000*, p. 405.

30. *Gansu nianjian*, 2000, p. 122.

31. *Siping nianjian*, 1999–2000, p. 55.

32. *Jinzhou nianjian*, 2000, p. 42.

33. *Wulumuqi nianjian*, 2000, p. 26.

34. *Zhengzhou nianjian*, 2000, p. 90.

35. *Wuhan nianjian*, 2000, p. 108.

36. *Jinan nianjian*, 2000, p. 41.

37. *Jinan nianjian*, 2000, p. 40.

38. *Jilin nianjian*, 2000 p. 89.

39. *Jilin nianjian*, 2000, p. 97.

40. *Jilin nianjian*, 2000, pp. 96–97.

41. *Zhejiang ribao*, July 30, 1999, p. 2.

42. *Guangzhou ribao*, August 3, 1999, p. A1.

43. *Guizhou ribao*, July 29, 1999, p. 1.

44. *Guizhou nianjian*, 2000, p. 143.

45. *Shenyang nianjian*, 2000, p. 99.

46. *Jiefang ribao* Web site, accessed by author December 15, 1999.

47. *Jilin ribao*, July 26, 1999, p. 1.

48. *Cheng ming*, no. 262 (August 1999), p. 6.

49. The list of 16 alleged deaths, illness, and insanity was published on the same day the ban was announced, in *Renmin ribao*, July 23, 1999, p. 4.

50. *Liaoning ribao*, August, 10, 1999, p. 2.

51. Xinhua, Chengdu, press release of August 5, 1999.

52. *Shandong nianjian*, 2000, p. 54.

53. *Xian nianjian*, 2000, p. 79.

54. *Suzhou nianjian*, 2000, p. 15.

55. *Shanghai nianjian*, 2000, p. 44.

56. *Haikou nianjian,* 2000, p. 74.

57. *Xian nianjian,* 2000, p. 79.

58. *Xian nianjian,* 2000, p. 79.

59. *Huangpu nianjian,* 2000, pp. 367-68, 373.

60. Zong (2002a), p. 67.

61. The series carried the authoritative signature of the "People's Daily Commentator," in the column "Chongxiang kexue, pochu mixin," published usually on Mondays, on June 21 and 28 and July 5, 13, and 19, 1999.

62. The series was published on June 29 and July 1, 6, 8, and 13, 1999.

63. This was published on June 25 and July 9 and 13, 1999.

64. Xinhua, Beijing, press release of July 23, 1999.

65. Xinhua, Beijing, press release of April 27, 1999.

66. Zong (2002a), p. 65.

67. Xinhua, Beijing, press release of June 14, 1999, translated in Ming Xia and Shiping Hua, eds., "The Battle between the Chinese government and the Falun Gong," *Chinese Law and Government* (September–October 1999), pp. 5-104, at pp. 19-22.

68. Xinhua, Beijing, press release of June 14, 1999.

CHAPTER 3

1. *Renmin ribao,* July 23, 1999, p. 1.

2. Zong Hairen, *Zhu Rongji zai yi jiujiujiu nian* [Zhu Rongji in 1999]. (Hong Kong: Mirror Books, 2001); translated in *Chinese law and government* (January-February, 2002) [hereafter Zong (2002a)], p. 68.

3. Zong (2002a), p. 68.

4. Zong (2002a), p 68. *Cheng ming* (August, 1999, p. 8) reported the arrests began on July 19.

5. Zong (2002a), p. 70.

6. These cities were Beijing, Tianjin, Shijiazhuang, Dalian, Shenyang, Weifang, Yiantai, Wuhan, Guangzhou, Shenzhen, Linyungang, Taiyuan, Datong, Changzhi, Zhangjiakou, Benxi, Yanchuan, Jinzhou, and four other unnamed cities. *Cheng ming* (August 1999), p. 8.

7. *Cheng ming* (August 1999), p. 8.

8. See chapter 5 for these distinctions.

9. Zong (2002a), p. 69.

10. *Jiefang ribao,* July 24, 1999.

11. *Shaanxi ribao,* July 27, 1999, p.1.

12. *Guangxi ribao,* August 21, 1999, p. 2.

13. *Hainan ribao,* August 18, 1999, p. 1.

14. Xinhua, Beijing, press release of July 24, 1999.

15. *Shanxi ribao,* July 310, 1999, p. 1.

16. *Liaoning ribao,* August 10, 1999, p. 2.

17. *Anhui ribao,* July 27, 1999, p. 1.

18. *Sichuan ribao,* August 19, 1999, p. 1.

19. *Hainan ribao,* August 18, 1999, p. 1.

20. *Guangxi ribao,* July 31, 1999, p. 2.

21. *Jiefang ribao,* August 1, 1999, p. 2.

22. *Hubei ribao,* August 9, 1999, p. 1.

23. *Jilin ribao,* August 21, 1999, p. 1.

24. *Liaoning ribao,* August 11, 1999, p. 1.

25. *Xinhua ribao,* August 7, 1999, pp. A1, A2.

26. *Xinhua ribao,* July 23, 1999, p. A1.

27. *Sichuan ribao,* July 23, 1999, p. 1.

28. *Henan ribao,* July 25, 1999, p. 2.

29. *Shanghai nianjian,* 2000, p. 43.

30. *Jiefang ribao,* July 24, 1999, p. 2.

31. *Jiefang ribao,* July 24, 1999.

32. Xinhua, Beijing, press release of July 22, 1999.

33. Xinhua, Beijing, press release of December 27, 1999.

34. *Zhongguo jiancha nianjian,* 2001, p. 392.

35. Zhonghua renmin gongheguo, Gonganbu "Gongan jiguan banli xingxi anjian chengxu guiding" [Ministry of Public Security, "Regulations on handling criminal cases by public security organs"], May 14, 1998, in *Zuixin gong'an paichusuo minjing gongzuo shouce* [The new manual for police work in public security precincts] (Beijing: Fulu chubanshe, 1999), p. 648.

36. *Zhongguo Jiancha nianjian,* 2001, p. 392.

37. *Zhongguo jiancha nianjian,* 2000, p. 516.

38. *Renmin ribao,* July 23, 1999, p. 5.

39. *Guangxi ribao,* August 21, 1999, p. 2.

40. *Fujian ribao,* July 23, 1999, p. 1.

41. *Shanxi ribao,* August 12, 1999, p. 1.

42. *Shaanxi ribao,* July 27, 1999, p. 1.

43. *Sichuan ribao,* July 27, 1999, p. 1.

44. *Heilongjiang ribao,* August 5, 1999, p. 4.

45. *Guizhou ribao,* July 30, 1999, p. 1.

46. *Shanxi ribao,* August 2, 1999, p. 1.

47. *Hunan ribao,* August 2, 1999, p. 3.

48. *Sichuan ribao,* July 27, 1999, p. 1.

49. *Shaanxi ribao,* July 25, 1999, p. 1.

50. *Shandong ribao,* July 25, 1999, p. 1.

51. *Guizhou ribao,* July 30, 1999, p. 1.

52. Xinhua, Beijing, press release of July 22, 1999.

53. *Fujian ribao,* August 6, 1999, p.1.

54. *Shaanxi ribao,* August 6, 1999, p. 1.

55. *Hubei ribao,* July 25, 1999, p. 2.

56. *Liaoning ribao,* August 7, 1999, p. 2.

57. *Hunan ribao,* July 28, 1999, p. 1.

58. *Jiefang ribao,* July 24, 1999.

59. *Guizhou ribao,* August 1, 1999, p. 1.

60. *Shaanxi ribao,* July 28, 1999, p. 1.

61. *Heilongjiang ribao,* August 3, 1999, p. 4.

62. *Shaanxi ribao,* August 7, 1999, p. 1.

63. *Guizhou ribao,* July 29, 1999, p. 1.

64. *Heilongjiang ribao*, July 24, 1999, p. 2.

65. *Hubei ribao*, August 1, 1999.

66. *Xinhua ribao*, July 27, 1999.

67. *Guangxi ribao*, July 31, 1999, p. 1.

68. *Fujian ribao*, July 23, 1999, p. 1.

69. *Taiyuan nianjian*, 2000, p. 106.

70. *Changchun nianjian*, 2000, p. 96.

71. *Shaanxi ribao*, August 15, 1999, p. 1.

72. *Henan ribao*, July 26, 1999, p. 2.

73. *Shanxi ribao*, August 12, 1999, p. 1.

74. *Guizhou ribao*, July 28, 1999, p. 1.

75. *Changsha nianjian*, 2002, p. 102.

76. *Heilongjiang ribao*, August 3, 1999, p. 4.

77. *Qian'an nianjian*, 2000, p. 73.

78. *Jinzhou nianjian*, 2003, p. 144.

79. *Shaanxi ribao*, July 27, 1999, p. 2.

80. *Renmin ribao*, July 27, 1999.

81. *Guangming ribao*, July 29, 1999, p. 5.

82. *Renmin ribao*, July 26, 1999, p. 5.

83. *Hainan ribao*, August 18, 1999, p. 1.

84. *Renmin ribao*, July 29, 1999, p. 5.

85. *Guangxi ribao*, July 30, 1999, p.1.

86. *Renmin ribao*, July 28, 1999, p. 4.

87. *Guangming ribao*, July 29, 1999, p. 2.

88. *Shaanxi ribao*, July 31, 1999, p. 2.

89. *Zhejiang ribao*, July 29, 1999, p. 1.

90. *Beijing ribao*, July 28, 1999; *Guangming ribao*, July 29, 1999, p. 5.

91. *Hainan ribao*, July 24, 1999, p. 3.

92. *Guangxi ribao*, July 28, 1999, p.2.

93. *Guangxi ribao*, August 4, 1999, p. 2.

94. *Xinhua ribao*, July 26, 1999, A2.

95. *Guangming ribao*, July 29, 1999, p. 5.

96. *Shaanxi ribao*, July 27, 1999, p. 2.

97. *Renmin ribao*, July 27-29, 1999; *Guangming ribao*, July 27-29, 1999.

98. *Renmin ribao*, July 29, 1999, p. 5.

99. These provincial capitals were Guiyang, Jinan, Nanchang, Shenyang, and major cities of Shanghai and those in Anhui, Yunnan, Fujian, Heilongjiang, Sichuan, Shaanxi, Guangxi, Gansu, Hebei, Henan, Shanxi, and Neimonggu. *Renmin ribao*, July 30, 1999, p. 5.

100. *Renmin ribao*, July 30, 1999, p. 4.

101. *Guangming ribao*, July 29, 1999, p. 5.

102. *Guangming ribao*, July 29, 1999, p. 5.

103. *Guangming ribao*, July 29, 1999, p. 5.

104. *Hebei ribao*, July 28, 1999, p. 2.

105. *Hebei ribao*, July 28, 1999, p. 2.

106. *Guangming ribao*, July 28, 1999, p. 2.

107. *Hainan ribao*, July 24, 1999, p. 3.

108. *Guangxi ribao,* July 28, 1999, p. 2.

109. *Guangxi ribao,* July 30, 1999, p. 1.

110. *Guangxi ribao,* July 30, 1999, p. 1.

111. *Huarong nianjian,* 2001, p. 117.

112. *Jinjiang nianjian,* 2001, p. 85.

113. *Wuhan nianjian,* 2001, p. 113.

114. *Huarong nianjian,* 2002, p. 100.

115. *Xiangtan nianjian,* 2003, p. 66.

116. *Huarong nianjian,* 2001, p. 117.

117. *Harbin nianjian,* 1999–2000, p. 324.

118. *Luoshan nianjian,* 2004, p. 274.

119. *Jinzhou nianjian,* 2002, p. 67.

120. *Jinzhou nianjian,* 2002, p. 67.

121. *Shenyang nianjian,* 2001, p. 94.

122. *Nenjiang nianjian,* 2001, p. 139.

123. *Hengyang nianjian,* 2001, p. 126.

124. *Xinyu nianjian,* 2001, pp. 111–12.

125. *Wanzhou nianjian,* 2003, p. 122.

126. *Fushun nianjian,* 2003, p. 184.

127. *Shenyang nianjian,* 2001, p. 94.

128. *Liling nianjian,* 2001, p. 103.

129. *Jinzhou nianjian,* 2000, p. 70.

130. *Huarong nianjian,* 2001, p. 103.

131. *Xiangtan nianjian,* 2003, p. 67.

132. *Guangzhou ribao,* July 24, 1999, p. A4.

133. *Liaoning ribao,* July 24, 1999, p. 3; July 26, 1999, p. 1.

134. *Shanghai nianjian,* 2000, p. 373.

135. *Dongying nianjian,* 2000, p. 116.

136. According to official government sources, Li Hongzhi's original birthday was July 7, 1952, which he changed to May 13, 1952, to coincide with the birthday of Sakyamuni, the founder of Buddhism; see Ju Mengjun, ed., *Chanchu xiejiao qiankun lang* [The universe will be bright after the cult is eradicated] (Beijing: Xinhua chubanshe, 2001), pp. 4–5. The date varies in the Gregorian calendar.

137. *Xiangtan nianjian,* 2003, p. 66.

138. *Nanjing nianjian,* 2000, p. 261.

139. *Ma'anshan nianjian,* 2000, pp. 88–89.

140. *Jilin ribao,* July 30, 1999, p. 2.

141. *Jilin nianjian,* 2000, p. 89.

142. *Jilin nianjian,* 2000, p. 89.

143. *Jinzhou nianjian,* 2000, p. 86.

144. *Shenyang nianjian,* 2000, p. 99.

145. *Liaoning ribao,* August 16, 1999, p. 2.

146. *Weifang nianjian,* 2000, p. 114.

147. *Dongying nianjian,* 2000, p. 116.

148. *Changchun nianjian,* 2000, p. 96 refers to 5,600 "person-times."

149. *Nenjiang nianjian,* 2001, p. 113.

150. *Hengyang nianjian,* 2001, p. 126.

151. *Huangshi nianjian*, 2000, p. 114.

152. *Qinhuangdao nianjian*, 2000, p. 112.

153. *Jilin ribao,* July 29, 1999, p. 2.

154. *Jilin nianjian*, 2000, p. 89.

155. *Shenyang nianjian*, 2000, p. 99.

156. *Hengyang nianjian*, 2001, p. 126.

157. *Weifang nianjian*, 2000, p. 114.

158. *Dongying nianjian*, 2000, p. 116.

159. *Dongying nianjian*, 2000, p. 116.

160. *Liaoning nianjian*, 2000, p. 69.

161. *Siping nianjian*, 1999–2000, p. 55.

162. *Jinan nianjian*, 2001, pp. 70–71.

163. *Jilin nianjian*, 2000, pp. 96–97.

164. *Fushun nianjian*, 2002, p. 166.

165. *Liaoning nianjian,* 2004, p. 85; www.xinhuanet.com/english/2003-07/21/content_985704.htm.

166. *Changchun nianjian*, 2003, p. 106.

167. *Liling nianjian*, 2003, p. 67.

168. *Huarong nianjian*, 2001, p. 117; *Xiangtan nianjian*, 2003, p. 66.

169. *Xiangtan nianjian*, 2003, p. 67.

170. *Yangzhou nianjian*, 2003, p. 81.

171. See library.minghui.org/topic/9,,,1.htm, accessed by author on December 2, 2006.

172. *Xiangtan nianjian*, 2003, p. 66.

173. *Xiangtan nianjian*, 2003, p. 66.

174. *Xiangtan nianjian*, 2003, p. 67.

175. *Zhongguo jiancha nianjian*, 2004, 2005, 2006.

176. *Shenyang nianjian*, 2001, p. 94.

177. *Jinzhou nianjian*, 2002, p. 114.

178. *Anshan nianjian*, 2002, p. 81.

179. *Fushun nianjian*, 2003, p. 184.

180. *Jinzhou nianjian*, 2003, p. 144.

181. *Shenyang nianjian*, 2002, p. 106.

182. *Weifang nianjian*, 2000, p. 114.

183. *Huarong nianjian*, 2003, p. 106.

184. *Shenyang nianjian*, 2000, p. 99.

185. *Shenyang nianjian*, 2001, p. 94.

186. *Xiangtan nianjian*, 2003, p. 67.

187. *Changchun nianjian*, 2002, p. 105.

188. *Zhujiang nianjian*, 2001, p. 64.

189. *Nankang nianjian*, 2003, p. 120.

190. *Nankang nianjian*, 2003, p. 119.

191. *Xuanwei nianjian*, 2003, p. 132.

192. *Ma'anshan nianjian*, 2001, p. 160.

193. *Xiangtan nianjian*, 2003, p. 67.

194. *Changsha nianjian*, 2003, p. 122.

195. *Changsha nianjian*, 2002, p. 110.

CHAPTER 4

1. *Renmin ribao*, July 23, 1999, p. 1.

2. *Zhongguo xinwen nianjian* 2000, pp. 205–6; *CCTV Yearbook*, 2000, p. 112.

3. Because of division within the Politburo, the media coverage on the 1989 Democracy Movement was not as unified or intense. For a longitudinal survey of communication campaigns, see Jianlong Wang, "Research on Chinese communication campaigns: a historical review," in Wenshan Jia et al., eds., *Chinese communication theory and research: reflections, new frontiers, and new directions* (Westport, Conn.: Ablex Publishing, 2002), pp. 131–46.

4. CCTV (2000), p. 114; Zong Hairen, *Zhu Rongji zai yi jiujiujiu nian* [Zhu Rongji in 1999] (Hong Kong: Mirror Books, 2001); translated in *Chinese law and government* (January-February 2002) [hereafter Zong (2002a)], p. 69.

5. Actually 115 minutes 13 seconds plus commercial breaks.

6. *Zhonghua remin gongheguo ziliao shouce*, 1949–99, p. 895; *Zhongguo guangbo dianshi nianjian*, 2000, p. 41.

7. *Zhongguo guangbo dianshi nianjian*, 2000, pp. 246–50. The "News and New Digest" program was inaugurated in April 1950; "National Network News" in May, 1951.

8. *Zhongguo xinwen nianjian*, 2000, p. 70.

9. The News Commentary Division produced two daily programs: *Focused Interview* (13 minutes) and *Eastern Time and Space* (40 minutes); and two weekly programs: *News Investigation* (30 minutes on Fridays) and *Plain Speaking* (40 minutes on Sundays). *CCTV Yearbook*, 2000, p. 124.

10. *CCTV Yearbook*, 2000, pp. 58–59.

11. *CCTV Yearbook*, 2000, p. 112.

12. *CCTV Yearbook*, 2000, pp. 59–60.

13. The 66 programs were aired from July 22 to August 25; *CCTV Yearbook*, 2000, pp. 112–114.

14. *CCTV Yearbook*, 2000, p. 113.

15. The Chinese title is "Li Hongzhi qiren qishi."

16. The Chinese title is "Si erwu feifa juji shijian zhenxiang."

17. The Chinese titles are "Youhuo yu caozong—toushi 'Falungong' heidong," "Jiaodian fangtan—kantou Li Hongzhi," and "Jiaodian fangtan—beilie pianshu, waili xieshuo." *CCTV Yearbook*, 2000, p. 113.

18. *Zhongguo xinwen nianjian*, 2000, p. 692.

19. *Renmin ribao*, July 23, 1999, p. 1. For an English translation, see Ming Xia and Shiping Hua, eds., "The battle between the Chinese government and the Falun Gong," *Chinese Law and Government* (September-October 1999), pp. 5–104 [hereafter Xia and Hua (1999)], at pp. 14–18.

20. *Renmin ribao*, July 23, 1999, p. 1; Xia and Hua (1999), p. 31.

21. *Renmin ribao*, July 23, 1999, p. 1; Xia and Hua (1999), pp. 31–32.

22. All these documents were published in the major national press. An exception if the *Gongren ribao*, which did not publish the Xinhua news report on the meeting between United Front Minister Wang Zhaoguo with leaders of minor political parties.

23. The July 24, 1996, notice banned the publication, reprinting, and distribution of five Falungong books—*Zhongguo Falungong, Falunzhuan, Falunzhuan II, Falung Dafa Yijie*, and *Shentong Dafa–Li Hongzhi he Zhongguo Falungong*; see Xinhua, Bei-

jing, press release of July 23, 1999, and Xia and Hua (1999), pp. 29–31, for an English text. The May 10, 1999, notice banned and confiscated copies of tapes and videos on the Falungong method; the June 1, 1999, notice banned four Falungong publications by the publisher Qinghai Renmin Chubanshe; the June 5, 1998, notice banned and confiscated copies of the *Lun Falun Fa;* the August 16, 1996, notice did the same for the *Zhuan Falun.*

24. Xinhua, Beijing, press release of July 23, 1999; *Renmin ribao,* July 23, 1999; Xia and Hua (1999), pp. 46–51 for an English text; and Yan Shi, ed., *Shiji jupian: Li Hongzhi* [Swindler of the century: Li Hongzhi] (Beijing: Dazhong wenyi chubanshe, 1999) [hereafter Yan (1999)], pp. 312–15, for the Chinese text.

25. Xinhua, Beijing, press release of July 23, 1999; *Renmin ribao,* July 23, 1999; Yan (1999), pp. 316–18.

26. These include a Ministry of Personnel notice forbidding state functionaries to practice Falungong; a United Front Department notice urging nonparty personages to uphold social stability together with the CCP; and a circular of the Central Committee of the Communist Youth League forbidding its members to practice the Falungong; see Xinhua, Beijing, press release of July 23, 1999, and Xia and Hua (1999), pp. 22–28, 51, for English texts.

27. These include an article signed by the Department of Policies, Rules, and Regulations of the NPB repudiating Li Hongzhi's doctrines for what it considered to be cosmological, biological, and religious fallacies that were contrary to established science, and two press conferences of the Ministry of Civil Affairs and the Ministry of Foreign Affairs. See Zong (2002a); Xinhua, Beijing, press release of July 23, 1999; *Renmin ribao,* July 23, 1999; Xia and Hua (1999), pp. 65–78; Yan (1999), pp. 325–27.

28. *Renmin ribao,* July 23, 1999, p. 1.

29. *Renmin ribao,* July 24, 1999, p. 1.

30. The list includes those from (1) the four headquarters of the military (Chief of Staff, Political Affairs, Logistics, and Equipment), (2) the CCP central organizations (the three central commissions: Disciplinary, Legal and Political Affairs, Central Committee General office; the four departments: Organizations, Propaganda, United Front, International Liaison); (3) three mass organizations (Trade Union, Communist Youth League, Women's Federation); (4) professional associations (Federation of Scientists, Artists, Writers, Reporters, Taiwan Affairs); and (5) mass media (Translation Bureau, Foreign Language Bureau, Xinhua Agency; Broadcast and Telecommunications Bureau; *Renmin ribao;* Qiushi Press; *Guangming ribao, Jingji ribao,* China Daily); as well as other CCP central bodies, including the China National Political Consultative Conference; International Propaganda Office, Central Taiwan Affairs Office; Central Editorial Office; Central Trade Union Commission, Central Party School; Central Teaching and Research Office; Central Documents Research Office; and Central Party History Research Office. *Renmin ribao,* July 24, 1999, p. 4.

31. The provinces were Hunan, Hubei, Tianjin, Zhejiang, Liaoning, Fujian, Sichuan, Jiangxi, Guangxi, Hainan, and Gansu; *Renmin ribao,* July 26, 1999, p. 1.

32. *Renmin ribao,* July 24, 25, 1999, p. 1.

33. *Renmin ribao,* July 24, 1999.

34. *Renmin ribao,* July 24, 1999; July 27, 1999, p. 4; July 28, 1999, p. 3.

35. *Renmin ribao,* July 26, 1999, pp. 3, 4; Xinhua, press release of July 27, 1999.

36. *Renmin ribao,* July 27, 1999.

37. The July 27 emergency notice was jointly issued by the NPB, the Ministry of Public Security, State Bureau of Industry and Commerce, Customs Administration, and the National Office to Eliminate Pornography; *Renmin ribao,* July 27, 1999, p. 5.

38. *Renmin ribao,* July 26, 1999, p. 5; July 27, 1999, pp. 4, 5; July 28, 1999, p. 4.

39. *Renmin ribao,* July 30, 1999, p. 1.

40. *Renmin ribao,* July 29, 1999, p. 5.

41. In television, the campaign against the Falungong was demarcated as (1) July 22–23, (2) July 24–29, and (3) July 30–August 2, 1999; *CCTV Yearbook,* 2000, p. 114. The press campaign was similarly partitioned in three phases but no begin or end dates for each phase were published; *Zhongguo xinwen nianjian,* 2000, p. 205.

42. As above, the numerical count is based on the number of stories on the Falungong listed as "important news" in the electronic version of the *Renmin ribao.*

43. The campaign began in February 1996, when State Councilor Song Jian attacked pseudoscience in his address to the National Conference on Popularization of Science."

44. These include, among others, *Bianzheng di lishi di weiwuzhuyi* [Dialectical historical materialism] (Beijing: Junshi kexue chubanshe, May 1999); *Zhongguo wushenlunshi ziliao xuanbian* (Song Yuan Ming bian) [Selections on the history of China's atheism—Song, Yuan, Ming periods] (Beijing: Zhonghua shuju, January 1999); *Bu zhidao di shijie* [The unknown world] (Beijing: Zhongguo shaolian ertong chubanshe, August 1998). All were included in the official anti-Falungong series of 120 books.

45. See James Tong, "Publish to perish: regime choices and propaganda impact in the anti-Falungong publication campaign July, 1999-December 2000," *Journal of Contemporary China,* 14, no. 44, (August, 2005), pp. 509–10, hereafter Tong (2005)

46. Tong (2005), p. 512.

47. Between 1978 and 1997, the number of newspapers in China increased from 186 to 2,149, and circulation from 12.8 billion to 28.8 billion copies. The number of periodicals increased from 930 to 7,918 in the same period, *Zhonghua remin gongheguo ziliao shouce,* 1949–99, pp. 910–11.

48. Chin-chuan Lee, "Chinese communications: prisms, trajectories, and modes of understanding," in Chin-chuan Lee, ed., *Power, money, and media: communication patterns and bureaucratic control in cultural China* (Evanston, Ill.: Northwestern University Press, 2000), pp. 9, 11.

49. *CCTV Yearbook,* 2001, p. 334.

50. *CCTV Yearbook,* 1999, pp. 253–56; *CCTV Yearbook,* 2000, pp. 324–29; *CCTV Yearbook,* 2001, pp. 339–46.

51. *Zhongguo gongchandang zhujishi zhiliao* [Organizational History of the Chinese Communist Party, hereafter *ZGZZ*), suppl. vol. 1, xia, p. 938.

52. *Zhongguo tushu nianjian,* 1999, p. 81.

53. *Zhongguo guangbo dianshi nianjian,* 2000, p. 335.

54. *Zhongguo tushu nianjian,* 1999, p. 79.

55. *Zhongguo chuban nianjian,* 2001 (Beijing: Zhongguo chuban nianjianshe, 2001), p. 84

56. The 16 NPB publishers are listed as the first 16 presses of the central publishing houses in *Zhongguo chuban nianjian,* 2000, p. 67; *Zhonghua renmin gongheguo ziliao shouce* [Handbook of information on the People's Republic of China], pp. 920–23.

57. *Zhongguo chubanshe nianjian,* 2000, pp. 67–71, 692–99.

58. *Zhongguo chuban nianjian,* 2000 pp. 66-71; *Zhongguo guangbo dianshi nian-jian,* 2000, pp. 505-6.

59. Yuezhi Zhao, *Media, market, and democracy in China: Between the party line and the bottom line* (Urbana: University of Illinois Press, 1998); Barrett McCormick, "Recent trends in mainland China's media: political implications of commercialization," *Issues and Studies* (December 2002/March 2003), pp. 175-215; Chin-chuan Lee, "Chinese communications"; Stephanie Hemelryk Donald, Michael Keane, and Yin Hong, eds., *Media in China: consumption, content and crisis* (London: Routledge/Curson, 2002); Yuezhi Zhao, "From commercialization to conglomeration: the transformation of the Chinese press within the orbit of the party state," *Journal of Communication* (Spring 2000), pp. 3-26; Feng Chen and Ting Gong, "Party versus market in post-Mao China: the erosion of the Leninist organization from below," *Journal of Communist Studies and Transition Politics,* 13 (1997), pp. 148-66.

60. *Zhongguo xinwen nianjian,* 2000, p. 208.

61. The contrition, confession, and conversion of the first set of Falungong Chief Station leaders were reported in the *Renmin ribao* on July 27, 28, and 31 and August 1, 3, 5, and 8.

62. For a case study of the problem of bureaucratic coordination and the policy-making process in the energy establishment in China in the 1980s, see Kenneth Lieberthal and Michel Oksenberg, *Policy-making in China: leaders, structures, and processes* (Princeton, NJ: Princeton University Press, 1988).

63. Xiaoping Li, "'Focus' (*Jiaodian Fangtan)* and changes in the Chinese television industry," *Journal of Contemporary China* 11/30 (February 2002), pp. 17-34; Alex Chan, "From propaganda to hegemony: *Jiaodian Fangtan* and China's media policy," *Journal of Contemporary China* 11/30 (February 2002), pp. 35-52.

64. Zong (2002a), p. 69.

65. *Renmin ribao,* July 24, p. 4; July 26, 1999, pp. 1, 4.

66. *Renmin ribao,* July 29, 1999, p. 5.

67. ZGZZ, suppl. vol. 1, xia, pp. 871-72, 939, and vol. 7, no. 1, pp. 230-31.

68. ZGZZ, vol. 7, shang, p. 230.

69. "Zhongyang xuanchuan xixiang gongzuo lingdao xiaozu" (in Chinese), ZGZZ, vol. 7, shang, p. 231.

70. *Zhongguo chuban nianjian,* 2000, p. 158. There was no reported NPB involvement in the joint *Renmin ribao* and *Qiushi* seminars on July 27, 1999, and that of the *Renmin ribao* and *Guangming ribao* of July 30, 1999, or the joint forum of the three agencies on November 4, 1999. *Renmin ribao,* July 28, 29, and 31 November 5, 1999; *Zhongguo xinwen nianjian,* 2000, pp. 205-7.

71. *Zhongguo xinwen nianjian,* 2000, pp. 205-7.

72. *Zhongguo xinwen nianjian,* 2000, pp. 30-51; *Zhongguo guangbo dianshi nian-jian,* 2000, pp. 198-209.

73. ZGZZ, suppl. vol. 1, xia, pp. 871-73, 938-39; *CCTV Yearbook,* 2000, p. 38.

74. Central Committee membership seems to reside with the institutional affiliation rather than the incumbent office holders: the heads of the CPBS, CCTV, SBBFT, and NPB have never been elected to the Central Committee, while those of the Xinhua news agency and *Renmin ribao* have generally been Central Committee members. The president of *Renmin ribao* in 1999 (Zhao Huazai) was a full member of the 15th Central Committee. His predecessor, Gao Di (1989-1992) was in the 13th Central

Committee (1987-92), Qian Liren (1985-89) was in the 13th Central Committee (1987-92), and Qin Chuan (1983-85) was in the 12th Central Committee (1982-87). From 1976 to 1982, *Renmin ribao* was under restructuring to purge the Cultural Revolution radicals, and there was no president.

75. In the anti-Falungong campaign, the media administrative agencies needed to deal with the ministers of public security (Jia Chunwang), state security (Xu Yongyao), and administration of justice (Gao Changli); Jia was a Central Committee member in 1999, and Xu and Gao were alternate Central Committee members. In addition, NPB and SBBFT also needed to work with the ministers of culture (Sun Jiazheng), civil affairs (Duoji Caiyang), personnel (Song Defu), and information production (Wu Jichuan), all of whom were Central Committee members in 1999. *Zhonghua renmin gongheguo ziliao shouce,* 1949-99, pp. 146-47.

76. Zong (2002a), pp. 53-58.

77. Zong (2002a), pp. 60-63.

78. Zong (2002a), pp. 60-63. Luo Gan held leading positions in the party and state in security and law enforcement, and served concurrently as a state councilor, as well as a member of the Politburo and the Central Secretariat. Ding Guan'gen was vice premier of the State Council and minister of propaganda.

79. *Zhongguo xinwen nianjian,* 2000, pp. 205-8

80. *Zhongguo xinwen nianjian,* 2000, p. 208.

CHAPTER 5

1. *Renmin ribao,* July 24, 1999.

2. *Renmin ribao,* July 24, 1999.

3. Ming Xia and Shiping Hua, eds., "The battle between the Chinese government and the Falun Gong," *Chinese Law and Government* (September–October 1999), pp. 5-104, [hereafter Xia and Hua (1999)], at pp. 51-55.

4. Xia and Hua (1999), pp. 52-55.

5. *Renmin ribao,* July 23, 1999, p. 1.

6. Xia and Hua (1999), pp. 14-18, 51-55.

7. *Xinjiang nianjian,* 2000, p. 61.

8. *Guangming ribao,* August 17, 1999, p. 2.

9. *Qinghai nianjian,* 2000, pp. 50-51.

10. *Jinjiang nianjian,* 2000, p. 38.

11. *Dandong nianjian,* 2000, p. 110.

12. *Guizhou nianjian,* 2000, p. 89.

13. *Meizhou nianjian,* 2000, p. 58.

14. *Baoding nianjian,* 2000, p. 85.

15. *Renmin ribao,* August 2, 1999, p. 4.

16. *Jinan nianjian,* 2002, p. 89.

17. *Chongqing nianjian,* 2002, p. 102.

18. *Zibo nianjian,* 2000, p. 55.

19. *Kaifeng nianjian,* 2001, p. 65.

20. *Renmin ribao,* July 31, 1999, p. 1.

21. *Hebei nianjian,* 2000, p. 61.

22. *Renmin ribao,* July 25, 1999, 4.

23. *Sichuan ribao*, July 26, 1999, p. 3.

24. *Renmin ribao*, August 2, 1999, p. 4.

25. *Guangming ribao*, August 11, 1999, p. 2.

26. *Shenyang nianjian*, 2000, p. 48.

27. *Jinan nianjian*, 2002, p. 89.

28. *Fujian ribao*, August 13, 1999.

29. *Shanghai nianjian*, 2000, p. 41.

30. *Fujian ribao*, August 13, 1999.

31. *Renmin ribao*, July 27, 1999, p. 4.

32. *Anshan nianjian*, 2002, p. 84.

33. *Daye nianjian*, 1998–2002, p. 135.

34. *Changsha nianjian*, 2001, p. 106.

35. *Daye nianjian*, 1998–2002, p. 135.

36. *Luanjiang nianjian*, 2001, p. 113.

37. *Nanyang nianjian*, 2001, p. 53.

38. *Jinan nianjian*, 2001, p. 70.

39. *Hengyang nianjian*, 2000, p. 137.

40. *Changchun nianjian*, 2003, p. 104.

41. *Xinjiang nianjian*, 2000, p. 61.

42. *Wuhan nianjian*, 2001, p. 113.

43. *Nanyang nianjian*, 2001, p. 53.

44. *Changsha nianjian*, 2001, p. 106.

45. *Jinzhou nianjian*, 2000, p. 71.

46. *Dandong nianjian*, 2002, p. 59.

47. *Daye nianjian*, 1998–2002, p. 135.

48. *Luanjiang nianjian*, 2001, p. 113.

49. *Anshan nianjian*, 2002, pp. 83–84; *Anshan nianjian*, 2003, p. 88.

50. *Jinan nianjian*, 2001, p. 70.

51. *Changsha nianjian*, 2001, p. 106.

52. *Dandong nianjian*, 2002, p. 59.

53. *Anshan nianjian*, 2003, p. 88.

54. *Nanyang nianjian*, 2001, p. 53.

55. *Daye nianjian*, 1998–2002, p. 135.

56. *Jinzhou nianjian*, 2000, p. 71.

57. *Renmin ribao*, August 8, 1999, p. 2.

58. *Guangming ribao*, August 11, 1999, p. 1.

59. *Guangming ribao*, August 11, 1999, p. 1.

60. *Guangming ribao*, August 10, 1999, p. 2; August 17, 1999, pp. 1, 2; *Huixian nianjian*, 2000, p. 103.

61. *Harbin nianjian*, 1999–2000, p. 323.

62. *Fushun nianjian*, 2000, p. 173.

63. Xiang Xiang, *Yunnan: Pojie Falungong* [Breaking up Falungong in Yunnan]. Kunming: Yunnan chubanshe, 2002 [hereafter Xiang (2002)], p. 146.

64. *Jingdezhen nianjian*, 2000, p. 101.

65. *Changsha nianjian*, 2001, p. 106.

66. *Hengyang nianjian*, 2000, p. 65.

67. *Luanjiang nianjian*, 2001, p. 113.

68. *Jinan nianjian*, 2001, pp. 70–71.

69. *Shenyang nianjian*, 2000, p. 99.

70. Xiang (2002), p. 147.

71. Xiang (2002), p. 214.

72. *Daqing nianjian*, 2000, p. 83.

73. *Xinyu nianjian*, 2001, p. 111.

74. Xiang (2002), p. 147.

75. *Jinan nianjian*, 2001, p. 70.

76. *Harbin nianjian*, 1999–2000, pp. 323, 338; *Heilongjiang nianjian*, 2001, p. 102.

77. *Dandong nianjian*, 2000, p. 109; *Anshan nianjian*, 2002, p. 84.

78. *Xinyu nianjian*, 2001, p. 111.

79. *Jinan nianjian*, 2001, p. 70.

80. *Xinjiang nianjian*, 2000, p. 61.

81. *Renmin ribao*, August 11, 1999.

82. Zhongguo shehui kexueyuan, "Shehui zhuyi fazhi shensheng buke qin-fan" [The sanctity of the socialist law cannot be violated], *Renmin ribao*, August 11, 1999.

83. "Zhonghua Renmin Gongheguo Zhi'an Guanli chufa tiaoli" ["Security man-agement penalty regulations of the People's Republic of China"] (1986). *Zhonghua renmingongheguo falu chuanshu* [Complete collection of laws of the People's Republic of China]. Changchun: Jilin renmin chubanshe, 1989, pp. 1529–1534.

84. For references to the Ministry of Justice Administration and the Heilongji-ang Provincial Labor Reform Bureau notice, see *Harbin nianjian*, 1999–2000, p. 338; for that of the Yunnan Provincial Party Committee, see Xiang (2002), p. 147.

85. *Heilongjiang nianjian*, 2001, p. 102.

86. More than 30,000 Falungong practitioners were registered by August 5, 1999, in nine Heilongjiang cities: Fushun, Jiamusi, Daqing, Neihe, Shuangheshan, Maodanjiang, Yilan, Qitai, and Wangqui. *Heilongjiang ribao*, July 27 and August 1, 3, and 5, 1999.

87. *Heilongjiang nianjian*, 2001, p. 102.

88. *Anshan nianjian*, 2001, p. 137.

89. *Anshan nianjian*, 2002, p. 83.

90. *Harbin nianjian*, 1999–2000, p. 338.

91. *Qinhuangdao nianjian*, 2001, p. 114.

92. These participating higher education and research institutions included the Yunnan University, Yunnan Provincial Social Science Academy, Yunnan Teacher Training College, Yunnan Institute of Ethnic Minority, Yunnan Observatory, the Hos-pital of Yunnan Medical College, and the Kunming Technical University.

93. Xiang (2002), p. 149.

94. Xiang (2002), pp. 151–52.

95. Xiang (2002), pp. 192–93, 213.

96. Xiang (2002), pp. 163–64.

97. Xiang (2002), pp. 192–93, 213.

98. Xiang (2002), pp. 192–93, 213.

99. Xiang (2002), p. 214.

100. Xiang (2002), p. 219.

101. Xiang (2002), pp. 180–82.

102. There are no exact figures for torture in Qinghai and Tibet, but since these two provinces also had reported cases of deaths resulting from torture, it can be inferred that torture occurred (see table 5.3).

103. See library.minghui.org/victim/i18334.htm, accessed by author on February 2, 2006.

104. See search.minghui.org/mh/articles/2006/9/11/137590.html, www.minghui.org/mh/articles/2006/9/13/137666.html.

105. See search.minghui.org/mh/articles/2002/4/8/28007.html.

106. See search.minghui.org/mh/articles/2003/5/5/49697.html.

107. See search.minghui.org/mh/articles/2006/7/5/132201.html.

108. See search.minghui.org/mh/articles/2006/4/19/125595.html.

109. See search.minghui.org/mh/articles/2004/4/8/28007.html.

110. See search.minghui.org/mh/articles/2004/4/8/28007.html.

111. See search.minghui.org/mh/articles/2002/4/8/28007.html.

112. See search.minghui.org/mh/articles/2002/6/1/31128.html.

113. See search.minghui.org/mh/articles/2006/4/19/125595.html.

114. See search.minghui.org/mh/articles/2002/4/8/28007.html.

115. See search.minghui.org/mh/articles/2002/11/6/39635.html.

116. See search.minghui.org/mh/articles/2002/5/6/29583.html.

117. See search.minghui.org/mh/articles/2004/2/1/66123.html.

118. See search.minghui.org/mh/articles/2004/10/31/88050.html.

119. See search.minghui.org/mh/articles/2004/9/15/84217.html.

120. See search.minghui.org/mh/articles/2004/9/15/84217.html.

121. See www.minghui.org/mh/articles/2006/9/13/137666.html.

CHAPTER 6

1. "Zhongyang zhian zhili huiyuanhui," in Chinese.

2. These were Xiao Yang (president of the Supreme People's Court), Han Xubin (chief procurator of the Supreme People's Procuracy), Jia Chunwang (minister of public security), Xu Yongyao (minister of state security), Gao Changli (minister of justice), Zhou Ziyu (deputy director of the General Political Department of the People's Liberation Army), and Wang Shenjun (chief of staff of CLPAC). Chen Jiping and Zhang Geng were listed as deputy chief-of-staff of CLPAC but not members; see *Zhongguo Falu nianjian*, 2000 [China law yearbook, 2000], p. 1269.

3. *Zhongguo Falu nianjian*, 2000, p. 1270.

4. Aside from Luo, Xiao, and Han, who were directors and deputy directors of the CSOUMC, Jia, Xu, Gao, Zhou, and Wang were listed as the top 5 of the 39 members, and Chen Jiping and Zhang Geng were listed as 22 and 23, *Zhongguo Falu nianjian*, 2000, pp. 1269–70.

5. Zong Hairen, *Zhu Rongji zai yi jiujiujiu nian* [Zhu Rongji in 1999] (Hong Kong: Mirror Books, 2001); translated in *Chinese law and government* (January-February 2002) [hereafter Zong (2002a)], pp. 54–55.

6. Zong (2002a), pp. 55–56.

7. Zong (2002a), pp. 60–61.

8. See Zhou Shiyu, "The '610 Office'—the primary organ mechanism of Jiang Zemin's State terrorism policy against Falun Gong," presented at the Panel Discus-

sion on China's State Terrorism at National Press Club, Washington, D.C., October 10, 2001 [hereafter Zhou (2001)]; and Zong (2002a).

9. Zhou (2001).

10. Zong (2002a), pp. 66–67. According to a Falungong source, the establishment of the office was first mentioned in a Politburo meeting on June 7, 1999; see www.epochtimes.com/gb/4/10/26/n700451.htm.

11. Zong (2002a), p. 67; *Cheng ming*, no. 262 (August 1999), p. 6, reports that an "April 25 Special Committee" was formed, headed by Hu Jintao, PSC member. It was probably referring to the same *ad hoc* committee but with mistaken identity.

12. Zong (2002a), pp. 54–56.

13. Jiang emphasized that sit-ins and demonstrations in the Zhongnanhai would be absolutely forbidden, that the regime had not been opposed to or ordered the banning of *qigong*, and that He Zuoxiu's article attacking the Falungong was a personal action where future discussions would be allowed; see Zong (2002a), pp. 56–57.

14. Zong (2002a), pp. 54–55.

15. See "Falungong zhenshi di gushi" [The true story of the Falungong], http://minghui.org/mh/article/2000/6/25/12501p.html.

16. See table of contents of *Zhongguo shehui zhian zonghe zhili nianjian, 1995-1996* [China Social Order Integrated Management Yearbook, 1995-1996] (Beijing: Falu chubanshe, 1998), pp. 1–29.

17. Kenneth Lieberthal and Michel Oksenberg, *Policy-making in China: leaders, structures, and processes* (Princeton: Princeton University Press, 1988), pp. 22–24.

18. Zhonghua renmin gongheguo, Guowuyuan "Guanyu jigou xieji di tongji" [State Council, People's Republic of China, "Notice on establishing organizations,"] (no. 12, April 30, 2003).

19. The "one organization" refers to a single legal person, a single financial account, a single leadership group, and a single office staff. The "two labels" refers to one name for the party office and another for the government office within the same organization. Examples include the State Council Taiwan Affairs Office and the Taiwan Affairs Office of the Central Committee of the Chinese Communist Party, the State Archival Bureau and the Central Archival Bureau of the Chinese Communist Party, and the State Council News and Information Office of the People's Republic of China and the Central External Propaganda Office of the Chinese Communist Party. See also table 6.6 below.

20. The time of the renaming differs from localities. Shandong renamed the institution in the latter half of 2002, and Changchun Municipality in Jilin before the end of October 2002, but Guangzhou Municipality only established its "Leading Group on Work to Maintain Social Stability" in March, 2006; see *Changchun ribao*, October 31, 2002, www.gz.gov.cn/vfs/content/newcontent.jsp?contentId=426903&catId=4077, and www.upholdjustice.org/news/610_25/2004-01/1074145409.html, accessed by author on December 3, 2006. The government office was renamed the "Office for Preventing and Handling Cults" (*Fanfan he chuli xiejiao bangongsi*) on August 2003; see entry on that office in zh.wikipedia.org/wiki.

21. See www.epochtimes.com/gb/4/10/26/n700451.htm, accessed by author on July 31, 2005. Liu Jing was reported to be the Director of that office on February 20, 2001; see Xinhua, Beijing, press release of February 26, 2001.

22. See www.epochtimes.com/gb/4/10/26/n700451.htm, accessed by author on July 31, 2005.

23. See www.epochtimes.com/gb/4/10/26/n700451.htm, accessed by author on July 31, 2005.

24. See www.epochtimes.com/gb/4/10/26/n700451.htm, accessed by author on July 31, 2005.

25. See www.epochtimes.com/gb/4/10/25/n699725.htm, accessed by author on July 31, 2005.

26. See 610bgs.fuyang.gov.cn/news/ZCWJ_5735/20049298018.aspx, accessed by author on August 6, 2005.

27. Xinhua, Beijing, press release of February 26, 2001.

28. See www.people.com.cn/GB/shizheng/19/20010227/404354.html, accessed by author on July 31, 2005.

29. Zhonghua renmin gongheguo Guowuyuan, "Guanyu jigou xieji di tongji" [State Council, People's Republic of China, "Notice on establishing organizations"], (no. 12, April 30, 2003).

30. State Council Press Conference, February 27, 2001; *Beijing ribao,* January 10, 2003; see www.epochtimes.com/gb/4/10/25/n699725.htm, accessed by author on July 31, 2005; Jiaoshezheng, no. 3, 2002, cited in www.zhuichaguoji.org/cn/index2.php?option=content&task=view&id=64&pop=1&page=0, accessed by author on December 1, 2006.

31. *Laiyang nianjian,* 2001, p. 86.

32. See www.epochtimes.com/gb/4/10/25/n699725.htm, accessed by author on July 31, 2005.

33. See www.epochtimes.com/gb/4/10/25/n699725.htm, accessed by author on July 31, 2005.

34. *Dandong nianjian,* 2000, p. 109.

35. *Xinjin nianjian* (1999–2001), p. 146.

36. See xinsheng.net/xs/articles/gb/2003/12/7/24648.htm and www.ruanyifeng.com/blog/2006/09/civil_servant_position_rank.html, accessed by author on July 31, 2005. For a classification of the 15 grades of state civil servants, see "Guojia gongwuyuan jinxing tiaoli" [Provisional Regulations on State Civil Servants," Arts. 9–10.

37. See www.hlj.gov.cn/ggzl/hljzb/drsyq/t22041218_8963.htm, gzw/jl.gov.cn/gzw_57_5/infocontent.jsp?infoid=286, www.hunan.gov.cn/zwgk/hnzb/swszfbwj/200501050127.htm, www.qt610.net/list.asp?id=40, www.henanrd.gov.cn/GB/200501/gb200501037.htm, and www.shanxigov.cn/gb/gzsx/zwgk/zfjg/zstsjg/gzw/nsjg/userobjectla, accessed by author on August 13, 2005; *Yunnan nianjian,* 2000, p. 103; *Sichuan ribao,* August 6, 1999, p. 2.

38. See www.zhejiang.gov.cn/gb/node2/node50/node52/node69/node122/node2124/userobject13ai6670.html, accessed by author on September 25, 2005.

39. See www.henanrd.gov.cn/GB/200501/gb200501037.htm, accessed by author on August 13, 2005.

40. *Yunnan nianjian,* 2000, p. 103.

41. *Sichuan ribao,* August 6, 1999, p. 2.

42. See www.shanxigov.cn/gb/gzsx/zwgk/zfjg/zstsjg/gzw/nsjg/userobjectla, accessed by author on August 13, 2005.

43. *Sichuan ribao,* August 6, 1999, p. 2.

44. *Sichuan ribao,* August 6, 1999, p. 2.

45. The new name can be found in Sicheng District of Beijing Municipality, Jiangmen Municipality of Guangdong Province, and Wuhai Municipality of Neimonggu. See big5.bjxch.gov.cn/pub/sch_quwei/jgsz/t20060113_617039.html and www.jmpj.gov.cn/ft/sjpw_news.aspx?guid=20050811111760332.

46. See www.sanya.gov.cn/party/party_6.shtml, accessed by author on July 31, 2005.

47. See www.hybb.gov.cn/ShowArticle.asp?ArticleID=130, accessed by author on July 31, 2005.

48. *Laiyang nianjian,* 2001, pp. 85–86.

49. *Laiyang nianjian,* 2001, p. 86.

50. *Xinyu nianjian,* 2002, p. 117.

51. See www.sanya.gov.cn/party/party_6.shtml, accessed by author on July 31, 2005.

52. See www.ordos.cn/danweizhineng/article/ShowArticle.asp?ArticleID=402, accessed by author on July 31, 2005.

53. See zfw.huizhou.gov.cn, accessed by author on July 31, 2005.

54. See www.hrbdongli.gov.cn/zz/qwsd610.php, accessed by author on July 31, 2005.

55. See www.hrbdongli.gov.cn/zz/qwsd610.php, accessed by author on July 31, 2005.

56. See www.hrbdongli.gov.cn/zz/qwsd610.php, accessed by author on July 31, 2005.

57. China had 1,567 counties, but 2,861 county-level administrative units. The latter also includes autonomous counties, county-level cities, banners, autonomous banners, and districts.

58. See www.longhui.gov.cn/mews/zwgg/Show.asp?ArticleID=13634, www.xianghe.gov.cn.bxjy/zzjg.zzjg.htm, and www.antu.gov.cn/government/class_index_xw.htm, accessed by author on July 31, 2005.

59. *Tonghai nianjian,* 1998–2002, p. 148.

60. See tahe.dxal.hl.cn/info/list.asp?id=238, accessed by author on July 31, 2005.

61. See www.hlraohe.gov.cn/zwgk/zfw.htm and www.gzdaozhen.gov.cn/dis/015.htm, accessed by author on July 31, 2005.

62. See www.antu.gov.cn/government/class_index_xw.htm, accessed by author on July 31, 2005.

63. *Tonghai nianjian,* 1998–2002, p. 148.

64. See www.sitang.gov.cn/open/Section/safety/200504/299.html, accessed by author on July 31, 2005.

65. See www.dljd.gov.cn/zwgk_gkzd_zoom.asp?Id=341, accessed by author on July 31, 2005.

66. *Shaanxi ribao,* August 21, 1999, p. 2.

67. See news/cau/edu.cn/sjpw[jp?id=0000000455, accessed by author on August 2, 2005.

68. See www.imau.edu.cn/dangban/dbwenj/dbwenjl.htm and mainpage.nwu.edu/cn/unit/udb.wdaqbds.htm, accessed by author on July 31, 2005.

69. See dwb.lzu.edu/shownews.asp?newsid=341, accessed by author on July 31, 2005.

70. See www.lzu.edu.cn/notice/meizhouxinxi/20031203371.htm, accessed by author on July 31, 2005.

71. See hustwb.edu.cn/kaw/ShowArticle.asp?ArticleID=154, accessed by author on July 31, 2005.

72. See www.bjmu.edu.cn/200411/article/2004-10/537.htm, accessed by author on August 1, 2005.

73. See www.xiangguangming.org/newcontent.asp?ID=4977, accessed by author on July 31, 2005.

CHAPTER 7

1. Xinhua, Beijing, press release of July 22, 1999.

2. In 1998 and 1999, official sources list 23 central party leadership and work departments, 46 State Council ministries and commissions, 31 provincial units, 11 military regions, 3 national headquarters of the Military Affairs Commission, 8 armed services, and 7 national-level mass organizations; see *Zhongguo gongchandang zhujishi zhiliao* (1921-1997) [Organizational materials of the Chinese Communist Party] (Beijing: Zhongguo dangshi chubanshe, 2000) (hereafter *ZGZZ*), vol. 7, shang, pp. 47-222; *Zhonghua renmin gongheguo zhengfu jigou wushinian* [Fifty years of the government organizations in the People's Republic of China] (Beijing: Dangjian duwu chubanshe, 2000) (hereafter *ZGZJW*), pp. 506-8; *Zhongguo zhengfu zhuji jigou* [Government organization of China] (Beijing: Gaige chubanshe, 1998), pp. 174-351.

3. These are 1997 figures from *ZGZZ*, vol. 7, xia, pp. 1224-45, 1344-49.

4. *Dangwu gongzuo shiyong shouce* [Practical manual on party work] (Beijing: Jingji guanli chubanshe, 1990), p. 268; Yang Xixiang and Pengyuan Yan, *Dang di jicheng zhuji gongzuo fangfa shouce* [Manual on work methods of the base-level organizations in the party] (Beijing: Zhongyang dangxiao chubanshe, 2000), pp. 278-79.

5. *Dangwu gongzuo shiyong shouce*, pp. 268-69.

6. *Dangwu gongzuo shiyong shouce*, p. 268.

7. Yang and Yan (2000), pp. 278-79.

8. *Dangwu gongzuo shiyong shouce*, p. 268.

9. Yang and Yan (2000), pp. 289-90; Xinhua, Beijing, press release of January 20, 2002; see also "Notice of the Anhui Provincial Party Committee and Provincial Government on simplifying meetings and documents" (January 24, 2002), in www.ah.gov.cn/zfgb/gbcontent.asp?id=2708, accessed by author on May 20, 2005.

10. The official Chinese Communist Party organizational history lists six mass organizations: (1) All China Workers Union, (2) China Federation of Women, (3) China Association of Science and Technology, (4) China Union of Literature and Art, (5) China Federation of Writers, and (6) China Union of Returned Overseas Chinese. See *ZGZZ*, vol. 7, shang, pp. 326-30.

11. For a classification of different types of meetings of the Chinese Communist Party and regulations thereof, see *Dangwu gongzuo shiyong shouce*, pp. 268-270.

12. Xinhua, Beijing, press release of July 23, 1999.

13. Xinhua, Beijing, press release of July 23, 1999; *ZGZZ*, vol. 7, pp. 263-69.

14. Xinhua, Beijing, press release of July 23, 1999; *ZGZZ*, suppl. vol. 4, pp. 385-426.

15. *ZGZJW*, pp. 506-8.

16. Xinhua, Beijing, press release of July 23, 1999; *ZGZZ*, suppl. vol. 1, pp. 675–742. The central state leadership organs also included the state chairman, the State Council, and the Central Military Affairs Commission. For the National People's Congress, it was its General Office of the Standing Committee that convened the meeting.

17. Xinhua, Beijing, press release of July 23, 1999. The list of 29 departments is taken from *ZGZJW,* pp. 506–8.

18. Ibid.

19. Xinhua, Beijing, press release of July 23, 1999; *ZGZJW,* pp. 517–1,098.

20. The party group of the Ministry of Agriculture has six members, those of the ministries of Information Industry, Science and Technology Industry, Labor, and Social Security each have seven, and the Ministry of Railway has eight. The data are listed in the organization section from the Web sites of respective ministries, accessed by the author on May 20, 2005.

21. Nationwide, 11 million of the 40.49 million cadres in China in 1997 were party members, who made up a larger percentage of the cadres in higher administrative strata. See *ZGZZ,* suppl. vol. 1, xia, pp. 1348–49, 1405–20.

22. *Renmin ribao,* July 26, 1999, p. 1.

23. *Dangwu gongzuo shiyong shouce,* p. 131.

24. The party secretary of the State Council's Overseas Chinese Office was Liao Hui, a Central Committee member in 1999; *ZGZZ,* vol. 7, shang, pp. 153–309.

25. Data for the provincial party committee, provincial government, provincial people's congress, and provincial party disciplinary committees are drawn from *ZGZZ,* vol. 7, shang, xia, which lists appointments that ended on September 1997. Data for the provincial political consultative conferences are drawn from the latter's Web sites, which list data for 2006.

26. *Fujian ribao,* July 23, 1999, p. 1.

27. *Hainan ribao,* July 23, 1999, p. 1.

28. *Hubei ribao,* July 25, 1999, p. 1.

29. The Anhui Provincial Organization Department convened a discussion meeting for all heads and deputy heads of bureaus within its department, and a separate meeting for the organization bureau chiefs of subordinate cities and counties, the work committees [*gongzuo weiyuanhui*] of the provincial party, and government agencies, as well as those of the provincial education establishment and the directors and heads of provincial departments; *Anhui ribao,* July 23, 27, 1999, p. 3.

30. *Hubei ribao,* July 28, 1999, p. 1; *Jiefang ribao,* August 5, 1999, pp. 1, 4; *Gansu ribao,* July 29, 1999, p. 1.

31. *Zhongguo Erlinglingling nian renkou pucha ziliao* [Tabulation of the 2,000 population census of the People's Republic of China] (Beijing: Zhongguo tongji chubanshe, 2000), vol. 1, table 1-1.

32. *Heilongjiang ribao,* July 23, 1999, p. 1.

33. *Guizhou ribao,* July 24, 1999, p. 1; *Hainan ribao,* July 24, 1999, p. 1.

34. *Harbin ribao,* July 23, 1999; *Hainan ribao,* July 25, 26, 27, and 29, 1999.

35. *Henan ribao,* August 1, 1999, p. 2; *Anhui ribao,* July 27, 1999, p. 3.

36. *Shanxi ribao,* July 29, 1999, p. 1.

37. *Guizhou ribao,* July 23, 1999, p. 1; *Hainan ribao,* July 23, 1999, p. 1; *Hubei ribao,* July 23, 1999, p. 1; *Fujian ribao,* July 23, 1999, p. 1.

38. *Dangwu gongzuo shiyong shouce,* p. 269.

39. *Guangdong nianjian,* 2003.

40. See, e.g., *Fujian ribao,* July 23, 1999, p. 1.

41. *Gansu ribao,* July 23, 1999, p. 1.

42. *Xinjiang ribao,* July 24, 1999, p. 1.

43. *Nanfang ribao,* July 24, 1999, p. 1; *Maoming ribao,* July 25, 1999, p. 1.

44. *Guizhou ribao,* July 23, 1999, p. 1; *Beijing ribao,* July 23, 1999, p. 1; *Hubei ribao,* July 23, 1999, p. 1; *Sichuan ribao,* July 23, 1999, p. 1.

45. *Henan ribao,* July 22, 1999, p. 1.

46. *Chongqing ribao,* July 24, 1999, p. 1.

47. *Gansu ribao,* July 24, 1999, p. 1.

48. *Yunnan ribao,* July 23, 1999, p. 1.

49. *Hainan ribao,* July 23, 1999, p. 1.

50. The lack of meetings of these provincial party committees may not mean the absence of such meetings or the lack of communications to lower levels. In some cases, the Falungong issue might have been raised in some other provincial meetings held around July 22, as appeared to be the case in Henan, Gansu, Chongqing, and Yunnan noted above, and in compliance with the party guideline that administrative meetings should be combined; see Yang and Yan (2000), p. 287.

51. *Shanxi ribao,* July 29, 1999, p. 1.

52. *Guangxi ribao,* July 25, 1999

53. *Dalian ribao,* July 23, 1999, p. 1.

54. *Dalian ribao,* July 23, 1999, p. 1.

55. *Fujian ribao,* July 23, 1999, p. 1.

56. *Hainan ribao,* July 25, 1999, p. 1; *Guangxi ribao,* July 24, 1999, p. 1.

57. *Hubei ribao,* July 24, 1999, p. 1.

58. *Jiangxi ribao,* July 24, 1999, p. 1.

59. *Dalian ribao,* July 23, 1999, p. 1.

60. See www.asial.com.sg/Harbin/1999/19990723/7.htm, accessed by author on November 30, 1999.

61. *Qiqihaer ribao,* July 24, 1999, p. 1.

62. *Qiqihaer ribao,* July 24, 1999, p. 1; *Jiemusi ribao,* July 23, 1999, p. 1.

63. *Maoming ribao,* July 25, 1999, p. 1.

64. *Tianjin ribao,* July 26, 1999, p. 1; *Maoming ribao,* July 25, 1999, p. 1.

65. *Maoming ribao,* July 27, 1999, p. 1; *Qiqihaer ribao,* July 27, 1999, p. 1; *Daqing ribao,* July 26 and 27, 1999, p. 1.

66. *Jiemusi ribao,* July 23, 1999, p. 1.

67. See www.asial.com.sg/Harbin/1999/19990723/7.htm, accessed by author on November 30, 1999.

68. *Lanzhou wanbao,* July 24, 1999, p. 1.

69. *Daqing ribao,* July 26, 27, 1999.

70. *Maoming ribao,* July 25, 1999, p. 1.

71. *Jiamusi ribao,* July 23, 1999, p. 1.

72. *Dalian ribao,* July 24, 1999, p. 1.

73. *Jiamusi ribao,* July 23, 1999, p. 1.

74. *Maoming ribao,* July 27, 1999, p. 1.

75. *Maoming ribao,* July 27, 1999, p. 1.

76. The Central Committee notice lists several items to be included in the study program: (1) the Chinese Communist Party Constitution, (2) Jiang Zemin's speeches, and (3) central party and state directives on the Falungong. These were mentioned twice in the Central Committee notice. A fourth item, "Why CCP members cannot practice the Falungong," was mentioned once; Xinhua, Beijing, press release of July 22, 1999.

77. *Lanzhou wanbao,* July 24, 1999, p. 1.

78. *Daqing ribao,* July 26, 1999, p. 1.

79. *Lanzhou wanbao,* July 24, 1999, p. 1.

80. *Lanzhou wanbao,* July 24, 1999, p. 1.

81. *Fujian ribao,* July 23, 1999, p. 1.

82. *Maoming ribao,* July 25, 1999, p. 1.

83. *Maoming ribao,* July 25, 1999, p. 1.

84. *Maoming ribao,* July 29, 1999, p. 1.

85. *Maoming ribao,* July 31, 1999, p. 1.

86. *Maoming ribao,* July 30, 1999, p. 1.

87. *Shanxi ribao,* August 8, 1999, p. 1.

88. *Dazhong ribao,* July 25, 1999, p. 1.

89. *Jilin ribao,* July 26, 1999, p. 1.

90. *Zhejiang ribao,* July 27, 1999, p. 1.

91. *Qiqihaer ribao,* July 26, 1999, p. 1.

92. *Jilin ribao,* July 26, 1999, p. 1.

93. *Jiangxi ribao,* August 17, 1999, p. 2.

94. These are 1997 figures, in *ZGZZ,* vol. 7, xia, pp. 1224–45, 1344–49.

CHAPTER 8

1. *Zhongguo chuban nianjian,* 2000 [China Publications Yearbook, 2000] (Beijing: Zhongguo chuban nianjianshe, 2000), pp. 66–71; *Zhongguo guangbo dianshi nianjian,* 2000 [China Broadcast and Television Yearbook, 2000] (Beijing: Zhongguo guangbo dianshi chubanshe, 2001), pp. 505–6.

2. *RMRB* editorials on the Falungong reprinted in the *GMRB* or *JFJB* carried Xinhua datelines; see *Guangming ribao,* July 23, 26, 27, 29, and 30 and August 4, 6, 9, 13, 18, and 20, as well as *JFJB* on the same days. *Qiushi* editorials were published in *RMRB* on August 1, 1999, and in *JFJB* on July 26 and 29 and August 1, 1999; the *JJRB* editorial published in *JFJB* on August 6, 1999, also carried Xinhua datelines.

3. Xinhua, Beijing, press release of July 22, 1999. The supplementary communications were made by the Communist Youth League, the Ministry of Personnel, the United Front Department, and the NPB. The press conferences were convened by the Department of Organization, the Department of Propaganda, the Ministry of Civil Affairs, and the News and Information Office of the State Council. Xinhua, Beijing, press release of July 23, 1999.

4. Xinhua, Beijing, press releases of July 29 and August 3, 4, and 12, 1999.

5. These are labeled as "Xinhuashe Pinglunyuan" (Commentator) or "Xinhuashe Teyao Pinglungyuan" (Special Commentator).

6. The July 31 and August 4, 5, and 6 Xinhua guest commentaries were published by *JFJB* in full text on the same day; those of July 27 and August 2 and 3 were excerpted.

7. The only exceptions were the July 23, 1999, *RMRB* editorial and the first of the series of 10 *JFJB* editorials.

8. *Renmin ribao,* July 28, 1999, p. 1; July 30, 1999, p. 1.

9. *Qiushi,* no. 275 (November 16, 1999), pp. 28–29.

10. The Xinhua anthology includes news items originally published in *RMRB,* July 22, August 18 and 20, and November 1, 1999; *GMRB,* February 26, 2001; and *JJRB,* August 5, 1999. See Ju Mengjun, ed., *Chanchu xiejiao qiankun lang* [The universe will be bright after the cult is eradicated] (Beijing: Xinhua chubanshe, 2001), pp. 123–29, 168–71, 257–59, 299–326, 338.

11. *Qiushi,* special issue on the Falungong, July 26, 1999.

12. Xinhua, Beijing, press release of August 12, 1999.

13. *Renmin ribao,* July 28, 1999, p. 1.

14. The two electronic stations also did not collaborate in covering other events. In the 50th People's Republic of China anniversary, CPBS and CCTV each set up its own 19 and 50 respective broadcast points at the National Day parade in Tiananmen Square; *Zhongguo guangbo dianshi nianjian,* 2000, p. 73.

15. *Zhongguo xinwen nianjian,* 2000 [China Journalism Yearbook, 2000]. Beijing: Zhongguo xinwen nianjianshe, p. 208.

16. *CCTV Yearbook,* 2000, p. 113.

17. Seventy-five divided by the sum of 210 and 170 minutes.

18. Seventy-five divided by the sum of 210, 170, and 116 minutes.

19. *Zhongguo xinwen nianjian,* 2000, p. 206.

20. *CCTV Yearbook,* 2000 [China Central Television Yearbook, 2000], p. 114.

21. The press campaign did not specify begin and end dates but did indicate that each phase was launched with an authoritative commentary from *RMRB;* see *Zhongguo xinwen nianjian,* 2000, p. 205. Since there were no special authoritative commentaries published in *RMRB* on July 22, 24, and 30, it is clear that the phasing of the press and television campaigns was not coterminous.

22. If we date the beginning of the publication campaign as July 30, when the NPB convened a preparatory conference to plan the series, or August 6, when the NPB issued the notice inviting the nation's publishers to submit publication proposals repudiating the Falungong, both sets of begin dates would not match those of the press and television campaigns. The end date of the publication campaign, where publishers had to commit to produce the anti-Falungong material in print by the end of March 2000, also did not overlap those of the other two campaigns. For a brief history and chronology of the anti-Falungong campaign and a list of the 120 titles, see *Zhongguo chuban nianjian,* 2000, pp. 158, 470–74.

23. *Zhongguo chuban nianjian,* 2001, p. 85.

24. *Zhongguo chuban nianjian,* 2001, p. 85. Zhou, a leading physicist, was president of China's Academy of Sciences from 1987 to 1995. Lu was his successor. Zhu earned a University of Michigan Physics Ph.D. in 1950 and had been president of China's Institute of Engineering of the State Council since 1994.

25. The 1999 publication plan was set in the National Conference of Publication Bureau Chiefs held in Beijing, January 23–26, 1999; see *Zhongguo chuban nianjian,* 2000, p. 156.

26. The Ninth Five-Year Publication Plan selected 1,209 titles to be published in 1996–2000. These titles did not include the anti-Falungong series. *Zhongguo chuban nianjian,* 2000, p. 156.

27. *Zhongguo chuban nianjian,* 2000, p. 78.

28. The first permanent Portuguese settlement was built in Macau in 1553. More than 50 titles commemorating the return of Macau were published in 1999; *Zhongguo chuban nianjian,* 2000, p. 78.

29. *Zhuan Falun pipan* [A critique of Zhuan Falun] (Beijing: Beijing chubanshe, 2001), 5,000 printed copies; Dou Wentao, *Falungong daqidi* [Great expose of the Falungong] (Beijing: Xiandai chubanshe, 2000), 5,000 printed copies; Wang Zhigang and Song Jianfeng, *"Falungong" xiejiaobenji mianmianguan* [Different perspectives of the essence of the Falungong cult] (Beijing: Lantian chubanshe, 2001), 6,000 printed copies; Yan Shi, ed., *Shiji jupian: Li Hongzhi* [Swindler of the century: Li Hongzhi] (Beijing: Dazhong wenyi chubanshe, 1999), 10,000 printed copies; Ju Mengjun, ed., *Xiandai huangyan: chanchu xiejiao qiankun lang* [The universe will be bright after the cult is eradicated] (Beijing: Xinhua chubanshe, 2001), first edition, two printings, 30,000 copies; *Bushi "zhen shan ren" er shi "zhen chan ren"* [It is not "truth, kindness, forbearance" but real cruelty] (Beijing: Xuexi chubanshe, 2001), first edition, two printings.

30. In the 2003 Book Purchasing Fair in Beijing, orders for the top 22 titles ranged from 100,000 to 4,000,000 copies. The top 100 titles each have a minimum order of 20,000 copies. This is an incomplete listing; www.chinawriter.org/haoshu/tsphb/tsphb000019asp, accessed July 15, 2003. Equivalent data for the 1999 Book Purchasing Fair are not readily available.

31. *Zhongguo chuban nianjian,* 2000, pp. 67–71, 699.

32. Xinhua, Beijing, December 27, 1999.

33. On July 24, 1996, the NPB banned five Falungong titles: Hongzhi Li, *Zhongguo Falungong* [Chinese Falungong] published by the Junshi yiwen chubanshe (1993); Hongzhi Li, *Zhuan Falun* [Revolving dharma wheel], published by the Zhongguo guangbo dianshi chubanshe (1994); Hongzhi Li, *Zhuan Falun,* juan er [Revolving dharma wheel, vol. 2], published by the Zhongguo shijieyu chubanshe (1995); Hongzhi Li, *Falun Dafa yijie* [Explanation of the meaning of the great doctrine of Falun], published by Changchun chubanshe (1995); and *Shentong Dafa–Li Hongzhi he Zhongguo Falungong* [The magic power of the great doctrine–Li Hongzhi and Chinese Falungong], published by the Shenyang chubanshe (1995). On August 16, 1996, the NPB banned *Zhuang Falun* [Revolving dharma wheel] published by the Hualing chubanshe (n.d.). On June 5, 1998, the NPB approved the Guangdong provincial NPB to ban Li Hongzhi's *Falun Fofa* [Buddhist doctrines of the dharma wheel] published by the Huacheng chubanshe (1997). On June 1, 1999, the NPB approved the ban by the Qinghai NPB of Hongzhi Li's *Zhuang Falun fajie* [Explanation of the doctrines of the revolving dharma wheel], *Falun Fofa–zai Xini jiang Fa* [Extolling the Falun doctrines in Sydney], *Falun Fofa–zai Ou Zhou fahui jiang fa* [Extolling the Falun doctrines in a doctrinal conference in Europe], and *Falun Fofa–zai Beimei shoujie fahui shang jiang fa* [Extolling the doctrines in the first doctrinal conference in North America], all published by the Qinghai renmin chubanshe. Xinhua, Beijing, press release of July 23, 1999.

34. There were many nationwide best book competitions, but several were discipline specific: literature, national minority, historical, ancient text, education video, art, and music multimedia products. Others are restricted to certain type of publishers, or market segments (women's literature, children's books), publication products

(education video, art, and music CDs), or specific disciplines—literature, national minority, history, and ancient classics. For instance, the NPB has a competition for best books produced by in-house publishers. *Zhongguo chuban nianjian,* 2000, pp. 164, 213-15, 217-19, 224-28.

35. *Zhongguo zhengfu jikou minglu* [Directory of government institutions in China] (Beijing: Xinhua chubanshe, 1996), vol. 1, p. 265.

36. The 1999 National Best Book Competition had three levels of awards. At the highest level, the National Book Honors Awards (*Guojia tushu jiang rongyu jiang*) were presented to 12 titles selected from all publication categories. The next highest awards went to 40 titles, including eight in social sciences, eight in science and technology, four in literature, four in fine arts, four in children's books, three in ethnic minorities, three in dictionaries, and three in ancient classics. At the third level, 96 titles were selected for the Honorable Mention Awards (*timing jiang*), with the respective numbers of titles shown in table 8.6. In total, 148 titles received the National Best Book Prize in 1999. *Zhongguo chuban nianjian,* 2000, p. 164.

37. The 2000 National Best Book Prize Competition had only one tier of awards for 214 titles.

38. Several of the books were jointly published by multiple presses.

39. *Zhongguo chuban nianjian,* 2000, p. 161.

40. These were the 1999 National Book Prize and Honorable Mentions, the 2000 National Book Prize, the 2000 China Book Prize, and the 1999 "Five Best Projects."

41. The winning title was a nature book series titled *Hong mayi zhiran congshu* [Red Ants Nature Books] (Beijing: Xiaonian ertong chubanshe, 1998), 6 vols.

42. *Zhongguo gongchandang zhujishi zhiliao* (1921-1997) (Beijing: Zhongguo dangshi chubanshe, 2000); *Zhongguo xiaosu minzhu gemingshi* [History of the revolution of the ethnic minorities in China]. (Guilin: Guangxi minzhu chubanshe, 2000).

43. Wang Binglin, *Deng Xiaoping lilun yu zhonggong dang shixue* [The Theory of Deng Xiaoping and the Study of the History of the Chinese Communist Party] (Beijing: Beijing chubanshe, 2000).

44. Jin Chongji, *Liu Shaoqi zhuan* [Biography of Liu Shaoqi] (Beijing: Zhongyang wenxian chubanshe, 1999); Li Dazhao, *Li Dazhao zhuanji* [Biography of Li Dazhao] (Shijiazhuang: Hebei renmin chubanshe, 2000); Qiaomu *Wen Cong* [Collected Works by Hu Qiaomu] (Beijing: Renmin chubanshe, 2000).

45. *Zhongguo renmin kangri junshi zhengzhi daxueshi* [History of the Chinese People's anti-Japanese military and political university] (Beijing: Guofang daxue chubanshe, 2000).

46. Five of the top 10 titles in the 2003 Beijing Book Fair were dictionaries. At least 10 of the top 50 titles were school texts and exam preparatory manuals. See www.chinawriter.org/haoshu/tsphb/tsphb000019.asp, accessed July 15, 2003.

47. These titles were either monographs or series; *Zhongguo chuban nianjian,* 2000, pp. 658-62.

48. The 385 titles include both new prints and reprints of books published in 1999-2000; *Zhongguo chuban nianjian,* 2001, pp. 614-620.

49. *CCTV Yearbook,* 2000, pp. 324-29.

50. *CCTV Yearbook,* 2001, p. 189.

51. *CCTV Yearbook,* 2000, p. 328. The winning title was not one of the five special anti-Falungong programs produced by CCTV under the direction of its editorial

board and referred to in the chapter on the media campaign; see *CCTV Yearbook*, 2000, p. 113.

52. *Zhongguo xinwen nianjian*, 2001, pp. 252–61.

53. *Zhongguo xinwen nianjian*, 2001, pp. 252–61.

54. See www.radio-tv.com.cn/pingjiang/ShowArticle.asp?ArticleID=84.

55. *CCTV Yearbook*, 2001, pp. 154–55.

56. One first prize winner was a Xinhua press release titled "The Prophecy of a Heavenly Cross Is Declared to Be Fake." A third prize winner was a *Zhejiang ribao* story titled "Don't Yield an Inch to Evil."

57. See section on labor reform institutions in chapter 5.

58. See the Minghui Web site (www.minghui.org).

CHAPTER 9

1. See www.people.com.cn/GB/channe11/10/20001229/365770.html, accessed August 26, 2006.

2. See section on Falungong allegations of torture in labor reform institutions in chapter 5.

3. Several hundreds among these laws were considered well conceived, policy salient, and sufficiently sophisticated to be referred to the nine special committees of the legislature for further deliberation and drafting; see www.npc.gov.cn/zgrdw/yajy/. While the titles of all the bills were not disclosed, the smaller subset of bills referred to the special committees were published, and these included proposing a law on inheritance tax, regulating hedge funds, protecting witnesses in court trials, and providing equal retirement benefits for both sexes.

4. Together with the Chinese Communist Party, the government, and the NPC, the CPPCC completes the four main governing bodies of the regime at different administrative levels. Sometimes, the fifth body, the party's Disciplinary Committee, is added to form the five governing bodies (*wu tau ban zi*). The CPPCC was established on September 20, 1949, just prior to the official founding of the People's Republic of China on October 1, 1949.

5. See www.cppcc.gov.cn/htm/ziliao/mulu91.htm, www.cppcc.gov.cn/htm/ziliao/mulu92.htm, www.cppcc.gov.cn/htm/ziliao/mulu93.htm, and www.cppcc.gov.cn/htm/ziliao/mulu94.htm.

6. *Zhongguo jiancha nianjian*, 2003, pp. 5, 22, 28, 115, 123, 130, 137, 143.

7. *Renmin ribao*, July 23, 1999, p. 1; Ming Xia and Shiping Hua, eds., "The Battle between the Chinese government and the Falun Gong," *Chinese Law and Government* (September–October 1999), pp. 5–104, at pp. 31–32.

8. *Renmin ribao*, August 11, 1999.

9. *Renmin ribao*, August 11, 1999.

10. *Renmin ribao*, August 11, 1999.

11. See *Minghui* (www.minghui.org), various sections on regime persecution.

12. See www.fayixing.com/casecontent.jsp?id=7978, accessed by author on September 1, 2006.

13. See www.hl.jcy.gov.cn/detail.cfm?newsid=218747952&id=228A438539EDFD, accessed by author on September 1, 2006.

14. "Guanyu banli zuzhi he liyong xiejiao zuzhi fanzui anjian juti yingyong falu ruogan jieshi" [Concerning certain explanations of specific legal applications on handling cases of the organization and use of crimes of cult organizations] (October 30, 1999), Xinhua, Beijing, press release of October 30, 1999.

15. *Dalian ribao,* July 24, 1999, p. 1.

16. See www.epochtimes.com/gb/4/12/30/n764897htm.

17. See www.epochtimes.com/gb/4/12/30/n764897htm.

18. See www.epochtimes.com/gb/6/1/4/n117212.htm.

19. Xinhua, Beijing, press release of September 22, 2002.

20. See www.bj148.0rg/newnews/pub/1050462192765.html.

21. See www.rsf/article/php3?ID_article=9309.

22. Xinhua, Beijing, press release of September 22, 2002.

23. See www.legalinfo.gov.cn/gb/ldjyglj/2003-05/13/content_27179.htm. The labor reform regulations prohibit the assault, rebuke, humiliation, and torture of inmates. For a compilation of laws and regulations on labor reform education, see www.legalinfo.gov.cn/moj/ldjyglj/node_222.htm.

24. Case of Li Yazhen at search.minghui.org/mh/articles/2005/7/21/106647p. html, www.minghui.org/mh/articles/2006/3/29/123963.html, www.minghui.org/mh/ articles/2005/4/12/99429.html, and www.minghui.org/mh/articles/2006/12/9/144304. html.

25. See www.minghui.org/mh/articles/2004/10/21/87114p.html, www.minghui .org/mh/articles/2004/10/21/87115p.html, search.minghui.org/mh/articles/2006/7/15/ 132948p.html, search.minghui.org/mh/articles/2006/7/26/134029p.html, and search. minghui.org/mh/articles/2005/5/23/102461p.html.

26. *Renmin ribao,* August 15, 1995, p. 3; September 26, 1997, p. 3; August 24, 1999, p. 10.

27. *Renmin ribao,* August 7, 1997, p. 4; May 9, 1999, p. 4; July 17, 1999, p. 2.

28. *Renmin ribao,* August 4, 1999, p. 3.

29. *Renmin ribao,* August 2, 1999, p. 4; August 4, 1999, p. 3.

30. See minghui.org/mh/articles/2005/11/4/113548.html.

31. See search.minghui.org/mh/articles/2005/11/4/113548p.html.

32. See search.minghui.org.mh/articles/2006/7/25/133885p.html.

33. See www.minghui.org/mh/articles/2004/10/21/87115p.html.

34. See search.minghui.org/mh/articles/2006/7/21/133578p.html.

35. See search.minghui.org/mh/articles/2006/7/21/133578p.html.

36. Gordon G. Chang, *The coming collapse of China* (New York: Random House, 2001).

37. Zong Hairen, *Zhu Rongji zai yi jiujiujiu nian* [Zhu Rongji in 1999] (Hong Kong: Mirror Books, 2001), translated in *Chinese law and government* (January-February 2002), pp. 3–93, at p. 63.

38. State Council, People's Republic of China, "Regulations on religious affairs" (March 1, 2005).

39. Crane Brinton, *The anatomy of revolution.* New York: Norton, 1938.

Bibliography

ENGLISH LANGUAGE SOURCES

Adams, Ian, Riley Adams, and Rocco Galati. 2000. *Power of the wheel: the Falun Gong revolution*. Toronto: Stoddart Publishing Co.

Arnason, Johann P. 1993. *The Future that failed: origins and destinies of the Soviet Model*. London: Routledge.

Baum, Richard. 1994. *Burying Mao: Chinese politics in the age of Deng Xiaoping*. Princeton: Princeton University Press.

Brinton, Crane. 1938. *The anatomy of revolution*. New York: Norton.

Bruszt, Laszlo, and David Stark. 1991. "Remaking of the political field in Hungary: from the politics of confrontation to the politics of competition," *Journal of International Affairs*, 45/1: 201-45.

Casil, Janice. 2004. "Falun Gong and China's human rights violations," *Peace Review*, 16/2 (June), pp. 225-31.

Chan, Alex. 2002. "From propaganda to hegemony: *Jiaodian Fangtan* and China's media policy," *Journal of Contemporary China* 11/30 (February), pp. 35-52.

Chan, Cheris S.C. 2004. "The Falun Gong in China: a sociological perspective," *China Quarterly* no. 179 (September), pp. 665-84.

Chang, Gordon G. 2001. *The coming collapse of China*. New York: Random House.

Chang, Maria Hsia. 2004. *Falun Gong: the end of days*. New Haven: Yale University Press.

Chen, Chiung Hwang. 2005. "Framing Falun Gong: Xinhua news agency's coverage of the new religious movement in China," *Asian Journal of Communication*, 15/1 (March), pp. 16-37.

Chen, Feng and Ting Gong. 1997. "Party versus market in post-Mao China: the erosion of the Leninist organization from below," *Journal of Communist Studies and Transitio Politics*, vol. 13, pp. 148-66.

China Daily, various editions.

Chirot, Daniel, ed. 1991. *The crisis of Leninism and the decline of the left*. Seattle: University of Washington Press.

Donald, Stephanie Hemelryk, Michael Keane, and Yin Hong, eds. 2002. *Media in China: consumption, content and crisis*. London: Routledge/Curson.

Edelman, Bryan, and James T. Richardson. 2005. "Imposed limitations on freedom of religion in China and the margin of appreciation doctrine: a legal analysis of the crackdown on the Falun Gong on other 'evil cults,'" *Journal of Church and State*, 47/2 (Spring), pp. 243-68.

Ekiert, Grzegorz. 1991. "Democratization processes in East Central Europe: a theoretical reconsideration," *British Journal of Political Science* 21(3): 285-313.

Elster, Jon, Claus Offe, and Ulrich Preuss, eds. 1998. *Instititional design in post-communist societies: rebuilding the ship at sea*. Cambridge: Cambridge University Press.

Fish, M. Stephen. 1995. *Democracy from scratch: opposition and regime in the new Russian Revolution*. Princeton, NJ: Princeton University Press.

Gill, Graeme. 1995. *The collapse of a single-party system: the disintegration of the Communist Party of the Soviet Union*. New York: Cambridge University Press.

Goldstone, Jack A. 1996. "The coming Chinese collapse," *Foreign Policy*, no. 99 (Summer), pp. 35-52.

Hancock, Bill. 1999. "China's internal war with the Falun Gong sect spills onto the Internet," *Computers and Security*, 18/6 (October), pp. 464-66.

Hong Kong Standard, various editions.

Hough, Jerry F. 1997. *Democratization and revolution in the USSR, 1985-1991*. Washington, DC: Brookings Institution.

Kaminski, Marek M. 1999. "How communism could have been saved: formal analysis of electoral bargaining in Poland in 1989." *Public Choice* 98(1-2): 83-109.

Karklins, Rasma, and Roger Petersen. 1993. "Decision calculus of protesters and regimes: Eastern Europe 1989," *Journal of Politics* 55(3): 588-614.

Kindopp, Jason. 2002. "China's war on 'cults,'" *Current History*, 101/656 (September), pp. 259-67.

Kuran, Timur. 1991. "Now out of never: the element of surprise in the East European revolution of 1989," *World Poiltiics*. 44(1): 7-48.

Lee, Chin-chuan. 2000. "Chinese communications: prisms, trajectories, and modes of understanding," in Chin-chuan Lee ed., *Power, money, and media: communication patterns and bureaucratic control in cultural China*. Evanston, Ill.:Northwestern University Press.

Leung, Beatrice. 2002. "China and the Falun Gong: party and society relations in the modern era," *Journal of Contemporary China*, 11/33 (November), pp. 761-85.

Li, Xiaoping. 2002. "'Focus' (*Jiaodian Fangtan*) and changes in the Chinese television industry," *Journal of Contemporary China* 11/30 (February), pp. 17-34.

Lieberthal, Kenneth, and Michel Oksenberg. 1988. *Policy-making in China: leaders, structures, and processes*. Princeton: Princeton University Press.

Lohmann, Suzanne. 1994. "The dynamics of informational cascades: the Monday demonstrations in Leipzeig, East Germany, 1989-1991," *World Politics*, 47/1: pp. 42-101.

Maier, Charles S. 1997. *Dissolution: the crisis of communism and the end of East Germany*. Princeton, NJ: Princeton University Press.

Mason, David S. 1992. *Revolution in East-Central Europe: The Rise and Fall of Communism and the Cold War*. Boulder, CO: Westview Press.

McCauley, Mary. 1992. *Soviet Politics, 1917-1991*. Oxford: Oxford University Press.

McCormick, Barrett. 2002/2003. "Recent trends in mainland China's media: political implications of commercialization," *Issues and Studies* (December/March), pp. 175-215.

McDonald, Kevin. 2004. "Oneself as another: from social movement to experience movement," *Current Sociology*, 52/4 (July), pp. 575-90, 665-81.

———. 2006. *Global movements: action and culture*. Oxford: Blackwell Publishing.

McTernan, Vaughan. 2003. "The Falun Gong: a virtual meeting of East and West," *Bucknell Review* 47/2 (June), pp. 104-28.

Montinola, Gabriella, Yingyi Qian, and Barry R. Weingast. 1996. "Federalism, Chinese style: the political basis for economic success," *World Politics*, 48/1, pp. 50–81.

Munro, Robin. 2002. *Dangerous minds: political psychiatry in China today and its origins in the Mao era*. New York: Human Rights Watch.

Nee, Victor. 1989. "A theory of market transition: from redistribution to markets in state socialism," *American Sociological Review*, 54, pp. 663–81.

Nee, Victor, and Lian Peng. 1994. "Sleeping with the enemy: a dynamic model of declining commitment in state socialism," *Theory and Society*, 23, pp. 253–96.

O'Leary, Stephen. 2000. "Falungong and the Internet," *Online Journalism Review*, www.ojr/ethics/1017964337.php.

Ownby, David. 2003. "The Falun Gong in the new world," *European Journal of East Asian Studies*, 2/2 (December), pp. 303–21.

Palmer, David. 2007. *Qigong fever: body, science and utopia in China*. New York: Columbia University Press.

Przeworski, Adam. 1991. *Democracy and the market*. New York: Cambridge University Press.

Rahn, Patsy. 2002. "The chemistry of a conflict: the Chinese government and the Falun Gong," *Terrorism and Political Violence*, 14/4 (Winter), pp. 41–66.

Remington, Thomas F. 1992. "Reform, revolution, and regime transition in the Soviet Union," in Gilbert Rozman ed., *Dismantling communism: common causes and regional variations*. Washington, DC: Woodrow Wilson Center, pp. 121–51.

Roeder, Philip G. 1993. *Red sunset: the failure of Soviet politics*. Princeton, NJ: Princeton University Press.

Shirk, Susan. 1993. *The political logic of economic reform in China*. Berkeley: University of California Press.

Stokes, Gale. 1993. *The walls come tumbling down: the breakdown of communism in Eastern Europe*. New York: Oxford University Press.

Stone, Alan A. 2004. "The plight of the Falun Gong," *Psychiatric Times* (November), pp. 1–13.

———. 2005. "The China psychiatric crisis: following up on the plight of the Falun Gong," *Psychiatric Times* (May), pp. 1–13.

Szakolczai, Arpad, and Agnes Horváth. 1991. "Political instructors and the decline of communism in Hungary: apparatus, nomenclatura and the issue of legacy," *British Journal of Political Science* 21(4): 469–88.

Szelenyi, Ivan, and Balazs Szelenyi. 1994. "Why socialism failed: towards a theory of system breakdown," *Theory and Society* 23(2): 211–31.

Thornton, Patricia. 2002. "Framing dissent in contemporary China: irony, ambiguity and metonymy," *China Quarterly*, no. 171 (September), pp. 661–81.

Tismaneanu, Vladimir. 1992. *Reinventing politics: Eastern Europe from Stalin to Havel*. New York: Free Press.

Tompson, William J. 1993. "Kruschev and Gorbachev as reformers: a comparison," *British Journal of Political Science*, 23/1, pp. 77–105.

Tong, James. 2002a. "An organizational analysis of the Falungong: structure, communications, financing," *China Quarterly*, no. 171 (September), pp. 641–65.

———. 2002b. "Anatomy of regime repression in China: timing, enforcement institutions, and target selection in banning the Falungong, July, 1999," *Asian Survey* (November-December), pp. 795–820.

Tong, James. 2005. "Publish to perish: regime choices and propaganda impact in the anti-Falungong publication campaign July, 1999-December 2000," *Journal of Contemporary China*, 14/44 (August), pp. 507–523.

Walder, Andrew. 1994. "The decline of communist power: elements of a theory of institutional change," *Theory and Society*, 23, pp. 297–323.

Wang, Jianlong. 2002. "Research on Chinese communication campaigns: a historical review," in Wenshan Jia et al., eds., *Chinese communication theory and research: reflections, new frontiers, and new directions*. Westport, Conn.: Ablex Publishing, pp. 131–46.

Wolf, Charles, Jr., K.C. Yeh, Benjamin Zycher, Nicholas Eberstadt, and Sung-ho Lee. 2003. *Fault lines in China's economic terrain*. Santa Monica, Calif.: Rand Corporation.

Wong, John, and William T. Liu. 1999. *The mystery of the China's Falun Gong: its rise and its sociological implications*. East Asian Institute Contemporary China Series, no. 22. Singapore: Singapore University Press.

Wyatt, Alex. 2002. "The global economy and the on-line world: consequences of WTO accession on the regulation of the Internet in China," *Melbourne Journal of International Law*, 3/2 (October), pp. 436–53.

Xia, Ming, and Shiping Hua, eds. 1999. "The battle between the Chinese government and the Falun Gong," *Chinese Law and Government* (September-October), pp. 5–104.

Xiao, Hongyan. 2001. "Falun Gong and the ideological crisis of the Chinese Communist Party: Marxist atheism vs. vulgar theism," *East Asia: An International Quarterly*, 19/1-2 (Spring-Summer), pp. 123–44.

Zeng, Jennifer. 2006. *Witnessing history: one Chinese woman's fight for freedom*. New York: Soho Press.

Zhao, Yuezhi. 1998. *Media, market, and democracy in China: between the party line and the bottom line*. Urbana: University of Illinois Press.

———. 2000. "From commercialization to conglomeration: the transformation of the Chinese press within the orbit of the party state," *Journal of Communication* (Spring), pp. 3–26.

Zhou, Shiyu. 2001. "The '610 Office'—the primary organ mechanism of Jiang Zemin's state terrorism policy against Falun Gong," presented at the Panel Discussion on China's State Terrorism at National Press Club, Washington D.C., October 10.

CHINESE LANGUAGE PRIMARY SOURECES

Central Government Publications

Dangwu gongzuo shiyong shouce [Practical manual on party work]. 1990. Beijing: Jingji guanli chubanshe.

Zhongguo chuban nianjian [China Publications Yearbook]. Beijing: Zhongguo chuban nianjianshe, 2000, 2001.

Zhongguo erlinglingling nian renkou pucha ziliao [Tabulation of the 2,000 population census of the People's Republic of China]. 2000. Beijing: Zhongguo tongji chubanshe.

Zhongguo Falu nianjian [China law yearbook]. Beijing: Zhongguo falu Chubanshe, 2000-2005.

Zhongguo gongan nianjian, 2000 [China public security yearbook, 2000]. Beijing: Chunzhong chubanshe, 2001.

Zhongguo gongchandang zhujishi zhiliao (ZGZZ) (1921-1997) [Organizational materials of the Chinese Communist Party]. 2000. Beijing: Zhongguo dangshi chubanshe.

Zhongguo guangbo dianshi nianjian [China Broadcast and Television Yearbook]. 2000. Beijing: Zhongguo guangbo dianshi chubanshe, 2001.

Zhongguo jiancha nianjian [Procuratorial Yearbook in China]. Beijing: Zhongguo jiancha nianjian chubanshe, 2000-2005.

Zhongguo minzheng nianjian, 2004 [China civil affairs yearbook, 2004]. Beijing: Zhongguo shehui chubanshe, 2005.

Zhongguo renmin kangri junshi zhengzhi daxueshi [History of the Chinese People's anti-Japanese military and political university]. 2000. Beijing: Guofang daxue chubanshe.

Zhongguo shehui zhian zonghe zhili nianjian, 1995-1996 [China Social Order Integrated Management Yearbook, 1995-1996]. Beijing: Falu chubanshe, 1998.

Zhongguo sifa xingzheng nianjian [China Yearbook of Justice Administration]. Beijing: Falu chubanshe, 2000-2005.

Zhongguo tushu nianjian [China Books Yearbook]. Wuhan: Hubei renmin chubanshe, 1999.

Zhongguo wushenlunshi ziliao xuanbian (Song Yuan Ming bian) [Selections on the history of China's atheism—Song, Yuan, Ming periods]. 1999. Beijing: Zhonghua shuju, January.

Zhongguo xiaosu minzhu gemingshi [History of the revolution of the ethnic minorities in China]. Guilin: Guangxi minzhu chubanshe.

Zhongguo xinwen nianjian [China Journalism Yearbook]. Beijing: Zhongguo xinwen nianjianshe, 1999, 2000.

Zhongguo zhengfu jikou minglu [Directory of government institutions in China]. 1996. Beijing: Xinhua chubanshe.

Zhongguo zhengfu zhuji jigou [Government organization of China]. 1998. Beijing: Gaige chubanshe.

Zhongguo zhongyang dianshitai nianjian [China Central Television Yearbook]. Beijing: Zhongguo guangbo dianshi chubanshe, 2000-2005.

Zhonghua renmin gongheguo, Gonganbu. 1999. "Gongan jiguan banli xingxi anjian chengxu guiding" [Ministry of Public Security, People's Republic of China, "Regulations on handling criminal cases by public security organs"]. May 14, 1998, in *Zuixin Gong'an paichusuo minjing gongzuo shouce* [The new manual for police work in public security precincts]. Beijing: Fulu chubanshe.

Zhonghua renmin gongheguo, Guowuyuan. 2003. "Guanyu jigou xieji di tongji" [State Council, People's Republic of China, "Notice on Establishing Organizations"] no. 12, April 30.

Zhonghua renmin gongheguo zhengfu jigou wushinian [Fifty years of the government organizations in the People's Republic of China]. 2000. Beijing: Dangjian duwu chubanshe.

Zhonghua remin gongheguo ziliao shouce, 1949-99 [Handbook of information on the People's Republic of China, 1949-1999]. Beijing: Shehui kexue wenxian chubanshe, 1999.

"Zhonghua Renmin Gongheguo Zhi'an Guanli chufa tiaoli" ["Security management penalty regulations of the People's Republic of China"]. 1986. in *Zhonghua renmingongheguo falu chuanshu* [Complete collection of laws of the People's Republic of China]. Changchun: Jilin renmin chubanshe, 1989, pp. 1529–1534.

National Newspapers

Gongren ribao
Guangming ribao
Jiefangjun bao
Jingji ribao
Renmin ribao
Zhongguo qingnian bao

Provincial and City Newspapers

Anhui ribao
Beijing ribao
Beijing wanbao
Changchun ribao
Chongqing ribao
Dalian ribao
Dagong bao (Hong Kong)
Daqing ribao
Dazhong ribao
Fujian ribao
Gansu ribao
Guangdong ribao
Guangxi ribao
Guangzhou ribao
Guizhou ribao
Hainan ribao
Harbin ribao
Hebei ribao
Heilongjiang ribao
Henan ribao
Hubei ribao
Hunan ribao
Jiamusi ribao
Jiangxi ribao
Jiefang ribao
Jilin ribao
Lanzhou wanbao
Liaoning ribao
Maoming ribao
Nanfang ribao

Neimonggu ribao
Ningxia ribao
Qinghai ribao
Qiqihaer ribao
Shaanxi ribao
Shandong ribao
Shanxi ribao
Sichuan ribao
Tianjin ribao
Xinhua ribao
Xinjiang ribao
Xizang ribao
Yunnan ribao
Zhejiang ribao

Local Gazetteers (Provincial, Municipal, County Yearbooks)

(Figures within parenthesis denote multiyear and single editions)

Anshan nianjian, 2001, 2002
Baoding nianjian, 2000
Changchun nianjian, 2000–2003
Changsha nianjian, 2001–2003
Changshan nianjian, 2001
Chongqing nianjian, 2002
Dandong nianjian, 2000, 2002
Daqing nianjian, 2000
Daye nianjian, 1998–2002
Dongying nianjian, 2000
Fushun nianjian, 2000, 2002, 2003
Gansu nianjian, 2000
Guangdong nianjian, 2003
Guizhou nianjian, 2000
Haikou nianjian, 2000
Harbin nianjian, 1999–2000
Hebei nianjian, 2000
Heilongjiang nianjian, 2001, (2004)
Hengyang nianjian, 2000, 2001
Huangpu nianjian, 2000
Huangshi nianjian, 2000
Huarong nianjian, 2001–2003
Huixian nianjian, 2000
Jilin nianjian, 2000
Jinan nianjian, 2000–2002
Jingdezhen nianjian, 2000, 2001
Jinjiang nianjian, 2000, 2001
Jinzhou nianjian, 2000–2003

Kaifeng nianjian, 2001
Laiyang nianjian, 2001
Liaoning nianjian, 2000–2004
Liling nianjian, 2001, 2003
Luanjiang nianjian, 2001
Luoshan nianjian, 2004
Ma'anshan nianjian, 2000, 2001
Meizhou nianjian, 2001
Nanjing nianjian, 2000
Nankang nianjian, 2003
Nanyang nianjian, 2001
Nenjiang nianjian, 2001
Qian'an nianjian, 2000
Qinghai nianjian, 2000
Qinhuangdao nianjian, 2000, 2001
Shaanxi nianjian, 2000
Shandong nianjian, 2000
Shanghai nianjian, 2000
Shenyang nianjian, 2000–2002
Siping nianjian, 1999–2000
Suzhou nianjian, 2000
Taiyuan nianjian, 2000
Tianjian nianjian (2004)
Tonghai nianjian (1998–2002)
Wanzhou nianjian, 2003
Weifang nianjian, 2000
Wuhan nianjian, 2000, 2001
Wulumuqi nianjian, 2000
Xian nianjian, 2000
Xiangtan nianjian, 2003
Xinjiang nianjian, 2000
Xinjin nianjian (1999–2001)
Xinyu nianjian, 2001, 2002
Xuanwei nianjian, 2003
Yangzhou nianjian, 2003
Yunnan nianjian, 2000
Zhengzhou nianjian, 2000
Zhujiang nianjian, 2001
Zibo nianjian, 2000

CHINESE LANGUAGE SECONDARY SOURCES

A group of China law workers. August 11, 1999. "Yu Fa Bu Rong, Yu Li Bu Tong" [Incompatible with law, illogical in reason], in minghui.ca/mh/articles/1999/8/11/5736.html.

Beijing zhichun (U.S.A.), various editions.

Bianzheng di lishi di weiwuzhuyi [Dialectical historical materialism]. 1999. Beijing: Junshi kexue chubanshe, May.

Bu zhidao di shijie [The unknown world]. 1998. Beijing: Zhongguo shaolian ertong chubanshe, August.

Bushi "zhen shan ren" er shi "zhen chan ren" [It is not "truth, kindness, forbearance" but real cruelty]. 2001. Beijing: Xuexi chubanshe.

Cheng ming (Hong Kong), various editions.

Dongxiang (Hong Kong), various editions.

Dou, Wentao. 2000. *Falungong daqidi* [Great expose of the Falungong]. Beijing: Xiandai chubanshe.

Falun Dafa Yijie [Explanation of the meaning of the great doctrine of Falun]. 1995. Changchun: Changchun chubanshe.

Falungong xianxiang pingxi [A critical analysis of the Falungong phenomenon]. 2001. Beijing: Shehui kexue wenxian chubanshe.

"Falungong zhenshi gushi" [The real story of Falungong], June 25, 2000, http://www.minghui.org/mh/articles/2000/6/25/12501p.html.

Ho, Pin. 1996. *Zhongguo xin zhuhou* [The new lords of the People's Republic of China] Mississauga, Ont.: Mirror Books.

Hong mayi zhiran congshu [Red Ants Nature Books]. 1998. Beijing: Xiaonian ertong chubanshe, 6 vols.

Qiaomu Wen Cong [Collected Works by Hu Qiaomu]. 2000. Beijing: Renmin chubanshe.

Jin, Chongji. 1999. *Liu Shaoqi zhuan* [Biography of Liu Shaoqi]. Bejing: Zhongyang wenxian chubanshe.

Ju, Mengjun, ed. 2001. *Chanchu xiejiao qiankun lang* [The universe will be bright after the cult is eradicated]. Beijing: Xinhua chubanshe.

Li, Dazhao. 2000. *Li Dazhao zhuanji* [Biography of Li Dazhao]. Shijiazhuang: Hebei renmin chubanshe.

Li, Hongzhi. 1993. *Zhongguo Falungong* [Chinese Falungong]. Beijing: Junshi Yiwen chubanshe.

———. 1994. *Zhuan Falun* [Revolving dharma wheel]. Beijing: Zhongguo guangbo dianshi chubanshe.

———. 1995. *Zhuan Falun, juan er* [Revolving dharma wheel, vol. 2]. Beijing: Zhongguo shijieyu chubanshe.

———. 1997. *Falun Fofa* [Buddhist doctrines of the dharma wheel]. Guangzhou: Huacheng chubanse.

———. 1999. *Zhuang Falun Fajie* [Explanation of the doctrines of the revolving dharma wheel]. Sining: Qinghai renmin chubanshe.

———. 1999. *Falun Fofa–zai Beimei shoujie fahui shang jiang Fa* [Extolling the doctrines in the first doctrinal conference in North America]. Sining: Qinghai renmin chubanshe.

———. 1999. *Falun Fofa–zai Ou Zhou fahui jiang fa* [Extolling the Falun doctrines in a doctrinal conference in Europe]. Sining: Qinghai renmin chubanshe.

———. 1999. *Falun Fofa–zai Xini jiang fa* [Extolling the Falun doctrines in Sydney]. Sining: Qinghai renmin chubanshe.

———. n.d. *Zhuang Falun* [Revolving dharma wheel]. Hualing chubanshe.

Shentong Dafa–Li Hongzhi he Zhongguo Falungong [The magic power of the great doctrine–Li Hongzhi and Chinese Falungong]. 1995. Shenyang: Shenyang chubanshe.

Tang, Zhongren, ed. 2001. *Tiaochu jingshen xianjing* [Jumping out from the spiritual trap]. Shanghai: Shanghai renmin chubanshe.

Toushi xiejiao jiepou Falungong [Cult penetrated—anatomy of Falungong] 2001. Beijing: Zhongguo qingnian chubanshe.

Wang, Binglin. 2000. *Deng Xiaoping lilun yu zhonggong dang shixue* [The Theory of Deng Xiaoping and the Study of the History of the Chinese Communist Party]. Beijing: Beijing chubanshe.

Wang, Zhigang, and Jianfeng Song. 2001. *"Falungong" Xiaejiaobenji mianmianguan* [Different perspectives of the essence of the Falungong cult] Beijing: Lantian chubanshe.

Xiandai Huangyan: Li Hongzhi wailixieshuo pingxi [Contemporary lies: a critical analysis of the crooked theories and evil teachings of Li Hongzhi]. 1999. Beijing: Zhongguo shuji chubanshe.

Xiang, Xiang. 2002. *Yunnan: Pojie Falungong* [Breaking up Falungong in Yunnan]. Kunming: Yunnan chubanshe.

Yan, Shi ed. 1999. *Shiji jupian: Li Hongzhi* [Swindler of the century: Li Hongzhi]. Beijing: Dazhong wenyi chubanshe.

Yang, Xixiang, and Pengyuan Yan. 2000. *Dang di jicheng zhuji gongzuo fangfa shouce* [Manual on work methods of the base-level organizations in the party] Beijing: Zhongyang dangxiao chubanshe.

Ye, Hao. July 31, 1999. "Youguan Falungong shifou you zuzhi di zhenxiang" [An Explanation on whether the Falungong was organized] *Minghui* Web site.

Zhao, Jianxun, ed. 2000. *Zui-e—Falungong shouhaizhe xuelei kongsu* [Crimes—the blood and tears accusations of Falungong victims] Beijing: Zhongguo minzhu fazi chubanshe.

Zhao, Jiemin. "Qiefa jianju jianghu pianzi Li Hongzhi cailiao" [Materials exposing the swindler Li Hongzhi], at www.xy.org/_ppfl/.

Zhuan Falun pipan [A critique of Zhuan Falun]. 2001. Beijing: Beijing chubanshe.

Zhuang, Fenggan. 2002. *"Falungong" xianxiang di xinli fenxi* [A psychological analysis of the Falungong phenomenon]. Beijing: Kexue chubanshe.

Zong, Hairen. 2001. *Zhu Rongji zai Yi Jiujiujiu Nian* [Zhu Rongji in 1999]. Hong Kong: Mirror Books.

———. 2002a. *Zhu Rongji zai Yi Jiujiujiu Nian* [Zhu Rongji in 1999]. Hong Kong: Mirror Books, 2001, translated in *Chinese Law and Government* (January-February), pp. 3–99.

———. 2002b. *Zhu Rongji zai Yi Jiujiujiu Nian* [Zhu Rongji in 1999]. Hong Kong: Mirror Books, 2001, translated in *Chinese Law and Government* (March-April), pp. 3–91.

Index